the Present or Quit-rent consisting of one hundred Pounds
Weight of good and merchantable Tobacco, to be delivered on
or before the tenth Day of October at the Forks of Assiniboine River and to the Chiefs and Warriors of the Killistine
or Cree Nation a like Present or Quit-rent of one hundred
Pounds of Tobacco, to be delivered to them on or before the said
tenth Day of October, at Portage de la Prairie on the
Banks of Assiniboine River. Provided always that the
Traders hitherto established upon any part of the above-
mentioned Tract of Land shall not be molested in
the Possession of the Lands which they have already cultivated and improved, till His Majesty's Pleasure
shall be known. —

In witness whereof the Chiefs aforesaid have set their
Marks at the Forks of Red River on the day aforesaid.

Signed. Selkirk. — Meche Wheash. — Mechkaduwikonaie

La Sonnant   La Robe Noire

Segnor   Ouckidoat
His   Mark   His   Mark

Signed in presence of   Romial alias Rajon Barbu

Thomas Thomas   Kayaye wekonabie
James Bird   His   Mark
F. Matthew Capt.   L'Homme Noir
P. d'Orsonnens Capt.
Miles Macdonell
J. Bte Chr. De Lorimier
Louis Nolin Sr.

LORD SELKIRK OF RED RIVER

LORD SELKIRK
of Red River

JOHN MORGAN GRAY

MICHIGAN STATE UNIVERSITY PRESS

1964

★ ★
★ ★
★

FOR MY WIFE, ANTOINETTE LALONDE GRAY

CONTENTS

ILLUSTRATIONS AND MAPS

(Courtesy of the Public Archives of Canada unless otherwise acknowledged)

STARTING OPPOSITE PAGE 196

The Selkirk house at St. Mary's Isle, Kirkcudbright
From a photograph courtesy of Sir David Hope-Dunbar

Thomas Douglas, fifth Earl of Selkirk; from the portrait believed to be by Raeburn

Jean, Countess of Selkirk
From Bryce: 'Life of Lord Selkirk', courtesy of the Musson Book Co.

Colin Robertson; portrait probably by Gilbert Stewart Newton, 1821

Colonists of the Red River poling and tracking York boats; from a water-colour by Peter Rindisbacher

Portaging between York Factory and Red River; from a water-colour by Peter Rindisbacher

Miles Macdonell
From a reproduction in the office of the Sheriff of York County, Ontario, with permission

Fort William about 1812; from a painting by Robert Irvine (real name Cruickshank or Crookshank)
Courtesy of the University of Toronto Library

ix

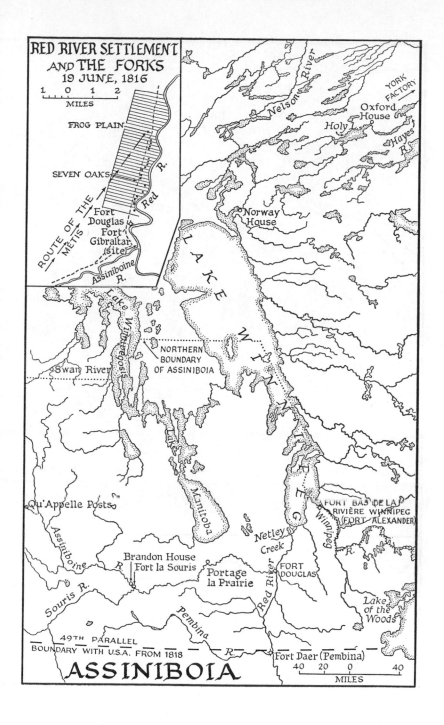

RED RIVER SETTLEMENT
AND THE FORKS
19 JUNE, 1816

1   0   1   2
MILES

FROG PLAIN

SEVEN OAKS

Red R.

ROUTE OF THE MÉTIS

Fort Douglas
Fort Gibraltar (site)

Assiniboine R.

YORK FACTORY

Nelson River

Oxford House

Holy L.

Hayes R.

Norway House

LAKE WINNIPEG

Lake Winnipegosis

NORTHERN BOUNDARY OF ASSINIBOIA

Swan River

Lake Manitoba

Qu'Appelle Posts

FORT BAS DE LA RIVIÈRE WINNIPEG (FORT ALEXANDER)

Winnipeg R.

Assiniboine R.

Brandon House
Fort la Souris

Portage la Prairie

Netley Creek

FORT DOUGLAS

Lake of the Woods

Souris R.

Pembina

Red River

49TH PARALLEL
BOUNDARY WITH U.S.A. FROM 1818

R.

Fort Daer (Pembina)

40   20   0   40
MILES

ASSINIBOIA

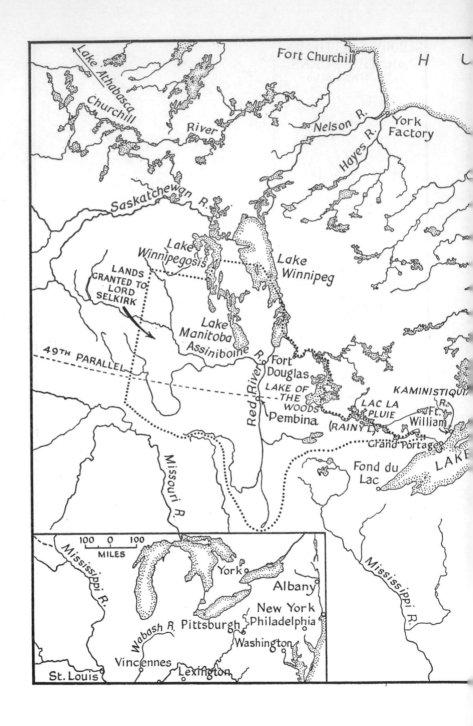

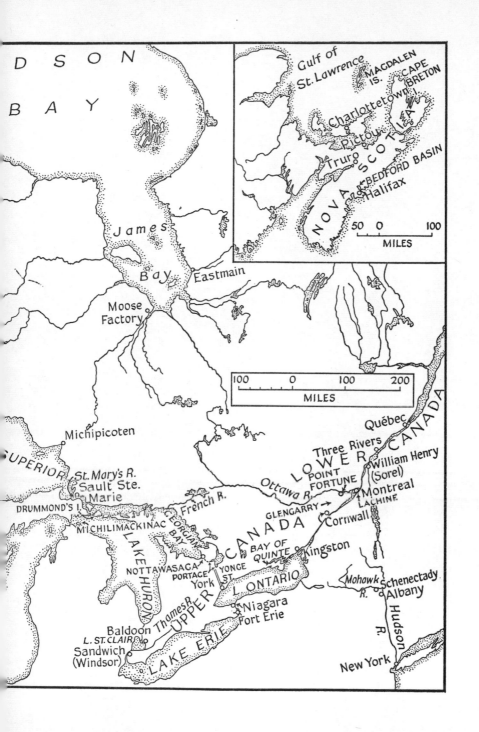

PREFACE

This book has grown out of an interest in the personality of Lord Selkirk, and a wish to get at the truth of his motives in forwarding Highland emigration. It is neither a history of the Red River Settlement nor of the Hudson's Bay Company or the fur trade in Selkirk's lifetime, though it touches all these topics at certain points. My interest in Selkirk came from a largely uninformed impression that he had had less than justice from the courts of Canada and perhaps from posterity.

There have been two admirable books touching this topic, to both of which I am under a heavy debt: Chester Martin's *Lord Selkirk's Work in Canada* (Oxford, 1916) and J. P. Pritchett's *The Red River Valley* (New Haven and Toronto, 1942). Nevertheless, it seemed worth while to make a fresh attempt to understand and to explain the rather baffling figure about whom Canadians tend still to have strong opinions and little information. That Lord Selkirk filled an important secondary role in Canadian history seems to me not in doubt. Whether he earned that place worthily, and deserves the affection in which he is held, my readers must decide.

The Scottish names scattered through the history of the fur trade have contributed a share of minor problems. Many will be found to differ in their spelling here from that in other books. As far as possible I have taken signatures on official documents or original letters as my authority for the spelling of all names. A further complication is the similarity in names; thus we have Alexander Macdonell of the North West Company, Alexander McDonell at Baldoon, and Alexander Mac-Donell the Sheriff of Red River. They represent the problem in its most extreme form – but not by much.

I have had more kindness and help with this work than can be adequately acknowledged. My greatest debt is to Dr. Kaye Lamb, Dominion Archivist, and to the expert staff of the Public Archives of Canada, in particular Mr. W. G. Ormsby, head of the manuscript division, and his predecessor, Miss Norah Story. I have had similar help on several visits to the Scottish Record Office in Edinburgh. In addition, Sir James Fergusson, Keeper of the Records of Scotland, has most kindly answered many inquiries and permitted me to draw heavily in one chapter on his valuable book, *The Sixteen Peers of Scotland*. Professor Fred Coyne Hamil of Wayne University has allowed me to use his extensive unpublished study of Lord Selkirk in Upper Canada and has answered various questions for me. The staff of the Toronto Public Library, especially Miss Edith Firth, have been uniformly patient and helpful.

I express my thanks to the Earl of Selkirk for allowing Messrs. Coutts to show me the record of the 5th Earl's banking with them between 1811 and 1820, and to the late Mr. Brooke-Caws of Coutts's for producing the information. The late Sir Basil Hope-Dunbar and his son, Sir David Hope-Dunbar of Kirkcudbright, descendants of Lord Selkirk, and Sir Basil's secretary, Miss Dorothy Gellatly, have all provided help. Mrs. Isobel Dobell of the McCord Museum, McGill University, kindly called my attention to Selkirk material not previously made use of. Miss Shirley Elliott, Legislative Librarian in Halifax, has provided important assistance in research. For reading parts of the manuscript and making valuable suggestions I am grateful to Professor W. L. Morton of the University of Manitoba and Professor Margaret Ormsby of the University of British Columbia. Professor E. E. Rich,

Master of St. Catharine's College, Cambridge, and formerly editor of the Hudson's Bay Record Society, has corresponded and talked with me about this study and provided both encouragement and help. Miss Irene Brown of the Ewart Library, Dumfries, kindly copied extracts from the *Dumfries and Galloway Courier*, 1816-18. Mr. Jules Bazin of the Bibliothèque Municipale, Montreal, has kindly provided help, and Mrs. Chester Martin showed me the late Professor Martin's Selkirk notebooks.

I am under a debt to the officials and staffs of many libraries and archives: the Provincial Archives of British Columbia, Manitoba, and Ontario, the National Library of Scotland, the Library of the University of Edinburgh, the Signet Library, Edinburgh, the Osler Library of McGill University, the Academy of Medicine, Toronto, the Library of the University of Toronto, and the Glenbow Foundation of Calgary. The staff of *The Beaver* magazine at Hudson's Bay House in Winnipeg has been helpful, as has Miss Alice Johnson, archivist of the Hudson's Bay Company in London. The library of the United States Naval Academy at Annapolis kindly lent me the microfilm of the correspondence relating to the John Paul Jones raid on St. Mary's Isle, Kirkcudbright. I wish I could name individuals in all these cases.

For assistance with research I owe thanks to Mrs. Joan St. George Saunders of London, England, Mrs. Mabel Good of Montreal, Dr. Bertha Wright of Exeter, Mrs. W. M. Brehaut of Charlottetown, and Mr. George Macgillivray of Fort William. Sir John Murray graciously allowed me to see the records of Messrs. John Murray's dealings with Lord Selkirk and Miss Jane Boulanger made a useful search for me. My son, John A. M. Gray, undertook research for me in the area of Pau, France, and we are both indebted to M. Pierre Bayaud, archivist of Pau.

Finally, I owe inexpressible thanks to my friends and long-suffering colleagues at Macmillan, to Mrs. Roy Ireland who typed my manuscript, and to my wife who for five years helped with and endured this book.

LORD SELKIRK OF RED RIVER

Chapter 1

THE SEVENTH SON

I

Late on an evening at the end of April 1778 a coach drew up
to an inn at Derby in the Midlands of England. The travellers
were Dunbar Hamilton (Douglas), 4th Earl of Selkirk, and his
two eldest sons, Basil, Lord Daer, and John. They were on
their way home from London to Kirkcudbright in Scotland
and it had been a long day. The Earl packed the boys of
fifteen and thirteen off to bed and doubtless intended to
follow shortly.

Their onward journey lay through Buxton whence they
would probably travel towards the Lake Country. The Earl
and his wife had half planned a meeting at Keswick and a
leisurely trip through the lakes in early May; she would be
ready to start on hearing from him. They were not young
lovers, these two, having been married twenty years, during
which time the Countess had borne him seven sons (two of
whom had died in infancy) and four daughters, and there was
to be another baby before long; but the warmth of affection
and mutual respect lay over their lives and the lives of their
children. The Earl could describe himself as 'having the dis-

I

advantage of a useless Scotch title', but otherwise being 'in all respects as much a Private Country Gentleman as any one can be. . . .' And he could think of his family as having 'never injured any person'. There was every reason over supper and a night-cap for thinking with contentment of the journey ahead. He had left Dunbar, his third son, at school in Hampstead, and was only a bit concerned to get Basil and John under their mother's care to clear up their colds.

As he sat contentedly, a garrulous waiter who did not know him casually dropped the news that an American privateer had raided Whitehaven on the west coast and burned some shipping. This in itself was a startling event, a thing not heard of in England for a hundred years; but there was more to follow. The raider had crossed the Solway to Scotland, the waiter said, and burned a nobleman's house – Lord Selkirk's house. It was news to make him doubt his hearing, to make the heart stand still. After the first startled questions and answers, the desperate, blank uncertainty of what to do, the Earl called for the newspapers. The story was inescapably there in a London paper; a dispatch from Edinburgh quoted a letter from Kirkcudbright written on April 23 – a week before. Lord Selkirk's house had been plundered, the letter said, and it added nothing about the safety of the family. He assumed the worst had been withheld, and the word 'plunder' suggested scenes of horror at once too dreadful to be faced and too probable to be put away: his wife far gone in pregnancy, the little children, the too-vulnerable older girls. A Whitehaven newspaper spoke of great columns of smoke having been seen across the Solway.

After the first stunned indecision, it was obvious he must somehow have more news. The nearest possible source was Buxton, where he had suggested letters might be sent. He ordered the best horses available and reluctantly roused the sleeping boys. At three o'clock in the morning they set off at dangerous speed to travel the thirty-four miles over very hilly country. Through the dawn and past the edge of sunrise his despair grew as the terrible clarity of exhaustion thrust itself upon him. The sweating horses clattered at last into the inn-yard at half past six and within moments he was holding letters he hardly dared to open.

In a letter from London was an enclosure written in the hand he might never see again. It was dated the twenty-third – the day of the raid. 'My dear love,' he read, 'nothing gives me the pain it does to think how uneasy you must be after you hear of this till you hear from me. . . . It is now some hours ago, and I am as much composed after as during the time.' It went on to outline the story of the raid – no one was harmed, and only the family silver taken – and ended, 'Adieu my love. Believe me easy and well.' After the shock, the hours of strain and grief, the sweet reassurance was too much; the Earl broke down.

He and the boys were a long time learning the whole story and though relieved of their worst fears they were not easy for many days. They pressed on to Manchester, looking for more letters, and on through Liverpool to Keswick and then towards home; clearly something had happened to delay the Countess. In fact, it was only a slowness of the mail. Just over the border, at Annan, they met the whole family bowling down the road: Countess, governess, four girls and two small boys, and servants – filling the coach and riding horseback they came, alive and well and hoping to get to Keswick in time. Together they turned back to Dumfries where the Circuit with its accompanying social gaiety was just beginning. And there they settled down 'to the great satisfaction of the girls, who got their fill of dancing', and to Lady Selkirk's 'tolerable degree of fatigue'.

The story of the raid could now be heard in all its detail; indeed, it had to be told and discussed endlessly, for everyone knew something of it. Just after breakfast on the twenty-third a heavily armed boat-party had landed unnoticed on the tip of St. Mary's Isle, where the Selkirk mansion stood, and had made its way up to the house while Captain Paul Jones stayed with the boats. They had met a gardener and told him that they were a Royal Navy press-gang, and from him they learned that the Earl was away from home. By the time they reached the house the gardeners and farm-hands had disappeared down the road to Kirkcudbright, fleeing the press-gang. As the women and children fled upstairs, and the servants down to the pantry, two officers entered and confronted the butler, demanding to see Lady Selkirk. They were shown into the parlour, and she came down to meet them with disconcerting coolness. They bluntly revealed their identity and their demands: they were from the United States frigate *Ranger*, Captain John Paul Jones; they had intended to take the Earl of Selkirk as a hostage (to exchange for American sailors); since he was not at home they would take the household silver as a prize of war. 'It was needless to expostulate as it was useless to resist,' Lady Selkirk wrote to her sister. With calm dignity she gave the necessary orders about the silver to Daniel, the butler, and offered her visitors a glass of wine.

It was all over in a few minutes. None of the sailors surrounding the house entered, or harmed anyone, though there were mutterings about burning the house and taking the linens as a reprisal for similar outrages along the New England coast. Twice while the silver was being collected in sacks the reluctant Daniel was found trying to hold some back and was made to disgorge by Lady Selkirk. The more junior officer was courteous and seemed to dislike his task; the other kept saying that the house was no longer 'that Lady's' but his, and everything in it was at his command. She thought him evil-looking, a dangerous bad man, and stayed with him as he walked through the house, to prevent any trouble with the servants, who had regained their confidence and become truculent. Then the sailors had formed up and shouldered the sacks of silver. The officers were civil to the last but clearly anxious to get away. Soon after the boat had put off from shore, and long before *Ranger* had stood out of the treacherous waters of Kirkcudbright Bay, volunteers from the town had come swarming over the isle dragging some old ship's cannon and taking up warlike postures – but *Ranger* did not return.

Such was the plundering of Lord Selkirk's house, the news of which had caused him great anguish – a harmless incident

4

but clearly one that might have ended very differently. The Earl, in justice, felt bound to tell on all sides how well behaved and under control the American sailors had been. The story was a nine-days' wonder, wearying and in the end embarrassing, for the tale of Lady Selkirk's calm courage had spread from Kirkcudbright to Dumfries and beyond. '. . . I had rather not shine,' she wrote uncomfortably. 'I have got all the fame I can desire on this occasion . . . more than I think I have a title to, so it shall satisfy me the rest of my life. I say more than I have a title to for it is not easy to determine on what one may value themselves since even their virtues are given them as much as any advantage of person or fortune, for my own share I frankly acknowledge my composure to be constitutional. . . .'

She regretted sometimes that she had not let the servants save some of the silver, though her lord swore that she had done everything exactly right. Still, she sighed over her lost silver, 'which tho' little I shall probably never be mistress of as much again'. She could not know that Captain John Paul Jones, captivated by his officers' account of her charm and courage and dignity, had already written, promising most gallantly the return of the plate.

The incident slipped quickly into the past so that by mid-May it seemed to Lady Selkirk that if it hadn't gone outside the family it would have been forgotten, 'except now and then when a scrimpness of knives and forks might have made us recollect at dinner and laugh a little about it'. In that sensible household, bound together in affection and laughter, the coughs which the boys brought home, and which persisted, were more important than the loss of the household silver. The Earl, too, had contracted a cough at Dumfries and more than a month after the raid he and Daer had both to be bled for their colds. The damp climate of the Solway was cause for worry when any chest weakness was present.

Lady Selkirk with her constitutional composure worried less than the Earl over her children. She looked to summer and warmer weather to make all things right. And certainly her five boys and four girls gave reason for happy confidence, and more. This lively, affectionate, and talented group gave promise of a resurgence, of a renewed splendour, for the great house of Douglas. John Paul Jones, who had been born John Paul in a parish near Kirkcudbright, had hoped to capture the Earl of Selkirk, because he believed him to be one of the greatest men in the kingdom. It was the understandably mistaken view of a village boy. But he was not wrong in thinking that the Earl bore one of the great names of Scotland, a name which at many moments in Scotch history had stood close beside that of the king.

Unless they were without imagination, the Douglas boys and girls must have been excited by this heritage. All round them in ruined castles and well-remembered legends were echoes to inflame the heart of the least romantic. In the River Dee near their home stood Threave Castle, a stronghold of the Douglases almost 500 years before. Archibald 'Bell the Cat', Earl of Angus – the only noble in Scotland strong and bold enough to lead opposition to James III – was a Douglas and an ancestor. So was Lord James – The Black Douglas – who led Robert the Bruce's army 20,000 strong into England. A red crowned heart stood in the Douglas coat of arms in honour of Lord James's attempt to carry out Bruce's dying wish by taking his heart to the Holy Land. In a desperate battle with the Moors in Spain, Douglas flung the silver case containing Bruce's heart ahead of him into the midst of the outnumbering enemy, crying, 'Pass first in fight as thou wert wont to do and Douglas will follow thee or die' – then fought his way to the case before he was slain.

In a land of long memories with its almost primitive admiration for physical courage, and fixity of purpose to the point of ruthlessness, the sons of the house of Douglas could not but feel called on to acquit themselves well as opportunity offered, and even to seek opportunity. Dunbar, the third son, was to go into the navy, Alexander (Sandy), the next in age, was to be a soldier. Tom, the rather frail, studious youngster, seemed least apt for an adventurous future, and in so numerous

6

a family the prospects of the youngest son were bound to be slight. Most of the great estate must pass to Basil, Lord Daer; John was to be trained in the law; something had to be thought of for young Thommy – quiet, shy, and delicate, and rather a favourite in the family.

So, in December 1785 when he was still fourteen – and after a period at Mrs. Barbauld's progressive school – he registered at the University of Edinburgh for a course in what we should call 'liberal arts', to be followed by training in the law.

Perhaps fortunately, going to Edinburgh where his family and many of their friends lived for part of each winter did not completely thrust the diffident boy out into the world. His youthful interests and ready affection developed still within reach of his numerous brothers and sisters. Though gradually, within the next few years, they began to move out of the family circle, they did not lose touch. Daer had already made his first trip to France a year or two before. The year after Tom went to Edinburgh, his sister, Lady Helen, married Sir James Hall of Dunglass, and their Edinburgh house in Hanover Street became another haven. The Halls were a popular couple, taking from the first a modest prominence in society; Helen was Queen of the great Haddington Ball the next spring. A year later, on New Year's Eve, Tom and Dunbar were staying overnight with the Halls when at two o'clock in the morning Sir James came leaping up the stairs and 'woke them with a rattle' to drink the health of a new nephew, Basil Hall. Meanwhile, Dunbar had already seen naval service and Alexander had started on his military career. The following summer, Daer, like other prominent young Britons, watched and cheered at the fall of the Bastille and even helped to liberate a prisoner.

The family was growing up and spreading out, but to Tom summer still meant vacation and expeditions into the country surrounding St. Mary's Isle. He enjoyed long hikes into the hills on foot or on horseback, sketching old castles, or studying the geological structure. And there was always the Circuit for the Quarter Sessions at Dumfries where, he reported to his university friend William Clerk, everyone was 'dancing like the devil'. In between times he was encouraged to try his hand at the various arts and skills of the country gentleman, making a plantation, building, studying crops and livestock. And he learned, too, if only by observing, the obligations of a laird to his tenants – lessons he never forgot. Imperceptibly, he moved from a boy writing William Clerk, 'Dear William', and signing himself, 'Farewell yours most affectionately', to the man who would presently write, 'Dear Clerk . . . Yours ever sincerely'.

He did not, of course, mature in a moment. The curriculum he had chosen, along with the brilliant and high-spirited company in which he was taking his place, developed his striking intelligence during five years, though he remained shackled in part by diffidence and by his comparative youth. He chose in progression three courses in classics, one each of mathematics, logic, rhetoric, and belles-lettres, two of natural philosophy, and three of ethics with the famous Dugald Stewart. It was not a crushing programme and the end product of it might be either a merely polite accomplishment or a full and ready man. And throughout his university terms the rich educational process of talk with others went on: talk in the streets, in coffee shops, in taverns – the talk by which the young teach themselves and alarm their elders.

In this, Thomas Douglas was more fortunate than most. His father, and at least Daer among his brothers, held rather advanced Whig views. They could not easily be shocked by even the wild talk of undergraduates, though the young men of the time were living in a world changed beyond belief from the one into which the elderly Earl had been born. The aftermath of the Rebellion of 1745 had destroyed the clan system in the Highlands and hurried on the changes in land tenure, which in turn were closely followed by the opening guns of the Industrial Revolution. On every hand were shifts of population and power and privilege, hardship to be contrasted with new wealth. From across the Atlantic, shared in by displaced kinsmen, came new notions of the rights of man; while nearer home, in France – always, and surprisingly, close to Scotchmen – the same ideas had burst into flame. It was an exciting

8

time to be young, and to be in an Edinburgh that was opening its arms wide to the future.

Scotland had its own stimulus to thought and action. The
Union of 1707 with England had not for long borne the appearance of partnership. Increasingly, through limited franchise
in elections for the House of Commons, and the selection of a
Government 'list' of Representative Scottish Peers, Scotland
was delivered in Westminster like a pocket borough; the
suave and capacious pocket was that of Henry Dundas, soon
to be Viscount Melville. In a time of awakening to liberty on
all sides, Edinburgh was stirring into a volunteer movement
of resistance that alarmed the moderate. This was familiar
and welcome debating-ground to a young Douglas; for the
Earl of Selkirk had been one of the leaders of the resistance to
the 'King's List' in recent elections of Scottish peers. In his
fiery, uncompromising speeches there was perhaps an echo of
old Archibald – Bell the Cat.

Thomas Douglas and his friends were part of a brilliant
group to which many would look back as to a golden age:
Francis Jeffrey, soon to be a founding member and later editor
of the *Edinburgh Review*; Walter Scott who was to remember
Tom Douglas as one of the most generous and disinterested
of men; William Clerk of Eldin and Adam Fergusson who were
for a lifetime to be the companions of Scott and feeders of his
genius. This coterie, with a dozen more, founded in 1788 'The
Club' which met monthly in rooms in Carruber's Close off the
High Street. Here, lively discussions were followed by livelier
suppers at a near-by tavern. Drawn casually together by
mutual interests and the rub of events, they were contributing
to a growing legend, as they strolled, arguing, to their club or
went singing up the High Street towards home – the legend of
Edinburgh as the Athens of the North. But they had nothing
to do with legends: to be young and alive was enough. In after
years Walter Scott liked to recall the stimulus of those carefree
days, with a certain suitable regret for time misspent; as ageing men with time growing short have always forgotten the
sheer pleasure that squandering time once was.

9

Whether or not they gave a thought to the making of legends, they walked always in the shadow of great moments in the past. Almost every event in Scottish history had touched the Royal Mile somewhere between Holyrood Palace and Edinburgh Castle; and there could have been few in the group to whom it spoke more than to Thomas Douglas. The Earls of Selkirk were among those traditionally privileged to have an apartment in the palace. He might recall the great and terrible day long past when the Douglases under the Earl of Mar had lined the High Street and fought for their lives against the more numerous Hamiltons; in the end they had slaughtered or driven out the Hamiltons with the help of Wedderburn of the Border, who had burst his way in to their assistance, smashing the gates of the city with sledge-hammers. There were reminders, too, in the Parliament House and the Law Courts that the splendours of the past did not all reside in the exploits of warriors, but in the concepts of life under law with justice, hard-won and worthy to be guarded.

The conditions of his life might by now be said substantially to have formed Thomas Douglas. Home environment and education had inclined and largely prepared him to perform valuable service in any one of several directions. He had a good brain able to take broad imaginative leaps and equally to engage itself, indeed to bury itself, in masses of laborious detail. With this went an impulsive generosity of spirit, a compassion that responded to every good cause – and doubtless to many bad ones – and that warred steadily with an intelligent caution, always lagging a little behind yet always certain to catch up. The tall, handsome youth with his ready smile, auburn hair, and searching blue eyes promised within the uncertain limits of his physical vigour to be heard from, perhaps in an unusual way. As yet life had neither much hardened him nor even tried him far, and there was no indication of what degree of strength or what quality of fortitude his still flickering interests and enthusiasms might command at some decisive moment in the future.

His approach to the law had been casual thus far. Indeed

his preparation for the future was strictly a by-product of his enjoyment of the present. He was probably no more idle than most young men and not much attracted to dissipation, but his keen mind had not yet developed a clear focus; unconsciously, restlessly, he was searching. His university career finished with two years of Scottish Law under David Hume, with Walter Scott still his classmate. But unlike Scott he did not matriculate or join the Faculty of Advocates.

It was at this stage and in this frame of mind that Thomas Douglas started on the series of travels that was to end his search. Towards the end of April 1792 he set out with a Mr. Gilmour on a trip through the Highlands of Scotland. He had probably crossed the Highland Line before and it is certain he knew much of the stormy and melancholy history of the Highlands, but this was to be an extensive exploration that was bound to be informed by the warmth of his ready interest in human problems. From Perth on May 2 he wrote his father that he 'had the honour' of watching a parade in Dundee to burn Mr. Dundas in effigy for opposing the reform of the Scottish boroughs; he thought the people had 'a dash of the French qui vive'. The same day, noticing many plantations of young trees probably set out as a result of Dr. Johnson's rude remarks on his tour of the Hebrides, he reflected on the debt due the great man for his acrimony. The traveller was just twenty-one but he was living on tiptoe and as he set out everything was of interest. There was matter for much more serious and painful reflection awaiting him farther north, in the glens and on the harsh borders of the sea where the grim story of an uprooted people was beginning to unfold.

Something of the changes taking place in the Highlands was already known throughout Scotland; but the general statements of changes in landholdings and agricultural policy conveyed little enough of the realities in human shock and suffering. People living on small holdings their forebears had cultivated since time out of mind were being forced by the hundreds to quit them, without alternative housing or employment being provided for more than a very few. The process had begun slowly when, after the Rebellion of 1745, ownership of the clan lands was vested by law in the chieftain. The former system of clan holdings had been unwieldy and increasingly unsound economically, but it had provided a marginal subsistence for a considerable population, and it was deeply rooted. Improved methods of agriculture along with improved markets and transportation began to open up possibilities of development for the Highland lands, subject to the small allotments being thrown together for large-scale cultivation and especially for sheep-farming. As the older Highland chieftains died off, there came a generation less inclined to question its moral right to dispose freely of the land it owned in law, willing to charge rent to those who had lived rent-free and to rent to the highest bidder. Temptation was confirmed by the arrival of outsiders willing to purchase or to work the land at handsome profits. The pace of eviction was quickening and the procedure becoming more cruel.

The precise record of the young Douglas's response to all he saw has been lost; only the general impression, which struck deep enough to colour his whole life, remains clear. Even a man less sensitive must have been touched by the kind of paralysed stupor with which the Highland people – largely illiterate, taught only to solve problems by direct action under the leadership of the chieftain – confronted a betrayal backed by the law. All the chiefs had not failed their people, nor were all who failed equally ruthless; but the helpless people, encamped in the path of a tidal wave that would ultimately spare none, awaited their doom with stubborn and incredulous suffering. It seems unlikely that Thomas Douglas took any conscious resolve to help – indeed he had not the means – but he did at least recognize the need.

Soon after his return from the Highlands he set out on the Grand Tour of the Continent, a normal part of the expensive training of elder sons in noble families but not usually of the younger ones. His father may have felt that the son's sympathy and wide-ranging interest in politics would ultimately lead him towards government service, and fostered his bent accordingly. At the time of his departure for France in November, Thomas was enthusiastic about forcing the acceptance of Scotland's demands for parliamentary reform by the widespread enlistment of volunteers, similar to the movement in Ireland. But in Paris the realities of an experimental republicanism in action somewhat cooled the enthusiasm for the revolution that he had shared with his Whig family and with the members of The Club. His travels took him on to Naples where he stayed for more than a year under the eye of Sir William Hamilton, British ambassador to the Kingdom of the Two Sicilies. Here was no struggle for liberty to be studied but rather the last flowering of an old and decadent order. It was not an atmosphere in which he could easily be happy. The events he had so recently witnessed in the Highlands and in France must make him impatient of the elaborate ritual of a society turning resolutely away from life; but he was perhaps more critical of his own shyness, his inability to play a part, than of the role he was called on to play. 'I am in company without making one of the company,' he wrote unhappily. 'Can I hope that time will cure me of this ridiculous timidity?' Sir William Hamilton spoke of him only as being a little reserved. Further on in his travels, in Switzerland, a change of society seemed not to change the 'shyness and cold temper' which he deplored.

But if his travels did little towards the conquest of this distressing weakness they did much in other ways to prepare him for the important changes in his life that were now approaching. He seems to have acquired grace and fluency in French and to have met leading figures in the capitals of Europe (his friendship with Talleyrand became the subject of North West Company mockery in later years). Nevertheless, his father, admiring his scholastic attainments, could still write in affectionate reproof: 'I have known many lads of sixteen who, as the vulgar saying is, could have bought and sold you in a market.'

In the early summer of 1794 there was little sign that the abundant life of the large family based on St. Mary's Isle was about to be overturned. The round of country-house visits, the Circuit of Dumfries, some shooting, the winter at Edinburgh broken by the occasional assembly or play, seemed as safe from sharp disturbance as from any great excitement; if it was a little dull it was at least serene. In June of that year Lady Selkirk went on a visit to William Hall of Whitehall. With the ample accommodation of the day, her son-in-law, Sir James, thought it necessary to send only a casual note of warning to his uncle; in addition to Lady Selkirk in the carriage there would be three daughters, and three servants on horseback, to be prepared for. Could anything be more serene than jogging through the rolling border country, pausing to admire a vista or a crop, a bridge or an improvement in planting since last they passed that way?

By late summer a dark cloud had crossed their sun. Daer's health, never very robust, seemed seriously to be worsening – Daer who from his youth had moved easily and gracefully into the position of leadership in the house and the countryside that was both his privilege and his responsibility. As summer progressed it was decided that he must seek a warmer climate for his health, and preparations were made for a trip to Madeira. Before the shock of this was even accepted, without warning, there came another blow. Alexander, posted to Guadeloupe with his regiment, had died there of yellow fever; Sandy and Thommy, the youngest, had been the only boys at home at the time of the Paul Jones raid – and now Sandy was dead. And then in November came news of Daer's death. The severity of his illness had prevented his making the trip to Madeira. Instead, he had gone to Ivybridge in Devonshire and from there the news of his suffering made the word of his death almost welcome – though it was 'a loss never to be repaired'. He was buried in Exeter Cathedral.

Daer and his father had been companions, had travelled much together, shared political enthusiasms which many found shocking: Edmund Burke and his views on the American war of Independence; Major Cartwright and his tireless, forlorn campaign for parliamentary reform. Doubtless, Daer was to have taken his father's place at the elections of Representative Peers for Scotland and spoken out against tame acquiescence in the wishes of ministers in London. Basil, Lord Daer, had been idolized in Kirkcudbright where he was not only the laird's eldest son but everything that a future laird should be. Now Basil was dead and John was the new Lord Daer. It was a sad loss, but in a sense less tragic than when fifty years before young Lord Daer, only son of the third Earl, had died suddenly 'of a dead palsie'. Dunbar Hamilton, a grand-nephew, had become the heir then and had changed his name to Douglas. At least now the succession was secure.

They had always kept in touch, passing news of each other as a close-knit family does: news of Alexander coming north to do some recruiting, and hoping to enlist some Highlanders; news from Lady Helen Hall that she was expecting her brothers from Edinburgh on a visit to Dunglass; news of Dunbar as a young officer going out in the ship that was to take the breadfruit trees to Jamaica and then to go on round the world. So they had written back and forth across the years of their growing up – keeping track of each other, proud of each other. They had been numerous and strong and bursting with life, but their number had shrunk grievously.

Then, just as it might have seemed that Death had done his worst, he struck them repeatedly. In 1796 came, again without warning, news of the death of Dunbar. He had died on naval duty at St. Kitts of the same yellow fever that had killed Sandy.

Whether it was a long resolve growing out of his father's taunt or an impulse in response to his changed circumstances, Thomas Douglas determined now to learn farming in good earnest. He obtained a farm from his father and worked it as if he were a tenant. It was the wonder of the countryside, and long afterwards the natives liked to point out a field that Tom Douglas had broken to the plough, driving the clumsy implement with his own slender hands.

It was experience he would stand in need of, for a year later John, Lord Daer, was also dead. The Douglas sons seemed doomed to die far from home, and death had overtaken John in Florence. Thomas Douglas, youngest and last of seven sons, was now Lord Daer and his father's heir – the hope of his house. He went quietly on with the working of his farm. It was good for his health and it was useful for the duties that must soon be his.

A year later the circle shrank further still with the death of Lady Mary Douglas, and in the following year, in 1799, of the old Earl himself. Thomas Douglas, who five years before had no expectations of either fortune or responsibility, at twenty-eight was suddenly the inheritor of both.

2

Thomas Douglas had had two years in which to get used to the notion of inheriting the title and all that went with it. He did not have quite the advantages of specific preparation that would have been Basil's or John's, but the rich educational opportunity of his years in Edinburgh and in continental travel together with his interest in the land and in people had broadened and cultivated his mind. Moreover, the accumulated sadness of the family disaster could not leave an intelligent and sensitive beneficiary otherwise than humble. He was of a liberal tendency of mind, yet his modesty did not suggest any fundamental doubts about the existing social structure or the propriety of his place in it; he was simply not inclined to be impressed with his own importance. Not long after this it was said of him that he was 'particularly averse to everything resembling cringing or studied servility. An independent mode of thinking and acting is the strongest recommendation to his consideration.' The observer, himself a commoner, added: 'With this knowledge of his disposition properly acted upon you may confidently expect his intimate acquaintance.'

The young Earl was, in fact, just as he appeared to others – sensible and steady; and his awkward shyness presumably came from over-seriousness about life rather than about himself; much less did it come from any fundamental insecurity expressing itself in over-assertiveness. For the moment, his changed status seemed to make no difference to his life. He was learning Gaelic and studying the development of events in the Highlands, which seems never to have been far from his mind once it had fastened on that unfolding and irrevocable tragedy.

For a generation there had been a steady trickle of emigration from the Highlands, and it was growing at what some thought an alarming rate. Selkirk seems to have accepted from the first that this could not be stopped: the people of the glens had become redundant population; he favoured their going where they had a better prospect of happiness and prosperity, so long as they were not lost to Britain. Emigration meant a new chance for people worth assisting; if this stream could only be so diverted as to strengthen Britain overseas, the end result might be gain all round rather than political loss.

As the basic scheme took shape in his mind, his eye ranged over maps that offered possibilities. Availability of good land in areas not too difficult to reach, with climate not too dissimilar: these were the considerations. And never far from his thinking was the element of political strategy. Since successful colonies were automatically political factors, it was merely wise to place them to strategic advantage – the human considerations being constant. His attention had already been called to North America; indeed, he had inherited a considerable tract of land on Lake Ontario, bought for the estate years before by an agent; but with boundary disputes now settled it was clear that this was within the northern borders of New York State and so unsuited to his emigration plans. Informed gossip was also suggesting the possibility of Britain's acquiring the Floridas or Louisiana. These Spanish possessions were said to be about to pass by secret treaty to France. Britain had considered earlier the idea of trying to acquire them by trade or seizure, and now the war with France offered interesting possibilities.

Just at this point, with Selkirk's hopes and ideas becoming clearer and directed always towards the aiding of his fellow countrymen, rebellion in Ireland caught his attention and momentarily changed his plans. The first response of his nature to a cry of distress was always a generous inclination to help – an attitude some people can always believe in and admire while to others it remains absurd, incomprehensible, or suspect.

Observing the harshness with which rebellion in Ireland was crushed, his immediate impulse was to put his Highland emigration schemes to the test on behalf of the unhappy Irish. He put the idea forward to the Colonial Office in the guise of an act of enlightened self-interest for Britain: given land and a chance to start again elsewhere, the most daring spirits would emigrate and would in the same moment become less disposed and less able to stir up effective trouble. It was a 'radical cure' for the troubles of Ireland.

Even as he made his proposal, Selkirk set out to travel for some months in Ireland, to study conditions for himself. Nothing he saw caused him to change his views, neither did anything he learned make him a sufficiently persuasive advocate. The Colonial Office did not like the scheme, regardless of where the Irish might go; they considered that a colony made up of people so intractable was foredoomed and unsuitable for their support, and they were in any case opposed to colonization *en masse*.

In all these negotiations, everything Selkirk stood for, his strengths and weaknesses, came out. The man who importuned unduly and acted impetuously – driven by his single-minded enthusiasms – was merely younger, more flexible, and less bitter than the man who fought desperately in much the same cause almost twenty years later. In 1801 or early 1802 he had come upon a description of the Red River country which so fired his imagination that he would contemplate no fundamental obstacle to the realization of his dream: this was to be the site for his settlement. He had already the fertility in planning with which he was later, single-handed, to keep the North West partnership off balance in the struggle that was to grow from their conflicting interests. And he had also now what he would never lose – a degree of obstinacy, a reluctance to withdraw when it was unreasonable and self-defeating to insist, which though an aspect of his strength was also a weakness he seemed unable to recognize.

The tone of the correspondence with the Colonial Office suggests that he seriously overplayed his hand. However, though apparently not convinced, he seems ultimately to have realized that their views were not to be shaken. Quickly he swung back to his old scheme and acquiesced in Lord Hobart's view. An Irish colony was not a feasible undertaking; very well, he would send Highlanders. He had succeeded in learning of a large migration of people from the Western Highlands – about 100 families, nearly 800 people in all, who having been evicted from their lands were on the point of going out to the United States. His observations of emigration patterns had already confirmed what he knew of deep-grained Highland tendencies to follow where friends and especially kinsmen had gone before them. To deflect a tide of emigration was like turning a stampede of cattle; a success might indefinitely command the flow in a new direction.

Strategy allied to compassion had ruled his first proposals for the movement of Irish colonists and had then driven him too hastily to organize his Highland group. Louisiana, Red River, and Sault Ste. Marie (the pass to the North-west that might fall to the Americans) could all be pressed as desirable strategically. Each in turn had failed. The government was unwilling to set aside the Hudson's Bay Company's charter claims which limited access to Red River, and Selkirk's personal expense in the Sault Ste. Marie venture promised to be prohibitive – his suggestion of a compensating grant of mineral rights around Lake Superior and Lake Huron having been brushed aside.

But his importunity had won a measure of acceptance for the broad scheme of helping Scottish emigrants to settle on British soil, and by the summer of 1802 success seemed to be in sight. Then, for some months, matters stood still; even an interview with the Prime Minister, Henry Addington, seemed to avail nothing. The government was fearful of appearing to initiate or even to encourage emigration. The Highlands were a fruitful source of recruits for the army and the uneasy peace that had followed the Treaty of Amiens was already coming to an end. In desperation, he talked of taking up land for his colonists in the western United States and the Government at last acted to meet his wishes: he was to have suitable lands in Prince Edward Island and Upper Canada on very favourable terms.

By the time the grant was confirmed in April 1803, he was already well forward with the complex plans and arrangements required for moving so large a group of people, and in July his three shiploads of settlers embarked.

3

The preparations for sea were merely the last in an intricate series of juggles that must have tried his nerve as certainly as they had tested his dexterity and determination. The probability of suitable land had forced him to commit himself to the most readily available group of emigrants who might demonstrate his theory. Yet by the time he had them the site for his colony had receded almost beyond grasp, and while he pleaded his case urgently in Downing Street through the late winter, his emigrants grew restless; they preferred in any case to go to Carolina where they already had friends and relations. A condition of their remaining bound to him required that he undertake to accompany them, to see his promises fulfilled; and if they were to move in 1803 he must contract for supplies and ships before he could know their destination or even be certain they would sail at all. And, when at last it was settled, he had to turn his back on Britain just as the menace of renewed war with Bonaparte laid him open to charges of desertion of which his enemies would one day take full advantage.

If it worried him, he scorned to show it, and once the coast of Scotland had sunk into the mists astern he had little enough time for remote problems. Sailing in the ship *Dykes,* slightly ahead of the *Polly* and the *Oughton,* he had locked himself up for five weeks with a shipload of the most lovable, disputatious, and immovably stubborn people ever to land in British North America, any one of whom, it may be assumed, would have been pleased to discuss land grants with him the whole way across the Atlantic, and many of whom probably did.

At this stage plans and discussion could only be theoretical, subject to adjustments when they reached Prince Edward Island. From the background of his long study of settlement problems and his knowledge of land, he had tentative ideas of how best to place the people on his grant. These were talked over with his agents and with the leaders of the groups on board, as a fair east wind blew them cheerfully forward on their great adventure. If the voyage was an omen, the colony seemed born under a lucky star, for on August 3, well ahead of expectations, the *Dykes* was in the Gulf of St. Lawrence. The wind failed them then for a few days, as they went slowly in past the Magdalen Islands and the North Cape of Cape Breton. In idle contentment the people looked at these outer fringes of the promised land while they fished for cod and mackerel over the side.

He had hoped to arrive first at the rendezvous, in order to have some kind of shelter ready for the other settlers. But, in spite of the *Dykes*'s swift voyage, the *Polly* with the people from Skye on board had arrived two days ahead of them. She rode gently at anchor in the agreed spot while the long and confusing business of unloading onto distant beaches by small boats went forward. Selkirk had now to lose still more time calling on the governor and being drawn reluctantly into Charlottetown's modest social round. Though he begrudged the time, it was not wasted. Between visits and callers, he poured into his journal an immense collection of detail about the land, its personalities and politics, the local customs and agricultural practice, the state of the roads, the postal service, sources of supply, and markets for produce. It was all noted down, and filed also in his memory; the colony would not fail for his lack of knowledge.

A few days later he sailed back to his grant and landed in Orwell Bay after dark. Word of his coming spread to a few of the settlers and they gathered to welcome him, like a Highland chieftain, at his landing. The scene at the water's edge brought back to Selkirk a memory of Seaforth being greeted by his people at Kintail, on his own first trip to the Highlands eleven years before. In his romantic nature there was always a lurking wish to be a Highland chief and he treasured the scenes that established some claim to the title. He looked now with pleasure along a mile of shore where his people had constructed scores of lean-tos out of evergreen boughs. Before each shelter burned a great fire round which the settlers moved with their pots and pans or squatted contentedly in the summer night. It was a wild and beautiful scene, this first ragged edge of settlement crouching between the forest and the water.

By morning the news of his arrival had spread up and down the shore and about breakfast-time the people began gathering round Jo McDonald's tent where Selkirk had slept. 'We had a hearty shaking of hands,' he wrote happily in his diary for that Sunday, August 14; 'they came in general round me with a keeness & warmth that perhaps had a little resemblance to the old feudal times.' But, though he could linger for a moment over a romantic fancy, it was never for long. The whole hard, practical business of establishing the settlement on a workable footing had still to be done. As quickly as possible the settlers had to be placed on lands to their liking, to get some seed in the ground, to begin the clearing of land; and for each family a small, tight cabin must be built against the winter.

There were a dozen things to see to at once. He started surveyors at work, arranged for the building of a storehouse for provisions, encouraged leading settlers to take parties over portions of his land, and set out to explore it for himself. For the next two months he travelled tirelessly, overland by stout

Canadian pony and around the shores in a canoe, planning and laying out in his mind's eye. Wherever he went he read the quality of the soil in what grew wild upon it. He might sleep on the ground, in a hammock slung between trees, or in the house of an established settler whom he would question searchingly on the problems his people must face: how best to clear land; the expectation of harvest in successive years; the application of his own knowledge of farming to these somewhat different conditions. By flickering candlelight or leaping flames it all went down in his diary in immense and careful detail.

In a few weeks he was in the way of being an expert on the island and its prospects, and in spite of difficulties his conclusions were encouraging. When one day in his explorations he met four of his own Highland lads, sharing his meal with them and trying his Gaelic, he was fresh from a visit to a man who in eight years, starting with nothing, had won for himself a well-stocked freehold farm – an example of what lay open to them. Afterwards, they followed him, talking companionably and heaving his boat through the muddy shallows. In incidents such as this, trust in him and confidence in the future was slowly built in a people whose trust had been betrayed and confidence destroyed. It was the making of a stable settlement and a lasting legend.

But the victory was not easily won. The settlers, having little money, were desperately determined to lay it out to the best advantage and suspicious of every effort to hurry their decisions. Against their natural caution, intensified into a set stubbornness, was the proprietor's need to get indications of probable purchases, as a basis of planning. Selkirk, for his part, was unwilling to set his price too low, both because he believed men did not value what they got for nothing and because the suspicious Highlanders might thereby be put off. He heard soon after, to his amused exasperation, of one large proprietor who had sought to lure Highland settlers with the offer of a free cow with each farm, and had no applicants because the Highlanders 'took against it', thinking the offer too good to be true.

In the present instance the situation was bedevilled by rival proprietors whose agents went among the settlers to lure them away with counter-proposals. And squatters on the grant, facing dispossession, spread unattractive accounts of the country to frighten the settlers off. For a few days there was talk of a large number going on to Quebec, and some were lured away to another part of the island. The leaders on whom he had counted to help reassure the people were in some cases among the most contrary; they wouldn't say no, but no one could hurry them into saying yes. Time, precious for planting and building, went by, while the settlers wavered and argued. Selkirk, who had offered lots at a dollar an acre for partially cleared land near the shore and half a dollar an acre farther inland, now undertook to require only half the purchase price in cash, the balance to be payable in produce. The settlers were impressed but not convinced. And then, as mysterious as the undefined reluctance, came success. Somehow the mindless near-stampede was turned, and men hurried to announce their decisions and claim their land. Everyone wanted some frontage on the shore, though Selkirk had hoped to establish the farms in a series of large wheels surrounding small villages. The result was a row of narrow farms with log houses at the front − almost a continuous village running for miles.

Finally, on the twenty-seventh of August, the *Oughton*, last of the ships, arrived with the emigrants from Uist. For a time it appeared that the whole inexorable process must be gone through again, complicated by Selkirk's wish to keep this latest group away from the earlier arrivals. There was some fever in one area newly settled, and there were differences in religion between the groups. Moreover, the *Oughton* had carried a number of very poor families which had to be guaranteed a year's subsistence on credit, and this could hardly be promised to all. These were people who had always lived by the sea and once any attempt to settle them inland was given up the process of settling them on shore lots went quickly and well.

With his promise fulfilled, to see his people settled, Selkirk prepared to leave in late September. Already in less than two months much had been done. It was wonderful to see how quickly the best of the men and women were learning the strange and demanding arts of the pioneer. The woods rang with axes, beginning to be handled with skill; no longer did men court destruction by hacking at a tree without any idea of where it would fall. The fires were disappearing from the shore and were being replaced by the less spectacular but more comforting glow from the windows of a hundred cabins.

The colony was launched, and with an easy conscience Selkirk took his departure.

4

Selkirk had planned a leisurely journey across Nova Scotia to Halifax. From there he would go by sea to Boston and traverse upper New York State to enter Upper Canada at Niagara. He intended to learn a great deal about general conditions and about immigrant problems and prospects. Though a large grant was waiting to be claimed in Upper Canada, he seems not yet to have decided what use to make of it.

The first days of his journey from Pictou in Nova Scotia and through the old settlement of Truro provided both interest and reassurance. Here, in rugged clearings along the half-opened road, he found people just such as those he had left in Prince Edward Island. The only difference was that these people had triumphantly survived the first hard struggle of the pioneer settlers; all had not prospered equally but all had improved their lot and succeeded more or less in proportion to their capacity and effort. So he had mistaken neither the opportunity nor the response to it of which both Highland and Lowland people were capable. He noticed in some detail the typical case of a man who had started with nothing, but having planted five bushels of potatoes had harvested sixty. On this, supplemented by a little corn-meal, he and his wife and child had managed through the first winter. Now, in the second year, there was the expectation of 200 bushels of potatoes from the planting of ten, and there would be some wheat. There was more land cleared as well and a cow almost paid for, along with adequate shelter and abundant fuel. None of it had been easy, but a man who had had nothing might face greater difficulties than these in good heart, knowing that the future was in his own hands.

Armed with his notebook, his easy manners and agreeable smile, the young Earl went in and out of the tiny cabins of recent arrivals and the substantial stone houses of those who had long since won their place. The tales he was told were certainly of hardships, of unremitting toil; but they had not the hopelessness of those heard in the Highlands ten years before and many times since. The copious notes he put together – on road-making and fencing, on crop yields, on markets and prices, and on individual experiences – were the memoranda of a practical colonizer and the foundations of a philosophy of emigration. Even the most insignificant fact was worth noting, and every circumstance bearing on results was considered.

There seems to have been no rebuff, no unwillingness to talk to one so patently interested. He doubtless had much to give in return; for his accumulated notes, added to his already deep knowledge, qualified him almost as an itinerant counsellor; knowing how one man had succeeded with this kind of soil and why such an experiment had failed elsewhere. Seeing land wooded with hemlock and pine and a little hardwood, with generally a good appearance of mould, he could reflect that on Tweedside this would be reckoned good turnip and wheat land. Both for the simple authority of its knowledge, and its echo of home, talk like this did not need to come from an earl to open the doors of isolated farm-houses.

In the third week of September Selkirk rode along Bedford Basin, which looked to him like a Highland loch, and into Halifax. There, for the next two weeks, he was caught in a succession of dinner parties, without wholly abandoning his notebook or ever losing sight of his objectives. He made exhaustive notes on government and on the needs of Halifax as a market for the farming community. The social life, as usual with him, seemed not to engage his interest sufficiently to be recorded.

Towards the end of his stay he called on Father Edmund Burke, the Roman Catholic Vicar-General, to whom he had a letter of introduction. In him Selkirk found a man of enthusiasms to match his own and of a most persuasive tongue. Burke shared Selkirk's views on emigration as an extension of national policy but lamented the choice of Prince Edward Island for his experiment instead of Upper Canada. In particular, the priest pressed the importance of the Lake St. Clair area and urged the establishment of a settlement of Europeans at the entrance to Lake Huron, as a bastion against absorption by overflow from the United States. Selkirk demurred; he had no more settlers to send and had an impression that a settlement by him in Upper Canada would not be welcomed by officialdom. But Burke's enthusiasm was contagious and in a second long talk he produced maps and pointed out key locations – especially the River St. Clair. If Selkirk hadn't settlers, he, Burke, would find some – Irishmen. They talked of desirable numbers, of the expense, and of the best routes. Though the Earl had misgivings about Burke's judgment, he was partially won over; they would correspond; and whatever men Burke sent to Upper Canada Selkirk would see placed.

After a week in Boston he struck out north-west for Albany and the Niagara frontier. Among other things, he was now trying out the route he had suggested to Father Burke that Irish immigrants might take. In general, he was more eager to learn, freer of prejudice, than most British travellers. The antipathy he felt towards Americans, dating back, he supposed, to the Paul Jones raid, was balanced by a genuine and sympathetic interest in their bold experiment in government and the remaking of society. Letters of introduction tended to throw him among the remnants of the old governing group – the Federalists – and from them he heard what he might have been expected to like: toasts to the King of England, in Boston; comments on radical defects in the American Constitution; distrust of an educational system that gave everyone facility of expression and confidence without maturity of judgment; the opinion that Britain had as much freedom as was consistent with stability in government. They were at any rate views with which he was not at once in disagreement. They went down in his diary, often without comment, sometimes with a dry aside. For he was not inclined to take all these opinions at their face value and was clearly prepared to allow for growing-pains. When his Federalist friends objected to voting by ballot, on the ground that it gave opportunity to unscrupulous election officers, he noted that their real objection was probably to the loss of control over their tenants and dependants.

Against the understandable and seemingly valid objections of the stand-patters, the unconscious Tories, he found promise for a society which in the name of liberty had released hope and boundless energy in men. Along the road he did not meet the 'brutal surliness' of which British and continental Europeans complained, finding instead that courtesy was met with courtesy and kindness. And he saw other signs of a practical democracy which he found convincing and hopeful. One day on the road he encountered a man in a wagoner's frock and looking like an English farm servant. As they talked, a third man drew up addressing the farmer as Colonel. Here was sport for the sharp pen of the usual traveller, but not for Selkirk: 'His address tho' homely was however easy – his answers very pertinent & distinct & his conversation very different from what would have come from similar dress and appearance in England.'

Though he greatly enjoyed the company of men like Alexander Hamilton, Stephen van Rensselaer, and General Philip Schuyler, in other men he noticed 'some of the peculiarities remarked in the American national character – particularly their sordid attention to money'. This he put down to the want of a landed aristocracy and the necessity for almost everyone to work for a living, so that it was scarcely possible for a man 'to feel that absolute *insouciance* about money from which the character of a *Gentleman naturally* arises'. He went on to reflect that a merchant might 'from reflection & a superior mind possess the sentiments of a Gentleman but they do not naturally spring out of his situation'.

It all went down in the voluminous notebooks, but neither the sympathetic interest nor the ultimate disillusionment with American government distracted the colonizer and farmer for long. Building materials and costs, the evolution of immigrants into land-owners, the planting and uses of Indian corn, the hazards of sheep-raising, and the reasons for ague among new settlers – these were the things of which he could never learn enough, more fascinating than the workings of patronage or the success of demagogues. Through the splendours of Indian summer he made his way up the Hudson and Mohawk valleys, pausing to sketch a bit of country – and being thought mad in the process – sleeping with near indifference in comfortable inns or poor log-house taverns, talking with everyone he met, observing everything.

On November 15 he crossed from Buffalo Creek to Fort Erie in Upper Canada. He was moving onto fateful ground and meeting the people with whom the main course of his life and its ultimate disaster would be closely bound up. There was no warning of this in his friendly, informative meetings with men like Thomas Clark and Robert Hamilton of Queenston, who between them controlled a large part of the carrying trade between Lake Erie and Lake Ontario. From them he learned a great deal about the as yet simple commerce of the infant province, and the bestriding importance of the fur trade. The dominant North West Company of Montreal had for six years been locked in a deadly struggle with the XY or New North West Company under Sir Alexander Mackenzie and his associates. Mackenzie, who as a North West clerk had reached the Arctic by Mackenzie River and had been first to the Pacific, enjoyed an immense prestige in England, but it had seemed only to stimulate the hostility of his former colleagues in the war now reaching its climax.

On November 20 Selkirk sailed for York and once again the

29

ubiquitous fur trade thrust itself memorably on his attention. His ship was becalmed towards evening until a group of Canadian *voyageurs*, belonging to the fur trade – with that gay competence he would one day know well – warped it ashore with the ship's boat. The little capital of Upper Canada, founded only ten years before, made no great impression as the *voyageurs* towed them in past Gibraltar Point to a waterfront prospect of ragged stumps and small scattered buildings.

For the next six weeks little York with its seventy or so pioneer houses was Selkirk's home. He came to know well the unpromising settlement with its 'roads called streets infamous & almost impassable'. Governor John Graves Simcoe had selected Toronto as a naval station and temporary capital ten years before and had changed its name to that of a royal duke. A group of reluctant officials, finding these pretensions both ridiculous and uncomfortable, had followed Simcoe from Niagara, and as yet the town contained little more than a garrison, government officers, and such servants as they could hold and maintain. But, impressive or not, York was the capital, and here if anywhere the ideas put forward by Father Burke must be tested and, if promising, acted on.

Selkirk was immediately at work making comprehensive inquiries about politics, communications, and costs, seeing quickly enough the mistakes that had been made in carving this town on the rim of the forest. And as always he talked land. From the first he was in and out of the Surveyor-General's office examining maps and deciphering surveyors' field notes, apparently drawn increasingly to the Lake St. Clair area. Father Burke had talked also about the Mississauga Tract on Lake Ontario, recommending it as a more promising speculation. This consideration Selkirk brushed aside; he wanted more space in one parcel than was to be found near by. Since February, a grant of 1,200 acres in any ungranted township had waited only on his claim, and he was to have a further 200 acres for every family he should settle (fifty of the 200 going to the settlers). In little more than a week after landing, he had made his choice. It was in Dover and Chatham townships on Lake St. Clair and it was made before Burn, his overseer, returned with his report on the area. The persuasions of Father Burke and considerations of strategy had undoubtedly pushed him towards a decision that was to prove disastrous to many, and to put a weapon in the hands of his future enemies.

Life in York was not all land administration or politics and in the crude little capital the niceties of social intercourse were scrupulously maintained. The handsome young Earl was eminently receivable and Judge William Dummer Powell observed that everywhere people acclaimed the visitor's charm of manner and his talents. Selkirk seems to have been on friendly terms with the Governor, General Peter Hunter, the Chief Justice, Sheriff Alexander McDonell, and all the leading figures in the community. He was also a frequent visitor at Colonel Isaac Brock's 49th Regiment mess and in Judge Powell's house. In spite of their unpromising exteriors the houses had surprising warmth and comfort and the visitor took pleasure in the furniture fashioned out of beautiful local woods: walnut and curly maple and cherry. In these surroundings the time doubtless passed swiftly enough; and the impossible streets, their ruts frozen to iron by the winter and their worst holes packed with snow, proved not at all impassable. He made friends and his affairs seemed full of promise.

Selkirk set out for Montreal on January 4. In a few short weeks he had made himself as much of an expert on land-holdings and on the influences shaping the new province as maps and industry could make him. During the journey he improved his knowledge, questioning and observing, and noting in immense detail when the weather held him stormbound and he could only write up his diary. For the first hundred miles east of York he found only scattered settlements joined together by hopeless roads which, for long distances, it was no one's responsibility to maintain. What progress could be found was almost always due to some Yankee settler whose superior energy, knowledge of conditions, and initiative were unfailingly impressive. The leading citizens of these groups he liked, but their followers he found grasping, ungenerous, and unreliable.

He was more than ever convinced that, in time, immigrating Americans must become the controlling influence in the province and that, regardless of the progress this might represent, it would be a sorry day.

Farther east he began to encounter the settlements of disbanded regiments from the American war and of homogeneous groups of American loyalists or immigrants. Here was more hope; for in the Bay of Quinte and Kingston, in Osnabruck and Cornwall and Glengarry, there were solid settlements based, however loosely, on some unifying principle other than money; religious or clan or regimental ties held the groups to some extent under elders, priests, chieftains, or officers, and progress, though slow, gave promise of a permanent and coherent society. Even among the people of Glengarry, the most recently arrived (and, being Highlanders, the most interesting to him), he found great reason for hope. The people stuck together and helped each other; and their mean first houses were still far better than the hovels from which they had been evicted in Scotland. The second houses were such as belonged to modestly prosperous small holders in the Lowlands; and growing civilization, especially in cleanliness, seemed to keep pace with the hard-won prosperity. It all confirmed confidence in his developing plans.

The most momentous event of the trip, pleasant but scarcely recognized as important, was Selkirk's meeting with Captain Miles Macdonell on his farm at Osnabruck just west of Cornwall. Macdonell had come out from Scotland to New York State as a boy, not long before the Revolutionary War. He had then been brought to Canada in the Loyalist migration and in due course had become a soldier and had risen to the rank of captain in the Canadian Volunteers. On the disbandment of his corps in 1802, Miles had flung himself into farming, and, as Selkirk learned, he was a very popular figure among his neighbours; men would work for Captain Macdonell when they would help no one else. This Selkirk saw no reason to doubt, finding him 'very much of a gentleman in manners & sentiments'. He was also impressed with the ambition and boldness with which Macdonell, untrained to the land, was attacking the improvement of his farm and buildings, which tenants had long neglected. He had met Macdonell's brother-in-law, Sheriff Alexander McDonell, at York, and had similarly been drawn to him. These Glengarry men with their commanding presence, their dignity and grave courtesy, represented much of what had always attracted him to Highland people. That what went with these qualities at this stage was frequently arrogance, an unaccommodating temper, and a lack of the staying power that was built into the less attractive Lowlanders, he either had not learned or would not recognize. These were the men he would always choose for his hardest tasks, and though they would carry a position or two with great dash they would fail before the rigours of a wearing siege – and he with them.

As he moved on to Montreal he found little to make him doubt Highland capacity. Here for the moment almost all the grandees with whom he found himself surrounded were Highlanders connected with the fur trade – the agents of the North West Company and their bitter rivals of the XY Company, whose war in the interior was just approaching an accommodation in Montreal. He found them interesting, prosperous, and hospitable, and they, with their open-handed ways, saw in this Scottish nobleman a most desirable guest. Following his invariable custom, he questioned them closely on their affairs, to an extent that they later chose to regard as an indication of sinister designs. They would doubtless have been more affronted than satisfied to find that in his notebooks he gave almost as much space to Young's brewery at Beauport, and more to affairs at York and democracy in the American states. For the moment they were flattered by his interest and for a week or two he enjoyed the splendours of the Beaver Club and listened in their impressive houses to fabulous tales of the North-west.

Much of his time went to dealing with an immense accumulation of European mail. Then he was off to Quebec where he made a shrewd estimate of British mishandling of relationships with the French Canadians, aggravated by the commercial success of his recently made Scottish friends in Montreal. Looking, like every traveller, over the battlefields of the Plains of Abraham, he commented dryly that in Wolfe's victory there appeared to have been 'fully as much guid luck as guid guiding'.

Through the winter and spring, the Earl went tirelessly on across Vermont to New York City and back again through Albany and Buffalo to complete a figure eight at York. We may be sure that he never ceased to observe and to question, to note the geological formation, to question a farmer, or to examine a new milling process; but except for rough entries and memoranda the notebooks were put away.

In early June he came to his grant on the edge of Lake St. Clair and flung himself into the excitement of planning a new settlement. It would be called Baldoon after his father's estate, and the home farm would be the finest in Upper Canada. There were to be all the essential mills on the property sooner or later – sawmill, grist-mill, brewery, and distillery – and a road was to run through the settlement to the River Thames. Selkirk hoped shortly to have a schoolmaster and a priest. Already eleven families of settlers were on their way out from Scotland, and they would have to be supplemented by picked workmen, overseers, and sheep-hands brought from Scotland or found on his travels in Canada and the States.

Selkirk had found the man he wanted as manager of the settlement in Sheriff McDonell of the Home District, and, after a good deal of uncertainty and wavering, McDonell, who had gone to Baldoon with him, accepted. Through July, planning and preliminary work went on. Contracts had been let for the first buildings by the end of July, when Selkirk set out for York and the long journey home.

At Queenston he met his settlers upward-bound and arranged that Thomas Clark would give them some work and care for them until Baldoon was more nearly ready. They were an unpromising lot, but doubtless he was encouraged to remember what Pictou and Glengarry had accomplished in a few years for people who came to them desperately poor, filthy, ignorant, and full of suspicion.

Selkirk stopped at York for last talks with his friends and with the Governor. General Hunter was not encouraging about the appointment of Sheriff McDonell, whose ability he doubted, though not his integrity or industry. His facile support of Selkirk's hopes – of securing the islands off his grant to complete his drainage plans and securing the Shawnee Township for its higher ground and water power – were later to prove illusory and seriously misleading. Similarly, when Selkirk offered to build a great road through the heart of the province, for $500 a mile and large land grants back of the road on each side, Hunter felt sure such a proposal would be seized on by the Executive Council, and at a much higher price. Here again Hunter was to prove quite wrong, or guilty of duplicity.

But all promised well as Selkirk set out for Montreal and onward to Prince Edward Island. Here, at least, the promise of a year earlier was proving no illusion. In spite of difficulties and squabbles the settlement was shaping well and a good small crop was being harvested in addition to the plentiful supply of fish that his people had obtained. Until mid-October he laboured, adjudicating complaints of every magnitude and encouraging arrangements for the bringing out of further settlers.

While there, he learned from one of his agents that the liberality of his terms had given great offence to some of the Highland proprietors and that the Emigrant Regulation Bill was a direct result of his success. It was even being said by his defamers that his real objective was not yet disclosed; possibly it was to be the fur trade – or copper mines. 'These ideas are probably the result of his own imagination,' wrote Selkirk, 'but attend.'

Almost the last rough note of Selkirk's trip recorded still another tribute to the character of Miles Macdonell. It was as though the gods themselves were determined to mislead him.

News of illness among the new settlers at Baldoon caught

him in Halifax before he sailed. It was still inconclusive but contained a grim warning. He sent what directions he could to Sheriff McDonell and turned homewards.

It seems Selkirk landed in the south of England and journeyed north by Exeter. The last enigmatic entry in the diary is a small, rough sketch of a part of the cathedral annotated 'D Shrine'. Basil, Lord Daer, had been buried there ten years before.

Chapter 2

THE YEARS OF SUCCESS

I

Only a stubborn and ungenerous opponent could have begrudged Selkirk some feeling of triumph on his return. He had
set out to demonstrate a theory, the fruit of almost ten years
of observation and reflection. It had been carried forward in
the face of hostility and disbelief, and at a heavy cost. A failure
would have laid him open to ridicule, if not censure, either of
which in his code might be more serious than any loss of
money. Possibly he had never contemplated taking risks on
such a scale but in the end he had had no choice. The pressing
forward of his views had produced an issue he could not avoid,
and he had accepted the challenge. Now the case, if not proven,
was in the way of being so, and he proceeded to consolidate
his success.

It was the essence of his scheme that it should end not in
personal triumph but in public acceptance and national policy.
At first he contemplated merely the publication of his sub-
missions of 1803 to the Colonial Office, expanded by an account
of his subsequent practical experience. In the end he decided

in favour of a book in which he might marshal the arguments that had convinced him long since: the congruence of Highlanders' needs and Britain's interests. Through the winter and spring he laboured steadily, setting out the case, reinforcing it, polishing the style. Reading it 150 years later, we cannot miss the impression of a man happily at work, moving from manuscript to reference books, certain of his objective and doubting only his capacity to present the case to full advantage. The result was to be a book men must notice for as long as the problem remained. When, ten years later, Walter Scott electrified Scotland with *Waverley*, he referred in his last chapter to the great changes that had taken place in Scotland and which had been 'traced by Lord Selkirk with great precision and accuracy'.

At the end of January a painful shock required him to face the darker side of his undertakings: that those who intervene to change people's lives may change them for the worse. A letter from Alexander McDonell after a tragic autumn at Baldoon was enough to cloud the pleasing visions that Selkirk had carried back with him from Prince Edward Island. When he had left Baldoon in late July everything promised fair; the main building – The Mansion House – and one labourer's cottage were well advanced. The crops that had been planted showed good promise. But throughout September and October drenching rains had impeded all work, ruined much of the partially reaped crop, and flooded the low-lying fields. Helpless and despondent, the emigrants crouched in cold and damp tents, which were presently filthy as well. This had proved a breeding-ground for malaria. The overseer and the wife of one of the shepherds were among the first to die, but before the autumn was out sixteen more had followed them, including the heads of a third of the families. McDonell, whose fate it was to be always too late with his cures for the ills of Baldoon, had arranged for fourteen houses to be built at once on a ridge of high ground, and had then set out for Sandwich in search of provisions and medical help.

Selkirk, having had some warning of disaster in Halifax in

November, had written quickly, directing the immediate removal of the settlers to a distance from the area and the issuing of lots on higher ground. At the same time he steeled himself, knowing his people and the experience at Prince Edward Island, to warn McDonell against pampering the settlers. To be kept busy and to have some responsibility for their own survival would promote both health and happiness. McDonell, snug in York, decided that nothing further could be done before spring and filed the letter to await his convenience.

Now, when the full tale of the tragedy reached Selkirk at the end of January 1805, there was nothing he could do immediately. He returned to the writing of his book, in which the Baldoon experiment may be inferred only in sombre warnings about difficulties to be encountered, the absolute disaster of illness in lonely places, and the preference for settlers developing their own farms, over indentured servants dependent on a landlord and lacking incentive. Through the spring the book drove steadily on and in early summer he was ready to go to London with his manuscript. It was to be called *Observations on the Present State of the Highlands of Scotland with a View of the Causes and Probable Consequences of Emigration.* 'Selkirk on Emigration', as it would soon be known, developed a seemingly unanswerable argument through the history of the Highlands and the character of the Highlanders. It exposed and overrode the obstructive attitude of the Highland Society, and set forth in the final chapter a modest but attractive account of success in Prince Edward Island.

Following a careful statement in some detail of his original plans and difficulties, he described his return to the island at the end of a year to find the people safely beyond want, with their first harvest gathered and an abundant supply of fish.

> Thus in a little more than a year from the date of their landing on the island, had these people made themselves independent of any supply that did not arise from their own labour.
>
> To their industrious dispositions and persevering energy, the highest praise is justly due. Without these, indeed,

every other advantage would have been of no avail: for if the arrangements that have been detailed have any merit, it may all be comprised in this, – that by their means the industry of the individual settlers was preserved unimpaired, was allowed full scope to exert itself, and was so directed as to produce all the effect, or nearly all, of which it was capable.

The book having been accepted for publication by Longman, he sat down in London in the month of June to write an introduction. It was a statement of reasons for writing on the subject and of his qualifications; and to assuage his own feelings of guilt it contained an explanation of his absence from the country at a time when invasion by Bonaparte seemed imminent. 'In other respects I have had no reason to regret my absence, as it has not only led me to sources of information, to which few have access; but I trust that my occupation in the meantime has not been wholly useless to my country.'

The launching of the book with its persuasive arguments and bold contradiction of 'the misrepresentations, which have been circulated under the sanction of respectable names' sealed his course. Others had sponsored settlements without enunciating a philosophy of emigration. They were either casual benevolences or adventures in investment; this was a declared attempt to shape national policy. In spite of sharp rejoinders from those he had challenged, he moved forward into the public eye with some confidence. In accordance with a custom he was to follow all his life, he sent inscribed copies of the book to acquaintances as various as Walter Scott, Talleyrand, and the Duke of Hamilton.

Since good reports continued to come in from Prince Edward Island, it seemed that he might put emigration on one side for the moment. But Baldoon, like a dead albatross about his neck, was there to remind him that success was not guaranteed at any cost. McDonell had returned in the spring to find everything much improved. For the moment the fever was gone and hopes were high. He decided to set aside Selkirk's instructions about moving the settlers. During the summer, when danger seemed to have passed, malaria returned and McDonell, too late, had taken all the people into the town of Sandwich, where they were maintained and cared for at heavy expense and where, nevertheless, two of the girls from the settlement died. Reading this with dismay, Selkirk wrote ordering Mc-Donell to close Baldoon and move the people to a healthier situation up the River Thames. McDonell was to dispose of the cattle, keep the buildings in repair, and try to arrange for the sheep to be looked after. Selkirk believed he had all but closed the book on a disastrous venture.

Much had happened in the world Selkirk knew since his return. Napoleon's army of England, camped about Boulogne, had already become so familiar as to lose its terror long before it began to be drawn away in the summer of 1805. After two years at sea Nelson came home briefly to demonstrations of near-adoration and left again in September for his last patrol. Then, in swift succession, came the glorious news of Trafalgar, with its saddening postscript, and word of the destruction of the Austrian armies at Ulm and Austerlitz and with them of Pitt's carefully wrought European Coalition. What seemed to men in England the heaviest blow of all was now prepared. Shortly after Nelson was carried in solemn triumph to St. Paul's Cathedral in January 1806, William Pitt, worn out by the weight of his burdens, was buried in Westminster Abbey.

With two of the country's greatest props removed and the genius of Wellington as yet undeclared, Britain faced a future full of alarming uncertainties. Selkirk's characteristic response was to begin at once a searching examination of the system of enlistment and training for national defence. But it was an academic study, for England under Lord Grenville – who with his 'Ministry of all the Talents' had succeeded Pitt – was more bent on peace than war. Selkirk, apparently receiving a momentary notoriety, remained in London, taking an increasing part in politics and improving his acquaintance with leading men. In addition to universal military service, he was taking a lively interest in the Spanish colonies in South America and the growing agitation against the slave trade.

Since he had inherited the title there had only been one general election, in August 1802, and, preoccupied with settlement and with the last illness of his mother, who died in November, he had neither attended nor voted in the Scottish peerage election. Now that he had put his ideas into practice abroad, there was nothing to be done but occasionally to watch over the results, and it was inevitable that he should seek an active share in politics, if only to advance the cause of directed emigration. A second and revised edition of his *Observations on the State of the Highlands of Scotland* came out in Edinburgh in the summer of 1806 under the influential imprint of Archibald Constable, and a further edition was called for in London. His defiance of the Highland Society was blazoned forth and the battle carried to its very gates. Whatever satisfaction his father had taken in being a private country gentleman, the son had resolutely put away from him. At least within the limits of his chosen field, he would be a public figure from now on.

He had not long to wait for an opportunity, though whether he sought it remains a mystery, as do most of the surrounding circumstances. Knowledge of his recent travels in America was doubtless widespread, as was the record of his father and Daer in the Whig interest. These circumstances, allied to his impeccable family connections and his recognized talents, were enough to recommend him to Grenville and Fox. It appears that in late February he was approached to go as minister to the United States, and accepted the appointment. By mid-March the news was out, at least in informed circles, so that Lady Bessborough could write to Lord Granville Leveson Gower: 'Lord Selkirk goes Minister to America. I suppose you know.' Meanwhile Charles James Fox had already written Anthony Merry, the minister in Washington: 'In consequence of your long continued state of ill-health, His Majesty is graciously pleased to grant you leave of absence to return to this country.' Merry was instructed to notify the American government of the change, which, it was not doubted, would be agreeable to them 'from the character and talents of the

Earl of Selkirk and the intimate knowledge which he possesses of the reciprocal interests of the two countries'.

The decision made in haste seems to have been repented at leisure. At the end of April Selkirk wrote his friend William Clerk that nothing was yet 'fixed' about his going abroad: 'I have been put off in a teazing manner, & the suspense is as disagreeable to myself as to our friend Edie, but we must have patience. Others of your friends are still worse off. . . .'

It is not clear why the decision was changed; whether the offer was withdrawn, or, on reflection, refused by Selkirk. The chief reason may simply have been that he wished nothing to interfere with his plans for colonization. Equally, his preoccupation with emigration schemes may have raised a doubt of his sufficient enthusiasm for the new appointment. He had applied for an immense grant – of 300,000 acres – in the colony of New Brunswick, near to Prince Edward Island, and until May it appeared that his application might be approved. However, remembering the loss of his colonists in the island to other land-owners, to his own heavy cost, he sought to attach to the grant conditions that were unacceptable. In the end, the new grant was refused, so perhaps he had given up a great opportunity to no purpose.

It is not certain whether by summer he had taken any definite decision about standing for election as a Scottish peer. In May and June he was still in London, staying in Upper Brooke Street, submitting his views on questions of the day to those more actively engaged in them, playing somewhat the part of the distinguished amateur. He was doubtless learning more about the differences between the youthful theories of The Club and the practice of the world of hard realities. In September Charles James Fox died and in October Grenville asked for the dissolution of Parliament. Shortly afterwards, a general election of Representative Peers for Scotland was proclaimed at the Mercat Cross in Edinburgh. The same proclamation had been made at Kirkcudbright in his father's day – the last such proclamation in a county town of Scotland – when he could not have guessed that it might one day summon him.

It was the custom to let it be known that one was standing for election as a Representative Peer – to solicit support, but with detachment. As the day approached, he had reason to be moderately confident, for he had friends in London; and, though the peers led by his father had fought fiercely against 'the King's List', the ministers had a way of making their wishes clear to good purpose. Still, the support of the government, supposing he could count on it, was by no means a guarantee.

At noon on Thursday, December 4, he stood among the peers near the entrance to the Picture Gallery of Holyroodhouse. Within the room was a scene which doubtless he could visualize from attendance at one of his father's elections, knowing in the end that one day he must take his place at the long scarlet-covered table. Back from the table on both sides stood rows of chairs filled with spectators, as were both crowded ends of the great room. Through the doorway came the continuous rustle and whisper of greetings and the exchanging of bows – suddenly hushed as the official procession entered the chamber, led by the bearer of the mace and followed by the Clerks of Session in wig and gown. Behind the Clerks moved the Royal Chaplains, Drs. Grieve and Somerville, the Keeper of the Records of Scotland, and the Baillie of Holyroodhouse. As the officials took their places and arranged papers at their table across the head of that of the peers, the thirty-six peers present moved forward to the long table, taking the only chairs that remained empty. It was the largest attendance of peers in twenty years and one of the largest in living memory, which warranted a little increase of tension as the Union Roll of the Peerage was laid upon the table and the chaplain rose to open the proceedings with a prayer. The election on which Selkirk had set his heart had begun, but it is doubtful whether anyone looking at that handsome, slightly cold face, above the cravat of a dandy, could have read there any sign of an inner excitement.

It was to be a long election: the large attendance of peers guaranteed that. Moreover, all but nine of those absent had submitted signed lists of the sixteen candidates for whom they wished to vote. After the reading of the proclamation announcing the election, the calling of the Long Roll commenced. At the head of the table the Deputy Clerk Register intoned, 'His Royal Highness the Prince and Steward of Scotland, Duke of Rothesay'; from his place the Earl of Lauderdale answered without rising, as proxy for the Prince of Wales. The voice moved down the roll: 'The Duke of Hamilton, the Duke of Buccleuch, the Duke of Lennox, the Duke of Gordon ...' The great names of Scotland passed in review, being answered crisply, 'Here', or, 'Proxy', or, 'List' from the clerk who held the signed lists for most of those not present or represented by proxy. As the reading went on the peers around Selkirk began the writing of their own lists of names of the sixteen candidates they supported, giving careful attention to precedence.

There can be no doubt that what followed was an ordeal: the moment when he must get to his feet and read his list approached. A slight and unusual delay took place while the senior earl, the Earl of Crawford, being partially paralysed and unable to write, voted through notaries. But the ritual marched steadily down the list of earls to the calling of his own name. It was characteristic of him that, having set his heart on election, he faced the embarrassment of some automatic laughter and doggedly read his own name among the sixteen for whom he voted. The low voice finished at last and he sat down to listen while the clerk read, 'The Earl of Selkirk votes for ...'; his list followed, including 'The Earl of Selkirk'. Though there was plenty of precedent for what he had done, he never again voted for himself.

For five hours the reading and rereading of lists continued, while round the table the more eager openly or surreptitiously tried to keep tally. As the afternoon passed, darkness grew beyond the tall windows on the courtyard and servants moved through the crowd to set candles on the table. Until the very end the issue was in doubt, for the vote was heavy, and, though his name was heard with gratifying frequency, so were many others. At last the reading, the counting, and the checking were finished and the Deputy Clerk Register stood up to announce the result. The long scarlet cloth glowed in the candlelight between the rows of anxious faces turned toward the head of the table. 'William, Earl of Errol, 44.' From the first name he must have known that he was elected, for he had been given forty-six votes. In any case, the interval of uncertainty was ended almost at once, for by precedence his name was fourth on the list of successful candidates: 'Thomas, Earl of Selkirk, 46.'

A few minutes more and it was all over. The officials followed the mace from the room and the pent-up excitement of hours could burst out in congratulations, in expressions of pleasure and disappointment. Peers, with their friends and families, surged through the doorway to gather cloaks against the winter evening and to summon from the milling crowd in the outer courtyard the carriages that would carry them to an evening's celebration.

Lord Selkirk, like the other successful candidates, had not long to stay in Edinburgh. Almost half the time before the opening of Parliament at Westminster would be required for the journey. There might be time for a meeting of the Friday Club with Walter Scott and for a few visits to old friends. There would be little time for rest before facing the formidable trip to London; but, at thirty-five, though not robust he was in the prime of life and the exhilaration of success would offset much fatigue. As he called on old friends and received congratulations his manner was probably calm, but no one who knew that intense inward nature could doubt that he was filled with excitement.

2

Selkirk entered on his new career quietly enough. After the administration of the necessary oaths on December 15, he with the other newly elected peers took his seat in the House of

Lords. For the present it rested with him to decide what part he could most usefully play there and how soon he might win the right to play it. To begin with, at all events, little was expected of him.

His turn did not come until the night of February 4–5, on the second reading of the bill for the abolition of the slave trade. The debate, though the issue was never in doubt, roused a fury of opposition from the Tories and brought forth one of Grenville's greatest speeches, largely in praise of Wilberforce who had given years to the cause, had fathered the present bill in the Commons, and now with others from the Lower House listened with deep attention from the gallery. Though this was a measure which roused all Selkirk's warm generosity of spirit, it was a formidable occasion for a shy man making his maiden speech in a chamber that had heard Chatham and the great men of other days. He rose to speak following a coarse and almost incoherent attack on the measure by the Earl of Westmorland. As always, his words were carefully chosen and tellingly phrased; yet the speech was not wholly a success. Wilberforce found it 'sensible and well principled' but delivered in so low a voice it could scarcely be heard. Still, he had made a modest mark in difficult circumstances and on a great occasion. And when the debate ended at five o'clock in the morning, with a majority of 100 to 34, he had earned a place in the weary but jubilant groups in which the long battle was fought again, as he would belong in the future whenever the occasion was remembered. Going home in the cold dawn, he could find satisfaction to offset whatever disappointment might trouble him about his own performance.

Later in February he spoke again in the House, and several times more during the spring. If it had not ceased to be an ordeal he seemed at all events to speak more freely. But both the manner and the matter bear the stamp of the literary man, perhaps too packed and too carefully balanced for effective debate, and above all too earnest. There was rather the solemn distinction of one who had done his preparatory work carefully and given much thought to its presentation than any real felicity of style or contagious spontaneity. However, he had no reason to doubt that he was winning favourable opinion. It might still be a question whether he possessed more than minor gifts, but even these were not negligible.

Though Whig in most of his sympathies and attitudes he was drifting away from his colleagues on the issues of the day. He was still – perhaps even more than in his youth – the idealist whose delayed responses were embarrassingly hard-headed and practical. On the question of Irish Catholic disabilities, and even more on the issue of national defence, he moved nearer to the Tory position. Convinced that England could not be considered immune from the threat of French invasion and that a standing army adequate to every danger was neither desirable nor feasible, he had worked out an intricate alternative scheme of national service. Characteristically, he had gathered the immense body of necessary information and had marshalled it with great care, testing his theories with a number of senior military men. In June the substance of it had been published under the imprint of Messrs. Hatchard of Piccadilly, and in August he presented it to the Lords in the most ambitious speech of his parliamentary career. The elaborate detail of the presentation could hardly have been made to sound interesting unless by an Edmund Burke, but it was bound to win respect. The original pamphlet, expanded, was published as a book in 1808 and found worth reprinting fifty years later.

Meanwhile, in April 1807, the Ministry of all the Talents had come to an end with its great promise unfulfilled. It had provided for the abolition of the slave trade and nothing more. Peace was as far away as ever. When he went north in May for the Scottish peerage election, Lord Selkirk could have had no certainty of re-election. Change was in the air and events were to show that the peers were not unaware of it. The election had been proclaimed for the twenty-second of June, barely six months after the previous one. Perhaps for that reason the turn-out was smaller and the business more quickly completed. Nevertheless interest was keen and the peers, so often accused of indifferently returning the same group term after term, rejected five of the eight peers who had been newly elected with Selkirk in December. Of the sixteen returned, only he and five others remained from the previous house. In a representation that seemed to have been basically changed on party lines, he appeared to have been given a gratifying personal endorsement.

It must have appeared to many that he had thrown aside his visionary emigration schemes like a new toy, although an expensive one. Baldoon in Upper Canada he had all but given up, in dismay at its lack of success and ruinous cost: but, pressed and reassured by McDonell, he had agreed to continue it for the moment at its present level while issuing stern warnings about curtailment of expense.

Indeed, his realism had caused him to look ruefully at the balance-sheet of his colonizing ventures. The result had been a submission in the spring of 1807 to Lord Grenville in which he showed that in return for an expenditure of over £30,000 he had acquired landholdings in Prince Edward Island and Upper Canada worth, at most, £10,000. On the other hand, he could point with some pleasure to almost 1,000 people whose lot had been improved to the advantage of British North America. He realized that he had no real claim on the government, but he hoped that some compensation might be considered reasonable. There is no record of a reply, but his appointment in March as Lord Lieutenant of the Stewartry of Kirkcudbright was perhaps the effective answer; whether it was the kind of answer he looked for or needed remains a question. His fortune was not so great that he could continue to sustain the losses of recent years without prospect of return; whatever land values in British North America might become, as liquid assets they were of little use. There had been irony and perhaps bitterness in his having to arrange the sale of his father's Baldoon estate to the Earl of Galloway, no doubt partly to defray the costs of Baldoon in Upper Canada.

In the spring of 1807 he had a direct reminder of Upper Canada in a visit from Judge William Dummer Powell, with whom he had been on friendly terms at York. A foolish adventure in South America had put Powell's son in prison and in danger of his life, and had brought the father to London. In spite of the hazards of the Napoleonic Wars, the judge was eager to go if necessary to Spain to plead for his son. It was injudicious but very human and appealing. Selkirk introduced Powell to Lord Holland, whose warm support in the highest quarters in Spain won the young man's pardon and freedom. The most Powell had hoped for was a change to a healthier prison and perhaps some shortening of the sentence, and the whole affair strengthened the bonds between the two men.

It is easy to see now that, by the early autumn of 1807, Thomas Douglas had reached a crossroads in his affairs. For the next four years, in all probability, he would be a member of the House of Lords with enough sense of mission to satisfy most men. His colonizing ventures had settled down; Prince Edward Island was growing steadily and bringing prosperity to his settlers with little intervention from him; Baldoon, though much less satisfactory, had been sealed off. As a colonizer he might rest indefinitely on modest laurels. Though he had accomplished less than he hoped, he had done much for the Highlands and was an acknowledged expert in his chosen field. But it was far short of his dreams and of what he probably regarded as his obligations. Belonging to the House of Lords – especially as an elected member – might give anyone a feeling of consequence, but there was a vast gap between being of consequence and being so regarded by the uninformed. He could not deceive himself that he had accomplished very much as a Representative Peer or was likely to do so. Though by temperament and upbringing a Whig, he was impatient of their unrealistic visions, without being able wholly to support their opponents. He had not the habits or mentality of a good party work-horse; neither had he yet discovered the reach and confidence that might make him a party leader.

He was ripe for something to change his life when love intervened. By now he was thirty-six and it may be supposed that society regarded him as a most eligible bachelor and that he himself was thinking along similar lines; but the event that mattered most in his life we know least about. The methodical keeper of papers and leaver of memoranda must deliberately have left no record of this vital side of his private life. Like all possessors of an ancient title and great estates, he was bound to think about his succession. Yet there is no evidence that he took any active steps or conducted any systematic search for a suitable wife. Perhaps there had been an unconscious quest, for when the choice was made it was right – almost the only major decision of his life that was to bring no regret.

The announcement that appeared in *The Times,* the *Gentleman's Magazine,* the *Edinburgh Weekly Journal,* and a few other papers in late November 1807 said simply, 'Married at Inveresk, on the 24th, the Earl of Selkirk to Miss Jean Wedderburn, only daughter of James Wedderburn Colvile Esq.'

Jean Wedderburn was only twenty-one and from what she was later to become we can infer the girl of quick wit and winning charm, with a bubbling and at times unmanageable sense of fun. She was a romantic with a high-spirited courage, and we may believe that her wedding to the handsome, shy, yet adventurous Earl of Selkirk appeared to her as the fulfilment of all her dreams. Years later she was to recall, as a moment of almost suffocating happiness, the first time he had shown his interest in her publicly in front of her rivals. For his part, from the moment of their marriage he wore near his heart a gold brooch that was a gift from her, until it was lost on a portage west of Fort William nearly ten years later – and the loss seemed to him irreparable. The letters that remain show them both as closing always to each other with a code signature of their own: 'O.O.L.' – 'Only One Love'? It is a guess but perhaps not far from the truth.

A few months later they had taken a house in Portland Place in London. The young Countess of Selkirk does not seem to have had any ambition to cut a great figure in the London of Beau Brummell, of Carlton House and Devonshire House, of Lord Byron and the splendid and exclusive assemblies at Almack's. She was first and always a good wife to a man whose interests were in public affairs, who did not much care for the theatre, and who, though he wore the snowy neckcloths made fashionable by Brummell, would have scorned to spend hours arranging them. Her sense of fun, which could never resist the target of pomposity and probably teased her lord out of many a solemn mood, was never at war with Lowland common sense. In addition to his political friends they had their families. Lady Katherine Douglas, Selkirk's favourite sister, and Jean Selkirk became fast friends; and the Earl seems from the first to have been warmly attached to her brother, Andrew Wedderburn Colvile, and her cousin, John Halkett. Andrew had been highly successful in the West Indies trade and Halkett, trained in the law, had served successively as governor of the Bahamas and of Tobago. Their wide-ranging talk and experience would appeal more to Selkirk than would the studied manners of the bucks or the futile desperation of the gamblers of Brooks's.

In his own way Selkirk was making the kind of place for himself that appealed to him and seemed appropriate. His book on national defence was recognized as a piece of solid good work, and in July he was elected a Fellow of the Royal Society. Not long after, he became a member of the Alfred Club (soon to be known as the "alf read') of Albemarle Street. Lord Dudley described the club as 'the most abused, and most envied, most laughed at, and most canvassed society that I know of, and we deserve neither the one nor the other. ... The eagerness to get into it is prodigious.' Byron found it 'pleasant; a little too sober and literary ... upon the whole a decent resource in a rainy day, in a dearth of parties, or parliament, or in an empty season'. In spite of its dullness, its overabundance of bishops among the members, Selkirk seemed to enjoy the Alfred and to value his membership there.

For some time before his marriage, and ever since, Selkirk's life had centred increasingly on London. Yet events already in train were beginning a slow process that would end by drawing him away – that would do even more than that. Probably he had never quite given up his original idea of a colony 'at the Western extremity of Canada upon the Waters which fall into Lake Winnipeck' – Red River. This had been his first proposal to Lord Pelham, six years before, but many things had intervened and there was no sign that he had thought much about it since. The rights of the Hudson's Bay Company under its charter had seemed an absolute impediment to such a plan. Now a combination of events was bringing it forward again in a new and promising shape. The shrinking of the fur markets in war-time and the aggressive trading of the North West Company had driven the value of Hudson's Bay shares from £100 down to £60, and it might not be difficult to secure a sufficient interest to provide a hearing for his plan. Probably Andrew Colvile and John Halkett encouraged him in this, or even suggested the new approach. By now it was clear that the government of Upper Canada would not support him in a large-scale colonizing venture. The failure of Baldoon had contributed to Upper Canada's indifference or hostility to his efforts, but the feeling went further back than that; a small clique – the forerunners of the Family Compact – controlled affairs in the province and welcomed no powerful new-comer. He was through with Upper Canada and if he was to start again it must be elsewhere. Where better than 'the Western extremity of Canada ... a country which the Indian Traders represent as fertile, & of a Climate far more temperate than the shores of the Atlantic under the same parallel'?

There was all this in the decision, together with the finding in June 1808 of a powerful partner, Sir Alexander Mackenzie. The nature of their association has never been quite clear, nor the degree of their intimacy. For quite different reasons each sought a powerful voice in Hudson's Bay Company affairs. They may have thought that their interests were not irreconcilable; Mackenzie wanted at least transit rights through Hudson Bay for the North West Company trade and perhaps a bargaining position for a division of the fur country. More probably, neither disclosed his whole purpose when together they started to buy Hudson's Bay Company stock on joint account, with Selkirk providing most of the capital since

53

Mackenzie's assets were tied up in Canada. There seems to have been no great haste in all this, nor were purchases substantial to begin with. Shares were not readily available and Mackenzie as a stockholder in a rival concern was not a welcome purchaser.

Selkirk, with his charming young wife and his parliamentary interests, was not yet fully caught up in the Red River scheme; it was merely a remote and intriguing possibility. During the autumn of 1808 he and Jean knew she would have their first baby in the spring. North America and colonization must for the moment have seemed remote and unimportant.

In politics the wind of reform was beginning to blow alarmingly. In the teeth of a Tory election success in 1807, Sir Francis Burdett, one of the leading reformers, had won the seat in Westminster. A variety of ill-focused hopes and uncoordinated efforts were springing up throughout the kingdom. Old Major John Cartwright, seeking with William Cobbett to give leadership to parliamentary reform and to find new and influential recruits, seems to have turned to Selkirk for support, invoking the memory of his father and of the admired older brother, Basil, Lord Daer. If Selkirk did not wholly know what he was in favour of, he had at least learned what he was not prepared to support. It may have been only the middle-aged view of the established in retreat from a generous and slightly irresponsible youth; but the change of view had filtered through a succession of disillusionments. The French Revolution, which in youth he had hailed, had quickly disappointed him. Likewise, American democracy which he had welcomed in theory had in practice ultimately repelled him.

During the winter and spring, while he waited with Jean through the last trying weeks for the birth of their child, he worked out a rationale of his views on the reform question. On April 22, at Blackheath, Jean Selkirk gave birth to a boy – Dunbar James, Lord Daer. Three days later he finished *A Letter Addressed to John Cartwright Esq.*, and sent it off for publication by Constable in Edinburgh and London.

He had arrived at a moderately conservative position and

stated it well to the elderly man, first recalling 'the sentiments of esteem, which I know to have been entertained towards you by my father and brother'.

> To Parliamentary Reform my father and brother were, as you well know, zealous friends; and all my own early prepossessions were in favour of such a measure. I saw with abhorrence the ascendancy which unprincipled and worthless characters often acquired through the influence of corruption. I lamented the public advantages so often sacrificed to the interest of individuals. I was struck with the glaring manner in which the practice of our Constitution appeared to deviate from its theory: and I flattered myself that if the representation of the people were put on a proper footing these abuses would be eradicated.

He went on to outline further his youthful conviction that with equalized representation, extension of the suffrage, and more frequent elections bribery could scarcely be applied with effect. He then described his disillusion with the practical application of his theories, notably in the United States where 'universal suffrage and frequency of election prove no bar to the misconduct of representatives' and where 'a political adventurer, raised to power by popular favour, is fully as likely to abuse that power, as is the purchaser of a rotten borough'. His disappointment with the American system and the influence of his Federalist friends appeared in all he wrote.

> Ask Mr. Cobbett, whether in the popular elections of America, the preference is more generally given to the man of solid judgment and tried integrity or to the artful knave, who, free from the restraints of truth and honour, can exert all his dexterity in the arts of deception. . . .
> If the notions of a radical and entire change are pursued with violence, moderate men will again be forced to believe that there is no alternative between measures of a Revolutionary tendency, and a resistance to every reformation whatsoever.

The writing of such a document – sensible, experienced, cautious – may have cost him some pangs for his lost youth, for Major Cartwright was thirty years older than he and still carrying the lance of a young crusader; indeed it ought to have done. But he left no record of a lament. In the next few months he took little part in the debates of the Lords. Presumably his home was more fascinating than ever, and the affairs of the Hudson's Bay Company were moving rapidly towards a crisis.

3

In May 1809 the Committee of the Hudson's Bay Company was forced to decide against the payment of a dividend on its stock, for the first time in twenty-five years. Though the financial position of the company was far stronger than its critics pretended, the closing of the continental fur market, increased taxes, and a worsened competitive position had at once reduced and frozen its assets. Within the company there were sharply conflicting views of what ought to be done and agreement only on the need for some drastic change.

Doubtless Selkirk had interested the shrewd and energetic Andrew Colvile in the problem and the latter seems to have accepted eagerly both the speculation and the challenge. In the next few months both Colvile and John Halkett joined Selkirk in buying Hudson's Bay Company stock. On November 29, 1809, Selkirk attended his first General Court of the company's stockholders and, at that time or shortly after, Andrew Colvile joined the directorate known as the Committee.

The choice for the Committee lay between a reorganized and more active drive for the trade in beaver, and a reduction of fur-trading in favour of timber and the whale fishery, at least while the war lasted. Inherent in the first of these was a suggestion that a colony might be started in the Hudson's Bay territory, which, by providing cheap food near the centre of operations, would reduce one heavy item of cost. There was already at Red River a straggling settlement of freemen –

Canadians who after some service in the fur trade had turned their backs on civilization and who, with their Indian wives, lived precariously by hunting and a little planting of crops. Perhaps it was natural that the suggestion of a colony was bound to be linked at once with Red River. The linking of the two, whether inspired or accidental, both crystallized Selkirk's remote plans and advanced them at a breathless rate. More precisely, what had been only a dream took shape as a distinct possibility.

On December 9, just over a week after the meeting of the General Court, Selkirk wrote to Miles Macdonell in Upper Canada. His letter spoke of the possibility of an advantageous situation developing for Macdonell and suggested that it might be necessary for him to come to England on short notice. This was not the first letter since their meeting five years before, and Selkirk had perhaps always hoped to find a suitable opening for the ex-soldier who was bored with his pioneer farm on the St. Lawrence. It was characteristic that he should now so eagerly jump to the conclusion that Macdonell was the man required for a post that was not yet even well defined, but which on reflection must indicate a requirement far beyond anything he yet knew of Miles Macdonell.

It was an incautious move, but having waited so long for this opportunity he was lifted by its sudden emergence to a pitch of excitement, so that for the moment he could not pause for nice calculations; they would come later. He did not at present seem to contemplate the kind of personal management of a colony at Red River (Assiniboia) that he had undertaken in Prince Edward Island and Upper Canada. The spark of interest in colonization already shown by the Hudson's Bay Company he would fan to a growing flame; and presumably he intended to put Miles Macdonell forward for governor, as a man of proven bravery, of capacity in commanding the support of Highlanders, with some administrative ability and an unimpeachable integrity. This would have been no more than just, and it was not easy to say what else was needed. But within a few months Lord Selkirk might have guessed at the need for other qualities – qualities hardly to be found with the others in any man: bravery alone, without enduring fortitude, would not be enough. Administrative ability and easy popularity would need to be combined with commanding intelligence, far-seeing and steady judgment, tact, and endless patience. It was to be a task for a superman and Miles Macdonell was but a man, with a share of man's weaknesses – foolish optimism, and enough vain pride to cloud his intelligence.

None of this cast a warning shadow in 1810 when the idea of the new colony on the coveted site crowded out caution. In February Selkirk wrote Macdonell that matters had not yet been fully clarified but that it might nevertheless be well for him to come to England; Selkirk would be responsible for the expense of his trip.

During that spring the arrangement with Sir Alexander Mackenzie came to an end. Mackenzie seems to have realized that Selkirk was intent only on colonization, anathema to every fur-trader. Neither their individual nor their joint purchases had been large: Sir Alexander had acquired shares to the value of £800, and Selkirk shares to the value of £4,087 – including £495 turned over from joint account by an irritated Mackenzie. Selkirk had stopped purchasing in May 1809, but at that point Andrew Wedderburn Colvile and John Halkett began to buy, and by the spring of 1810 had holdings of about £4,400 and £3,700 respectively. The three of them together now owned stock worth just over £12,000. It was far short of control in a company with a capital of £104,000 but they might at least prove an influential group in the company's affairs.

Some whiff of danger from all this seems to have momentarily roused the North West Company's representatives in England and consideration was given to moves that might block the proposed colony. But they were not sufficiently alarmed to take defensive action. Mackenzie's purchases had intended just the opposite. After debate, a decision was taken not to proceed with the buying of Hudson's Bay shares. Selkirk's ideas of colonization would only mean danger if he had a decisive voice in their rival's affairs, but this did not at present appear as a possibility. It is clear that whatever stock Selkirk and Mackenzie had purchased even the major share was not large. He had irritated the Nor'Westers by blocking Sir Alexander, but he had not thereby become formidable in his own right.

Apart from the slightly comic notion of a colony at Red River, they might have recognized a purposeful stir about the offices in Fenchurch Street. The old company, never in recent years a serious rival but rather a convenience to hold the northern line against independent traders, was growing tired of its costly role. Under present conditions the comfortable pace of trade beside the Bay, with Indians who came hundreds of miles to their posts, had been strangled by the aggressive Nor'Westers. They intercepted the Indians on the rivers leading to the Bay or arrived in their villages with rum and trade goods. When, lethargically, the Hudson's Bay traders had moved towards the North West Company's choicest source of beaver, Athabasca, they had been beaten back, bewildered by a combination of guile and violence in which their rivals had had a long schooling. They had now the simple choice of so reducing their fur operations as virtually to abandon the field to their rivals and making good their losses with other commodities, or of matching their competitors in toughness and enterprise. The colony, under the sponsorship of Selkirk and Andrew Wedderburn Colvile, was an integral part of the more resolute policy.

At this point the group who were in favour of fighting it out found a convincing supporter in the person of a former Nor'Wester, Colin Robertson. When the old and new North West companies had ended their bitter war by uniting in 1804, they had shortened the horizon for many of their active young men – clerks who had joined one or other company in the expectation of winning a partnership. Some continued to find satisfaction in turning their propensity for aggression on the comparatively mild Hudson's Bay men, whose conditions of employment did not encourage retaliation. Others, like Colin

Robertson, found it mean work with no future. Leaving the North West Company with a generous testimonial he did not intend to return actively to the fur trade, but saw an advantage, and perhaps a personal satisfaction, in putting his knowledge of the trade at the disposal of the Hudson's Bay Company. He believed he could show them how to defeat the Nor'Westers and, what was just as hard, persuade them to act on his advice.

Robertson had found his way to the Committee through William Auld, one of the company's senior traders and one of the few advocates of meeting the Nor'Westers' force with superior force. Auld, superintendent of the Northern Department, which included Red River, was in London on leave and for consultation in the early part of 1810. He was a hard, opinionated man, but not without ability and courage, and he possessed experience that commanded attention.

Thus, at a decisive moment in their affairs, when a tentative decision to withdraw from active fur-trading had been taken, the Committee faced powerful advocates of the opposite course. And the spokesman of those advocates quickly became Andrew Colvile whose nature and whose judgment opposed this abdication, this tame abandonment of time-honoured and legal rights. For the strength of the Hudson's Bay Company position was that they could theoretically exclude others from their chartered territory (the area watered by the rivers flowing into the Bay), but they had the same rights in unchartered territory as the North West Company, or any other trader who could make good his position there.

A series of discussions reversed the earlier mild decision. They were not prepared to go as far as either Auld or Robertson advocated but neither would they leave the field to the Montrealers. Robertson had pleaded for the enlistment of French-Canadian *voyageurs* right in Montreal and an advance in strength – a bold challenge – along their opponents' channel of communication. This appeared to the Committee recklessly provocative. Nor were they ready to follow Auld in enlisting large numbers of bullies for the purpose of frightening their

60

rivals from the field. The Nor'Westers would not give up easily and the result must be large-scale violence, in itself deplorable and perhaps damaging to the company's privileged position under its charter.

So Auld went back to the Bay in the summer of 1810 with the promise of reinforcements; they were to be men of a sturdier cast than the mild Orkneymen formerly employed, though less numerous than he had asked for. He was also instructed to set about the establishing of a company colony at the Forks of the Red River. Robertson, having failed of his hopes – an agency for the Hudson's Bay Company in Montreal – went into a business partnership in Liverpool, hoping to do some business with Andrew Colvile, and already on the way to being dedicated to the service of Lord Selkirk – whatever it might require of him.

4

By the time the Nor'Westers learned that a colony was really to be formed in Assiniboia, it was too late to stop it, or to smother it at the source. There would be stages on the road when it might be blocked and they no more doubted their ability to block it than they doubted the necessity of doing so. If they knew of the instructions to Auld to form a colony, that step did not concern them much; for fur-traders of whatever company agreed only in this, that settlement was bad for the trade and to be 'discouraged'. Auld, in fact, was hardly given time to demonstrate the lack of enthusiasm that he had probably voiced. In early winter, when there had been time only for mail announcing his arrival at the Bay – before he had had time to act – the Committee decided to press on with the formation of a colony by different means.

Probably Selkirk, impatient of the unsatisfactory results to be expected from Auld's reluctant compliance with instructions, had forced the issue. Early in 1810 it had been suggested

61

that he might become a member of the Committee, but delicacy had dictated a refusal. He was nevertheless given access to the Hudson's Bay Company's accounts and papers and he frequently joined in Committee deliberations. To many of the older members this was probably unwelcome, for, though in theory a colony as a place of retirement for company servants was to be recommended, colonization on the scale contemplated by Selkirk was not. Nevertheless, late in 1810, the Committee invited the Earl to submit a proposal under which he would undertake to form a settlement that would satisfy his aims while safeguarding theirs. By the first week of February 1811 it was ready.

The plan had about it a breath-taking boldness. In return for an immense grant of land – almost as large as Britain and Ireland together and five times the size of Scotland – for which he was to pay a nominal ten shillings, Selkirk undertook to supply the company with 200 servants a year and to develop an agricultural colony. The colonists were prohibited from trading for furs and from distilling more alcohol than they required for their personal use. On the face of it the scheme was open to devastating attack, but it put squarely in issue the question of whether the directorate seriously intended a colony. If it did, and wished to avoid the expense of its development, someone had to be offered suitable inducement to shoulder the heavy costs.

Selkirk loved land. He was an improving landlord who had seen – and proved for himself – what land could do. And to anyone with the love of land in his blood the prospect of such an acquisition – a kingdom – must have been irresistible. In January Jean had given birth to her second baby, Isabella, and she must have listened with affectionate amusement – perhaps with growing dismay – as he worked out his scheme. It was a scheme that would provide a new life for hundreds, indeed thousands, of dispossessed Highlanders – but at what a cost! Gently, now or later, she teased him about his Kingdom on Red River, but there is little doubt that his obsession with the vast scheme alarmed her. Even at this stage its difficulties were evident, and its possible cost was frightening. She probably knew that his enthusiasm was outrunning that of her brother Andrew and of John Halkett and many others. But, whatever his misgivings, Andrew was grimly supporting his brother-in-law, and there was little doubt that their conviction would carry all before it.

In this confidence Selkirk already had his recruiting agents at work – Colin Robertson in the Hebrides, Roderick McDonald in Glasgow, and Miles Macdonell in Ireland. His plan was to send out an advance party under Miles to reach Red River in the late summer of 1811, and to prepare crops and buildings for the first party of settlers who were to arrive in the autumn of 1812. The leaping imagination, harnessed to great administrative talents, recognized but saw almost too easily past the difficult preparations, the voyage itself – the hard, 600-mile journey inland from the Bay – and the harsh winter to follow, which would test every arrangement and sound every man's strength to the bottom.

But it was not to be so easily managed. Once Selkirk's plan was accepted by the Committee, Sir Alexander Mackenzie demanded that it be laid before a general court of the stockholders. This could not with propriety be refused and a meeting was called for early May. By now the more violently opposed directors had been brought round so that when the Committee faced the stockholders it was announced that they deemed the grant to Lord Selkirk to be advantageous. The details of the arrangement were made known and the General Court was adjourned to meet again on May 30. Too late, but, roused at last, the North West representatives in London did what they could to marshal opposition and publicly discredit the plan. At least a year before, Sir Alexander Mackenzie had given them grim warning. Speaking of Selkirk, he had written: 'He will put the North West Company to a greater expense than you seem to apprehend, and, had the Company sacrificed £20,000, which might have secured a preponderance in the stock of the Hudson's Bay Company, it would have been money well spent.' Certainly, Selkirk and his associates, for far less money, appeared to have secured an effective preponderance on the one issue.

There was no doubt that at the decisive meeting the North Westers would bring every possible gun to bear, and in the last few days Edward Ellice and John Inglis, North West Company agents, secured some Hudson's Bay stock. They would not be qualified to vote but they must at least be heard. Meanwhile, as when eight years before Selkirk had sailed for Prince Edward Island, costly arrangements must proceed as though the plan were unopposed. If the advance party was to reach Red River before the cold weather, it must be away soon after the meeting. Messages flew back and forth in both camps. Selkirk was preparing a prospectus of the new colony that might call forth some of the financial support its full development would require. The Nor'Westers were contemplating further means of blocking the man they had until now thought it sufficient to ridicule. On May 25, Simon McGillivray wrote his brother William, the head of the North West Company in Montreal: 'His Lordship is a designing and dangerous character – and Sir Alexander has not been sufficiently aware of him.'

When the adjourned General Court met on the last day of May it produced a 'protest' sponsored by three Nor'Westers and three other shareholders which might have been more effective had its origin been less suspect. The sound basis of the protest was that a valuable territory was being disposed of without adequate return, or prospects of return, to the shareholders. If it were to be sold, this should at least be done at public auction. But as the argument mounted in fury it diminished in force. Parts of the protest were both manifestly untrue and unfair in the light of Selkirk's record in promoting emigration to British North America, and the disgruntled and furious Nor'Westers witnessed the confirming of the grant of Assiniboia to Lord Selkirk by more than two-thirds of the votes of the shareholders, by all the members of the Committee, and by a simple majority of those present.

On June 12 the documents were signed that formally conveyed the grant to Selkirk and appointed Miles Macdonell its first governor. Two weeks later the first gun in a North West counter-attack was heard when an article in the *Inverness Journal*, signed 'A Highlander', assailed Selkirk and described the hardships of the journey to Red River and the terrors to be faced at the journey's end. It was to be the first of many, and it exhausted neither the Nor'Westers' will to damage the settlement nor the range of their malice.

In Selkirk's last talk with Sir Alexander Mackenzie there had been no cordiality, but neither had there been any outward expression of anger. Miles Macdonell fared less well. When as the governor of Assiniboia he called on Mackenzie, he was met by a tirade against Selkirk and the colony: it was a mad scheme aimed against the North West Company. He was warned that the Nor'Westers would not tolerate the colony and had the power to set the Indians on it. Ellice loosed his rage and frustration at Selkirk himself in even more explicit terms. Having said that the North West Company would neither fail to thwart the settlement, nor be restrained by any principles of equity or honesty,

> he described the wintering partners of that Company as a set of men utterly destitute of all moral principle, or the feelings of honour prevalent in civilized society, men who were in general of the lowest origin, selected from among the indigent relatives of the leading partners ... that their feelings and manners were not more correct than those of the Indians. ... While in the station of clerks they were taught never to hesitate at any act which would recommend them to their superiors ... [as] partners they would not scruple to commit any crime which was necessary to effect the views of their associates in the concern.

Selkirk, with pawky humour, merely noted that he 'had not previously heard so correct a description of the North West Company'.

As Macdonell set about final preparations for departure he could not claim that he had not been warned. Yet it was probably impossible to take the warnings at their face value. Besides, he would not be alone. Though quite separate from the

Hudson's Bay Company, the colony could surely count on support in any open rupture with Indians or Nor'Westers. And, though the group he was taking out was as yet a sorry crew, he planned to turn them into good men capable of taking care of themselves. Bidding good-bye to Selkirk, Miles Macdonell assumed a confident air, yet both knew that this was no journey to be undertaken casually. Macdonell was to sail from Yarmouth early in July and to embark his party at Stornoway a few days later. By Christmas-time Selkirk should have news of their arrival at York Factory, but there could be no news from Red River for almost eighteen months.

Chapter 3

A MOST UNFORTUNATE BUSINESS

I

There was little to lift a commander's heart in the group that embarked with Miles Macdonell in July. Rumour and evil report had spread through Scotland and the Western Isles, so that few were willing to enlist for the unknown Assiniboia, and those few were mostly hard cases in whom necessity silenced alarm. Crowded now into the hastily chartered *Edward and Ann,* an old ship of doubtful seaworthiness, they found little to claim their loyalty or calm their fears.

Miles, Roderick McDonald, and Colin Robertson had been hard-pressed to find even the motley collection of 125 Irish, Orkneymen, Glaswegians, and Highlanders who had made their way to the rendezvous. About twenty of these had been lost at Stornoway before the ships sailed and only a scrambled embarkation and hasty departure had prevented the desertion of others. If Macdonell had doubted the seriousness of the North Westers' threats he had no reason to doubt it now. During the loading of supplies, the customs inspector – Reid, a connection of Sir Alexander Mackenzie – had imposed every difficulty provided by the regulations and a few of his own devising. He had visited the ship and in the most solemn manner called on the enlisted men to state if any were not sailing of their own free will: all were free to go ashore, none might be coerced. The ranks wavered and some broke away as Miles sought to hold them to their commitments and reminded them of debts to Lord Selkirk already contracted. Ashore, Captain McKenzie, a recruiting officer who was Reid's son-in-law, persuaded some of the men to take the King's shilling, then proceeded to arrest them as deserters. Others of the men went ashore on various pretexts and were not seen again. Miles Macdonell, watching his already discontented force melt away while he waited for late arrivals, decided to wait no longer. Abandoning a part of the supplies lying on the docks – supplies that would be sorely missed at Red River – he begged the captain to put to sea as quickly as possible. A hasty letter to Selkirk gave an account of his troubles and carried an echo of weary exasperation, 'This my Lord has been a most unfortunate business.'

The hundred-odd men who remained had all been enlisted as Hudson's Bay Company servants. A proportion of them would be told off presently for the service of Lord Selkirk, to prepare buildings and put in crops at Red River. The remainder under Hillier would man fur-trade posts – not as aggressors but to give a show of strength, the demonstration of a new policy, to the North West Company. Macdonell himself had an appointment from the Hudson's Bay Company as Governor and chief magistrate of Assiniboia, but he was also Lord Selkirk's employee in charge of the settlement. These ambiguities were in time to baffle even those who wished to recognize a difference between settlement and fur trade. The North West Company, never admitting the distinction, would find the confusion to its purpose.

As the *Edward and Ann* moved out on its hazardous venture, Macdonell determined to do what he could to knit his company into an effective and contented whole. Among other things he proposed to use the weeks at sea in training them to the use of arms, for hunting, and for their own defence; but he was to find them as unhandy and raw as any group that ever broke a sergeant-major's heart. Across the heaving waters, in discouraging contrast, the *Prince of Wales* and the *Eddystone*, trim and well-found ships, seemed to face the approaching Arctic with confidence. They were the ships of a company to which braving icebergs and northern storms had been routine for almost 150 years. They would have been heartening companions were there not already evidence that the established Hudson's Bay men were reluctant to associate themselves with Selkirk's people. Not least of the evidence was the cruel contempt to be found in the ship considered good enough for such people, though all three vessels stood out together into the same unwelcoming sea.

The voyage that began so badly never came right. Contrary winds beat back the ships, and the squalid quarters which did not improve with the weeks at sea added to the general discontent. The officers' mess on the *Edward and Ann*, more comfortable than other places, was not noticeably happier. Unaccommodating tempers were only slightly improved by the manufactured cheerfulness of a tipsy Catholic priest, Father Charles Bourke, who had embarked without the consent of his bishop and who, Miles was determined, would never be parish priest at Red River. In spite of wrangles, Macdonell seems to have convinced himself that all would be well once they landed; it could not, at any rate, be much worse. Departure had been later than planned and the voyage was proving to be the longest on record. They would be hard put to it to reach Red River before freeze-up, yet, if they did not manage that, the object of their over-hasty arrangements would be largely lost. When the ships finally anchored at York Factory on September 24, and hope of getting inland was all but gone, Macdonell forced himself to report cheerfully to his superior:

> I was aware of considerable difficulty in prosecuting this scheme, which a desire to forward your Lordship's view led me to undertake. The troubles attendant on it have already exceeded my expectations: I feel a confidence however that we shall surmount every difficulty, although

much retarded in the progress hitherto, the object is very attainable. Your Lordship need not be under any apprehension for us.

Almost at once it was apparent that to travel inland to a location where neither food nor shelter waited would be folly. It was equally clear that the party could not be housed at York Factory and was not welcome in the vicinity. Reluctantly, the new arrivals trekked twenty-three miles up the Nelson River, where at least there was plenty of wood, and under a sheltering bank built a line of crude huts just before the fist of the northern winter closed on them. Had it not been for the supplies of York Factory, furnished at Lord Selkirk's charge but always grudgingly issued, the party would have starved to death. They were inexperienced hunters, and game was scarce. As it was, by spring they had become somewhat trained to axe and gun, and though living on the brink of disaster and surviving scurvy they had come through well.

This experience – an accomplishment in which they might have taken pride – should have welded them into a united and formidable band, but the winter had been one long quarrel which was to leave its scars. There had been trouble between Hillier's and Macdonell's men, an ugly fight between the Irish and the Orkneymen, and an armed insurrection against Macdonell's discipline, which split the camp for weeks and only ended when the mutineers were starved out. But the most serious breach occurred between the Nelson Encampment and York Factory. Governor Auld, whom Miles Macdonell had in a sense supplanted, was not disposed to approve either the settlement or its leader. The assistance he was under instructions to provide was given reluctantly, and the Hudson's Bay officers were not above fomenting discontent among Macdonell's men.

A winter mercifully milder than usual was succeeded by a long, cold spring. Macdonell's party for Red River, originally thirty-five to Hillier's seventy, had been further reduced by the sending back of some for discipline and the death of one from scurvy. The remnant waited impatiently for the ice to go out of the rivers and so to open the road inland. In some years this happened in May, but in this fateful year the ice still held at mid-June, while the precious planting-time at Red River came and went. Not until the end of the first week in July did the party finally embark its stores and push the last clumsy boat out into the Hayes River. It was the last lap of a journey that had begun almost a year before.

After all they had suffered, the last lap should in justice have been comparatively easy, but the new country had still some lessons to teach them. Provided they were careful and lucky, they might look to coast the last 260 miles down the eastern shore of Lake Winnipeg and into the mouth of Red River. But the first half of their journey south lay upstream; first, be-tween low-lying and often slippery mud-banks along which they had often to haul the boats against the current, and then through deepening rock and shoaling water where they would be fortunate if they had only to struggle waist-deep in the icy stream, dragging or 'tracking' the boats. More often, the river plunged at them through a narrow gorge with a force they could not match and in water too deep for wading. Then came the labour of the portage when the cargo and sometimes the boats had to be carried up rocky paths and along the crest above the rushing current – when a whole back-breaking day might go to the winning of a few hundred yards. With care it was not dangerous, but carelessness might be fatal, and nothing could short-cut the time or much lighten the labour. Selkirk had been told that Hudson's Bay Company men made the journey to Lake Winnipeg in sixteen to eighteen days, and repeated the information with comfortable assurance from an arm-chair in London. To Miles Macdonell's inexperienced hands it was grinding work, with lean fare and the roughest of beds at the end of the day.

The worst of the journey was over when they came at last through a network of rivers, lakes, and small streams to Holy Lake – beautiful and serene, like a reward for all they had endured. Here at the Hudson's Bay Company's Oxford House they recruited four men, including an Indian guide. Many had left them to join the Hudson's Bay ranks, and their party had shrunk to nineteen before receiving this welcome reinforcement. Here, too, they acquired a bull and a cow which they christened Adam and Eve – the settlement's first livestock, and, as it proved, its most durable.

The party went on then in better heart down Jack River to Lake Winnipeg. This was a point that would one day hold bitter memories for them. Now it was only a milestone of good omen. They had still the length of Lake Winnipeg to travel, but the treacherous lake was in one of its good moods, and through uneventful and peaceful days they ghosted along its shore, nearing their journey's end.

Not until the end of August did they step ashore at Red River. The country, as they approached, had appeared richer and more welcoming. They entered the river through a maze of reed-beds swarming with water-fowl and travelled the last forty miles up the tawny, slow-moving stream without difficulty. Their troubles seemed to be at an end, and the smiling land – the endless miles of light brush and buffalo grass and wildflowers – seemed the promised land of dreams. From the east bank they looked across to a group of log buildings within a stockade – the North West Company's Fort Gibraltar, which stood in the elbow formed by the junction of the Assiniboine River with the Red. This was 'The Forks'. Neither in the fort opposite nor from the small group of Hudson's Bay people gathered round them was there any sign of hostility. A few days later, on September 4, Miles Macdonell held a carefully planned ceremony of 'seizin' in which the grant was formally declared to be taken over, in the name of Lord Selkirk, from the Hudson's Bay Company. The announcement was solemnly read in English, and parts of it also in French, while bemused freemen and half-breeds and Indians looked on and listened. Afterwards, two cannon were fired and the flag was raised. Among those who took part on this occasion, whatever their reservations, were two or three representatives of the North West Company – among them John Wills, commanding at Fort Gibraltar, and Alexander Macdonell, Miles's cousin and brother-in-law. Afterwards, light refreshments were served to the gentlemen and a keg of spirits was broached for 'the people'.

In the next few days Miles Macdonell explored the immediate area to fix a location for the settlement, where the first buildings would be placed and the first land put under cultivation. Lord Selkirk had left him quite free to decide, even suggesting that he might prefer a location on Lake Winnipeg to one on Red River, specifying only – with bitter memories of Baldoon – that the place must be dry, and clear of woods yet near enough for fuel and building supplies. The plans did not suggest that they should shelter near a Hudson's Bay post, nor give any hint that fear of Indians was a factor in the thinking of either man; they only directed that, as soon as possible, negotiations should be started with the Indians with a view to quenching their title to the land on an agreeable basis.

Miles found what he sought, in a fine point on the west bank round which the river swept in one of its many loops. It was two miles north of Fort Gibraltar, and he named it Point Douglas. Here, in due course, he planned to build Fort Douglas and make it the heart of the settlement. He set men to work at once, clearing ground to get some planting done. He had hoped to find supplies for his people left at the direction of the Hudson's Bay Company, but it had been a bad winter, with general shortages as a result, and the Bay men had nothing to spare. At Auld's order, they had planted potatoes; but, for this welcome supply, Miles in his bitter disappointment gave them no credit, complaining to Lord Selkirk that no arrangements had been made.

Sixty miles farther south, at Pembina, there was an established buffalo-hunting area where in a normal year ample supplies of fresh meat were to be had all winter. The North West and the Hudson's Bay companies both had posts there already, and he decided to winter his people with them. There would be little enough time, for already the nights were growing chill, and before winter he would have to have shelter for his own people and for the first large party of settlers.

73

2

In the grip of his intense enthusiasm for the Red River scheme, it was not easy for Selkirk to wait out the long intervals between incoming news and outgoing instructions and reinforcements. Though there were a variety of political and domestic demands on his attention, the long, thoughtful letters to Miles and to others about the colony speak of deep concentration and of an object never long out of his mind. He and Jean spent the autumn of 1811 in Scotland, part of it at St. Mary's Isle and part in the Highlands trying to assess the damage done by the North West campaign, and taking a hand in recruiting. By spring when he was back in London he knew of Miles's troubles at Stornoway on setting out. A further savage attack in the *Inverness Journal* forced him to revise his hopes of recruits from the Highlands; the attacks were doing damage.

The most serious damage of all may have been their share in angering Selkirk and affecting his judgment. Though he wrote coolly enough of them, as certain in the long run to be exposed and likely then to react in his favour, they underlined a hostility that ought not to have been ignored. He was spending long days at Hudson's Bay House in London steeping himself in the company's affairs, and there the record of the meaning of North West opposition was quite clear. The Hudson's Bay traders had never experienced the full weight of it, but the samples handed out to Peter Fidler and others who had ventured into Athabasca in recent years were sufficiently convincing.

It seems now that he had a simple choice. He could concentrate on making the settlement into an armed camp and on preparing elsewhere for the violence that was to be anticipated. Or he might have taken extraordinary measures to convince the Nor'Westers that the colony, though unwelcome in fur country, would never become an active extension of the Hudson's Bay trading effort. It seems certain that he had said as much to Sir Alexander Mackenzie and doubtless his pride hindered him from doing much more. But, free as he was to sacrifice his own heavy investment to his pride, his obligation to the people he had sent out and those about to follow required his unconditional concern for their welfare – if necessary, a sacrifice of pride.

He had once produced a neat statement during a debate in the House after the fall of Grenville's ministry. 'If they did not take sufficient care to explain themselves,' he said, 'they have no right to complain that their expressions were misunderstood.' If this was not his own choice now it might rapidly become so, and if he did not take sufficient care to explain himself he would have no right to complain that he was misunderstood. For he ought to have recognized that he was confronting a dynamic trading organization placed in an intolerable situation. The proposed settlement lay across their main trade route, their life-line. If his intention was to take advantage of this, or to allow the Hudson's Bay Company to do so, the North Westers must destroy the colony or be destroyed; and they must act while they still had the preponderance of man-power. Thus, they would never have been easy to persuade that they were not menaced, but unpersuaded they were bound to act.

It was one of the puzzles for Selkirk's contemporaries, as well as for those who came after, that his affairs, the great venture of his life, should drift into an unmanageable chaos. His recognized humane and patriotic impulses were linked with a lucid brain at once capable of directing intricate matters on a large scale and of making mistakes that lesser men would not have made.

The truth seems to have been that his demanding dreams were in control, clouding the central problem. He was quickly enmeshed in detail regarding supplies, recruiting, transportation, jurisdiction, and administration. Was it the old story of a wood not seen for the trees? Or was it that he could not give a convincing undertaking without inhibiting his plans and shortening his horizon? Was it simply the act of a proud man in his conscious innocence, unwilling to risk the derision of coarser opponents by offering what it was not in them to accept, and taking an alternative risk while he rushed forward the proof of his good faith?

In any case the moment passed quickly, perhaps unrecognized, while he divided his attention between the responsibility of the settlement and the bewildering shifts of the political scene. The mental illness of the King during the late winter had brought on a long struggle to establish a regency adequately safeguarded. The bitter divisions on that issue, the Peninsular War, the insoluble problems of Ireland and Catholic disabilities, drew Selkirk increasingly into the centre of events against the pull of Red River affairs. In March appeared the dazzling possibility of a cabinet post being offered him in the not distant future. Jean Selkirk, watching a struggle which to others might seem uncertain, was in no doubt as to the outcome. 'I do not see at present the least probability of Lord Selkirk taking office,' she wrote Lady Katherine Douglas; 'he seems too much wrapt up in his Transatlantic schemes to give in to any such idea.' As usual where he was concerned, she was right. The day before her letter to Katherine, he had written Miles Macdonell about the settlers he would send in the summer and of the probability of his coming out the following year, 1813, with a much larger party.

Neither the affairs of Red River nor their own apparent want of interest could entirely separate the Earl and his Countess from the great world to which they belonged by right and by obligation. But the glimpses that survive do not suggest that they gave it much more than the service of their station. At the Prince Regent's glittering fête on the nineteenth of June 1811 – when 2,000 guests led by the exiled French royal family thronged Carlton House – the Countess of Selkirk was one of a very few singled out by the reporter of *La Belle Assemblée*. He wrote of her 'white satin round dress, with beautiful silver embroidery', of her head-dress which was 'a very full plume of white feathers, and superb coronet of diamonds; diamond earings and necklace etc'. Similarly, the Earl attended a levee at the palace a few months later wearing the uniform of a lieutenant-general, as became the Lord Lieutenant of the Stewartry of Kirkcudbright. These cannot have been their only appearances at formal occasions, but the letter- and memoir-writers of the period scarcely mention them; and it seems unlikely that this would either have surprised or much troubled the Selkirks.

In May the leader of the government, Spencer Perceval, was assassinated in the lobby of the House of Commons and it seemed that the hard-won political equilibrium of the spring was destroyed again. When, after various alternatives had been explored, Lord Liverpool took over the leadership in June, and many of Sidmouth's supporters were included in the cabinet, Lord Selkirk was already on his way to Ireland to speed his outgoing settlers.

As he set out for Sligo, Selkirk not only turned his back on politics and a possible advancement, but left to Jean a painful domestic problem that had much occupied them in recent months. Sir James and Lady Helen Hall's youngest son, James William, had suffered a mental breakdown some months before, one of the distressing symptoms of which was a turning against his parents. Both for the better opportunity of treatment in London and because for the moment 'poor William' trusted them, the Selkirks had made themselves largely responsible for him. Regardless of other demands, this was too grave a responsibility to be put aside; and it was one more distraction about which they had serious talks together and medical consultations before Lord Selkirk left. The young aunt, scarcely older than her nephew-patient, took up her charge with well-founded misgivings.

Though these matters sank into the background in the excitement of the gathering at Sligo, Selkirk can hardly have known peace of mind there. He had closed the door on a career most men coveted, at its most promising moment, and he had left Jean to grapple with a distressing problem that required and deserved his help. Yet the problems at Sligo would not be solved by less than his best efforts and even those might not be adequate. Parties under recruiting agents began to arrive about the middle of June and at once he was involved in the insistent

77

clamour of questions and decisions. These were settlers rather than indentured servants and until the last moment some were engaged in bargaining for advantages in the colony, in playing their own hand as shrewdly as possible. Others, with the weight of failure already on them, faced the unknown with misgiving. Some had come from the Highlands of Scotland – from Caithness and Sutherland and Argyll – others from the area of Sligo; and, though Selkirk thought the Scots more promising, the group as a whole was ill-assorted. In addition to Hudson's Bay Company servants recruited by Selkirk's agents, there were in all about eighty settlers including half a dozen families with a number of young children. Determined by his experience at Baldoon to send settlers who must fend for themselves rather than hired servants, Selkirk was taking risks in sending families into country which he still knew only from fur-traders' accounts. They were what the settlement needed for stability – if it could support them.

The claims and questions pressed in from all sides. He had to settle them with too little knowledge and without an informed adviser. A man of judgment and decision was needed to command the party to Red River. In Owen Keveny, an Irishman, he saw firmness and decision; inferring judgment as well, he appointed Keveny to the command. In order to persuade finally a wavering settler of some social pretension among the Scots, he granted a township of 10,000 acres at Red River to Alexander Maclean and gave him a dozen valuable Merino sheep which were waiting with others to be embarked, and promised him also subsistence for a year for family and servants. So he went on from day to day making such disposal as he could of indifferent material, making what he hoped was the best of what he ought to have recognized as a bad job.

In between times, with that unhurried air that was his outward response to pressure, he wrote long and careful letters of instructions to Auld, to Hillier, and to Miles Macdonell, covering settlement matters and announcing some Hudson's Bay Company policies for the year ahead. It was of a piece with his appointment of Keveny and his concessions to Alexander Maclean that they should be set out in meticulous detail and elaborately justified, yet based on a fundamental error. His instructions on their attitudes to the North West Company and on their basic legal position under the charter showed a failure to understand the Nor'Westers and a grievous ignorance of the problems of law enforcement in that empty land.

The Committee had decided that Hillier should lead a strong party to the upper Churchill River, more for the purpose of establishing legal jurisdiction and resisting North West encroachment than in the hope of successful trading. Having talked with Peter Fidler at Sligo about the latter's experiences in Athabasca, Selkirk wrote to Hillier:

> You know how anxious we are that in repelling the violent aggressions of the Canadians, you should never exceed the bounds of moderation, or allow any provocation to lead you into an imitation of their lawless proceedings. The principles of the Law of England on the subject of self-defence, and its proper limits, are not abstruse or difficult to be understood but seem to be engraved by nature on the hearts of Englishmen. These will be your guide and you will study on all occasions rather to do less than more than you would be justly entitled to do. . . . You must give them [the Nor'Westers] solemn warning that the land belongs to the Hudson's Bay Company and that they must remove from it; after this warning they must not be allowed to cut any timber either for building or fuel. What they have cut should be openly and forcibly seized, and their buildings destroyed. In like manner they should be warned not to fish in your waters, and if they put down nets seize them as you would in England those of a poacher. We are so fully advised of the unimpeachable validity of these rights of property, that there can be no scruple in enforcing them whenever you have physical means. If they make a forcible resistance, they are acting illegally, and are responsible for the consequences of what they do, while you are safe so long as you take only the

79

reasonable and necessary means of enforcing that which is your right.

From the legal opinions secured, this was merely a statement of the proper attitude. But the last paragraph, which envisaged the Hudson's Bay territory as a landed estate, took insufficient account of both practical difficulties and public opinion. It would be taken down out of context and used in evidence against him, as proof of aggressive intentions and trading ambitions for which the colony was only a mask and a cloak.

To Miles he wrote of the impending war with the United States, which, unknown to them both for weeks, was declared while he sat writing at Sligo. It was the letter of an amateur general and a romantic. In spite of his letter to Hillier he assumed that in the event of war, with central Canada lost, men of the rival companies and the settlement would unite under Miles Macdonell to hold the North-west. From this he sketched a military appreciation in which, mounted on horses from the fur-trade posts, Miles and his men should fade back into the prairies ahead of any strong American military force and ultimately find support from the Spanish colonies of New Mexico: 'If by these methods you can hold out for a while, & let me know where you are to be found reinforcements shall come to you through one route or another, & it will go hard with me, but I will have a share in your adventures.'

In his eagerness to forward the settlement, he had pushed, and been pushed, into the foreground of Hudson's Bay Company affairs, required to expound the law and make *ad hoc* decisions on matters he little understood. All his energy and attention was required for Red River, which needed simple ploughs before costly Merino sheep. His own grant measured 116,000 square miles and was only a small fraction of the Hudson's Bay territory. Absentee landlords had failed before now to understand the problems of estates much smaller and less remote.

There were, at all events, as loading and embarkation proceeded, none of the distractions of the year before at Stornoway. The *Robert Taylor*, which was to carry the settlers, was a good ship and she was sailing in company with the *King George* and the *Eddystone* of the Hudson's Bay service. At the last minute Selkirk decided to hold back for further training a promising young Scot, Archie McDonald, who had acted as a recruiting agent and was to have sailed. In the same piece-meal way he secured Dr. Thomas McKeevor from Dublin to accompany the settlers, and personally recruited a vigorous-looking man called Langston in Sligo. By the twenty-fourth all was in readiness, though with the difficulties of Sligo Bay it seemed unlikely the *Robert Taylor* could get out that day. Selkirk and other well-wishers from Sligo dined on board about four o'clock and drank to the venture amid mounting optimism. Above them could be heard the trampling of feet and the rattle of gear as the crew worked the ship down the bay. From time to time came the sound of shouted orders and the murmur of water along the hull. The ship seemed already straining towards Hudson Bay.

At six, without warning, the captain, who had been studying his sails and the weather, came below to announce that he wished to put to sea at once. There were hasty farewells and good wishes as Selkirk and his companions went over the side and their boat was cast off. Even as the boat dropped swiftly astern the two parties seemed to cling, waving and calling – the settlers gazing back at the rugged and beautiful coast that many of them were not to see again. By the time the boat regained the harbour it was dark and the tiny figures of people had been swallowed in the outline of a ship, gleaming in pale moonlight, sailing to the west.

3

Back in London Selkirk managed to convince himself that Red River arrangements were going forward in promising fashion. In July he was able to write of the settlers who had gone out, 'This, I think, will prove a very good nest-egg.' At that moment Miles Macdonell had only started for Red River from York Factory; and at sea, in the *Robert Taylor*, Keveny's harsh management was provoking a mutiny. So far from being well advanced, the settlement was only moving with difficulty up to its start-line, and the future was full of uncertainty.

In Selkirk's absence, William Hall's condition had worsened and his resentment had now fastened on the Selkirks. For some days he had been lost, while Jean lived in fear of the harm he might do himself or others. He was found at last with no damage done and seemed to improve in lodgings of his own and under a new medical attendant, but he remained a constant and painful worry through the summer and into the autumn.

Their new protégé, Archibald McDonald, was a favourite with them both, and Selkirk set about his education eagerly: 'He seems indeed a very fine young man and of the best dispositions. His heart is certainly uncorrupted and I only wish (before putting him into the situation which I have in view for him) to ascertain that his principles are sufficiently rooted to bear up against every temptation, a point which is not easily judged of, as it depends more on early habit and education than natural disposition.' It were well had he been able to test similarly Miles Macdonell, Keveny, and others. For Archie McDonald was to prove staunch in the troubles ahead.

In August the Selkirks made ready to go north to spend some time quietly at St. Mary's Isle and to prepare for another election of Scottish peers in November. 'Archibald McDonald remains here to continue his studies principally directed to medicine and the sciences which relate to it. ... I have given him a few lessons in mathematics which I believe have also been lessons in humility.'

The autumn and early winter in the north passed uneventfully. In September at St. Mary's Isle Selkirk was in good health and found himself with time on his hands. He did not rest and relax easily and when an advertisement for two Seaforth farms in the Highlands came to his attention he was at once interested: playing with the idea of what? Of demonstrating that Highland property could be run to advantage without evicting the tenants? He asked Alexander McDonald of Dalilia to inquire about price and the nature of the properties. But a few months later he had decided that a venture of this kind was not for him: 'I must not allow myself to be tempted ... the notion of a Highland estate was but a passing thought, which I laid aside on cooler reflection.'

In early November they went to Edinburgh where the election of Representative Peers was to take place on the thirteenth. This time he had no doubt of being elected, and in the voting he sat comfortably near the middle of the list, his seat never in danger. The first excitement and novelty of these elections had long since worn off but on this occasion there was a particular pleasure in seeing his old friend Walter Scott acting as Deputy Clerk Register, knowing how Scott with his love of history and ritual would be savouring his part in this ancient ceremony and with what gusto he would describe it to their friends. Afterwards there was a dinner for a glittering company at Fortune's Tavern in Princes Street – a chance to see old friends and to answer questions, spoken and unspoken, about his venture in America, and the whispers that were travelling so swiftly through the Highlands.

His return to London before Christmas after the refreshment of Edinburgh was something of a shock. He found 'whole quires to wade through' – the full story of Macdonell's winter of 1811-12 at the Bay, and various accounts of the *Robert Taylor*'s voyage. Many things had occurred to bring the latter close to disaster. The returning ships had brought back with the dispatches four settlers rejected for bad behaviour or attempted mutiny, the leader of which was the man Langston whom he had recruited. And the mail was full of conflicting accounts of Keveny's lack of tact, of his brutality as a commander, and of the mischievous and unyielding attitude of Langston and his companions. They had fomented discontent between Irish and Scots by suggesting that the

83

latter were better treated. Keveny's answer to all problems of discipline was to put the culprits in irons or to make them run the gauntlet between lines of their fellow settlers armed with clubs. Langston had endured the gauntlet several times before hatching his plot to take over the ship and sail it to an enemy port and sell the cargo. It was discovered just in time, and Langston had spent the rest of the voyage in irons railing against Keveny.

Selkirk's response, as always, was one of loyalty to his men – of eagerness to assume the bad reports exaggerated. 'My Irish Supercargo ... appears to have been rather rough in his proceedings ... as far as I can make out the complaints of ill usage were destitute of foundation, but the existence of such complaints must have a disagreeable effect.' He knew too well how swiftly such reports would be seized on and circulated. The miserable circumstances of last year's departure from Stornoway were already on everyone's lips, blown up and bodied forth with circumstantial detail – how poor Highlanders seeking to swim ashore had been hauled back by boat-hooks, and all the rest of it. Against criticism, he held himself coldly aloof, but the campaign of lies and calumny, of misrepresentation of his purpose, endangered the whole venture.

Moreover, he already knew that the Committee of the Hudson's Bay Company was wavering in its support of his plans, and of the next stage which called for Colin Robertson to go out to Montreal and recruit a brigade of Canadian *voyageurs* for Athabasca. It also called for a substantial improvement of the river channel from York Factory to Red River and for the building of a winter road. For this latter purpose he had offered to surrender part of his grant in exchange for land along his right of way. He had no option but to put off again his own trip to Red River until this difficulty was overcome. He could have little sympathy with the Committee's horror at the mounting cost of active opposition to the Nor'Westers. His own personal account at Coutts Bank had shown a turn-over of about £20,000 in each of the last two years since he had embarked on the Red River scheme; and he had to admit that as yet he knew nothing of what the expenditure had accomplished – nor was there any end in sight. In eighteen months, thanks to the first winter's delay at York, there had been no real progress and there could be no news from Red River until the ships returned next autumn – almost another year. It was as though when his parties sailed for the Bay a blind had been pulled down.

And yet, it was not quite so. The returning ships in both years had brought back a variety of reports from officials at the Bay, especially from William Auld. These, by innuendo and direct charge, together with Miles's and Keveny's letters, made clear how little the traders liked the idea of the colony and how reluctantly they gave it even the minimum support required of them. To anyone who knew the exposed position of the people sent out to the mercy of prairie winters, added to North West hostility, these would have been upsetting to the point of panic. Fortunately for him Selkirk could not fully imagine the predicament of his people, who through the winter of 1812-13, now passing comfortably enough in London, were living on the edge of starvation, struggling through blizzards in search of the buffalo herds, existing like savages, and remembering with longing the miserable existence they had traded for this. Many of the agricultural implements that would have helped with crops in the spring had been left at York Factory to make room in boats for the Merino sheep, half of which died of disease or were killed by dogs.

Keveny's party had not had an easy journey from York Factory, but they had faced merely routine hardships. At the Forks they found only the men Miles Macdonell had left to make a beginning at Point Douglas. They had no choice but to push themselves for a further sixty miles in weather already growing cold. On October 27 they reached Pembina, with a reserve of spirit which promised well for the future colony – which was indeed to be its hallmark and its final salvation. Grumbling and fatigue were put aside as they rounded a last bend in the Red River, and came to land with flag flying, and with a piper playing in the leading boat.

Selkirk was possessed by his dream and armed against anything that might challenge its reality. He had only to pour in sturdy settlers to a land of unquestioned fertility and the thing was done, the demonstration completed, and the whole made strong beyond the capacity of hostile natives or rival traders to budge it. Given that strong core, it could grow to any size, more unshakable with every increase. For the moment he was in the grip of a kind of gambler's fever, backing his luck, trebling his stakes. Jean Selkirk, who was to confess afterwards that she could never turn him from a course once he was set on it, looked on with mounting dismay; but every objection was affectionately brushed aside or answered with 'some sanguine calculation'. Andrew, never as enthusiastic, seemed to have cooled in his attitude to the costly venture and Auld with growing boldness missed no opportunity, in writing to Colvile, of commenting on the folly of the settlement and the incapacity of Miles Macdonell. If any of it shook Thomas, Earl of Selkirk, he gave no sign.

Just as he had seen the settlement as serviceable in the event of war, so did the war now appear to provide the means of enlisting government support for the colony. During the spring he was in communication with the Duke of York as Commander in Chief and with Lord Bathurst who as Secretary of State for War and the Colonies might be doubly interested in his proposal. For a moment it looked as though the government would sponsor a battalion of Fencibles from Sutherland for Red River. In despair at having been turned off the lands they had occupied for generations, the Kildonan people, after an ineffective riot, had sent a delegation bearing a petition to London. Selkirk, meeting the delegation after Parliament had turned it away, found in them all the qualities he admired and sought to preserve in the Highland people. While proposing his regiment, he sounded the Kildonan people on the idea, and applications poured in. Before the submission to the Commander in Chief was finally turned down, there were no fewer than 1,100 men, women, and children with the smell of burning cottages in their nostrils ready to go to Red River. Selkirk's

86

idea was that not more than 200 married men should go out at once as soldiers, with their families to follow in two or three years' time. But the momentary excitement came to very little. In the end the government provided about twenty-five muskets and bayonets and some light artillery for the settlement, and that summer the Royal Navy convoyed the Hudson's Bay ships at the commencement of their voyage.

In spite of the let-down Selkirk could find satisfaction in the quality of the settlers who did go out in the ships in 1813. He was present at the final selection and saw them off from Stromness on June 28. There were over ninety people, mostly from Kildonan, including about forty sturdy young men. It was the most homogeneous group he had yet sent out and by all odds the best. With them went young Archie McDonald after his year of training, as second-in-command to a Dr. Laserre. If these people did not make good settlers the whole idea was a failure. But Selkirk was not in doubt, nor was he wrong about the calibre of the people. Through the summer and autumn he waited for word of their arrival and for news from Miles of the first year at Red River. No matter how great his anxiety, he could never have been prepared for the tale of disaster that came back in November 1813 with the returning ships.

On the voyage out, ship's fever had broken out among the settlers on the *Prince of Wales* and five settlers and several members of the crew had died, including Dr. Laserre, and the command had devolved on Archibald McDonald. Captain Turner of the *Prince of Wales*, anxious only to be rid of his charges, on arrival in Hudson Bay had sailed straight across to Fort Churchill and discharged them on the shore, where no one was ready to receive them and where two more died of typhus, while Miles Macdonell and Auld, with supplies, waited for the ships at York Factory. Auld sailed at once to Churchill to storm at the stubborn captain.

Finally, at Auld's insistence, the settlers were re-embarked and then, deliberately or not, the ship was run aground on a sand-bar. The last hope of a move to Red River or even to York Factory before winter was gone. Selkirk learned only that they had removed fifteen miles inland, carrying the sick, and there in the woods had built themselves rude cabins. Dreading scurvy if not starvation he sought consolation in reflecting that no precaution had been omitted for the health of his unhappy people. 'I am quite in despair at this most unexpected stroke.' The group with which his highest hopes had travelled – the group of whom he had said that he took as much interest in their success as if they were in his own employment – were stranded in a dangerous wilderness. And a year must pass before he learned their fate.

Good news from Red River might have softened the blow, but squarely faced it offered no satisfaction. True, Miles Macdonell, who tended to put the best face on unpleasant news, confirmed all that had been reported of the wonderful goodness of the soil. But Selkirk could no longer deceive himself that this was enough, and Miles's letters had other things to report. It was clear that the winter had been a desperate struggle for the poor people unprepared for such a contest; poorly clad, undernourished, ignorant of snowshoes and winter bivouacs, they had survived – but little more. And the struggle that might have drawn and riveted them together in adversity had driven them apart in suspicious, discontented cliques, united only in their misery. A letter from the settlement's surgeon, Dr. Edwards, full of accusations against Macdonell for mismanagement and high-handedness and far too great intimacy with the Nor'Westers, filled in details that were hardly needed to complete the picture of an unhappy colony not yet out of danger. The same bundle of letters contained one from Auld to Andrew Colvile so full of vituperation against Macdonell and the colony as to diminish any hope that Auld might be brought to a cheerful support of the colony under Miles.

There was something else. Just before the ships sailed back Miles wrote from York Fort that he had been discussing with the Hudson's Bay Company officers the question of safeguarding supplies for his people. For years the North Westers had been taking out pemmican and buffalo-grease in sufficient quantities to provision their brigades for Athabasca. Since much of it was coming from territory to which Lord Selkirk had absolute title, this was patently wrong while the settlers in the grant lived close to starvation. 'I am now determined the North West Company shall not take more provisions from [here] than will carry out their people who winter in Red River.'

On top of so much disaster, this decision threatened still more. Selkirk's first impulse may have been to applaud Miles's determination to assure the safety of his people. But further consideration of all that it meant could not be comforting. To anyone who knew the Nor'Westers it was clear that they would not accept this quietly, and the trouble it would give rise to could destroy all he had sought to build. He could only hope that the letters written to Miles from Stromness would sufficiently control his acts. There was at least one worse danger than another hungry winter. Whatever Selkirk had said to Hillier the year before, Miles must by now have his letter saying: 'I would wish you to be very cautious ... and always to remember that any violent overstretch of authority would be extremely pernicious to our cause.'

And the next day, thinking about Miles and his problems, he had written: 'The distance at which we are placed and the long period which must intervene between communications leaves a sort of melancholy impression of uncertainty over our correspondence.'

Feeling that way in June, he must doubly have felt it now. He was to know nothing but melancholy uncertainty for months, and it was to become a crushing burden. For the moment there was nothing to do but brood, and the brooding made him ill. Through the winter and spring life crawled by. He kept to their new house in Upper Grosvenor Street much of the time and took no part in the Lords debates. There was always Jean to cheer him when that was possible, and the children playing in front of the fire with a toy farm given them by John Hall. Red River would darken their growing-up years soon enough; meanwhile they chattered incessantly, and perhaps occasionally diverted the sickly and unhappy man who could think of little else.

4

The summer and autumn of 1813 had seen real progress at Red River. The buildings were not yet impressive, but the settlement was assuming the appearance of a village and the long, peaceful summer found people in possession of their own lots, working contentedly and with growing skill. The sense of community, so long in coming, was beginning to be felt. In spite of all, it was still necessary to retreat to Fort Daer at Pembina before winter in search of buffalo meat. Once again the buffalo stayed far out on the prairie, but it was an open winter and with growing confidence the settlers ventured after them like old hands and brought plenty of meat home. There were neither North West nor Hudson's Bay traders at Pembina that winter, and this, with Miles's hard-learned tact and the departure of Edwards to Churchill, did much to quiet the discontent of the year before.

On New Year's Eve, in the excitement of a rare party about to begin, an express came in from York Factory. It brought Lord Selkirk's letters from the *Prince of Wales*, finally taken from the ship at Churchill and sent on after being read by all the officers at York. One letter, which was marked for Miles only, to be returned in the event of his death, had been callously returned to England. Cheerfully, Miles read the letters from home, then joined his people in a party that lasted until dawn.

During the previous summer at York, while they waited for the ship that didn't come, he and Auld and the others had discussed the problem of supplies for the settlers. Someone, perhaps playfully, had suggested an embargo on provisions, and the idea had grown. Whether Auld suggested it or merely fostered an attractive notion once it had taken root, he certainly welcomed a measure that would serve his turn whatever its result. It could hamper or even destroy the North Westers' trade, or it could end the colony and destroy its governor.

It is probable that Miles, having taken up the scheme into which Auld had led him, was held to it by pride if not by his own conviction. Perhaps he had strutted a bit at York Fort. Certainly he had hinted, with a wink or its equivalent, that though the embargo would have to apply to both companies its interpretation would be up to him. He said later, ingenuously, that it was never intended to injure the Hudson's Bay Company but merely to avoid the appearance of discrimination.

He was not a clever man but he could not have been in doubt as to the seriousness of the dilemma he faced on reading Selkirk's letter of June 13. His devotion to Selkirk and his dependence on him should have allowed that quiet authoritative voice to break through his pride: 'I would wish you to be very cautious . . . and always to remember that any violent overstretch of authority would be extremely pernicious to our cause.' His instructions were clear, if perhaps his duty was not. He was, after all, governor, and had an absolute duty to the settlers. His people had never been secure against the danger of starvation since they arrived, and by the end of the next summer he would have double the number – 200 – to provide for, including the people now stranded at Churchill, and a great many more if Selkirk came out as planned. His proclamation prohibiting the export of all but a minimum of provisions for outgoing traders was already made out. 'It had been written before the receipt of your Lordship's letters, and notwithstanding the caution recommended in the instruction I issued it on the 8th of January, judging that remission might always be granted according to circumstances.' He seems to have lingered for a week in doubt, paying, perhaps, for having remained aloof too long from his officers, by having no one of standing whom he could consult, with trust in his motives and confidence in his judgment. It was one more burden for a man already pressed beyond his strength.

The step he was about to take would lead to disaster, and he must have known that it might. But to do nothing might also mean disaster. His sheriff, Spencer, one of the few to defend him afterwards, implied that Macdonell had had little choice: '. . . his wants I do assure you were equal to his needs, nay far surpassed them'.

91

The Nor'Westers, however, were not interested in his needs nor at all inclined to see them satisfied at their expense. As the proclamation began to appear, tacked up on the gates of their forts, the first response was incredulity. Resentment, like a slow-burning match, was not far behind. Though the act was of the sort they had expected from the beginning, Miles Macdonell had not so far insisted on Lord Selkirk's claims or on his own authority; there had been the initial ceremony of taking possession of the land – nothing more. Now they were faced with the reality of ownership in the soil, the use of which had always been free to them, and a change to which they could not easily, if ever, adjust.

The proclamation, after restating Lord Selkirk's claim and defining the boundaries of the grant, went on to outline the needs of the settlers at Red River together with those to be added to their numbers before the end of the summer. It stated Miles Macdonell's duty to provide for their support and the view that the game in the grant was no more than adequate for their welfare, in the present uncultivated state of the country:

> ... wherefore it is hereby ordered, that no person trading in furs or provisions within the territory for the honourable the Hudson's Bay Company, the North West Company, or any individual, or unconnected trader or persons whatever, shall take out any provisions, either of flesh, grain or vegetables, procured or raised within the said territory, by water or land carriage, for one twelve month from the date hereof; save and except what may be judged necessary for the trading parties at this present time within the territory, to carry them to their respective destinations, and also may on due application to me, obtain licence for the same. The provisions procured and raised as above, shall be taken for the use of the colony; and that no loss may accrue to the parties concerned, they will be paid for by British bills at the accustomary rates.

The proclamation was signed for Miles Macdonell by John Spencer as secretary to the Governor of Assiniboia.

It was not at first apparent what the result of the proclamation might be. There would in any case be no movement of supplies until the brigades went out in the early summer. Auld, travelling through the country as superintendent, wrote gleefully about what he learned of North West response. He claimed that John Pritchard, in charge of the North West fort at La Souris believed that Macdonell was within his legal rights, and that John Wills at Fort Gibraltar did also, though he might not admit it. Others, including John McDonald (known as 'One-Eyed', or 'Le Borgne') would resist the embargo by force. Auld had also heard what Miles apparently did not suspect: that in a show-down the settlers would not support him; this heartening information had reached the Nor'Westers from the leading settler, Alexander Maclean. In spite of this, the letter assured Macdonell that 'the Bourgeois will bluster and strut a bit and that will be all'.

Auld ended by begging Miles not to quote him, and offered Hudson's Bay Company help in enforcing the regulations. Miles, whatever his misgivings, declined the offer, saying that he had sufficient strength and that he regarded the present as 'the last struggle of an expiring party and when once foiled in it they can never trouble us more'. But by now it was late April and already there was evidence that the last struggle – if it was the last – would be formidable. As the rivers opened, the supplies of pemmican that had been traded for and cached during the winter began to move down the waterways guarded by parties that looked both strong and determined.

There could now be little doubt that a quarrel that might outrun all controls was in prospect. In the weeks ahead, brigades from Swan River, Turtle River, River La Souris, and Qu'Appelle were due to pass down the Assiniboine and swing into the Red. At the Forks of the Red River they would pass below the stockade of their own Fort Gibraltar and turn north for Lake Winnipeg, but before they gained the lake and turned east into the Winnipeg River they must pass for two miles or more along the front of the settlement and under the guns of Fort Douglas. The logistics of the fur trade, long established, required that they go out laden with pemmican. For not only must they supply their own wants over the 400-500 miles that lay between them and Fort William, but they must also supply the brigades now swinging down out of the great fan that lay over Athabasca, the handle of which rested on Fort Bas de la Rivière Winnipeg. Usually the tough northern men arrived short of rations, and sometimes actually starving. To withhold what they needed and considered their right might be thought inhuman, and was certainly dangerous. The North West Company had only once encountered a rival almost as tough and determined as itself – the XY Company. The two having merged ten years before, the Nor'Westers' toughness (and their view of what was due them) had been by that much supplemented.

Into the arms of this formidable crew, the proclamation had delivered a reinforcement Miles would have given – and had given – much to win for himself: the half-breeds. These sons of the fur-traders with their Indian mothers lived an unsettled life between Indian camp and fur-trade post – hunting, trading, and guiding – knowing no other life, having no other occupation. Some of them had been glad enough to hunt and trade for the settlement, but the Nor'Westers were their fathers, however much resented, their main source of income, and their masters. Whatever threatened the Nor'Westers threatened them. And a regulation based on the ownership by Lord Selkirk of the land they had roamed over without hindrance all their lives was a regulation they could hardly understand. A few of their leaders had been given some education in Montreal or in Scotland and served as North West Company clerks. Thus, those who might have been brought to understand how a man they had never seen, living 4,000 miles away, could claim their land, were tied to the opposing interest. Easily roused, rootless, the half-breeds or *bois brûlés* closed in behind the North West phalanx. On their swift ponies, from which they could shoot with deadly effect at the gallop, they were as dangerous and could become as unmanageable as a prairie storm.

Whatever gifts of leadership he lacked, Miles Macdonell was a brave man. If by now he regretted the pemmican embargo, he had no choice but to see it through. The needs of his settlement were not less because the regulation was resented, and a success that might still be confirmed would solve all his problems. Grumbling, but observing the regulations, the Hudson's Bay traders brought in their surplus pemmican and deposited it at Fort Douglas. The Nor'Westers were not impressed, suspecting that what came in the front door could be issued to friends from the back. They sent in no pemmican. Miles decided to act. Knowing that a large supply of pemmican had been gathered in at La Souris, he sent a strong party under Sheriff Spencer to demand its surrender. John Pritchard, commanding the post, refused them entry from behind a locked gate. Without being resisted, Spencer's men cut three pickets out of the stockade, forced the store-room door, and carried away 400 bags of pemmican. It did not help appearances that they were accompanied by Howse of the Hudson's Bay Company, and that the pemmican they could not carry away was stored at the Hudson's Bay's Brandon House near by.

There was no longer any doubt that whatever pemmican Miles was to secure, under a regulation that he believed to have the force of law, would have to be seized. The settlers, who had disliked the dangers of the proclamation, took heart at this tangible success. Macdonell felt the ground firmer beneath his feet and sent Spencer out again to meet a party said to be descending the Assiniboine with large stores. This time success was less satisfactory. The word of Spencer's coming had travelled across the plain, and at first he found only an abandoned boat. The pemmican was finally found and gathered in after an ignominious search. The Nor'Westers responded by arresting Howse for burglary at La Souris, and Miles Macdonell in turn covered all entry and egress from the river, by mounting cannon. Two miles away, at Fort Gibraltar, the North West wintering partners gathered, backed by a growing crowd of *voyageurs* and half-breeds. Some of the brigades from Athabasca waited near by, ready to join the rest. By now Miles

Macdonell was outnumbered, and by men who had always carried everything before them. One of the last to come in was John McDonald of Garth, overland from the Pacific by canoe. He was on the point of retirement, but, as brother-in-law of William McGillivray and as a fearless leader in bygone fur-trade wars, his prestige was immense.

Miles Macdonell was the same kind of man as those he faced – of similar background and temperament, stiffened by the same pride. Though trained in a less hard school, he was not soft, and for the moment he had more at stake. But his chief assets were intangible: the authority of his office as governor, the weight of the Hudson's Bay charter, and the backing of the Earl of Selkirk. The Nor'Westers might challenge and rail against them all, but they would not flout them as casually as they would the claims of a rival trader. Through several days of parleying, peace trembled in a balance that a loss of temper might at any moment upset. Miles's pleas on behalf of his settlers carried weight with men who had all known hunger on the frozen plains. Equally, the *Bourgeois* claims for the immediate needs of all brigades were unanswerable.

The agreement they reached was a credit to them all, though it was to be repudiated with fury at North West headquarters at Fort William. Macdonell gave up all but 200 bags of the North West pemmican. In return, the partners undertook in the autumn to send canoes to York Factory to bring back oatmeal for the settlement and to supply 175 bags of pemmican to the settlement the following winter. They might in turn send to England by Hudson's Bay ships such furs as they carried on the trip to the Bay and thus avoid the American threat to the fur-trade routes. Both parties had in a measure saved face while avoiding what must have been a bloody struggle. On June 28, 1814, John McDonald of Garth, the reckless old warrior who had turned peace-maker, signed first for the North West Company, followed by Duncan Cameron, John McDonald (Le Borgne), John Wills, and John Dugald Cameron. The ninety-pound bags of pemmican were hefted down the bank below Fort Douglas to the waiting canoes and the brigades swept out of the river heading for Fort William. As the *voyageurs* broke into song they did not sound or look like an expiring party.

Miles Macdonell was left to contemplate his measure of victory, and to recognize the magnitude of failure. The settlers who had begun by fearing and disapproving the embargo had changed when they believed it might succeed. Now everyone was free to criticize the final result; to have had the pemmican and given it up seemed to these simple people the height of folly. The Hudson's Bay traders who had not resisted the embargo had got nothing back, and their distrust of Macdonell was sealed in anger.

Just before the North West brigades departed, young Archie McDonald reached Red River with the first contingent, fifty strong, of the settlers who had survived the winter at Churchill. It was the only bright spot on Miles's horizon. Leaving the settlement under the command of Peter Fidler and Archie McDonald, he set out for York Factory. There the long strain overtook him and his nerves broke. Before leaving Red River he had written Lord Selkirk begging to be relieved of his command. Now for a time the Hudson's Bay officers, moved to pity in spite of their anger and dislike, took his weapons away from him lest he destroy himself, as he believed he had destroyed the settlement.

Chapter 4

HERE IS AT THEM!

I

Through the early months of 1814 the dream of the Kingdom of Red River hung in the balance. So far the history of the settlement had been one of complete misadventure in which no one could claim that the North West Company had played a large part. Certainly their propaganda had been harmful and the delay at Miles's starting had contributed to his failure to reach The Forks that year, to forward matters against the arrival of Keveny's party. But so numerous were the mishaps, and so serious, that it seemed much greater forces fought against the plan: ship-fever and contrary winds at sea; prairie fires that destroyed the grazing and drove the buffalo far from Pembina, when in normal years they scratched their woolly backs against the posts of the stockade and grazed within gun-shot; the first crops, for lack of a plough, had been planted shallow in newly burnt-over soil and the ashes had spoiled all but the potatoes and turnips. There had been mistakes in planning, and too much haste, and there had been grievous faults of leadership which no amount of deliberation by Selkirk could have overcome; but in the most testing requirements of a normal world Miles Macdonell and Keveny and young Archie McDonald were counted good men. If they all failed in the Red River venture, who could hope to succeed? The whole scale of the project and the obstacles to be surmounted – the northern sea, the long haul inland, and the hard country at the end of the journey: were these in combination too much for mere men? The lack of permanent settlement until now seemed to answer that they were, but against this was the almost routine ease with which the North West people and even the Hudson's Bay men moved through the country, living where they would.

These were the questions that plagued Selkirk throughout 1814 when disaster seemed to have answered his every move and a fortune had already been poured out in vain. From almost any point of view the course of wisdom was to give up the fight. In any calculation of money he must still be better off to cut his losses and conserve what remained; success for the colony now would not in a lifetime repay its cost. As to the people, many had died (perhaps many more than he knew) and none were yet out of danger; but, as long as a chance of success remained, were they not better off? They might die more slowly back in Scotland, but not less miserably; they were redundant outcasts with nothing to lose; they had been short of food at Red River but not shorter than in the Highlands. And what of his honour, his reputation staked on success, his belief that a strong settlement would be valuable in the national interest?

By April he had turned back with stern determination to drive the experiment through, and, though still unwell, he settled himself to Red River affairs. If the failure was largely Miles Macdonell's, he must be fully supported or replaced. Auld, who had blocked, undermined, and misled the venture, must go – Auld, who had turned his officers against Macdonell, written home of him that he had 'never by any chance done a single thing right', described him 'standing alone like the poison tree'; and, finally, Auld who had taken on himself and persuaded his associates to return to Selkirk one of his confidential letters to Macdonell, 'for reasons too impertinent and absurd for the most petulant school boy'. Nevertheless the letter that was to bring Miles news of Auld's dismissal was not to leave him in any doubt of how disappointing his own results appeared. The settlement accounts were in chaos, and Selkirk, reviewing the first year with exasperation, wrote that it was a satisfaction to have it behind them, he found no other cause for congratulation. 'It is mortifying to compare this with the great value of labour and expense.' Moreover, the requisitions for the year ahead called for £5,000 worth of goods for at most 200 people.

But the letter was not confined to criticism. He had long, minute directions for catching and smoking fish, for driving large numbers of buffalo into a pound, Indian fashion, and freezing the meat against need. He proposed also the segregating of a group of buffalo cows for breeding to the settlement bull, Adam, and the production of a domestic strain. Meanwhile, he had written to Upper Canada directing the expenditure of £1,000 for the driving of 100 cows through the Sioux country to Red River. (His letter characteristically set out the proposal in detail and contained an injunction against the cattle being driven too fast.)

As it happened, there was little room for settlers in the ships going out to the Bay in the summer of 1814, and it was perhaps a relief not to have to risk another large venture until the fate of the Kildonan people at Churchill was known. And in the circumstances there could be no possibility of his going as planned. Of the group that sailed in June there were only fourteen men for the settlement. Now there was nothing to do but wait through the months until the ships came back in early November with news of Archie McDonald's party and the results of Miles's reckless determination to control the export of pemmican from the grant. This last made him uneasy but he had discovered a measure of justification and precedent in the practice of colonial governors forced to take emergency measures for the safety of their dependants. Meanwhile, a blessed summer at St. Mary's Isle, in the soft air above the Solway, did much to restore his health and spirits.

He was back in London waiting impatiently when the packets of mail came in from the Hudson's Bay ships. And with the ships came Hillier and Dr. Edwards with first-hand news of all that had happened since 1811. Their reports, especially Edwards's, were to be taken with reserve, but they could fill in countless details of the outline sketched with painful slowness these three long years.

At first hearing, the news was all good, wonderfully good. The people huddled in their mud-floored cabins above Churchill had come through well. Thanks to oatmeal and an abundance of ptarmigan in the woods, they had escaped the scurvy he had dreaded. In the spring the first group under young Archie had marched the 150 miles to York Factory across frozen swamps and through light bush in thirteen days, then on to Red River by boat. Four more people had died of consumption or other complaints. The rest were now at the settlement, alive and well and at work in good heart. He had not underestimated their quality.

Apart from a nagging uneasiness about the Pemmican War, which might not yet be over, news of established growth at the settlement was at last reassuring. 'The progress of the former settlers is such as to [leave] no further doubt of their success,' he wrote McDonald of Dalilia; and he added that Miles had held his temper and handled himself well in the pemmican business – and made his point: '. . . at the same time it would have been more consistent with my views and my instructions if he had tried to avoid any such collision.' Still, the settlement was established – on a firm basis at last. He was in no mood now to have his dream again disturbed. Even the distressing word of Miles's breakdown seemed to be cancelled by Edwards's and Hillier's report. All was well.

Yet the dream was threatened within the month. Ships, sailing much later from Montreal than was possible from the Bay, brought letters from Colin Robertson. From Fort William had come word of instructions to the wintering partners of the

North West Company to incite the Indians against the settlement. He could not take the threat too literally, but such a degree of enmity as Miles had aroused was alarming. The Indians had always been prominent in the North West Company's most dire predictions, though they had never in fact shown the slightest hostility. He wrote Robertson that the North West threats gave him no small uneasiness, 'though I hardly think they can venture on a step which would brand them with indelible infamy – and expose them to a charge of High Treason'. He went on:

> If you can find means of seeing Mr. John Macdonell I beg of you to tell him that some circumstances . . . make me very anxious that he could take a trip as far as Red River with the first open water, to see his brother & assist him with his advice, in the delicate circumstances in which he may be placed . . .

It was a shrewd move, if only it could succeed. John Macdonell was a former North West wintering partner who had at one time been stationed at Red River. His presence there, among old friends, and standing by his brother Miles, might cool the temper of both sides.

John Macdonell had already recognized both the danger and the opportunity, for a month earlier he had written to a friend:

> From reports that have reached me from a source I cannot doubt . . . I have reason to fear that my brother's life and the safety of the infant colony in the Red River are in a perilous situation. My greatest fear is from treachery and machinations to prejudice the natives against the colonists. Some of the wintering partners of the N.W. Co. think favourably of the undertaking and will go all lengths consistent with their duty and interest as N.W. partners to prevent its destruction. The strongest argument I have heard used to raise a jealousy in the natives is by inculcating upon their minds a belief that they are robbed of their lands without any indemnification, this I have heard a year ago from the mouth of a principal and one of the chief instigators of this enmity.

He went on to deplore the pemmican embargo, adding: 'I certainly wish more moderation was used by both parties – I dread of hearing something disastrous from that quarter next year.' If he could liquidate his property at Point Fortune on the Ottawa River and realize on his North West Company shares, he proposed to go up to Red River. If only because his term 'natives' comprehended half-breeds as well as Indians, it is a pity John Macdonell failed to make the journey, for he understood the danger.

Meanwhile, events were moving swiftly at Red River. Even as Selkirk was writing cheerfully in the confidence that the colony was at last established, one of his settlers was sending a letter to Duncan Cameron of the North West Company at Red River:

> Honoured Sir
> I understand that your honour has proposed to relieve a poore distressed people By taking them to Montreal next spring I hoap that you will count myself and family in the number, as I assure you that it is well known that I was still against the taking of the pimiken . . .

2

The situation at Red River had changed dramatically during the autumn of 1814. During the previous two years there had been expectations of trouble and at times the North Westers had seemed to play the part of vultures waiting for their prey, apparently confident of the outcome. A few had shown a measure of patronizing good nature, if not kindness, as when Duncan Cameron had written a colleague: 'I would advise you to let Capt. McDonell have some wheat and potatoes on his own and Brother's account as I don't look on him or his Colonists as opponents in trade, besides he may as well be obligated to you for it as another . . . should an opportunity offer you'll give him my compliments.' Others had been less well disposed and had made the most of the colonists' misery to stir discontent; this was mischief-making, though not aggressively hostile.

But those who came back from Fort William at the end of the summer were no longer divided in their attitudes. The waiting period was over. Whether they had waited for the colony to fail or for a pretext on which to attack it, those who wished it ended were now at one. It was probably only the wintering partners and clerks who had been at all divided. When the colony first started, Simon McGillivray, having failed to stop it in London and in Scotland, had passed on his conviction that it must be stopped at Red River. 'It will require some time, and I fear cause much expence to us as well as to himself [Selkirk], before he is driven to abandon the project; and yet he must be driven to abandon it, for his success would strike at the very existence of our trade.' A year later, in 1813, as John Macdonell had learned, the process of rousing the resentment of the natives had already begun.

With the pemmican embargo, Miles Macdonell had played directly into his opponents' hands. News of all that had passed and of the compromise solution in June had been carried swiftly ahead of the brigades to the North West depot at Fort William. The arrival there was usually a signal for celebration and gaiety; this year, those who came from Red River were received with cold disapproval. While some were singled out for reprimand, all were made to feel that they had submitted the organization to insult and loss of respect. Dr. McLoughlin wrote bitterly that they had 'had their Belly full'. There were explanations and heated arguments and the case was tried a hundred times – among partners, among *voyageurs*, among half-breeds and Indian hunters and freemen – until in the mounting heat the verdict became unanimous and the sentence obvious to all. It was the way they were accustomed to, the only law they knew. Every insult had to be repaid with interest, and those whose sacred honour had been impaired might redeem it in the forefront of the battle.

There were two exceptions. No one hinted at any lack of courage in John McDonald of Garth; he was retiring and was allowed to go down to Montreal in peace, though he may have had a few hard words behind closed doors with William McGillivray. 'We ought to have fought for our *taureaux*,' he wrote to Dugald Cameron. 'So say all who were not there, this year you must bid all defiance. ...' John Pritchard, who had allowed his fort at La Souris to be entered and his pemmican confiscated, was publicly branded a coward. As he was in any case leaving the service, he was permitted to leave in disgrace after a searching examination by McGillivray and the provision of a long statement designed to incriminate Hudson's Bay Company and colony alike.

The posts of 'honour' were given to Duncan Cameron, who as a partner was to have the command at Red River, and to Alexander Macdonell, a clerk who was to marshal the half-breeds. Cameron had an amiable side which anger and appeals to his pride had for the moment put down. Macdonell, though perhaps not evil, was dangerous because he was stupid and vain – a loaded gun ready to be pointed by McGillivray. By 'early August' they were on their way back to their posts. And Whiteheaded Macdonell, off to the wars, couldn't resist striking an attitude, though all had been warned to silence:

> You see myself and our mutual friend Mr. Cameron so far on our way to commence open hostilities against the enemy in Red River – much is expected from us if we believe some – perhaps too much –. One thing certain that we will do our best to defend what we *consider* our rights in the interior – something serious will undoubtedly take place – nothing but the complete downfall of the colony will satisfy some, by fair or foul means – a most desirable object if it can be accomplished – so here is at them with all my heart and energy – general censure was *by some* thrown out against me (behind my back if you please) at Headquarters.

It was customary for the *Bourgeois* to carry hangers and dirks – for the maintenance of discipline. This was now to be improved on. Although the American war was over Duncan Cameron appeared at Red River in a captain's scarlet tunic and began styling himself 'Captain, Voyageurs Corps, Commanding Officer, Red River'. He also carried warrants for the arrest of Miles Macdonell and John Spencer, signed by Archibald Norman McLeod, J.P., of the North West Company. Miles Macdonell was still at York Factory as the curtain rose on a farce at which few would laugh.

The settlement watched the events at Fort Gibraltar uncomfortably. To some of these old soldiers a captain's uniform commanded obedience, and, moreover, the captain spoke Gaelic and could make himself very agreeable. While they wondered uncertainly about him, Duncan Cameron pounced, arresting Sheriff Spencer. The settlers drew together angrily then, and, given a leader, would have freed Spencer and ended the farce. But Peter Fidler, the senior man, was mild, and Archie McDonald was young and unsure; both recommended caution. When, a few days later, Spencer was carried down-river a prisoner before their eyes, the settlers were with difficulty restrained; one impulsive lad did fire across the bows of the leading North West canoe, but that was all. As the canoe bearing their sheriff disappeared, their bewilderment was complete; and the moment for rousing them to action had also passed.

The fabric of the settlement had never developed the texture to give it resistance to the strains now tugging at it. Among the settlers who had been there from the first were some who had begun to feel at home, who were putting down cautious roots; but there were many to whom the struggle seemed hopeless. The bigness, the harshness of the country, the violent changes of climate; the withering heat and the bright glare, followed unpredictably by stunning electric storms; the hot dry air of the summer and the shrivelling cold of the winter – this combination was too much for men to bear.

Years of subsisting meanly but with little effort in Highland glens had unfitted many for grappling with the prairie. If they had not wholly recognized their longing to be gone, they recognized it quickly enough when opportunity offered. It began to be whispered that there was free land to be had in Upper Canada, where life was easier; it was over a thousand miles away but Captain Cameron would help them to get there. There was a whisper, too, that Governor Macdonell had been outside the law in taking the pemmican and that they might be in trouble as well. Rumour found Captain Cameron kind, free with food and drink, sympathetic to their troubles. More and more visited Fort Gibraltar, and were tempted.

When Miles Macdonell returned from the Bay with confidence somewhat restored, he knew all was not well, but he was to be a long time in learning how far the trouble had spread. In fact, it was not yet unmanageable. But it needed wise and steady handling, and a confidence in his leadership which he had failed so far to win.

The star that had shone on Miles Macdonell at his first meeting with Selkirk seemed to have been extinguished. The popular Captain Macdonell, whom everyone liked and trusted and knew for a brave man, appeared drawn by a magnet to his own undoing. In his distracted state he either made wrong moves or right ones at the wrong time. In the previous summer, flushed with triumph in the pemmican negotiations, he had forbidden the half-breeds to hunt the buffalo on horseback, since they drove the herds far out on the plains. All those less well mounted – Indians, colonists, freemen, and even North Westers – cheered the regulation, but it confirmed the half-breeds' hostility. This had been followed in the autumn of 1814 and the spring of 1815 by notices to quit the premises, tacked on the North West forts within the grant. It was a matter of legal form, suggested by Selkirk to break any claim to land that might be established by occupation too long unchallenged. It could have waited a few months or been explained to the Nor'Westers; instead, they were allowed to suppose that they faced forcible eviction.

For the first time in its short history the colony remained for the winter of 1814-15 at the Forks of the Red River. A party of hunters went down to Pembina for supplies of buffalo meat, and that winter the colony was not in want. The Kildonan people, whatever their misgivings, had gone to work with energy, and everyone was safely if not splendidly housed. For the moment it seemed that the rot was stopped. Things were indeed better; but it was easy enough in the early darkness for settlers to make their way the two miles to Fort Gibraltar where they were sure of a welcome, and a drink, and sometimes even a dance. It was much gayer at Fort Gibraltar; and there a man could express his worries and grumbles and be sure of a sympathetic hearing. Messages and invitations were carried back in the darkness, and there were more hints of what might happen in the spring.

Macdonell and his officers could not have been wholly unaware of what was going on, but it is clear they did not understand its magnitude. Otherwise Macdonell's calm departure for Pembina in the spring was both blindness and folly. There were rumours that the Sioux were on the war-path and that Pembina was in danger; Miles went down to take command. He was a brave man, at his best in the face of recognizable danger. But he had an unfortunate tendency, as now, to face the wrong way.

In his absence, Duncan Cameron's campaign of subversion went on at an increased pace. There were threats now, about the dangers from Indians and half-breeds, to give point to the promises of land and free transportation. 'I have no interest whatever in making you these promises, but what humanity points out to me,' wrote Cameron. In March this was followed by a letter answering the worries of some of the indentured servants whose time was almost up and to whom money was owed. 'The surest way is to get whatever you can out of their store, and I will take any article that can be of use here off your hands, and pay you in Canada for them. . . .'

But Duncan Cameron was not having things all his own way. The North West and Hudson's Bay people might join in reviling the settlers as dirty, ignorant, indolent, and stupid, but, after all they had been through, they were not easily frightened, and some had an inconvenient dislike of treachery.

Against this sturdy wall, the undertow of Cameron's efforts broke and fell back a little. His honour would not be repaired by the carrying away of a handful of settlers; the objective was nothing less than the destruction of the settlement. He prepared a master-stroke that required active assistance from within, and he found his man in George Campbell, one of the leaders of the Kildonan settlers. Campbell had already been energetic in spreading disturbing rumours and was ready for the next step. Word was passed among a select few that so long as Fort Douglas possessed cannon no one would be allowed to leave in the spring. The cannon must be handed over to Duncan Cameron for safe-keeping.

The move was carefully planned and quickly executed. About one o'clock on April 3 a horse-drawn sledge was stopped outside the building that housed the field-pieces. One man stood guard with a loaded musket while a party quickly entered and brought out the field-pieces and howitzers. A few bystanders held back whoever attempted to interfere. As the horse drew away Cameron appeared, backed by an armed party. The cannon were convoyed to Fort Gibraltar and there the triumph was celebrated with a dram.

Through April and May the pressure mounted. The half-breeds under Alexander Macdonell arrived and established a camp north of the settlement at Frog Plain, and the night became filled with the sound of galloping ponies and Indian war songs and stray shots. Still the bulk of the colonists held firm. A battery of their own guns was erected by Cameron within range of Fort Douglas, and a raiding party took several of the isolated settlers prisoner and brought them into the half-breed camp. One day there was an open attack on the settlement, in which four men were wounded and one died of his wounds. Threats of Indian massacre became general and peremptory letters were sent by Cameron to some of the more stubborn settlers, demanding the surrender of their muskets 'in the King's name'. The fabric began to give way. Duncan Cameron was determined to break resistance by the arrest of Miles Macdonell.

My Lads

... I think it necessary, once more for all, to advise you as a fellow-subject to pay due respect, submission, and obedience, to the law of our blessed constitution. – And I further declare, that any person or persons who shall be found in future attempting, by any means, to rescue and screen the prisoner from justice, shall immediately be considered as accomplices in his crimes and treated accordingly. That your own good sense and judgment may dictate to you, free of party spirit, a true sense of the impropriety of violating or acting in direct opposition to your country's laws, is my Lads, the sincere wish of your well-wisher,

Red River	D. Cameron
Indian Territory	Capt. Voyageurs Corps,
June 7th 1815	Commanding Officer, Red River

Simultaneously, both the settlers and Miles Macdonell were made to feel that the Governor was the only real culprit. If he would surrender, the settlement would be safe. Worn out, doubting his own wisdom, Miles Macdonell at last crossed the empty plain towards Fort Gibraltar; half-way there he met the triumphant Cameron, splendid in the King's uniform, and gave himself up. A few days finished the business. There was a last campaign of terror under which all but the hardiest settlers wilted and gave way. When the prisoner, Miles Macdonell, went by Point Douglas on his way to Fort William, he went with a brigade of North West canoes that carried 140 of his settlers.

Cameron's departure with the bulk of the people left the field to Alexander Macdonell and the half-breeds. Some sixty settlers remained, fearful but steadfast, under the immunity earned by Miles's surrender. That pledge proved as valueless as the pemmican treaty of the year before. Notice was quickly served on them to quit the colony and never again be found in a colonizing way at Red River. The half-breeds began to ride down the crops and then to gallop from house to house putting all to the torch. Hastily snatching up their few possessions and gathering their children, the settlers took to the boats and steered north for Lake Winnipeg. Behind them on the prairie was a roar of flame and a sky filled with the smoke of their houses and the main fort buildings. Governor's House, mill, barns, stables and settlers' houses, all were gone – about thirty buildings, built with infinite pains, and with what hopes! Within a few weeks only a few charred timbers and one small isolated building east of the river might identify the spot where there had once been a settlement. The buffalo would browse on the new grass soon to spring from the ashes, and the prairie would claim its own.

3

In the ten months required to complete the Nor'Westers' mission, the rest of the world was locked out of Red River. There had been no worry about interference on the one side or hope of assistance on the other. In London Lord Selkirk, startled by Colin Robertson's warning, had taken such precautions as he could but had pushed forward arrangements for a new group of settlers to go out in June 1815, and a new governor to take station over Miles Macdonell. This would be a strong group of over eighty. And the Governor, Robert Semple, was a vigorous man who would have a general responsibility for both colony and Hudson's Bay concerns; he would be chief magistrate for the whole chartered territory. There was no real thought that Macdonell would not be there when Semple arrived, or that the large contingent of settlers would merely replace those who had been bribed and bullied into leaving the colony – the one group leaving Red River as the other left Scotland in the expectation of joining them there.

This stubborn pressing forward in the face of threats was not Selkirk's only answer. Colin Robertson was to go up as early as possible in the spring from Montreal with his Hudson's Bay brigade of Canadian *voyageurs* a hundred strong, bound for Athabasca – a bold and costly experiment by the English company and one that might be in time to check any threat to the colony. In addition, Selkirk carried the threat of Indian attack on the colony – on British subjects – to Lord Bathurst at the Colonial Office. Though Bathurst had difficulty in accepting the reality of the danger, he finally wrote in March 1815 to the acting governor of Lower Canada, Sir Gordon Drummond, instructing him to 'give such protection to the settlers at Red River as can be afforded without detriment to His Majesty's Service in other quarters'. Selkirk doubtless felt that all was now well and the safety of the settlers provided for. He was to learn more of the power and respectability of the North West name, and of the hard geographical realities of Red River's isolation.

With a war for survival just ended and with limited troops to meet his commitments, Drummond was reluctant to undertake the control and supply of a detachment at Red River. In addition, with the conflicting rumours in Lower Canada, he was not convinced of the danger to the settlers. The Honourable William McGillivray had just been made a member of the Legislative Council and it seemed sensible to appeal to him as head of the North West Company for an assessment of the danger at Red River. Drummond, if not accustomed to guile, was not a fool, and in requesting McGillivray's reassurance he also laid on him the responsibility of seeing to it that no such danger should arise.

Shortly before, in London, Henry Goulburn, under-secretary of the Colonial Department, perhaps from slightly different motives, had made Lord Selkirk's fears known to Simon McGillivray. William's brother wrote on June 19 to Lord Bathurst of 'the suspicions in which his Lordship labours to excite against the N. W. Coy of instigating the Indians to hostile proceedings. . . . I know these accusations to be utterly unfounded.'

Similarly, in Montreal on June 24, William McGillivray answered the Governor's question out of that injured innocence that carries the conviction of sincerity: 'I can not express the feelings of indignation to which this calumny gives rise. I deny in the most solemn manner the allegation whereon this shameful accusation is founded.'

He went on in a rising tone to further assertions of innocence, and an ambiguity just in case it might be needed:

> I am an utter stranger to any instigations or any determinations of the Indian nations to make any attack on the settlement in question; but I will not take it on me to say that serious quarrels may not happen between the settlers and the natives whose hunting grounds they have taken possession of.
>
> The arrogant and violent conduct of Lord Selkirk's agents, cannot well fail to produce such results as the quarrels above mentioned.

It was less than a week after this that the settlement went up in flames, not burned by the Indians – McGillivray was right – but by the North West Company's half-breed servants. Indians and half-breeds were to prove useful again in the future in the game of obfuscation.

The colonists leaving Red River for Upper Canada may at first have believed in Cameron's compassion for their predicament. The illusion ended at Fort William where the uncontrolled jubilation of the Nor'Westers showed them the part they had played. When George Campbell, ringleader of the disaffected, received £100 for his share in the destruction of the colony, the guilt and cupidity of the less-well-paid whipped them to a terrible anger. Campbell sailed east in a schooner with the nabobs of the company while the lesser, resolute men – those who had at last been intimidated and driven out – rowed heavy boats in all weathers the length of the Great Lakes. From Sault Ste. Marie Dugald Cameron wrote to Duncan that they were 'mad with rage. ... I am not able to write their complaints were I to write all night.'

Before they reached Upper Canada, William McGillivray was blandly reporting their arrival to the government, with the same assurance he had used in denying its imminence two months before:

> The disorders excited in the country by these acts of violence, the disgust given to the settlers by the extensive disadvantages of the country, as well as the violence and tyranny of their leader, and the dread of the natives, Indian and mixed breed, all contributed to break up the colony. Some few of the settlers (about fourteen families) have returned to Hudson's Bay, and all the remainder threw themselves on the compassion of the North West Company.
>
> Under these circumstances, partly from compassion towards these poor people and partly from a dread of the consequences of their remaining in the interior . . . the North West Company has offered these settlers a conveyance to this province . . . the number brought to Fort William was about 140 souls.
>
> Hopes certainly have been held out to them of obtaining lands from the government of this country . . . the North West Company only promised these people a conveyance to Canada, and subsistence for the journey; this promise has been performed . . .'

McGillivray may have thought that this ended the story of the Red River settlement, and very satisfactorily too. But before the autumn was out they knew better at Fort William, and by spring they knew better in Montreal.

Colin Robertson's brigade upward bound had passed Miles Macdonell and the departing colonists west of Fort William and had hurried on to Red River. There, things were less hopeless than they might have feared. The crops ridden down by the half-breeds had sprung up again and flourished. A heroic band of three men under John McLeod had saved the small blacksmith shop east of the river, with some stores, and defended it against all comers. When the half-breeds left, McLeod and his men had sallied out and commenced rebuilding. In a matter of weeks Robertson had persuaded the surviving settlers to come back to their land from the north end of Lake

Winnipeg. When Robert Semple's expedition reached the settlement in November it became almost as strong as it had ever been, and better prepared, and twice as determined.

And on September 8, Selkirk, roused at last to take a hand in the game, sailed from Liverpool for New York.

Chapter 5

A STORM TO THE NORTHWARD

I

The landing of the Selkirks at New York in late October 1815 was the opening of a new and decisive chapter in Red River affairs, and indeed in the Earl's life, for by this time the two were hardly to be separated. The great experiment was beginning to threaten his fortune along with his peace of mind, and he had come to believe that both the test of his capacity and his good name hung in that distant balance. But sailing into the Hudson River had more immediate and practical satisfactions. Jean Selkirk had stood the trip well, and for young Dr. John Allan, his personal physician, just released from the navy, the Atlantic crossing had been routine. To Selkirk, racked with desperate sea-sickness, it had been a long and debilitating misery. The streets of Manhattan felt firm and welcoming as strength and confidence returned.

It was a moment for which fate had poised a shrewd blow. Even as they planned their departure for Montreal where they would winter, they learned that the settlement had been destroyed in June. Details were lacking or contradictory, but there seemed all too little reason to doubt that anything of the settlement remained, though Semple must already be approaching Red River with his large party – and what of Colin Robertson? The desertion of his own people made the blow hard for Selkirk to bear and as yet he knew little of the heavy pressure, the bullying and intimidation and bribery, which had torn the weaker ones loose and propelled all but the hardiest in their wake.

In Montreal, while the party sought accommodation and settled in, they learned more of the destruction of the settlement. Hearing that the deserting settlers had been brought down by the North West Company, the Earl looked for some of the partners to wait on him with some explanation, however contrived; but none appeared. In uneasy silence the presence of Selkirk in Montreal was ignored, while his anger mounted. Outwardly he remained admirably composed, going about his affairs with an icy calm which though it may have been ominous gave little hint of its tendency or its force.

Selkirk's agents in Montreal, Messrs. Maitland, Garden and Auldjo, had not yet succeeded in finding him an adequate house. With a splendid assurance he applied to Sir Gordon Drummond in Quebec for permission to occupy temporarily the Government House in Montreal, Château de Ramezay. It was granted even as he negotiated the rental of Sir John Johnson's large stone house which lay close to the St. Lawrence River between Maitland and Garden's offices and the Bonsecours Church. This was near the heart of old Montreal and within a short walk of the offices of the North West Company in St. Gabriel Street, though the great houses of the principal agents lay farther west in the newer and more fashionable districts: Archibald Norman McLeod out on St. Antoine and William McGillivray on Côte St. Antoine – the latter's house the finest in the city.

Within a week of arriving in Montreal, after conferring with James Stuart and Samuel Gale, his solicitors, Lord Selkirk lodged a formal complaint with the Governor about the destruction of the settlement. He anticipated McGillivray's charge that the disturbance had resulted from the actions of Miles Macdonell in the pemmican embargo and argued coolly that Macdonell's offence, if any, might have been tested a year earlier before the Privy Council. It was a point well made, for the Nor'Westers' record of using the law to their own purposes and avoiding it when it might prove inconvenient said much for their adroitness if little for the administration of justice. Their admirers, and those involved in their acts, could only shake their heads wonderingly over North West smartness. Those who had suffered at their hands, an ever-increasing number, watched the performance of years in help-less rage. It was not difficult to find bitter enemies of the North West Company in Montreal, but evidence that would stand up against bribery and intimidation was rare. In the present instance there was already a substantial body of affi-davits from disgruntled settlers who had not found Duncan Cameron's easy promises fulfilled; and it was said that many more might be obtained at York in Upper Canada.

For the moment, Selkirk's air of quiet strength, his chilling confidence, and his apparent command of resources shook the Nor'Westers' customary assurance. This was neither their climate nor their tempo. They usually did what had to be done by hard work and good management. More stubborn opposi-tion they swept aside with an overpowering conviviality or crushed by whatever degree of toughness was required. Now they were off stride, because they were uneasy over events at Red River – and some of their members openly ashamed – and because it appeared that Selkirk might be strong enough to call them to account. Having long had things their own way, they were quick to cry out over any challenge that could not be met by their accustomed methods; belief that Selkirk might have a measure of government support both enraged them and moved them to self-pity. They began taking up unac-customed postures – poor but honest men trampled by a lord; the label 'the trading lord' became increasingly attached to all their references to Selkirk, along with 'the Bible peer' and 'Lord Moonshine'. Increasingly the suggestion was heard that

Canada's main source of trade was menaced by the rapacity of the Hudson's Bay Company led by Lord Selkirk disguised as a humanitarian colonizer. This was indeed a new note and a measure of the Nor'Westers' loss of easy mastery; not since the early days of the French fur trade had the Hudson's Bay Company been looked on in Montreal as a serious rival.

Montreal society found itself involved in all this. Many of its leaders were participants in the struggle, and in the provincial metropolis no one could easily ignore the high-born and attractive Selkirks. Thus, through a stimulating if uncomfortable winter, they confronted each other: the North West agents led by William McGillivray and Archibald Norman McLeod – aggressive good fellows – and the irreproachable John Richardson – rather careful of outward appearances but working tirelessly behind the scenes for a North West victory and quick, in the end, to claim his share of the salvage; Selkirk aloof and having as yet apparently put forth only a token effort – an unknown and somewhat alarming quantity. Informed circles in Montreal were already repeating the gossip that Colin Robertson had passed on to Selkirk that the all-powerful North West Company was not as strong as it looked; more than one wintering partner with his savings invested with the agents McTavish, McGillivrays and Company had been unable to draw out cash on demand. It was understood that the collapse of fur markets due to the Napoleonic Wars was the chief cause of the difficulty; but it was also known from the wintering partners and servants who came down on rotation that the contest for furs in the interior was not going the accustomed way. The North West Company's share was diminishing, and even that won at ruinous cost. In the circumstances, it was perhaps not to be expected that the onlookers could separate the contest over the colony at Red River from the fur-trade struggle. Selkirk, as the potential agent of North West Company destruction, was regarded by turns with respect or with disapproval amounting to hatred, depending on the individual's allegiance.

It was not a promising atmosphere for negotiation, but Sel-

119

kirk had come out authorized by the Committee of the Hudson's Bay Company to discuss terms for amalgamation of the two companies or some division of the fur forest between them. His own interest, the Red River settlement, might be saved by such an arrangement, but from the first he was not optimistic and quite possibly his heart was not in it. From what he heard it appeared to him that 'the natural arrogance and violence of Mr. McGillivray's temper' had been increased by his triumph at Red River – 'such as it is', said the Earl contemptuously – and by 'the vindictive spirit which he feels it necessary to keep up among his followers'. To arrogance and violence Selkirk seems to have opposed a cold distaste and between these rocks there was little room for a spirit of accommodation to make its way. Negotiations were opened in the greatest secrecy through the good offices of John Richardson and during November and December notes with outline proposals and accompanying maps were exchanged. But whatever real hope of success had ever been present diminished with every note. The Nor'Westers bargained from the premise that the rich Athabasca territory was theirs by right of discovery; Selkirk, from the assumption that the validity of the Hudson's Bay Company charter was beyond dispute. A proposal that the North West claim to monopoly in Athabasca should be granted in return for recognition of the charter he refused to treat seriously, remarking later to an acquaintance that 'the North West Company might as well expect a valuable consideration for recognizing the title of the House of Brunswick'.

Still in a tone of near-desperation turning to menace, the Nor'Westers pressed for a division of the trade. But they could afford no major concession, and without it the talks were doomed. Apart from Athabasca and the Hudson's Bay territory there was little worth dividing. As Christmas arrived there was a final proposal for the amalgamation of the two companies. Two days later the Nor'Westers delivered their last note, in which they predicted that their employees, seeing their means of livelihood 'attacked and threatened with annihilation', would develop an energy and resource in self-defence 'the extent of which it is not easy to estimate'.

It was the same unctuousness barely concealing an ugly threat with which in June McGillivray had denied a danger that was at that very moment unfolding at Red River. No one who knew his style or his record could doubt the draftsmanship of the final paragraph of the Nor'Westers New Year's resolution:

> Upon the whole it is a painful reflexion for the North West Company to find themselves obliged to abandon further negotiations at present as hopeless, and to see that a pecuniary contest is forced upon them which they cannot shrink from and must continue – until the Hudson's Bay Company shall entertain a different view of their interests.

Although both parties had been pledged to silence on the negotiations, Selkirk came to feel that advantage had been taken of his pledge. Through the spring a rumour was current in Montreal that he aimed at nothing less than the ruin of the North West Company. He was stung into answering openly: 'My object is, and always has been, confined to the maintenance of my legal rights and those of the body with which I am connected. If our adversaries come to ruin, it will only be from their own unprincipled conduct, and immeasurable ambition.' Nevertheless he had moved forward in the mounting quarrel and taken up a more active position than before. More than he showed outwardly, the destruction of the settlement – almost the destruction of his life's work – had stirred in him a passionate resentment that would not soon be appeased. He was now determined that the North West posts must remove from the grant and that there must be compensation for the affront offered to Hudson's Bay charter rights. In the circumstances, the negotiations in his hands were perhaps bound from the first to fail. But there is no sign that the Committee disagreed with the position he took or that the two companies could have drawn closer together even if the mild and conciliatory Governor Berens had himself been in Montreal.

The little circle of Selkirk's adherents was not apt to narrow the widening breach between him and the Nor'Westers. James Stuart, the senior of his legal advisers, was renowned equally for his ability and for a contentiousness that approached malevolence. Stuart as leader of the popular party in the assembly had for long waged a war of his own against the 'English' party in which Nor'Westers and their friends were prominent, and he had recently taken a lead in the impeachment of Chief Justice Sewell, which had left ugly scars. If Selkirk's quarrel was to Stuart's purpose, it may be doubted that the reverse was true. Stuart's partner, young Samuel Gale, however, was from the first a devoted Selkirk supporter. There is some evidence that he found Selkirk a little formidable but he was always Lady Selkirk's amusing and tireless slave. Lacking Stuart's hard mind, his enthusiasm could sometimes cloud his judgment, and, though the support of someone so transparently good-hearted was valuable in a public way, his enthusiasm for the cause did not in the end always help Selkirk's party to face facts.

In all this he was gaily joined by Dr. John Allan. Still only twenty-five, Allan had been found by Selkirk on the point of retirement from the navy in 1815 and was engaged as medical adviser. At once he flung himself into the contest with passionate zeal and vied with Samuel Gale in paying playful court to Jean Selkirk. Unlike Gale, he was ready to argue with Selkirk himself where he disapproved of his decisions, but his scorn of the Nor'Westers and their adherents was fierce and unremitting.

The agents, Maitland, Garden and Auldjo, seem never quite to have joined this inner circle. They had belonged in the other camp before being engaged by Colin Robertson and though they did their work loyally it was with somewhat less enthusiasm. Mr. and Mrs. Garden did at least succumb to Lady Selkirk's charms and to her they became firm and warm friends even though they stayed somewhat aloof from the struggle.

Against the North West's social and political power the little group stood isolated and relatively puny. But it had the strength that lay in knowing what it fought for and liking what it knew.

In the late winter Selkirk took the road that wound to the west along the shore of the St. Lawrence towards York, in Upper Canada. It was an arduous trip over 350 miles of primitive roads at the best of times, and in the depth of winter to be travelled only of necessity. York had grown since he last saw it in its raw beginnings ten years before, but its chief buildings had been sacked and burned by the Americans in 1813 – and the burning of Washington as a reprisal had not noticeably improved the appearance of York. It was still only the size of an English village with an untidy, hustling, self-important air in lieu of a village's calm serenity. He was not impressed. But the trip was useful in providing further evidence of what had taken place at Red River the previous summer. Many of the settlers brought down in North West canoes were now established on Yonge Street, north of York, and were ready enough to testify to the persecution they had endured. Perhaps those talks were otherwise salutory, for the settlers' hardships were not all of North West devising.

At the same time, Selkirk pushed forward arrangements for the supplying of a large expedition which he proposed to lead to Red River in the spring. The news of his intentions spread quickly and to his friends they seemed reckless and full of danger. Thomas Clark of Queenston, who had prospered greatly since their meeting twelve years before and was now a member of the Legislative Council, was overseeing supply arrangements; in March he wrote, most earnestly begging Selkirk to reconsider and if possible to make some compromise with the Nor'Westers, which he felt sure would be welcomed by them. Even Chief Justice Scott wrote of 'the personal danger and extreme risk your Lordship will encounter if you persist in the idea of going to Red River next summer'. None of these warnings swerved him from his course even for a moment, but they were not unheeded. Meanwhile there was much to see to: Alexander Wood was acting as his agent in York and was already gathering supplies. Selkirk himself was coming to an arrangement with D'Arcy Boulton, the Attorney-General of Upper Canada, to represent him in legal matters when Boulton was not acting for the Crown. Woods of Sandwich would act in the Western District. It all took time and energy, and it took a great deal of money. Selkirk's credit was as yet unassailed, but cash was short on all sides and this added to the difficulties and increased the already alarming costs of the expedition in the summer. In the hope of realizing cash, Selkirk gave orders for the sale of the lands he had inherited in New York State, but this could not be put through in a moment.

He returned to Montreal determined to push on with the arrangements. But signs of the strain he was under began to appear. Apart from the worry of mounting expense, the news from England was not heartening. There had been some question of his being given the rank of Governor by the Hudson's Bay Company, but Colvile wrote that they thought it unwise to invest with the powers of a judge the person most directly interested in the questions at issue. It would be open to criticism 'and from the tone taken by Lord Bathurst, it is necessary to be cautious and respect appearances'. He would have occasion to remember that letter. By the same mail young Basil Hall had inadvertently conveyed a dampening impression of how little interest there was in England in a case which Selkirk felt should call forth general indignation on behalf of his dispossessed settlers as British subjects. 'I am interested', wrote Basil ingenuously, 'more than many about me in the difficulties of your situation.'

But the news was not all discouraging. Colvile passed on a virtual assurance of the arrangement he had been seeking: that the Hudson's Bay Company would for the next seven and possibly ten years buy produce from the settlement on favourable terms, and would even agree to the surplus beyond their demands being sold to the North West Company at lower prices. It was not yet certain but it was probable, and it would make all the difference to the colony's prospects.

Best of all was the news brought in by a messenger from Colin Robertson. Jean-Baptiste Lagimonière, a true descendant of the *coureurs de bois,* reached Montreal on foot on March 10, having travelled the 1,800 miles through the Nor'-Westers' country in the depth of winter. It was a heroic feat worthy of the great news he carried: that in late October the colony was re-established, that it was now abundantly supplied and flourishing, that Semple with his strong reinforcement of settlers was about to arrive, and that Duncan Cameron at Fort Gibraltar – having been captured wearing his uniform, and lectured and released – was for the moment as mild as a lamb. The half-breeds were now convinced that the North West Company had used them the year before, and Robertson seemed to have won them over. It was splendid news at the moment when it was most needed.

As Lagimonière rested for his return trip, Selkirk wrote Robertson expressing his pleasure and gratitude, but issuing certain cautions. Though his unforgotten anger over the destruction of the colony in June was apparent, he was determined that his people should not resort to North West methods:

> There can be no doubt that the N.W. Co. must be compelled to quit all their intrusive possessions upon my lands and particularly the Post at the Forks: but as it will no doubt be necessary to use force for this purpose I am anxious that this should be done in a regular manner, under a legal warrant from the Governor, so that there may be no grounds for charging us with illegal violence similar to the conduct of the N.W.C. For the reasons which I stated in my letter last year to Capt McDonell ... you should abstain from unnecessary interference with the freedom of trade and I would regret it if the provisions of the N.W. Co. were stopped in coming out of the river provided they pass through the country in a peaceable manner without committing a trespass on my lands.

This may have seemed moderate and entirely reasonable considering the 'unimpeachable validity' of the charter and his rights of property. But to pass through his broad lands without committing at least a technical trespass was almost impossible. Moreover, his wrath had broken through at one point with an instruction that largely undid the caution: 'I have to entreat your most particular attention to secure the persons of Duncan Cameron and Alex MacDonald in the first place, and next to them of Seraphin LaMar, Cuthbert Grant and Mr. Shaw. . . .' It was not clear how this was to be done legally by Robertson, or without violence by Semple.

Charged with these exhilarating if slightly contradictory instructions, Lagimonière slipped out of Montreal in mid-April, bound for Red River. He was to travel light as far as York and there from Alexander Wood he could obtain his outfit for the long journey back. But the delights of York won easily over the hard prospect of the trip ahead of him, and Wood in vain tried to speed the traveller. Lagimonière's good resolutions kept failing him; meanwhile he talked too much in that small town where news travelled much faster than he did. Before he was finally set on the road, his plans and his mission were well known to the Nor'Westers.

Selkirk's busy winter and spring included two other main efforts: if he did not intend the destruction of the settlement to go unpunished, neither did he intend the true character of North West trading policies to remain so carefully beyond public scrutiny; and he meant to hold Sir Gordon Drummond to Lord Bathurst's direction about military aid for the settlers. The former task was the simpler, for Montreal was filled with both the oral tradition and the record of North West brutal high-handedness; even the company's power and lack of scruple had not always prevented conviction in Montreal courts. They had at least avoided the full consequences of their practice and had thus additionally embittered their accusers. Selkirk appears to have started writing *A Sketch of the British Fur Trade in North America with Observations on the North West Company of Montreal* before leaving England, and, though his journey added to the difficulties of his work, it produced an abundance of shocking material. With time he might have had much more, for, even as he wrote, Montreal was excited over a case in the lower St. Lawrence region in which the Nor'Westers had destroyed the gear and the oars of some French-Canadian fishermen and set them adrift in an open boat, for daring to fish near a North West post. And a few miles out of Montreal a poor *engagé* named Joseph Leger skulked in hiding, having been beaten and bribed by turns into staying away from Montreal for most of eleven years, lest he give damaging evidence against the company. If Selkirk missed these cases he found and recited many others and the book that was published later that year in London by James Ridgway of Piccadilly was the most telling indictment the North West Company had ever faced. In fact, they never attempted to answer it, but tried instead to smother it and all charges with the general and widespread suggestion that Selkirk was an unscrupulous liar. The book circulated in French as well as English and, making much of the exploitation and debauching of the French Canadians by the partners, merely said openly what had been whispered in the parishes of the St. Lawrence for a generation.

The book did even more. It seriously undermined the belief that the North West Company had played a gallant part in the taking of Michilimackinac in the War of 1812; it had in fact been represented in the action by four sailors. The patriotic and much-lauded gesture of forming a Voyageur Corps was shown up as a device for keeping the company's canoemen on the government pay-roll between seasons, and thus saving the trouble of recruiting for the fur trade in the spring. And, finally, the notorious case of the trial of John Mowat for the murder of Aeneas Macdonell was recited at length, with its record of North West faithlessness and the shameless perversion of justice – at the hands of a grand jury that included several North West partners, and a bench of which two of the judges had close family ties with the company. It was a terrible indictment, parts of which were so well known in Montreal as to give weight to the whole, and a charge of conduct so scandalous – if unanswered – as to tarnish beyond clearing the glittering North West pretensions to honour and patriotism

127

and splendid enterprise. Yet answered it never was. For the rest of its life the North West Company's high-toned talk of honour and respectability would not deserve the kind of challenge at which the partners were quick to raise fists or sticks or blades; it would merely deserve a snicker.

Even as he delivered this formidable blow, Selkirk persisted in his attempts to secure a military force under government to maintain order in the interior. The acting governor was no more able than he had been, and even less willing, to commit troops to such a difficult and distasteful service. Through the spring Selkirk returned stubbornly to his request, changing it at last to a plea for a personal bodyguard in view of the persisting rumours that his life would be endangered if he went to Red River. Apparently worn out by this respectful importunacy, Drummond agreed to the bodyguard, for Selkirk's personal safety – this reminder contained a cold and clear warning against further troubles and more than a hint that both Selkirk and the North West Company were being very tiresome. Then almost at once the promise was revoked because the de Meuron Regiment which was to have provided the bodyguard was ordered disbanded.

This appeared to be a disaster, for the season of departure for the interior was approaching and there was little time to look elsewhere for a sufficient number of reliable men. But disaster was turned to triumph when it appeared that some of the de Meurons – most of them Swiss and German mercenaries – were interested in taking land in the new world. It was an opportunity ripe for Selkirk's ingenuity. In secret, with four of the officers, he worked out a plan for engaging about ninety of the men to go to Red River; they would be paid for the upward journey and there they would have the choice of land as settlers or a free passage to Europe. The bargain was struck and quietly Captains Matthey and D'Orsonnens picked out and enlisted their men. It was a brilliant improvisation, and meanwhile in Upper Canada the gathering of an immense quantity of food supplies and munitions went forward.

In Matthey and D'Orsonnens, who were to be his close companions and guardians for more than a year, Selkirk had made a fortunate choice. D'Orsonnens would prove himself a rigid soldier, useful in the field and probably a bore in the mess; he carried out orders and controlled his men. Matthey was a gay blade with more than a touch of recklessness, adored by the men. Though perhaps less durable than D'Orsonnens he never wavered in his devotion to Selkirk and, in fact, when all others wrote his Lordship as 'Your most humble and most obedient servant', Matthey the charmer was always 'devotedly, Matthey'.

Though the two went swiftly and quietly about their work of selecting men, some word of the plan must have leaked out. Indeed, with ninety men in barracks sharing a secret, it could not long be kept from their comrades. The North West brigades were already preparing for the Upper Country and permission had already been secured for two de Meuron officers, Lieutenants Brumby and Missani, to go on a trip to the Indian Territory as guests of the company. Also two or three de Meuron N.C.O.s had already been employed, among them Sergeant de Reinhart of whom much would be heard.

Everything was moving forward now towards a completion of arrangements, but time moved even faster in the short season. In York, Alexander Wood and Thomas Clark wrestled with supply arrangements, finding great quantities of corn, a ton of flour, 100 barrels of prime pork, a ton of lard, 500 gallons of high wines, more than a ton of gunpowder, a hundred muskets and bayonets, four light six-pounder guns and two nine-pounders (to replace those that had been stolen and to restore the colony's defences). There were sawmill irons and saws and countless smaller items. In all, twelve boat-loads of supplies in addition to some ninety men.

On the fourth of June the de Meurons were finally discharged in Montreal; and under Matthey the men for Red River marched to Lachine 'with as much precision as if they had still been under military law'. Selkirk, watching the redcoats with their brisk bearing swing along at the end of their march, was pleased with his bargain. He believed he had found security for his settlement. Miles Macdonell, on bail awaiting trial, had already started with a small advance party; the main body would leave on the morrow and he would follow soon after.

A peculiarly vexatious attack from an unexpected quarter added to the worries of the departure. The Reverend Dr. John Strachan, rector of York and a fellow Scot, had a few months before published in England and Scotland an open letter to Selkirk on the Red River Settlement. Strachan had come into possession of Selkirk's prospectus, though it had not been given general circulation, and used it as the basis of a shrewd attack, the more upsetting because it fastened on some of the acknowledged weaknesses of the scheme and attacked others as yet in the balance: the uncertainty of the commercial possibilities for the colony, its extreme isolation, the dangers of massacre by Indians. This was objectionable enough, but the personal attack on Selkirk as an unscrupulous land-jobber was much more so.

At this moment the pamphlet was issued in Montreal, widely advertised and winning much attention. Strachan was known to be friendly with the Nor'Westers and indeed William McGillivray had furnished much of the information for the pamphlet. It was easy to assume that Strachan wrote out of interested motives since he was married to the widow of Andrew McGill, who had an income presumably from the fur trade. Also, the rector certainly disliked seeing the tide of Scottish immigration diverted from Upper Canada. But, whatever his motives, his capacity for doing damage was not in doubt, at a time when Selkirk's load was almost beyond bearing.

And now there were last conferences with solicitors and agents and the final parting with Jean and the children. Daer was old enough to be frightened and to grieve; Isabella hardly yet. And Jean? Though doubtless he knew it well, and witnessed it again now, he had yet to learn the full quality of her courage and steadfastness. He intended to return in the late autumn but they must both have known that many things might delay their reunion. She remained a hostage in the enemy camp and before the winter was over she would bear another child. Meanwhile neither could know what lay ahead for him; but he was going into the Indian Country ruled by men who had reason to wish his death and of whose wishes no secret had been made.

2

The successive relays of canoes and boats – North West and Selkirk parties – were making their way to the Upper Country with little idea of what they would find. Through the winter, Red River, locked like a fish in a block of ice, had given no hint of the life it nourished. In turn, it could only guess what was proposed for it from the outside world; and Lagimonière, making his way upwards with news, would not be allowed to complete his mission.

The colony that Robertson re-established in October 1815 was not numerous but it was resolute and, though its buildings were gone and replaced only by temporary shacks, it had found new strength. The settlers who had proved most stubborn before were the nucleus now. And it was clear that from this time on no one would talk them out of their land; they could only be beaten out of it. With the arrival of Governor Robert Semple and his party confidence had grown to match their determination. Semple had won – perhaps without quite earning – a reputation for great capacity which seems largely to have been based on his energy and self-confidence. About the country in which he now commanded and the men who opposed him, he had come to hasty conclusions on his arrival at York Factory. On reaching Red River where he found all quiet he was confirmed in his misjudgments, failing to understand how much of this apparently easy recovery was due to Colin Robertson – and how quickly it might all change. Through the winter the continuing quiet and comparative prosperity gave him little realization of what had gone before. Robertson's rough handling of Duncan Cameron had been selective and shrewd. Semple's similar attempts to quell disturbance by the thunder of his voice had no such effect and were not likely to have.

If the restoration of the settlement had not wholly surprised the Nor'Westers it had badly shaken their confidence. Within a few days of its destruction in June they had learned of the approach of Colin Robertson and his formidable contingent, and although there was a rumour – based on normal North West assumptions – that the proprietors had made plans to stop Robertson's party 'by main force', it had moved unimpeded up the North West right of way. Robertson, after all, was one of their own, trained in 'the North West spirit', and they knew what to expect. Even so, his capture in October of Duncan Cameron – who was represented as a peaceful man taking a quiet stroll on the prairie in front of his own fort – and, just for good measure, the recovery of two of the cannon stolen from Fort Douglas, defined the difficulty facing them. No doubt this step had seemed to Robertson merely good tactics, but news of a North West attack on Fort Qu'Appelle had provided a justification; and Cameron's release and the return of Fort Gibraltar had only followed Cameron's promise of good behaviour – no more plotting, no more aggression by the North West Company.

In the previous August Kenneth McKenzie had sent out a warning from Fort William to Cameron: 'You will require to be very careful this year in your actions respecting H.B. people do not for God sake commit yourself in either action or writing – prudence prevents misfortunes.' As news of the capture of Cameron spread along the North West Company network prudence was forgotten – uneasiness, anger, a sense of oncoming retribution rushed together to startle the masters of the posts into careless talk. Across the great plains messengers moved back and forth, running tirelessly on their snow-shoes behind the straining dog-teams, stumbling through blizzards into the snug forts all but buried under snow, where the leaping fires bespoke a capacity for survival on which the hurried questions cast an implicit doubt.

The North West partners were divided among themselves. Few were devoted in any sense to the Montreal agents who were considered to live in state on the hard labours of the wintering partners and their servants. For a straight trading struggle with the Hudson's Bay Company all were ready enough; this was less distasteful than other aspects of a trade that some found loathsome. But the pemmican embargo, though resented by all, had involved them in a war on poor settlers, their countrymen, which was hard to stomach. Most of them did not want the settlement but neither were they prepared for the drastic alternatives. James Hughes probably spoke for many when he expressed pleasure at the settlers' having gone down to Canada, 'but could not help thinking that had I been in our good Cap^{ns} place I would have left their miserable huts standing'. That wanton brutality had weakened their support from outside as well, and had played into Selkirk's hands. And another partner recognized that 'every neutral person thinks we are in the wrong by bringing out the colonists and destroying their houses, two things I believe had we not done everything else would be in our favour'.

They had not often as a group faced the consequences of their system, a system that corrupted too readily the kind of strong, simple, uneducated men who alone were apt to its purpose. They were even recognizing that the Indians, of whose friendship they made great boast and whose champions they claimed to be, welcomed the colony and would not be used against it. 'It would appear to me the day of retribution is drawing nigh,' wrote John McDonald, Le Borgne; 'they can then say we have lost the support of our friends by our selfishness.'

McDonald was right, for the Indians, hearing hints of plans for renewed North West aggressions in the spring, passed the word along to Colin Robertson. These confirmed Robertson's fears without giving him enough information for countermeasures. He was still a Nor'Wester trained, and exulted in the slogan, 'When you are among wolves, howl.' If he lacked information he knew where it was to be found – at Fort Gibraltar and in North West letters. Knowing that the North West winter express was about to arrive, he struck quickly in March and caught Duncan Cameron, in spite of his promises, in the act of writing a letter calling for support against the colony. When, a few hours later, a crack dog-team of the North West Express trotted with bells jingling into the stockade lit by welcoming torches, the couriers found themselves in Robertson's hands and dispossessed of the mail, their sacred charge.

In the face of outraged protests Robertson promised that the mail might go forward if he found no evidence of designs against the colony. He was in little doubt of the result, for Cameron's letter being prepared for the express was to James Grant at Fond du Lac and referred to the Indians in that neighbourhood: 'I wish that some of your *Pilleurs* who are fond of mischief and plunder, would come and pay a hostile visit to the sons of Gunpowder and riot, they might make a very good booty if they went cunningly to work, not that I would wish them to Butcher anyone *God forbid.*'

Among the letters from the express there was evidence still more grim of what the settlement faced. A long letter from Alexander Macdonell to Cameron contained news of the failure and tragic consequences of the Hudson's Bay expedition to Athabasca, the expedition Robertson had organized and led to Norway House where the command was given to John Clarke while Robertson turned south to restore the colony. 'Glorious news from Athabasca,' wrote Macdonell exultantly. Clarke, reckless of consequences, had pushed into the fur country without provisions, and North West exertions combined with a terrible winter had seen to it that he found almost none. Sixteen of his people had died of starvation and the costly expedition had failed completely. Speaking of Red River, Macdonell went on:

> I remark with pleasure the hostile proceedings of our neighbours – I say with pleasure because the more they do, the more justice we will have on our side a storm is

gathering to the Northward ready to burst on the rascals who deserve it – little do they know their situation last year was but a joke – the new nation under their leaders are coming forward to clear their native soil of intruders and assassins.

And in another letter, to Dugald Cameron, Macdonell had written, 'We will see some sport in Red River before the month of June is over.' He reported that 'Sir William Shaw', one of the half-breed leaders and son of a North West partner, had ordered all the half-breeds to prepare for the field: 'It is supposed . . . they will together form more than one hundred – God only knows the result.'

Even Robertson, the bold giant, could not read this without acknowledging its gravity. He decided to hold the express, retain possession of the fort, and keep Cameron in custody. The situation at The Forks had been clarified, but no one could think it much improved.

3

As events moved towards some resolution at Red River, the parties from Montreal, setting out during May and June, knew only that 1,800 miles away a conflict was probably in the making. Whether their interest was in fomenting or in stopping it, they had, alike, half a continent to cross before they could intervene.

The first away was Archibald Norman McLeod, one of the most active of the Montreal agents and the prototype of a Nor'Wester. Vigorous and violent, a magistrate for the Indian Country – on whose blank warrants Miles Macdonell and Spencer had been arrested and in whose scarlet uniform Cameron had befooled the settlers – McLeod believed that North West ends justified any means. He was on his way now to take command in Athabasca, but first he meant to look into the situation at Red River.

His early departure found the lakes not clear of ice, but McLeod had the best as well as the worst of the North West spirit and was not to be put off. Through Lake Huron his canoes fought the drifting ice which tore at the light craft without stopping them, and in the narrow throat of the St. Mary's River the danger was even greater. Lieutenants Brumby and Missani, out on a pleasure cruise, must have wondered about the wisdom of their decision. At the Falls of St. Mary's, above the worst of the ice, the party heard a rumour that the North West's Fort Gibraltar at Red River had been captured by the Hudson's Bay Company. What little caution was in McLeod's nature was flung off.

By the second of June he was at Fort William, and he at once rushed off a dispatch to James Grant at Fond du Lac, the post nearest which Lagimonière and his Indian guide were expected to pass. Having expressed a crushing surprise that the runner had moved east through their country undetected the previous autumn, he made it clear that the mistake must not be repeated.

> The Earl of Selkirk has been all winter in Canada and means to use his best endeavours to drive the N W Co out of the Indian Country. We have now fully ascertained that he has no more the support or protection of Govt than we have. Govt never guaranteed the Colony's success it merely permitted the Emigration of British subjects and as for the charter of the Hudson's Bay Company they know it to be invalid and useless.
>
> The Hudson's Bay Company has now proceeded to such lengths that no half measures will do and we must act by them as their conduct towards us warrants. – Lagimonière must not be allowed to proceed or forward letters ...

The next day he wrote again. This time, on an even graver matter, he was joined in signing by two partners, and the letter was not only to James Grant but to his clerks, Morrison and Roussin.

> After various consultations we have come to the resolution

of forwarding an express to you to request you will as soon as possible assemble as many of the Indians as you can by any means induce to go to Red River to meet us there. We also mean to take a few of the Lac La Pluie Indians with us: we shall and will be guarded and prudent, we shall commit no extravagancies but we must not suffer ourselves to be imposed upon. Possibly and probably their appearance will suffice, but in any case they shall be well and fully recompensed for their trouble. ... We shall be in Red River about the 17th of June.

Grant and his assistants may well have reflected on the lack of caution in these extraordinary notes and on the situation that produced it. For, as Grant well knew and was to tell Lord Selkirk later, when matters of a certain delicacy had to be seen to, the chosen instrument of their execution had a private talk in William McGillivray's office at Fort William before starting on his mission. Caution was the watchword in a company that had much to conceal. But caution was forgotten now and, as the party at Fort William made hasty preparations for departure, Robert Henry, equally reckless, dashed off a note to his uncle in Montreal telling him of the plan to raise the Indians: 'We start to-morrow about fifty men and Gentlemen. I would not be surprised if some of us should leave their bones there. ... I am very much afraid it will be a serious business ... if it comes to a battle many lives must be lost.'

Of these events Selkirk's people were mercifully unaware. Miles Macdonell was not far behind McLeod, and the de Meurons were just setting out from Montreal. The news could only have disturbed the Earl without materially adding to his determination. For at Kingston, during a pause, he wrote to the newly arrived Governor in Quebec, Sir John Sherbrooke, to inform him that he intended to institute 'criminal prosecution' against several of the partners of the North West Company 'for their conduct last year in respect of the settlement on Red River'. He planned to bring down witnesses in the fall and hoped special arrangements for trials might be made.

That done, his Iroquois canoemen bent to their paddles. He

had to pick up the last of the provisions and a small authorized bodyguard at Drummond's Island and overtake his main party at the Falls of St. Mary's at the entrance to Lake Superior.

4

The irony for the people of Red River was that the relaxing of winter's grip in 1816 merely opened the way for what threatened to be a more severe test. The cloud bearing down on them was not wholly dark but it was unquestionably an oncoming danger of serious proportions. The time of the event was more easily identified than its precise nature; it was the time of the final pemmican controversy of 1814 and the destruction of the settlement in 1815. By the end of June the North West partners must be well on their way to Fort William; and by the third week in the month some of the brigades, moving eastwards from the wintering grounds, would be passing the settlement. For two years now their passing had meant its peril. At the sweetest moment of the year – the moment of new crops, of wild-flowers and bird-song – the hour of danger would strike.

It was ironic, too, that the horrors originally held up to deter the settlers – Indian massacre, starvation, and death by freezing – had all been faced and brought to terms. Between them and the Indians there was mutual trust. Their labours on the land and a growing skill in hunting had reduced the danger of food shortage to a normal pioneer hazard, and they had survived in all weather. To these tough and resourceful people the only real danger now lay in open attack and against this the rebuilt Fort Douglas had not been made adequately strong. Two miles away, the captured fort – Gibraltar, with its stockade of oak palings – was stronger, and a continuing danger. If it fell again into enemy hands it would provide a base of operations on the doorstep of the settlement. To garrison both forts was to split and weaken the defence. In purely tactical terms the choice in Semple's dilemma was obvious: to destroy Fort Gibraltar and base his defence on a strengthened Fort Douglas. Earlier in the spring Colin Robertson had advocated this, but Semple was not then ready to take so lawless and provocative a step.

At this point John Bourke, the settlement storekeeper, and some others in charge at Fort Daer, found Colin Robertson's bold example of the spring too intoxicating for them. Thirsting to establish or retrieve their reputations for military ardour, they fell without warning or justification on the North West trading-post at Pembina. It was lightly held by half-breeds and in no state of defence – an embarrassingly easy prize – and so unprovoked an attack did much, then and later, to make the colony appear equal aggressors with the Nor'Westers. The half-breeds, kept neutral for some months by Robertson, had begun again to move in behind the North West banner; now the pace of the movement quickened. Robertson, watching the collapse of his policy as the result of blunders against which he had warned, grew increasingly exasperated. These men under Semple were the effective guiding body of the colony and he had no official voice in their deliberations. On his first arrival Semple had welcomed Robertson's active leadership and approved his judgment; now all was changed. Daily the breach between the two men widened, and with its widening the confidence of the settlers changed to an uneasiness approaching panic.

After a final altercation with Bourke, during which the latter threatened him with a pistol, Robertson decided to quit the settlement, since he was held powerless to avert a fate he saw too well. It was a dispiriting ending to a year of notable achievement and was to leave Robertson open to the charge that his highest loyalty was ultimately to his own pride. And doubtless the charge contained some truth in his case as in that of many involved in the controversy – especially the Highlanders. Peculiarly trapped in their own mythology, they placed personal boldness, synonymous with honour, above all virtues, no matter how dishonourable its accomplishments might be. A fight won by a ruse – which other people would consider treacherous – was glorious; backing down was the ultimate, almost the only, weakness. It was a childlike state of mind which in action could produce heroic results, but as a major factor in policy-making led often to wrong-headed and even shameful decisions. It explained both what the Nor'-Westers had accomplished and the poor thing they had become. And it accounted for the remarkable achievements and ultimate failure of men like Miles Macdonell and the extraordinary Colin Robertson.

But when he left the Red River Settlement, sailing north for Lake Winnipeg and York Factory, he left in a mood of bravado. With him went Duncan Cameron, bound as a prisoner for trial in England, and at his mast-head he flew a pemmican-sack. To many of the sober settlers this gesture was an unbecoming act of levity, but it was Robertson to the life. Though his going removed from the defence something far more important than one able-bodied man, it did reduce controversy. The colony, weakened and sobered, set about its too-long-delayed preparations for survival – though Robert Semple seems still not to have believed that that was the issue. Lord Selkirk's title to the land, and the Hudson's Bay Company charter, he took to be settled law and from them flowed a frame of ordered behaviour that approximated the life he had known elsewhere. He regarded himself and his settlers as living securely beneath the everlasting arms of a wise, just, and all-powerful government. An open attack by the half-breeds should be unthinkable, since in his view a severe retribution was even then preparing against them for their actions the previous year. He was to be spared the bitterness of learning how little the Colonial Office knew or cared about events in the Indian Country.

When Robert Semple arrived at York Factory in September 1815 and learned something about the dispersion of the colony in June, he wrote to the Committee of the Hudson's Bay Company. His letter spoke of the attack by the half-breeds as an instance of 'such lawless ferocity as can be paralleled only in the annals of Indian Warfare'. Since this had been openly and avowedly perpetrated under officers of the North West Company, it was useless to collect further proofs of their minor atrocities. But, if it was allowed to pass unpunished by the British government, it would be 'desiring us to seek redress at our own hands'.

In the circumstances, and considering it 'almost a moral certainty that redress will be attained at home for past aggressions and security against the future [he wrote] I shall pause before committing the company, through me, in any dispute even in the most legal forms with the Officers of the N.W. in this country'. It was a strangely prophetic letter in many ways:

> It would be useless in my opinion to enter into a war of Posts when a decisive and open attack has been made on a great point of the Company's Territories in open violation of all law. ... The disputes with the North West Company no longer rest with your servants here or are dependent upon the form of Justice in Rupert's Land.
>
> The general interests are now committed entirely into your hands and all here rely with perfect confidence upon the wisdom and fairness with which they will be maintained – Should our Government refuse to interfere the inevitable consequence will be that two great Trading Company's of the same nation will be reduced nearly to the state of Two Indian Tribes at war and scenes of bloodshed and Confusion will mark the whole of our tracks from the center of the Honourable Company's Territories to the extreme limits of Athapascow.

He asked that his determination not to fight at once should be understood and not interpreted as unwillingness to take risks for the cause: 'That such is not the case I may probably here after have full occasion to evince should a refusal to grant us redress compel us to resort to legal violence.' He closed in a mood of prophecy, reflecting on the wickedness of arming the half-breeds 'and thus to disclose to that lawless race the dangerous secret of their own strength'.

It had been a fair analysis except for its basic assumption

that there was a will to correct evils in the western territory that could act in time to be of help. He was, in fact, grimly on his own, without even the support of good advice, and by June he knew it. Still he clung to the hope of legal forms. The chief magistrate of Rupert's Land was not, surely, to be treated like any other man. He represented in his person the whole force of the law; as such he was the pivot on which civilized living turned. In this Robert Semple was not unduly puffed up. He and his officers did not find it easy to talk to Indians or half-breeds or freemen; he would have given them justice but he could not readily give them his hand or pretend to any approach to a social relationship. Otherwise, Robert Semple, the man, did not stand aloof, but he had a clear notion of what was due Robert Semple, the magistrate, as well as what was required of him. These things defined a mode of living outside of which lay chaos.

As the dangerous month of June began, it seemed that chaos was lapping at the colony's edges. Semple tried uneasily to maintain the forms he believed in, while seeking an alternative should they fail. The settlers knew in late May that a half-breed force was approaching, behaving more like a war-party than a fur brigade. They had ambushed the Hudson's Bay brigade from Fort Qu'Appelle, taking their furs and pemmican and holding the leaders prisoner. Then by a ruse they had taken and plundered Brandon House, pretending to ride by before turning and pouring through the gate in a flood of ponies at the gallop. The field leader in all this was Cuthbert Grant, young captain-general of the half-breeds. In the background, just out of sight, was Alexander 'Whiteheaded' Macdonell of the North West Company. '. . . little do they know', he had said of the settlers, 'their situation last year was but a joke'. If that did not prove true it would not be for want of Macdonell's trying.

By June Semple had accepted the necessity of destroying Fort Gibraltar and his men went to it with a will. What could be used to strengthen Fort Douglas was saved and rafted down the river. While eager hands seized the new timber and worked belatedly at making Fort Douglas strong, what remained of Fort Gibraltar was burned to the ground. There was nothing to do now but to wait and keep watch. They seemed to have reached the melancholy point foreshadowed incredulously by Semple: they were reduced nearly to the state of an Indian tribe at war. North from the fort along the bank of Red River stretched the little farms of the settlers and the temporary shacks flung up to replace those burned the year before. A rough track – the Settlement Road – ran for two or three miles through the partly cultivated farms to Frog Plain. It was a perilously strung-out flock to cover from the fort, and at night many of the settlers slept within the stockade. They could not live indefinitely like this, penned up together, but it was all too certain that the waiting would not be long.

All round them the prairie teemed with life, but the normal movements of people had almost stopped. The freemen who had not gone away to join the half-breeds, having watched the destruction of Gibraltar, knew it for a prelude to battle. In living memory no such affront had been offered the Montreal traders, and far less had been punished unforgettably. Everyone knew what had happened to the Hudson's Bay Company brigade that only last winter had defied the Nor'Westers in Athabasca. On both sides of the river men went to the farms in the early mornings warily, as men had not tended farms in the Canadas for more than 100 years – since the days when the Iroquois lurked on the outskirts of Montreal.

On June 17 two Indians came in to the fort asking for Governor Semple; they came from the west whence the half-breeds must also come. Their story was soon told. They were of the Sauteaux tribe and their information was that in two days the settlement would be attacked. They had encountered Macdonell and other Nor'Westers with the half-breeds. They had been told that the half-breeds intended to drive the intruding settlers away; if the settlers resisted, 'the prairie would be drenched with their blood'. Macdonell had invited the Indians' support. Politely but firmly they refused. Macdonell made it clear that it would be done whether they helped or not, but he would be glad to have some of the braves with him. They refused again, and left.

Now they offered the help of the Sauteaux to Semple. Tempted or not, he does not seem to have hesitated. It was his turn to refuse. He thanked them for their offer of help. The settlement might have come much nearer the status of an Indian tribe at war than he would have believed possible, but he had not abandoned the forms he had lived by – and by which he was soon to die.

The two remaining days moved slowly along. No plan of action seems to have been developed against the various possible eventualities. Semple appears to have clung to the notion that reason and the rule of law might yet prevail. On the afternoon of the nineteenth he rode through the settlement on a general tour of inspection, perhaps hoping by his calm example to bring some heart to his people. And he must partly have accomplished his purpose while winning unknowingly, and almost certainly unsought, a respect for his steady courage – creating a legend that remembers a brave man and overlooks what he was not. At the Frog Plain, while he talked to the settlers, one of the freemen sidled up to him – out of mischief or awe?

'Mon Gouverneur,' said the man, Bellegrade, 'are you not afraid? It is said the half-breeds are coming to make you prisoner.'

'No, I am not afraid,' Semple answered, 'I have a paper I will go and read to them and afterwards if they choose to kill me they may.' Then Robert Semple rode back to Fort Douglas. On his right, as he rode, the sun sliding down the great sky glowed at the farthest edge of the infinite plain while hawks swept low above the burnished grass. His horse's hooves thudded softly in the dust of the track. Danger seemed far away. Outwardly there was no sign of anything that threatened the summer evening's quiet. In a little while the frog chorus would begin and the drowsy hum of the insects, and later still, as night came down, the squeak of bats.

At the last moment the quiet evening was snatched away.

A boy in the loft that served as a watch-tower called out urgently that there were riders going by, west of the fort. Semple and some others climbed hurriedly to the loft and took the telescope; there was no mistake. Perhaps a mile and a half away a line of horsemen was moving north-east on a slanting course that would cross the Settlement Road near Frog Plain. The line numbered about thirty-five and though little detail could be made out it was certain that these were the half-breeds come at last. The tension, which had mounted in recent weeks, was almost at breaking-point in the people who had run from every doorway at the call from the watch-tower. As the men climbed down they were pressed with frantic questions; the need for reassurance was desperate. There were nearly 150 people in the enclosure, of whom perhaps half were able-bodied men and boys; the rest were old men and women, many of them with small children. Some of the women were crying, and every face held at once questions and a frightening knowledge. The hour of danger had struck.

Some rough plan of going out to face the half-breeds had apparently been in Semple's mind; he had told Bellegrade he would read them a paper. Now, reassuring to the last, he called for volunteers to go out with him to 'see what these fellows want'. It sounded innocent enough – at any rate, less than a call to battle. All the men seemed eager to go, but Semple asked only for twenty. Someone suggested that they take the three-pounder field-piece with them, but Semple refused on the ground that they were not going out to fight. In the end, twenty-six or twenty-seven went, with no clear instructions about arms or ammunition; some had a few rounds, some a good many; a few men even had bayonets. Semple left Alexander MacDonell, the sheriff, in command of the fort, and the little party straggled out of the gate amid farewells and, no doubt, admonitions to caution.

A short distance from the fort Robert Semple formed his men into a line of march and led the way down the Settlement Road. Almost at once they met some settlers running in panic from the farms and crying out that the half-breeds had come.

Though there are many and contradictory accounts of what followed, they say little of that half-mile, ragged march – whether the men moved in silence or exchanged nervous banter as the dust puffed around their tramping feet. About ten minutes after they started some clumsiness set off a gun in the column. In the silence following the explosion Semple turned angrily on the culprit and, with a severe reprimand, warned them all to be careful, and then led on. Shortly after, they came in sight of the half-breeds. A group of them were sitting their horses at the edge of a grove of oak and willow trees – a place called Seven Oaks; and, even as the settlers looked, taking in the fact that the riders were dressed like Indians and were in war-paint and feathers, more rode out from behind the trees. In addition to guns, some carried lances and all had tomahawks or knives. Semple had halted his men and some must have realized then, if he did not, the desperate folly of this unplanned venture. As other half-breeds came into sight it was evident there were many more than had been seen from the fort; the settlers were outnumbered almost three to one.

It is not easy to see any coherent plan in Semple's next moves. Realizing his disadvantage for either parley or fight, he ordered John Bourke to return to the fort to bring out a cannon. For a few minutes, it seems, the two groups contemplated each other in silence, and then, unaccountably, Semple ordered the march resumed. The half-breeds had broken into two divisions and for the moment rode away from Semple's party, the one group moving east towards the river which lay on the settlers' right, the other west into the open prairie. Semple's column spread out in a ragged line and began too late to fall back towards the fort. At this point the half-breeds turned and, schooled in the tactics of the buffalo-hunt, rode in a crescent toward the retreating men. The line of withdrawal began to swing, conforming to the flanking movement of the horses, and the settlers were now backing toward the river. War-whoops began to break out along the advancing line.

A lone rider moved out ahead of the half-breeds and advanced on Semple, waving his arm. Those near by heard him

call out, 'What do you want?' and Semple answer, 'What do
you want?' It is doubtful that any who heard clearly the
exchange that followed lived to report it, except the rider
François Firmin Boucher – a doubtful witness. Fear and the
excitement of the moment made every word dangerous, any
gesture enough to touch off an explosion. And still the settlers
seem not to have realized the extent of their peril. The North
West Company had taught the half-breeds the dangerous
secret of their own strength but not the dangerous secret of
their instability. Boucher may have tried to explain to Semple
that the half-breeds were only carrying supplies to meet the
brigades from the Upper Country. But the time for explanations had gone by. Between the lines the shouting voices rose,
Boucher calling Semple a 'damned rascal', and Semple, reply-
ing 'Scoundrel, do you tell me so', seized Boucher's bridle and
the butt of his gun. Someone fired and the exposed Boucher
slid off his horse, out of the line of fire.

The watchful half-breed line came instantly into action with
terrible effect. At the first shots, Lieutenant Holte of Semple's
party fell dead and Semple himself went down, his hip broken
by a ball. The settlers seem either to have stood paralysed or
to have closed on the fallen men, to be themselves shot down
without a semblance of effective resistance. The flaming crescent closed in, whooping and mad with excitement. Four
settlers broke for the river; one went down – shot on the run
like a buffalo. Bourke, coming in sight of the dreadful scene
with his cannon on a wagon, turned the horse in time to save
the gun and galloped back to the fort, himself severely wounded.
The half-breeds were off their horses now, finishing the ghastly
work. Rogers, one of Semple's officers, wounded but still alive,
begged on his knees for mercy and was killed where he knelt.
The half-breeds, wild with blood-lust, were finishing their work,
scalping some, ripping open others, and bashing in skulls with
gun-butts. John Pritchard alone of Semple's party on the field
survived to see the mutilated bodies stripped of their blood-
stained clothing. When the firing began he had claimed the
protection of a half-breed he had once befriended.

Cuthbert Grant, who seems to have tried to save the wounded Semple and moderate the fury of his men, was now determined that the fort must be given up. Late at night Pritchard carried his terms to Sheriff MacDonell: surrender and leave Red River under half-breed safe-conduct, or every man, woman and child would be killed. MacDonell at first refused. But, contemplating the demoralization wrought by the massacre on his people and pressed by Pritchard – himself in a state of shock – he at last gave in.

On the following evening a rider galloped with the news into Alexander Macdonell's camp at Portage la Prairie. 'Sacré nom de Dieu,' shouted Macdonell to the half-breeds and freemen, 'bonnes nouvelles – vingt-deux Anglois de tués.' Having kept his discreet distance, he made ready to ride into Red River and take over.

Robert Henry, who had gone up with Archibald Norman McLeod's party, wrote to his uncle in Montreal: 'I thank heaven the battle was over before we got there as it was our intention to storm the fort. Our party consisted of 100 men 70 fire arms and two field pieces.' He omitted to mention that Lieutenants Missani and Brumby and the other de Meurons had put on their uniforms at McLeod's request so the Indians would know the King was on their side.

John Rowand of the North West Company, who had been given a sword by Duncan Cameron for his part in the destruction of the colony in 1815, described the Seven Oaks affair to his father: 'So far,' he wrote with satisfaction, 'the N.W. are acting on the defensive only. . . . What do you think of Robertson seizing the N.W.Co. Winter Express and reading and opening all private and general letters . . . no Law.'

Chapter 6

FORT WILLIAM: RECEPTACLE OF PLUNDER

I

The ripples running outward from the events at Red River carried their news first to Archibald Norman McLeod's party, upward-bound from Montreal and swollen by reinforcements of such Indians as could be bribed or dragooned from Fond du Lac and Lac la Pluie. They had expected to reach the settlement about the seventeenth of June but had come three days late to their rendezvous with the half-breeds at the entrance to Red River. Having waited there uneasily for a day, they moved onward, and almost at once came in sight of a large flotilla moving downstream. It was like nothing they were prepared for and certainly bore none of the outward signs of a war-party; but McLeod's men stood on guard as the boats moved down the current towards them, bearing the helpless settlers from one frightening experience to the next.

Once it was certain there was no fighting to be done, McLeod the warrior quickly became McLeod the magistrate – a guise in which he was only slightly less dangerous. The settlers were convoyed to the recently left Nor'Wester camp at Netley

Creek. There for two days they huddled in fear and discomfort while a rough-handed search and an examination by Magistrate McLeod went on, with the wheels of justice being oiled by frequent and blood-curdling threats. The death of Semple and the escape of Robertson drove McLeod into a rage and no delicacy prevented a thorough search of what remained of Semple's possessions – his gun and pistols were even then being sold by half-breeds to North West partners at Fort Douglas.

At the end of two days most of the settlers were released after an unsuccessful attempt to make them take an oath never to return to Red River. A few, including the wounded Bourke, were kept as prisoners or witnesses and sent off to Fort William on the warrants for which McLeod was becoming famous. The Nor'Westers then went on to the settlement where they joined with Alexander 'Whiteheaded' Macdonell in drinking the half-breeds' health, congratulating them on their spirit, and scolding the Indians who had refused to help. They then rode in triumph to the 'battlefield' and viewed with satisfaction some of the grisly remains, though the Indians had buried most of the bodies. It was a great day. As Norman McLeod listened to François Deschamps, an old freeman, describe in sickening detail his pleasure in ripping up some of the wounded, he was moved to exclaim: 'What a splendid old man he is.'

Miles Macdonell with the Selkirk advance party had made good time from Montreal and come hard on the heels of McLeod; but he had come too late. Having fought through the last dangerous stretches of the journey, the miles of white water of the Winnipeg River, he was within a day's hard travel of Fort Douglas when he learned from some Indians that the settlement was no more. His own small party could accomplish nothing; the need now was to warn Lord Selkirk and to turn him back.

Hastily, Macdonell wrote an account of what he had learned and sent off a messenger who might get through if he failed. He counselled a return to Montreal: '... I conceive your present force inadequate to the enterprise, and all our resources in Red River are either destroyed or in the possession of the enemy. If we lose you my Lord all is lost.'

Then he turned his canoes eastward and drove the paddlers mercilessly. If Selkirk's flotilla had moved into Lake Superior before he met them, they might easily be missed in that inland sea, and unless turned back they faced a perhaps fatal disaster. One day in the last week of July, just at dusk, Macdonell saw the de Meurons' boats moving towards the south shore of the lake not far from the Falls of St. Mary. It was the main brigade, which Selkirk and John Allan were to follow by canoe in a day or two; they were still at St. Mary's at the house of Charles Ermatinger – trader and Justice of the Peace. Miles's messenger not having arrived, the bad news had to be broken, and Matthey and D'Orsonnens agreed to follow him back. When Macdonell arrived at Ermatinger's, Selkirk was already asleep and Dr. John Allan, having listened to the news, declined to waken him. As darkness covered the last remnant of flaming sky – far out on the water, beyond the de Meuron boats, beyond Fort William itself – the men sat talking of the news that must be broken in the morning.

When the time came, although Selkirk received the news with what the romantic Miles called 'a spirit becoming a Douglas', there was no concealing the gravity of the blow. Selkirk was certain that Semple was not the man to provoke an attack. If he had not done so, then this second destruction of the colony raised the question of whether it could ever be established beyond danger. The answer to that could only lie with the government – the government of Britain, for that in the Canadas seemed wholly incapable of protecting its people. Yet there was hope to be found in all this, for Selkirk was now certain that all the North West skill in circumventing the law was not equal to avoiding the consequence of these latest crimes. They were outside the law, but not beyond it; powerful as he knew them to be, he could not believe that. His ultimate faith in the law, and all he had learned of government, cried out against the proposition.

Slowly the discussion and the canvassing of alternative

plans carried them towards a decision that involved grave risks. Selkirk refused stubbornly to return to Montreal. He proposed to winter among the Indians near Fond du Lac, though opposed by Miles Macdonell who, knowing the northern winter, considered the idea unrealistic and exceedingly hazardous. John Allan opposed it with equal vehemence from a doubt that the delicate Earl would survive so rigorous an experience; apart from that, he believed the Nor'Westers capable of arranging his assassination. Their arguments flattened themselves ineffectively against the adamant in his nature. They were learning what Jean already knew, and perhaps the North Westers guessed: the rock-like strength of his determination. In this case Selkirk was supported by the de Meuron officers, confident in the size of their party, and not understanding that it was easier for a large party than a small to starve in the woods.

Out of the first decision grew another: since they were not returning to Montreal they had plenty of time; they would go to Fort William where, Miles had learned, some colony people were being held prisoner. Once more preparations for departure were made and this time they included a letter from Selkirk to Sir John Sherbrooke:

It is with feelings of the most anxious concern that I have to add the information recently received here of the success which has this season attended the unprincipled machinations of the North West Company who have again effected the destruction of the settlement on Red River, with the massacre of about twenty of the settlers and servants of the Hudson's Bay Company. The circumstances attending this catastrophe, and those which immediately led to it, have, as yet, reached me only in a very imperfect manner, and through channels which cannot fully be depended upon. I have no doubt that the North West Company are in possession of more accurate information, but the interest they have to misrepresent the facts, must be too evident to require any comment. Of this I am confident, that Mr. Semple was not a man likely to act in a

violent or illegal manner, so as to give any just ground
for such an attack as appears to have been made. I trust
that, in the course of a few days, I may obtain more complete information on this subject, at Fort William, where
now are assembled many persons who must have direct
knowledge of the facts, and on whom I propose, as a
magistrate, to call for information. In the delicate situation in which I stand as a party interested, I could have
wished that some other magistrates should have undertaken the investigation. In this view I have applied to
two very respectable gentlemen in this neighbourhood,
who are qualified as magistrates for the western district
of Upper Canada, and the only persons so qualified who
could be expected to go such a distance. Both of them
however have avocations which render it impossible to
comply with my request; I am therefore reduced to the
alternative of acting alone, or of allowing an audacious
crime to pass unpunished. In these circumstances I cannot doubt that it is my duty to act though I am not
without apprehension that the law may be openly resisted
by a set of men who have been accustomed to consider
force as the only criterion of right.

It was not a letter to reassure a branch of government already weary of the controversy and disposed to think well of
the partners of the North West Company. The news of the
massacre would be startling enough without the disquieting
knowledge that Lord Selkirk, with a strong force and in the
state of mind thus revealed, was about to confront the most
formidable set of men the Canadas possessed, on their own
doorstep.

While preparations for departure went forward, a letter
from William McGillivray arrived at Sault Ste. Marie for Mr.
John Johnson, another trader. It had been written the week
before at Fort William and gave McGillivray's account of the
massacre. It came to this: that a group of Indians and half-
breeds had been peaceably passing Fort Douglas on June 19
when Semple and his party emerged and without provocation
made a wanton attack on them. Unfortunately, Semple, four

of his officers, and sixteen of his men had been killed in the 'battle', as had one of the half-breeds. McGillivray added that none of the North West people had been within hundreds of miles of the clash (though his letter referred to the presence of Cuthbert Grant, leader of the half-breeds and a clerk of the North West Company). McGillivray said piously that he had no doubt the Nor'Westers would be blamed for the tragic event, but these were the facts.

A day or two later the brigades moved out under the frowning magnificence of Lake Superior's north shore. Ten days of tugging at the oars brought the heavy *bateaux* to the rendezvous only a few miles east of Fort William where there was a last council of war on the very threshold of the enemy keep. The de Meurons were eager for action and doubtless the officers were laid under stern reminders of their responsibility; in so far as there might be action on the morrow it would be in aid of the civil power, and breaches of discipline could bring disgrace on the whole party. The short summer night passed quickly. Hardly, it seemed, had the last colour been quenched in the western sky before the new day crept towards the sleeping camp across the miles of water they had traversed. The day that approached, whatever happened, must be filled with grave consequences.

The canoes bearing Miles Macdonell and Selkirk and the guard from the 37th Regiment were the first to reach the entrance to the River Kaministiquia and turn in, moving swiftly past the watchers at the fort. They continued upstream for almost a mile before landing on the opposite shore and making camp. An hour or so later the beating of drums announced the arrival of the main party; boat after boat crammed with scarlet-coated men moved into the river under the eyes of the startled *voyageurs,* the freemen, and the Indians. Undoubtedly the de Meurons intended to look formidable, and did. The boats came on and landed above Lord Selkirk's camp. Then came the bustle of making fast, of disembarking, of putting up tents and posting guards, of landing essential supplies. Before the commotion had subsided, a canoe crossed over to the fort bearing a note for the partners and agents of the North West Company.

The note that was delivered to William McGillivray stated that Lord Selkirk considered it his duty as a magistrate to inquire why certain of the colonists from Red River and certain employees of the Hudson's Bay Company had been brought to Fort William as prisoners. He had been informed that this was the case and that, among others, Pritchard, Pambrun, Nolin, Macpherson, Bourke, and Heden were still detained there. McGillivray blandly replied by note that he did not consider the first four as prisoners, and they were being sent over forthwith. Bourke had already been sent to Montreal as a prisoner, with Heden accompanying him as a witness. Presently the four men arrived; although according to McGillivray they had not been regarded as prisoners, two had been in close confinement and one in irons. Excitement ran high as the men made their way through the lines to Lord Selkirk's tents. For his part, he was seeing for the first time men he knew much about – owed much to.

The interrogation of the four men went on through the day and far into the night. Only Pritchard had been at the scene of the massacre and it was still fresh and horrible to him, as indeed it remained for long afterwards. Pambrun, who had been held a prisoner at Portage la Prairie by Alexander Macdonell's party, had seen the half-breeds set out. He had details to add which heaped up the grim witness to events and the guilt of the North West partners. Louis Nolin, the young interpreter, had not gone out with Semple's party but had seen some of the action from a distance and had been a victim of the events that followed.

When the last good-night had been said and the last candle extinguished in the sleeping camp, Selkirk had much of the evidence he had come in search of, and knew what must next be done. Early on the following morning John McNab, late of the Glengarry Fencibles, was called to the Earl's tent and ordered to bear a warrant for the arrest of the Honourable William McGillivray. In the afternoon, with another constable and an armed boat-party of seven men, McNab crossed to the fort and served the warrant on the head of the North West Company in his own room. McGillivray showed the mettle that had confirmed him for more than twelve years as the effective head of a great concern in a cut-throat trade. He accepted the warrant with quiet dignity – 'like a gentleman', McNab said afterwards – asking only for time to finish a letter he was writing. He then asked two of his partners, Kenneth McKenzie and Dr. John McLoughlin, to accompany him as bail. At their request the three partners were permitted to cross the river in their own canoe and the Honourable William McGillivray appeared before the Earl of Selkirk in his tent. There he was charged with treason and conspiracy, and as an accessory to murder. He asked if he might be bailed and was told the charge was too serious to permit bail. McKenzie and McLoughlin were then shown warrants against them and Mc-Nab was instructed to place them, too, in arrest.

A short time later McNab was given orders to return again to the fort, this time with warrants for all the remaining partners then at Fort William. Dr. Allan went also, with a warrant to search for and seal the partners' papers. Whether Selkirk anticipated resistance or merely sought to head it off, the constables were accompanied by twenty-five de Meurons under Captain D'Orsonnens and Lieutenant Fauché. And formidable trouble was clearly a possibility. News of the arrest of William McGillivray had spread and there were perhaps 200 Canadian *voyageurs* and Indians clustered around the gate of the fort. In the open gateway itself stood the men McNab had come for, among them John McDonald (Le Borgne), Hugh Mc-Gillis, Simon Fraser, and Alexander McKenzie (The Baron). He crossed the wharf and made his way to the gate accompanied by his fellow constable, Macpherson, Dr. Allan, and the de Meuron officers. The men remained in the boats on the alert for a call.

The first two warrants were served and accepted quietly. But as the constable attempted to serve his warrant on John McDonald the latter shouted that there would be no more submission until Mr. McGillivray was released. He called for the gates to be closed and one leaf was swung to. The constables became entangled in the attempt to shut the other leaf and McNab called on Captain D'Orsonnens for support. At a shout the de Meurons tumbled out of the boats on the run and blocked the closing of the gate. D'Orsonnens then ordered the objecting McDonald to be seized and placed in one of the boats, and, in spite of his violent struggles and with damage only to his dignity, this was done. Meanwhile at the call of a bugle Captain Matthey crossed with the remaining de Meurons. He found all quiet. D'Orsonnens' men had quickly entered the stockade; some had seized and manned the two guns that covered the gates while others took post in strategic positions. The North West Company servants were quickly dispersed and the threatening moment had passed. The remaining partners resigned themselves to the situation. After seals were placed on desks and boxes of papers, the whole party returned to Lord Selkirk's encampment. De Meuron sentries paced back and forth in front of the powder magazine and the gun house, and guards were mounted on the cannon and the gates. The partnership that had flouted the law with impunity for years was gripped as in a vice. For the moment they and their employees were stunned. That the Honourable William McGillivray could be arrested, and Le Borgne hauled unceremoniously by the scruff of his neck into a boat at their wharf – above all that strangers should give orders at Fort William – was beyond belief. Many things might come of the day's happenings, but the North West Company of the high hand would never be quite the same again.

When all had been charged in due form, the partners were offered their parole, and all accepted. The only condition was that on their word of honour as gentlemen they would do nothing to obstruct the execution of the law and would undertake no hostile act; this was freely given. On this understanding they returned to their quarters. The sun went down at last behind the Selkirk camp and darkness settled on the lake, swallowing the great fort. Cooking fires flared up along the river, then died out. As night took over, the calls of the changing guard within the fort alone testified that an era was coming to an end.

The outward calm and quiet of the night of August 13 at Fort William was delusory. The kitchen fire in the basement of the mess-hall was blazing high with papers, and the seals of certain boxes and desks lay broken. If any of the partners called attention to the honour they had damaged with the seals, the protest went unrecorded. Yet there must have been objectors. Some had had serious misgivings from the first and others when the colony was destroyed in 1815. The news of Seven Oaks meant much more guilt than most were prepared to shoulder. There had been bitter differences of opinion on the company's attitude, the public appearance of it all, and their personal responsibility. At the worst, the group seems to have behaved as if morality were a matter of being found out; judged on this basis they were guilty of a great wrong. Their alarm and outrage at finding their chief antagonist sitting unassailably in judgment drove them beyond bounds that most of them, alone, would have been ashamed to pass. It is even possible that many of them slept while the honour of the group was dragged in the mire. Only one thing seems certain: no part of the group would have taken such drastic action without the knowledge and general approval of the Honourable William McGillivray.

While steps were being taken to obstruct the law in the mess-hall, measures of a hostile nature went forward in the darkness outside. In spite of sentries, numbers of moccasined men moved silently among the buildings, smuggling out gunpowder and fire-arms.

But few secrets were kept for long in Fort William, where loyalty was not the only response to a ruthless system. Alexander Fraser, a half-breed blacksmith who had been coerced into renewing his indenture when his time expired, witnessed the burning of the papers and the movement of the arms; he was told that the latter were for an attack on Lord Selkirk's people. In the early morning he crossed the river with the news and was conducted to Lord Selkirk's tent. Outwardly, no immediate action was taken, but a search warrant was issued for arms and munitions outside the ammunition magazine and the gun house. During the day the *voyageur* camp was ordered to move across the river from the fort and the de Meurons took their place outside the stockade.

Some hours later a search disclosed eighty-three loaded guns concealed in the loft of a barn outside the fort, and a barrel of gunpowder was found hidden at the edge of a swamp. Their seizure was to bring on Selkirk a charge of theft.

The partners were given notice of a court of inquiry to be held in their Council House on August 15. They were advised that any of them might refuse to make a statement. Notes would be taken of the answers given at the hearing and individuals would be allowed to read over and approve the notes before signing them. Proper care was given to the composition of the court. All the gentlemen of Lord Selkirk's party were included and those of his de Meuron officers not on duty. In addition, Lieutenants Brumby and Missani, the North West sightseers, were invited to attend, and some of the North West clerks. All parties seemed now to be conscious that they were both discharging public responsibility and acting in the public eye. The result was a gravity of demeanour in everyone and an air of solemn decorum about the court, which the fuming partners might otherwise have denounced.

It was clear that the hearing of William McGillivray would be of much greater importance than any other or indeed than all the others put together. His shrewdness and experience guaranteed this, his cool nerve in the face of difficulties, above all his ultimate responsibility for all the North West Company did and was. Moreover, what McGillivray said today, Montreal would say tomorrow – and the Colonial Office, it seemed, the day after. Whatever the Earl thought about McGillivray, however much he disapproved of his conduct or despised his principles, he did not underrate his abilities. As they faced each other across the table, with Selkirk in McGillivray's accustomed place, they must both have reflected on the odd twist of events that had brought them to this moment. In other circumstances they had thought well of each other, might even have become friends. Now Selkirk was in the position of judge on an issue about which he could not pretend to be impartial. McGillivray was facing the impeachment and perhaps the destruction of his life's work, and of everything he stood for as a leading citizen.

If Selkirk expected to learn much from the examination, he was to be disappointed. Though McGillivray could not disclaim all responsibility so completely as the wintering partners had done before him, his adroitness made the questioning of almost as little effect. He was a master of the side-step and the half-truth, and all that emerged from his answers was a clear foreshadowing of the North West Company's future defence: that the attacks on the colony had been provoked by those in charge of the colony and that the North West Company had no concern in such attacks 'as far as known to me'; that the half-breeds resented the colony and resented controls such as Miles's order forbidding them to hunt the buffalo on horseback. He contrived to half-defend and half-disown the actions of Duncan Cameron and Alexander Macdonell, denying Cameron's direction of an attack on the colony and questioning Macdonell's responsibility for arresting the half-breed clerks, since he presumed them to have acted in self-defence rather than as murderers. It was obvious that the idea of arresting Cuthbert Grant was not to be lightly contemplated: 'It would have been very dangerous for any man to have arrested Mr. Grant.'

'Would you approve of continuing a salary to Mr. Grant as a clerk, after imbrueing his hands in murder?' asked Selkirk.

McGillivray hesitated; '... that question requires some latitude for an answer,' he said carefully, and then proceeded to take the latitude without providing the answer. And, when a further question about Macdonell stung him to an approval of him 'for preserving our property from attack', he hurried on to justify North West actions 'on the principle of retaliation'.

When the court reminded him that this principle was not accepted in law as a justification of criminal acts, he replied that he did not know on what other terms a man was to act to protect his property in the North-west.

The short, sharp exchange was over and McGillivray calmly concluded his summary of events with his bland certainty outwardly unshaken: 'One seizure has brought on another till the late unfortunate affair of Mr. Semple and his people who by an extraordinary infatuation went out to attack the half-breeds.'

The defence, if less than honest, had been more than shrewd, and there can be little doubt that McGillivray bore himself proudly as he was escorted from the room.

2

In the days that followed, the pulse of Fort William began to beat to a different rhythm. The atmosphere of roaring activity normal at this season was muted, and an air of stunned caution took its place. Outside the fort, instead of the usual clutter of teepees and upturned canoes, the de Meuron tents stood in review order, with their *bateaux* on the shore near by. Across the river among the ragged stumps, the transplanted *voyageur* camp had lost some of its careless swagger and bursting vitality. At meal-times, *engagés* and Indians crossed over in relays and lined up to draw their food under the watchful eyes of the de Meurons. Outside the Council House, where Lord Selkirk had taken up his residence, all could see the pacing sentries of the 37th Regiment, and those who had business with his Lordship had first to pass his bodyguard. The essential work of the fort went on, but lists of work-parties had to be submitted and approved. A stranger of unpredictable menace stood astride the lifeline of perhaps 2,000 fur-traders and canoemen; it was unbelievable. The Nor'Westers were facing what others had faced at their hands – the knowledge that Fort William and the fur trade could be as far beyond the rule of law as the man in charge there chose to make them.

If proof were needed, it lay in a silent and guarded bunkhouse alongside the mess-hall where, as all knew, the unseen partners awaited his Lordship's pleasure. There was no one to argue that this was indeed the rule of law, not merely a successful move in a power struggle. That there could be a law at Fort William beyond the wishes of the partners was a notion never contemplated. Meanwhile, strangers paced the gallery before the mess-hall, mild enough looking except perhaps for the de Meuron officers, but unquestionably in possession. There was no roaring and cursing, no knocking down and thrashing of men. The climate had changed, but things got done – and promptly. In the evening the partners were not to be seen making their way to the coffee room for a conference over a pipe and a glass. And the mess-hall no longer blazed, nor did it rock to the lilt of the fiddle and the beat of hundreds of moccasined feet. Instead, in the darkness, the de Meuron guards moved quietly on their ceaseless rounds. Rumour said they disdained rifles and carried only naked bayonets in their hands.

The period of waiting was not long. On August 17 three canoes had been made ready and the necessary *voyageurs* warned for a trip by order of Lord Selkirk. On the eighteenth the arrested partners took their places for what promised to be the strangest of home-comings. Lieutenant Fauché, late of the Regiment de Meuron, was in command of the little brigade. No record remains of the departure, or the form of send-off for the canoes. They usually left on a festive note, as the agents, and the partners going down to Montreal on rotation, exchanged banter and took last messages from those who were left behind; but there had never been a departure like this. To be sent off from their own fort under the eyes of their people, with only their parole standing between them and shackles, was a disgrace and a thing they would never forget.

Only one partner remained behind – Daniel McKenzie. Selkirk's informants had long known that this wreck of a man was the least solid of all the partners, in his attachment to the company. The partners, well aware of his weakness, had done what they could to compel his silence on Selkirk's arrival. But he had purposely been left to the last during the examinations, and the lateness of the hour had prevented his being questioned; his hearing was still to come. Daniel later claimed that Kenneth McKenzie, suspecting him of informing on the group, had threatened just before his departure for Montreal: 'If ever I am acquitted, I'll blow out your brains.' The 'if ever' in that threat was significant; not long before it would have been 'when'.

As the canoes disappeared to the east, the great depot settled down to its new and still uneasy routine. Selkirk seemed not to have decided what was to happen next. His plan had been, once investigations at Fort William were complete, to move on with his whole party to the Fond du Lac country, though Miles Macdonell and John Allan remained strongly opposed.

Meanwhile the search for evidence at Fort William was not completed. On August 20 Selkirk issued a search warrant, as a result, Allan believed, of special information. On formal demand the North West clerks opened, successively, the buildings under their charge. In one, the searching party came on a pile of fur-packs, thirty or forty in number: stolen goods. Although they had been repacked and marked 'R.R.' (Red River), the original mark 'Q.R.' was plainly discernible. They were the furs from the Qu'Appelle River, taken from Pambrun and Sutherland in May by Cuthbert Grant – the furs of which the Honourable William McGillivray, under examination, had stated he did not know what had been taken, or by whose orders, or what had become of it.

The same day that the stolen furs were found, still another North West partner, John McGillivray, arrived at Fort William, and instead of being welcomed by his friends was promptly arrested. The papers in his canoe were seized and sealed up in his presence for delivery to the authorities in Montreal.

Perhaps it was from revulsion at the finding of the stolen

furs that Selkirk undertook then to examine Daniel McKenzie before North West witnesses as well as his own supporters. The wretched prisoner, whose constitution and nerves had long since been undermined by hardship and excessive drinking, was badly frightened. There was already evidence in Selkirk's possession of his having tried to enlist the Indians at Sand Lake to attack the settlement the year before. Either the first questions threw Daniel into a panic or Kenneth McKenzie's threat still rang in his ears. He tacked uneasily through a feeble maze of denials, contradictions, and refusals to talk, which wore out the patience of the court and brought him close to a charge of contempt. He was marched out between guards with fixed bayonets and committed to the fort jail, an old, disused privy. Its last occupant had been the wounded Bourke, storekeeper from Red River, who was confined there for two weeks, but McKenzie was outraged. ('Bourke was a dirty blackguard. And will your Lordship say that a place where *he* might be confined, was fitting for a gentleman, a partner of the North West Company?...' McKenzie wrote later.)

The search went on and as yet no decision had been taken on what would follow, but time was getting short. There was leeway if they were returning to Montreal, abandoning the settlement. A move west, if it was to be made at all, must be made at once; already the nights were getting cold. And then on the twenty-first came a find that changed everything. In the equipment office lay bales of clothing directed to the Red River department and with them a list of thirteen half-breeds for whom the bales contained gift outfits over and above normal trade equipments. Near by, in an account book, in the handwriting of Alexander Macdonell, was a list of the half-breeds rewarded by Archibald Norman McLeod, on behalf of the partners, after the massacre at Seven Oaks. Following the list there were thirteen names of those who had not yet received their reward – the same names as those on the invoice of habiliments for Red River. The callous record was complete.

Lord Selkirk promptly announced a decision to winter at Fort William, as he considered himself bound to deliver it only to government, 'since it had been used by the North West Company as rendezvous of robbers and murderers and the receptacle of their plunder'. He told Allan and others that he conceived he had a right in law to hold in his possession the property of the North West Company contained in the fort, as security for the damage done to his property and that of the settlers under his protection. If his companions disagreed with either his reasoning or his feelings they seem to have made no protest.

There had never been any real doubt of the North West support of attacks on the settlement, but neither had there been complete evidence. Now Selkirk's quiet anger burned so deep that he called on Allan, the de Meuron officers, Miles Macdonell and the rest, to unite in a pledge that they would not give up the fort except to a party of the King's troops.

Meanwhile Daniel McKenzie, under guard in his cell, ill, frightened, and miserable, asked to see the doctor. Allan, looking at this wreck of a man, listened to a babble of questions that reflected McKenzie's fear for his health and for the consequences of his criminal associations: would a court take an Indian's word against a white man's? John Allan – honest, sensible, and careful – answered as best he could, prescribed for his patient, and gave him a sharp lecture on his drinking. He then reported to Lord Selkirk that he thought a prolonged period in the jail would seriously injure McKenzie's health, though his present illness seemed chiefly the result of his intemperance. Selkirk, listening with steady, attentive gaze, suggested McKenzie's drink should be cut off or so reduced that he could not get drunk. The doctor thought any sharp reduction of so rooted a habit might have serious results. Selkirk seems to have shrugged then; if the man could be well neither with it nor without it what was to be done? Allan thought his lecture might have a useful effect, and the topic was left.

Next morning Daniel McKenzie asked to be examined again. He seemed to have taken some resolve and, without any promise of immunity, but with the undertaking from Lord Selkirk that he would be recommended to the Crown as a witness, he began haltingly to unfold a disconnected but damaging story of North West guilt. At the end of a somewhat incoherent examination he asked to be allowed to go to his own room and write down what he knew; the request was granted. It was the end of his two-day imprisonment and the beginning of a long period of wandering at large, buttonholing members of Selkirk's entourage to bore them with his jumbled memories and to try to convince them of his good intentions. It would have been well if matters had ended there.

From his arrival at Fort William, Selkirk had been in an equivocal position. His letter to Sherbrooke from Sault Ste. Marie, announcing his intention of going to the fort, made it clear that he knew the dangers of such a move – the dangers at least of misrepresentation. The dangers of temptation he had perhaps not faced or quite believed in. At first glance it appeared there was no real difference between what as the aggrieved proprietor of the Red River Settlement he might think appropriate, and what as a magistrate his duty would require. Later his actions would be misrepresented: that was anticipated and accepted. But the behaviour of his people had been correct in the hard context of law enforcement, and he had succeeded to a considerable extent because of the moral strength of his position. The North West clerks had accepted the situation with no outward resistance. Stores that were required by Selkirk's people were requisitioned and issued on a voucher as though this were routine business. Clerks who had questions about operational matters sought audience of Lord Selkirk in the Council House (which many of them were entering for the first time, after years of service – this being the partners' sanctum); they found their problems discussed and a ruling given, not cordially, doubtless, but in a suitable atmosphere of mutual dignity.

Perhaps for this reason the first departure from that judicial atmosphere – cool but till now correct – was a shock. McTavish and Vandersluys waited on Lord Selkirk. This was the time, they said, when they normally sent off the canoes for Lac la

Pluie and Red River with the season's supply of provisions and trade goods. The outfits were ready; they wanted only permission to release the necessary canoes and detail the men. The request was refused. Lord Selkirk said coldly that he considered all North West people in the Red River district to be rebels in arms against British subjects and he could not consider sending supplies and munitions to support them in this. It was perhaps not an unreasonable position for a magistrate to take; but it was the most direct interference yet with the routine of North West trade, and it was unfortunate that he must appear the principal beneficiary of his own decision.

That Selkirk fully realized the awkwardness of his position was shown in the letter that he wrote to Sir John Sherbrooke on September 3. After describing his action, he went on:

> It is not improbable that my having stopped the supplies destined for these miscreants may be misrepresented as an act of aggression against the North West Company, or an interruption of the freedom of trade. But I trust that your Excellency will not be disposed to lend too easy an assent to the allegations of interested individuals, and that in this (or any other part of my conduct) I shall not be condemned without an opportunity of explanation ... when I am placed in circumstances that expose my conduct to misrepresentation.
>
> It would be a very great satisfaction to me if the load of responsibility under which I am now obliged to act could be alleviated.

This plea for government commissioners to look into matters and for troops to keep the peace in the interior was to be repeated in almost every letter, until finally, and all too late, it was in a measure granted.

Each day now, and even more markedly each night, the formidable winter of Lake Superior drew closer. Before the end of August the nights under canvas had become too cold even for the rugged de Meurons and they were moved into fort buildings. With them went the Hudson's Bay Company supplies which had lain until then in the boats. Two old Canadians were enlisted to teach the idle soldiers the secrets of fishing in the area, and a thriving fishery was soon established which provided quantities of dried lake trout and whitefish to help supply the needs of so large a group during the months ahead. As the Selkirk party settled in for the winter, more and more of those who were not staying set out on their journeys, and with each departure those who were left behind drew closer together. Within a few days most of the North West clerks left for Montreal. Before they went, an elaborate routine of sealing the room in which the company's business papers were kept was completed by Dr. Allan and McTavish. John McGillivray had already been sent off to York under escort of Lieutenants Missani and Brumby. Meanwhile, a proclamation, issued by the Governor General, and calling on both parties to cease all hostile activity, had reached Fort William by express canoe.

John Pritchard set out to carry the proclamation to the interior and everyone knew this might be the most hazardous trip of all. He was heading into what could only be regarded as enemy country, and the bearer of a proclamation calling for peace might be dead before anyone knew his mission, or – equally – soon after. With each departing canoe went *voyageurs* and Indians, and the haphazard camp across from the fort had shrunk until it housed only the few score of defeated men and their families – the people who couldn't go home to Lower Canada – and the canoemen for the interior who had been forbidden to go.

Before McTavish and Vandersluys left for Montreal, Selkirk proposed to them an arrangement for arbitrating the 'material' differences between him and the North West Company – the mutual damage to property. At first this seemed to appeal to the clerks and there was a warmth between the two parties that had not been present in their meetings until now. When Vandersluys suggested that Selkirk should seek to intercede for the partners he had sent down, the moment of cordiality was ended. Selkirk answered crisply that the law must take its course, and the offended clerk rejoined that they could not in the circumstances discuss arbitration – or any 'arrangement'.

As the canoes disappeared to the east the blank immensity of the inland sea stared back at the watchers in the fort. There was nothing in sight beyond the islands but endless water; for a hundred miles to the south, and across an arc of 350 miles east and west, there was emptiness, and at this season nothing to expect. There would be no more up-bound fur-traders until the next May or June. At best there might, miraculously, be mail from Montreal, a gesture from a world already so remote it was hardly real. For the rest, the pacing sentries would stare out at the polished or torn steel of the lake or at their companions fishing; they would wait wearily for the end of their duty, and then wearily kill time until they were posted for duty again.

The schooner that appeared on the horizon a week later was an unlooked-for and graceful vision. They watched it come on, bending under a press of canvas, standing in for their wharf. The duty officer had his men under arms. It was the North West Company's *Invincible* from the Falls of St. Mary with John Johnson, the independent trader, in charge. He came as an emissary from the North West Company with a formal demand for the return of their fort; but neither he nor Lord Selkirk seemed to take this with more than formal gravity. More disturbing was his news.

The canoes bearing the North West partners had got into trouble in a high wind just west of the Sault. Two had with difficulty reached an island but the third had overturned in the broken water just off shore. In spite of help from the now-lightened canoes which boldly put off to the rescue, nine men had been drowned, including Kenneth McKenzie, a de Meuron sergeant, and an old Iroquois chief famed as a canoeman. They would wait months for Lieutenant Fauché's account of the circumstances. But they might have anticipated the North Westers' swiftness to blame the mishap on Selkirk, who would be openly charged with callously overloading the canoes.

Johnson appeared in no hurry to be gone. His attitude to

the North West men seemed to be an amused and tolerant cynicism developed across years of association and rivalry. During his stay, two more discoveries piled up the mounting score against the North West associates, as though to show their friends as well as enemies the true nature of their operations. One of the *engagés*, Perrault, who had been going freely about the fort, came forward and confessed to taking part in the Red River massacre. He was brought before a court such as the partners had faced, with Johnson taking part, and described in horrible detail the events of those few minutes at Seven Oaks, of his own firing of several shots into the defenceless and screaming huddle of colonists. This story of a North West employee added nothing of importance to Selkirk's knowledge, but it underlined everything for someone outside the controversy.

John Allan's discovery did much the same. He had pried open a locked press in the Council Room to find at first that it appeared to contain only discarded wrapping-paper. But his groping hand came on a roll of birch bark, overlooked by the partners, and in the birch bark the letters of which Lagimonière had been robbed – their seals had all been broken open. Tait, a North West clerk, remembered an Indian boy arriving with the package and taking it to the now-dead Kenneth McKenzie, who had refused to open it. When next Tait had seen the package it was lying opened in the Council Room with its contents scattered about, and the partners had joked uneasily about mice nibbling the seals.

Selkirk now put in train the plans he had decided on, the taking of the North West posts between him and Red River, to be followed by the recapture of Fort Douglas in the spring or sooner. Restraining hands were shrugged aside. It was folly, he said, to worry about what the Nor'Westers would say of him; they would make the worst of whatever he did – and invent what he did not – as they always had. So fighting patrols of de Meurons and *voyageurs* moved out towards the forts at Fond du Lac and Lac la Pluie; the former move was especially reckless for Fond du Lac was on the border but probably in

U.S. territory, and, though it had been a North West Company post and used against Red River, it had during the summer become part of John Jacob Astor's South West Fur Company.

Within the waiting fort, Daniel McKenzie wandered about at will, bothering whoever he could with his troubles and his wildly veering hopes. At one moment he had some notion of going to Red River (where he had a son) to reason with the half-breeds among whom he had influence. At another, he speculated aloud on what his partners would think of him for aiding their enemies. No one seems to have spent much time comforting him, but Miles Macdonell was more willing than most to listen. Presently McKenzie came out with a pressing worry: he had bought up all the supplies at Mackinac for the North West Company just before the arrival of Selkirk's party; the supplies had been bought in the name of the partnership – in order to deny them to Selkirk. What if his partners turned on him now and left him obligated for the £1,200 he had spent? Dr. Allan tried to reassure him; the partners for their own good names must surely discharge the debt. The fussing McKenzie then asked whether Lord Selkirk could help in this; Allan said sharply that he thought not. But McKenzie was not to be put off and finally asked the question directly of Selkirk; the supplies were at Fort William, Selkirk needed supplies, McKenzie needed to unload his debt. Wasn't the solution of this easy, and satisfactory all around?

In getting the answer he sought, Daniel McKenzie could not have guessed the sequence of events he was putting in train. Selkirk, with his ardent nature concentrated for years on his great schemes, had been goaded beyond calm judgment by the successive stages of North West opposition. He had begun by conceding that they had some rights, at least in common law, but every step had moved the contest out of that reasonable framework. He could no longer suppose coexistence with the North West Company possible, and from what he now knew he could not conceive of a government allowing such a lawless and rapacious organization to continue if only its true nature

171

could be known. He welcomed Daniel McKenzie in 'with gently smiling jaws'.

Though he had his moments of doubt and hesitation, McKenzie claimed the right to act as a partner on behalf of all the partners of the North West Company. Had he not bought supplies without power of attorney? Very well, he could similarly sell them, and other things, and make agreements on behalf of the partners. There is little doubt that he liked the Earl and that, for the moment, he felt like a king himself. He was at least half convinced that the trouble with Selkirk and the legal results of their now-discovered violence had jeopardized, if they had not already ruined, the North West Company. The old resentment of a wintering partner against the Montreal agents flared up; this was a chance to save something out of the wreck for himself and his fellow partners. Guilt, cupidity, and muddled logic led him on in a series of conferences with Selkirk or Miles Macdonell and through the drafting and signing of mutual agreements. When the process was finished nothing remained on paper to the North West Company of its great depot at Fort William but the shell of the fort buildings and stockade.

There was probably some uneasy muttering within the Selkirk party; John Allan, for one, disliked the whole transaction and foresaw the use that would be made of it. But Selkirk brushed his objections aside. It would be absurd to refrain from doing anything for fear of misrepresentation by the Nor'-Westers. They would 'invariably misrepresent his conduct however unimpeachable it might be'. Besides, these arrangements would be judged by men of unassailable rectitude. As the forms had been drafted, this was true. Moreover, for two days the documents were left with McKenzie for his final consideration before fair copies were made.

Shortly before eleven o'clock on the morning of September 19, the senior men of the fort began to gather and to make their way into the Council Room. Across the table, Lord Selkirk and Daniel McKenzie faced each other while Pritchard fussed over the fair copies of various agreements. Behind Mc-

Kenzie stood Kennedy and Tait, clerks of the North West Company; Selkirk was supported by his own people. For the next hour there was a steady whispering of paper and the scratching of pens as documents were signed and passed to the witnesses. When it was finished, there was an agreement to submit claims for damages between Selkirk and the North West Company to arbitrators to be appointed by Chief Justices of the Courts of King's Bench and Common Pleas at Westminster; this was to have no bearing on any criminal prosecutions between the two parties. Meanwhile the North West furs at Fort William and the conveyance of one of Selkirk's estates were to be consigned to the arbitrators, to be disposed of by them if necessary for the payment of claims; the furs were valued at £60,000 and the estate, which produced £3,000 in rent a year, was considered to be roughly equivalent. There was, further, an agreement conveying all the movable property at Fort William except the furs to Lord Selkirk at a price equal to their invoice cost plus the cost of transportation to Fort William.

On the completion of the sale, McKenzie received the keys of Fort William from Mr. Tait, with whom they had been left by John Johnson; they were then formally surrendered to Selkirk. It was no longer the North West clerks who would come and go freely to the Indian shop, the ammunition magazine, the equipment shop, or the blacksmith's shop. As an earnest and a first instalment on the purchase of goods, Daniel McKenzie was paid £50 in gold before the meeting ended. With the yellow coins lying on the table between the two men, there must have been a few witnesses to reflect that thirty pieces of silver would seem to many more appropriate.

Chapter 7

MEANWHILE IN MONTREAL

I

Montreal, child of the fur trade, was not easily surprised by happenings in the Indian Country. During the city's infancy, before the trade moved inland, the summers were made vivid and often horrible by the gathering of Indians from all quarters, come to trade their furs and drink the traders' brandy. Along the shores of the St. Lawrence River an untidy satellite town sprang up for a few weeks, a town of birch-bark tents edged by hundreds of canoes, and peopled by Indians and *coureurs de bois*. Brandy facilitated bargaining, and the traders were not scrupulous, so the annual fair had more often resembled a debauch than an orderly market – a debauch that flowed into, and often threatened to overwhelm, the town, turning half its houses into bistros and spawning cabarets in every street. When from the press of competition the traders began to move west to meet the Indians, the fair disappeared from Montreal. It left the memory of an evil trade – but a trade still important to the prosperity of the city. It was a thousand miles out of sight but never long out of mind. And Montreal's rather flexible morality was still to be seen in such views as that of a magistrate who, when asked for a warrant against the killer of an Indian, answered that it was not yet determined that the killing of an Indian was to be considered a crime.

For a generation – in which control of the trade passed from French to English and Scottish hands – activity had centred at Grand Portage, and then Fort William. In the process, Fort William had become a place of legend – over the horizon and beyond appeal. The people who saw the brigades off in the spring saw them leave for Fort William with a kind of desperation, on a journey that might at any moment become dangerous. And it was for the brigades from Fort William, the homecoming men, that they waited each autumn in excitement and fear. Between the two, every crumb of news from the Upper Country was seized on and passed from house to house. There were few who could pretend indifference to what happened there.

In the autumn of 1816 everyone longed for news. The secret of Lord Selkirk's departure in June with a strong body of soldiers was long since out; and probably most people considered that if his Lordship were looking for trouble he would find it at Fort William. The first news to reach Montreal was of the massacre at Seven Oaks and the second destruction of the settlement – provoked by the settlers, it was said. It was horrible, but it was remote – hardly real – and it need not alarm Montreal. Then came news of what was called Selkirk's 'sack' of Fort William, and in late September the unbelievable happened: six partners of the North West Company, led by the Honourable William McGillivray, came home under arrest. It hardly mattered that they were met and led discreetly to a magistrate's house and there freed on bail. These, the town's most powerful citizens, were to be tried as accessories to murder. Murder in the Indian Country was not really surprising, but that these men should be brought to book was unthinkable.

For the North West partners it was bad enough to be openly accused of crime and put to the bar of justice, but a way of life, a social order, stood impeached. Formerly their affairs had been managed with a suave and powerful dexterity. Though there was whispering aplenty, little had been generally known against them since the war with the XY Company fifteen years back; what the grand manner and the right connections had been unable to manage, bribery and intimidation had taken care of. But now they found themselves cutting a poor figure in a public brawl and, for the moment, rage drove them beyond caution. No canard was too mean and no charge too far-fetched for their purpose – the ultimate discrediting of Lord Selkirk.

After listening and watching the spectacle during that autumn and winter, a friend of Selkirk's wrote him from Montreal that the enmity of the Nor'Westers to him personally would incline them to the commission of any act however atrocious to avenge themselves against him. Regarding him as the greatest obstacle to their views, they 'would willingly remove it by any means however diabolical'.

The energy and inventiveness that had carried the North West flag with honour to the Arctic, to the Pacific Coast, and round the Horn to China itself, having been momentarily paralysed by guilt and by Selkirk's bold action, began to stir again into purposeful motion. For the moment everything must be directed to the humbling of Lord Selkirk and the regaining of Fort William, nerve-centre of their affairs; both pride and dire necessity required this. At first their recent brush with the law hampered their efforts; an expedition was fitted out but preparations went forward as secretly as was possible in a matter of so much public interest. Application had been made for a warrant for the arrest of Selkirk on charges of the theft of eighty-three guns and of forcible entry to Fort William, and an order for the fort's restitution was sought. This time no brigade with trade goods set off to cheers and good wishes; but individual canoes slipped away at intervals and under cover of darkness, with crews composed of Iroquois and the North West bully boys – the *batailleurs* – and cargoes of weapons and ammunition. They were to rendezvous at Sault Ste. Marie under the partners, led by McGillivray himself, and there await the warrants. Exact details of what was happening were not known but general knowledge of the expedition and its intentions were soon an open secret.

2

In the great tradition of the French traders from whom they had taken over, the North West partners had always made it their business and their pleasure to establish friendly relations with the leaders in the colony – above all with the governor. It came easily to them and they did it well. With their big houses and lavish parties, their natural high spirits added to the beaming confidence of their station, the good opinion of successive governors was usually an easy prize. But it seemed that in this, too, something had gone awry. While Lord Selkirk was overmatching them in the way they best understood at Fort William, Lady Selkirk had taken their accustomed place by the Governor's fireside.

The place had been won as a consolation prize, a by-product of a trip to Quebec on Selkirk's behalf. The news of Seven Oaks and with it the word that he was on his way to Fort William had reached Lady Selkirk in Montreal on August 10. If something desperate had not already occurred, it might be happening even now. Knowing her husband's ardent nature, his stubborn devotion to his dream, she could not suppose he would easily be turned aside in his determination to seek justice for his settlers. How could she help? What would effectively support his efforts in this unlooked-for crisis? There were few to whom she could turn for advice. Meanwhile, the massacre was being reported in the Montreal papers as a clash over provisions between servants of the North West and Hudson's Bay companies.

After watching irresolutely for almost a week, she forwarded Selkirk's letter announcing his decision to go to Fort William to Sir John Sherbrooke. Her own covering letter was full of passionate concern that the Governor take action to control events. She pointed out that Selkirk had now the greatest power in the interior, but no authority from government to put an end to the disturbances. Above all, she pleaded the cause of the settlers: 'It cannot surely be intended to allow these people to be sacrificed to the imagined interests of any set of merchants, they have nothing to do with the fur trade.'

She awaited Sherbrooke's answer in a torment of indecision. James Stuart had convinced her that somehow the Governor must be persuaded to send envoys with authority to the Upper Country – and at once. On August 20 the Governor's reply was handed to her: 'After consulting the best informed persons I can meet with here ... I find it will be impossible to take any steps likely to prevent further mischief for the present. .... In any way in which I *can* be of service ...' So she had failed; and it was said that Sherbrooke would leave Quebec in a few days for Upper Canada. If he did not change his mind before then, she wrote her brother Andrew, 'the game was up for this year'. That night, taking Daer and Isabella, she caught the boat for Quebec; it was one of the new steamboats still so much a novelty that the timings of their journeys were fully reported in the newspapers.

To the children this must have seemed merely a splendid excursion, a joyful outing. For two days the paddle-wheel steamer thrashed its unhurried way through the reed-beds, which in places seemed to turn the broad and tranquil St. Lawrence into a meadow. Great cranes and herons stood like sentinels in the shallows, while myriads of ducks, water-hens, and sandpipers flashed or cruised in purposeful leisure. But that scene of quiet beauty, the sleepy old villages lying beneath the rising banks of the north shore, the solemn cows standing belly-deep in the lush meadows to the south, the joyful cries of her children as they raced about the deck – none of this could have served to quiet Lady Selkirk's apprehension. She sat writing yet another letter to Sir John Sherbrooke putting forward James Stuart's arguments in her own persuasive style.

She was doing a bold, even a rash thing, but this was not the time to distrust her instinct. Besides, she had not the habit of failure, nor indeed of being lightly turned aside from her course. The vessel came at last under the cliffs fronting the Plains of Abraham, panted below the Citadel fortress and the Château St. Louis, home of the Governor, and came to rest at the docks of the Lower Town.

They had landed in the late morning of the twenty-third and it was one o'clock before she was settled into her 'nasty hotel' with the children. Already her letter had been carried by messenger to the Château St. Louis. Two hours later the Governor himself called on her. That first interview went well and her hopes soared – 'he spoke most frankly and certainly has imbibed no prejudice against us'. He said he had considered sending commissioners inland and though he had given the idea up would reconsider it. That night, above the murmuring St. Lawrence, as she settled the children and prepared for bed, success seemed nearly in her grasp.

The morning brought a letter from Sherbrooke that blasted her hopes. The Governor regretted that the matter of the commissioners could not at present be reopened. 'This cruel note shuts my mouth,' she wrote to Andrew, 'it would be a bad return . . . to pester him further.' In no mood for social chat, she went to call on Lady Sherbrooke. 'I never felt less able to make conversation. I made an effort however and perhaps looked more savage than distressed.' Sir John, looking 'troubled', joined the uneasy party for a few minutes before retreating. Back at the hotel the Countess faced the prospect of three days in wretched quarters, being called on by the curious, until another steamer should permit a withdrawal. Just as she was sitting down to dinner with her children, the excited waiter burst into the room announcing the Sherbrookes. And before she could rise they were seated on either side of her begging her to join them for an early dinner at the Château and to sail with them on the *Malsham* that night.

When the steamer landed at Montreal two days later, the foundation of a lasting friendship had been laid. The crowd that had gathered to welcome the new governor to Montreal included several Nor'Westers, whose first intimation of her presence in the party was the sight of Lady Selkirk walking up from the shore on Sir John Sherbrooke's arm. Mr. Garden, she reported, 'chuckled amazingly'. 'This, dearest Lou,' she wrote Andrew, 'is a triumph quite to your taste, is it not?'

But it was only a consolation prize. She had not secured the promise of commissioners to go to the interior, and James Stuart was 'most grievously disappointed' at her want of success.

3

A life of hard soldiering had broken Sherbrooke's health; he suffered from a dangerous liver complaint that worried his doctor and made his own work a heavy burden. At fifty-two he wanted only peace and quietness, and the appointment to the Canadas had filled him with apprehension. Not long before sailing from Nova Scotia, where he had been governor, he wrote Sir George Murray that he felt quite unable either to command military operations or control constitutional problems. He was no longer General Sherbrooke, distinguished, if over-rash, at Talavera, and Sir Arthur Wellesley's second-in-command; much less was he the hard-drinking and reckless Colonel Johnny Sherbrooke of the British Army in India. This was a tired man, unwell, crossing that shaky bridge between the strength and boundless confidence of youth and the cautious and limited certainties of old age.

Doubtless he had been briefed on the local problems when taking over from Sir Gordon Drummond. Doubtless he had some of the military man's contempt for what seemed to many a squabble between two trade interests. But the North Westers were not unattractive, or without just grievances, and their friends were all round him – their leader William McGillivray sat in his Legislative Council. Over against them was a man he did not know but would expect to like, a noble-man of fortune and great parts, a man generally esteemed and against whom nothing was known – until now. Alongside him stood a woman of charm and spirit; impossible to think of her being interested in a trade brawl, or, equally, to detect any faltering in her support of the justice of Lord Selkirk's cause. Who was to judge – how even to get at the truth of the case? Before anything, there must be a period of calm, a settling down, an attempt at reasoned discussion. But time pressed and winter would literally freeze the situation in its present confused and dangerous state.

Various suggestions had been put forward and they continued to pour in on the bewildered Governor; those who had an interest, along with those merely offended by lawlessness – all had solutions. Lady Selkirk at their first meeting and Lord Selkirk in almost his first letter had suggested the appointment of a royal commission to investigate claims and the injuries done. Now, with Fort William taken, even the North Westers began to invite the intervention of government which until now they had strictly avoided. The suggestion had merit but also presented great difficulties. Commissioners equal to the task were not easy to find; and, being found, how many of the necessary calibre were free and physically equal to this emergency? A trip to the Indian Countries involved hardship and danger. Swift rivers knew nothing of royal warrants, and embattled half-breeds little more. Besides, most of the men of stature in Lower Canada were allied in some way to the Nor' Westers. Sherbrooke invited Lieutenant-Governor Gore of Upper Canada to name commissioners to represent the Crown in the interior. Gore replied hastily that he had no one of the necessary quality available.

Finally, in mid-October, knowing that it was already late in more ways than one, the Governor General approached the Honourable William Bachelor Coltman, a member of the Executive Council of Lower Canada. Coltman, a man of legal training and with a reputation for common sense and principle, seemed in many ways an admirable choice. He accepted, but the invitation must have alarmed while it flattered a man whose fat body and fussy manner were little suited to the harsh journeys and rough company that would be his.

News of the Commission pleased everyone and, when it was known that Coltman would act, James Stuart wrote to Lady Selkirk that the choice of Mr. Coltman 'exposes the Cause of Justice, which is that of his Lordship to little hazard'. In the midst of this general satisfaction, the Governor General wrote Lord Selkirk of the appointments as though he had acted on his suggestion: 'I have much pleasure in acquainting your Lordship that I have been enabled to meet your wishes in this respect.' The task of the commissioners was 'to quiet the existing disturbances'. It was good news – but it was not to reach Fort William until March of 1817, five months later.

The second commissioner, in so far as he was known, was less approved of. John Fletcher, a police magistrate from Quebec, was not an impressive figure except, like Coltman, in sheer bulk. He had served in the late war, but near home, and it was to appear that lack of brisk encounters with the enemy had left him with a burning thirst for martial glory. He and Coltman were to have a military escort, and were to be, respectively, Major and Lieutenant-Colonel. Fletcher's first act, and almost his last sober one as a commissioner, was to put on his uniform and throw back his shoulders.

While the commissioners went about the preparation for their journey, other matters were put in train. All Commissions of the Peace and appointments as magistrate for the Indian Countries and Canada West were revoked. Until further notice there would be no one to represent the law in this area but the commissioners, not even excepting the Hudson's Bay Company officials in their chartered territory. Precise directions for the Commission were prepared and they were given various personal and official letters for Lord Selkirk at Fort William.

A desperate game was now being played in grim earnest by both sides, and it contained a deadly condition imposed by the difficulties of communication. It required three to four weeks for picked canoemen in a light craft to travel between Fort

William and Montreal – the normal time was six weeks or longer. So letters could not be answered in less than two to three months.

The haste of both parties was feverish – Selkirk, so to demonstrate North West villainy as to force official notice and action at once; the North West agents, to re-establish their trade and prestige and to retrieve their capital locked up in furs; the need of both was a decision before winter. Theoretically, a letter might be answered in two or three months, but only if it was sent two or three months before freeze-up. Whatever remained undone or unsettled when the iron hand of winter closed on the north would advance little before the ice went out in the spring – and the closing of the hand was an unknown date. The final warning might be no more than a cruel wind from the north, a whiff of frost-crystals in the clear air, a rim of ice creeping out from a lake-shore. Then came a morning of piercing, clean cold or of heavy skies full of snow; and those who travelled far from warmth and secure shelter travelled at their peril.

It had been possible for Lord Selkirk's first moves at Fort William to seem legal, if startling, but the transactions with Daniel McKenzie, as now explained by McKenzie and his partners, were hard to defend. To go through the motions of an elaborate legal transaction with a notorious drunkard – now described as a 'retired partner', obviously not competent to act for the North West Company – was surely a travesty. There were many who considered (and as many to suggest) that the Earl – the 'Bible Peer' – with his vaunted idealism, had now shown himself 'in his true character'. He was said to have kept a drunken old man in detention from August 13 to October 11, and during that time to have coerced him into signing away an immense property for the obvious purpose of ruining the North West Company. Not many knew that, as recently as June, McKenzie had been entrusted with the responsibility of buying supplies far and wide for the Nor'Westers. And fewer still knew that, only months before, the Honourable William McGillivray had presented McKenzie's name to the acting Governor General, Sir Gordon Drummond, as that of 'a fit and proper person to be made a Justice of the Peace', as a result of which he had been appointed. (Sir Gordon Drummond, after all, had turned to William McGillivray for assurances as to the safety of the settlement a few days before its first destruction, because of his confidence in McGillivray as a man of honour and experience.) Who knew that McKenzie had been Selkirk's prisoner for two days only, weeks before the sale, and that the latter had tried to keep him sober?

More especially, the news of the dealings with McKenzie stunned Selkirk's friends. Within hours of his arrival at Sault Ste. Marie from Fort William, the confused and frightened McKenzie, confronted by his partners, had denied his damaging revelations of North West activity in the interior. Within a few days his total repudiation under oath before Dr. Mitchell, J.P. of Drummond's Island, dated November 11, together with a charge that he had been kept in a state of inebriety and actual derangement of mind at Fort William, were on the way east by express canoe.

But the most startling news from Fort William was still to come – news of a crime for which no kind of explanation ever appeared, as senseless as pulling the wings off a fly. In late July Owen Keveny, bringing calves from Fort Albany to Red River, had fallen into Archibald Norman McLeod's hands and been arrested. At first he had been sent in the direction of Fort William, then taken back when Selkirk's presence there became known. The prisoner was now something of an embarrassment. He was passed from hand to hand – taken east again, then west, then released, and again picked up. Alexander Macdonell, Cadotte, Cuthbert Grant, and Archie McLellan all had charge of him at one time or another, but his constant escort had been an Indian named Joseph and Sergeant de Reinhart. Joseph was in no doubt that the instructions from the first were to kill the prisoner, and in the end he carried out orders, shooting Keveny and leaving Reinhart to finish him with a sword. In all the weeks of indecision and argument only some Indians who had given him refuge while he was released and two North West canoemen – Faye and LaPointe – had shown Keveny any pity.

Faye and LaPointe had been at Rainy Lake with Reinhart when D'Orsonnens captured it. Their uneasy demeanour had led him to question them closely; but the horrifying story had only come out fully before Selkirk at Fort William, with details of how Reinhart and Joseph had washed and shared Keveny's blood-stained clothing, and of Archie McLellan reading the victim's papers in his canoe the next day before sinking them in the water with stones. Reinhart admitted his guilt, pleading only that he acted under McLellan's and Cuthbert Grant's orders. So another North West partner faced a charge of murder.

In cooler moments the story might have afforded some grim comfort to the men waiting in Fort William. The very madness of the act, the backing and forthing, the changing of instructions, the revulsion of some of the North West people, all provided a picture of confusion and fear to the point of madness – the behaviour of cornered rats.

A few weeks earlier Alexander Macdonell had written from Bas de la Rivière that they must hope for better times: 'worse we cannot have. The surprise of headquarters is a serious loss and a disgrace to the concern.' It was never easy to follow Whiteheaded Macdonell's thought-processes, and the last paragraph of his letter was in his best form: 'The North West Company and their adherents are as loyal subjects to their King and country as his Lordship and his – but will never submit to his tyranny and oppression.' It was only a few weeks since his 'glorious news from Athabasca' of fifteen Englishmen starved, and after Seven Oaks – 'Sacré nom de Dieu! Good news, twenty Englishmen killed.' Loyalty to King and country and resistance to tyranny and oppression clearly demanded flexibility.

At the entrance to Lake Superior, as autumn drew back and gales whipped the evergreens and tore the remaining leaves from the birches, the Nor'Westers' armada saw time run out in dissension, impatience, and lack of confidence. A year – a few months – earlier, nothing could have held them inactive; it was not mild men who had criss-crossed the wilderness. Now they waited for a warrant.

The warrant had been refused at York, first by Mr. Justice Campbell, and then by the Chief Justice. Now another was being sought at Sandwich on the evidence of North West clerks Vandersluys and McTavish who had been at Fort William during Selkirk's occupation. The waiting force at the Falls of St. Mary began to disintegrate; groups slipped away, hoping to get home before freeze-up forced them to abandon their canoes and cover the remaining distance on foot or horseback.

At this point, a constable, Robinson, arrived at Sault Ste. Marie from York with a warrant lacking only a signature to give it authority; someone hit on a brilliant solution, ready to hand. At Drummond's Island near by lived Dr. Mitchell, Justice of the Peace, one of those sad expedients of pioneer law enforcement, a man whose superior education seemed serviceable enough to outweigh his known weaknesses. Mitchell had already been useful in the matter of Daniel McKenzie's statement. He was elderly and 'never by any chance sober after mid-day', which made him useful to those who found fuddled authority to their purpose. Mitchell obediently signed as requested, and Robinson, accompanied by McBean, a North West partner, and Robert McRobb, a clerk, set out for Fort William.

The sighting of the single canoe with its crew of twelve *voyageurs* approaching was a matter for surprise at the fort, but not apprehension. There could be no menace in a lone canoe. Arrived at the gate in the stockade, Robinson asked to be taken to Lord Selkirk. He was shown into a room where his Lordship was writing, and there served his warrant. Selkirk examined the warrant and answered that he did not believe it was genuine; the differences in handwriting and Dr. Mitchell's reputation went far to convince him that the warrant was spurious or had been obtained surreptitiously.

No doubt he wanted to be convinced. He had already stated

more or less formally that he and his friends were determined not to give up Fort William except to a party of the King's soldiers. Besides, Keveny, the last person who had surrendered to a North West warrant, had been coldly murdered – a man whose death accomplished nothing for the North West Company. Since the warrant was issued at Drummond's Island, he asked whether the party brought any instructions for his detachment from the 37th Regiment which had come from there; they had none. He then formally refused to recognize the warrant. After some futile argument, the party, having spent two nights, withdrew angrily. They appeared to have paddled 300 miles for nothing and now must paddle the long journey back again over the forbidding waters of Lake Superior.

While Robinson's party was at the fort, the last Montreal canoe of the autumn arrived. It brought an accumulation of mail – letters written between July and October 9. With winter now bearing down on them, the last mail was the final proof of their isolation. News from loved ones, official letters on various matters – there would be no more for months. Nothing, it seemed, was going to be changed at Fort William before spring. The long wait stretched before them.

Before mid-November a canoe with the last budget of dispatches and personal letters followed Robinson's party east from the head of the lakes. It carried to Sherbrooke Lord Selkirk's summary of what he had done at Fort William, and to Lieutenant-Governor Gore of Upper Canada an explanation of the reasons for refusing submission to Dr. Mitchell's warrant. And it bore for the Governor General and for Selkirk's counsel copies of all the documents demonstrating North West Company violence that had not already gone down, including the statements relating to the Keveny murder. In summing up, Selkirk asserted that the North West Company could lay no criminal charge against him; at most he might be charged with a civil trespass. Once again he begged that a body of troops be sent to Red River in the spring, sufficient to maintain law and order, a request he had made repeatedly in London and Montreal for the past three years.

Having outlined to Sherbrooke his reasons for detaining the North West Company furs at Fort William, Selkirk added: 'No one (I trust) will imagine that I had any idea of appropriating to myself the property of others.' He then offered a somewhat lame justification of his dealings with Daniel McKenzie. It was, as he afterwards said, 'but an impudent avowal'.

It was some time after this before the arrangement that I refer to, was suggested. Mr. McKenzie was induced as I believe to take up the idea from motives of his own, into which I did not conceive it to be my province to scrutinize. But as he expressed himself as willing to enter into an arrangement, & as I was convinced he had a right to act in the name of his partners, I certainly did think it an object of importance to have the arrangement carried thro & I do not pretend to deny that I was glad to have it so framed as to keep a part of the Capital of the NWCo. in a state of inaction, till the question between us should be decided, so as to limit in some degree their resources for carrying on a system of lawless violence against me. On this account I could easily anticipate that it would excite indignation among some individuals of the greatest influence in the Concern, but on the other hand the arrangement seemed to me to provide for the fair interests of those who have property embarked in the Capital of the Company & whose object it is to preserve their property.

Of this I am convinced, that Mr. McKenzie did nothing but what he sincerely thought for the interests of the Company for which he was acting & in fact some points of the arrangement which were at first suggested were relinquished, because he could not be persuaded that they were advantageous to the NWCo. ... Tho' some of his partners may now wish to represent him as a drunken dotard, he has always managed the affairs under his charge in a satisfactory manner, & this very year Mr. McG. pressed him to undertake the management of the NWCo. department at Red River. I have also in the course of the evidence which has passed thro' my hands seen good

188

grounds for a persuasion that he is actuated by a principle far more honorable than the majority of His partners:—

The NWCo. may find it to their purpose to represent the agreement which Mr. McKenzie made on their part as having been entered into under duress or improper influence, yet I think the agreement itself or the nature of the stipulations cannot well be said to have the features of a leonine contract.

But the North Westers had not quite given up hope of reaching Fort William. A warrant for Selkirk's arrest and the restitution of the fort and contents had finally been issued at Sandwich and was now on its way to meet the North West canoes at the Falls of St. Mary. Smith, an under-sheriff, was already hurrying up Lake Huron, spurred on by a North West promise of $800 if he should succeed in arresting Selkirk. He caught the last of the brigade just turning for home and the decision was taken to make one final effort to win through.

The schooner *Invincible* was armed and provisioned and the remaining fur-traders and *voyageurs* came aboard. It would be a near thing, for already a great storm was sweeping across Superior, tearing the tops off the waves and hurling them against the rocky shore. Only desperate determination took a small ship out in such weather. Doubtless the sentries at Fort William huddled into their greatcoats as they squinted into the storm, or carelessly turned their backs, knowing nothing could come against them until the wind died. Though they underrated the North West spirit, they were right in the result. The little schooner was hardly on her way before the giant waves drove her back and smashed her on the rocks. Winter had finally closed the gate.

A few days later at Nottawasaga on Georgian Bay the commissioners were persuaded that it was too late for them to proceed farther west before spring. Colonel Coltman wrote a courtly letter to Lord Selkirk announcing his appointment as commissioner and explaining his predicament; he was enclosing various communications from Sir John Sherbrooke at

Quebec and from Francis Gore, Lieutenant-Governor of Upper Canada – which was to prove momentous. Having regretted 'the early severity of the season', Coltman left the letters to be sent forward when possible in the spring while he returned to York.

It was a disarming, fair-spoken, even friendly letter – this was Coltman's way. But it was a way that in time was to seem tricky, and in the present case was a good deal less than candid. The day before writing, he had taken a long sworn statement from Daniel McKenzie, setting out at great length the version he now offered of his transactions with Selkirk at Fort William. Attached to his statements were various drafts of the letters he claimed to have been coerced into writing – or into merely copying and signing – and draft suggestions for the final agreements, in the handwriting of Miles Macdonell. There is little doubt that he had done these things gladly enough at the time and welcomed help from a clearer head and a steadier hand, but it made an unpleasant story even more damaging; and it appeared to Coltman in that light.

Back at York in this mood, Coltman met Robert McRobb of the North West Company on December 17, at the end of a long hard trip from Fort William. From him came a statement even more serious than that of Daniel McKenzie, and one that was to have a decisive effect on Selkirk's affairs in Canada. It was a simple account of the refusal of the Earl and his chief supporters at Fort William (Captain Matthey and Dr. Allan) to yield obedience to Constable Robinson's warrant. Within a very short time a messenger was on his way to Quebec with a preliminary report by Coltman and Fletcher, and with copies of the affidavits of Daniel McKenzie and Robert McRobb.

The eventful year 1816 moved towards its close, but it was not yet finished. At Fort William nothing of consequence was happening or could happen for months. Some half-hearted festivities were planned, but the thoughts, the longings of all were elsewhere. Meanwhile, they could swap stories of other days and speculate endlessly about what was happening in the world beyond the frozen horizon: to the colonists; to Colin

Robertson, who must long since have arrived in England with his prisoner, Duncan Cameron; in Montreal and Quebec.

At Jack River, huddled around Norway House, the surviving colonists were enduring a severe and hungry winter and recovering slowly from the shock of Seven Oaks. It was a winter they would never forget, in which misery was finally pierced by the knowledge that Lord Selkirk was at Fort William, triumphant, and wild hopes of a return to Red River were reborn. Some of their number, in despair, had enlisted in the Hudson's Bay Company; most had been determined to return to Scotland. Meanwhile, there was nothing to do but fish through the ice in shrivelling cold, crouch over their smoking fires and wait.

The year-end found Colin Robertson not in England but at Moose Factory on James Bay. A late start and the necessity of calling at the south end of the Bay had proved his undoing. Ice had caught the ship at Eastmain and he had moved back to become an unwilling and unwelcome guest. Still wrought up over the events of recent months, he dreamed frequently of ambush and capture by Archibald Norman McLeod and of the loss of the papers he still carried and guarded fearfully – the papers he had taken from the North West Express in March.

At this moment of loneliness and indecision he heard on December 29 the news of Lord Selkirk's seizure of Fort William. It was a stroke of boldness after his own heart and one of which he better understood the consequence to the North Westers than anyone outside their own ranks. With his shrewd judgment, informed by his unfailing ear for gossip, he speculated on the internal effects as between the McGillivray and McLeod party – which he thought of as the 'violent group' – and the McKenzies (presumably led by the dead Kenneth), whom he called 'the moderates'. But to anyone with his sense of strategy and skill in tactics it was news such as he might have made the subject of a wild New Year's wish.

Two days later, on the last day of the year, Miles Macdonell and D'Orsonnens forced their way through to the plains and,

from the edge of the bush opposite Pembina, cautiously recon-
noitred Fort Daer. With their contingent of twenty-five de
Meurons and fifteen Canadians enlarged by Indian enlistments,
they had made their way over the old War Road of the Indians from the south-west corner of Lake of the Woods. The
reconnaisance showed no sign of strength or evidence of alarm,
and a swift rush easily bore down the token resistance. The
fort was retaken without anyone escaping to warn Fort Douglas of their approach. The path to the settlement lay open.

At Montreal on New Year's Eve, while all the world danced,
Lady Selkirk opened her desk and sat down to write to her
husband. She was heavy with the baby that must be born
within a few days, but for an hour or two she felt able to share
her troubles. The loneliness of recent months had been almost
unbearable, but the time and distance apart – not only the
delay before a letter would arrive, but before it could even
start its journey – withered attempts to forward casual news
or communicate the little passing moments of affection and
longing.

Montreal 'Hogmenay' 1816
The only comfortable way I can find to finish this old
year and usher in the new one is to write to you my own
dearest love. It has been a chequered year, more troubled
than any we have passed together, agitated beyond any
of my life, yet I acknowledge that the blessings have far
preponderated. At the moments when everything looked
blackest when I have been on the very brink of despair,
suddenly the clouds have dispersed and some unexpected
good has arisen. It was on the 17th of August that I
ventured on my first letter to Sir John Sherbrooke, who
would have guessed that by that bold step I was to gain
such friends. . . . Our babe's name if it is a girl is to be
Katherine Jean, what say you to that? Lady Sherbrooke
is Godmother, her name is Katherine, which is too great
a favourite with us not to be caught at. If it is a boy you
know it was to be Basil, and I had a great fancy to have
added Sherbrooke, which would have sounded very mag-
nificent before Douglas, but I am scared by the North

West. I wonder if you will be frightened at my *Envelopes and Seals*. I think not the most daring North Western will venture to meddle with them. ... We have much to be thankful for, of late the interposition of Providence on our behalf has been very marked. The health we both enjoy at this time, you in the midst of fatigue and hardships unusual to you, and me in spite of anxiety and I must own at times a misery of depression such as I never suffered before. Then the children have been healthy and stout all summer though it has been reckoned a particularly sickly season here, and at the very moment when I thought myself lost among strangers I find warm friends. Everything in your expedition turns out for the best, and last of all the great armada, with all the warrants and constables, partners, clerks, Iroquois and guns and Congreve rockets, melts away and disappears, and a little canoe comes dropping in now and then, and one after another of the partners return to Montreal looking very foolish, while all the world are laughing at them. They were to make a *second Moscow* of Fort William, they were to march you down on snowshoes, they were to bring you prisoner with a rope about your neck. In short the gallant things that were to have been done were innumerable, and they have only gained the loss of the Schooner and *'la risée de tout le monde'* this last failure has made a great impression. The Commissioners are on their way back to Quebec the ice having prevented them from embarking on Lake Huron, they have made one foolish step, in arranging an express all North West, to set forth their powers and commissions which supersede yours and all others. It was quite out of Sir John's plans that this should be done before they were on the spot to act themselves, but whether he will interfere now I do not know. I have my doubts if this express is not stopped, whether they may not make use of it to serve their warrants from Sandwich upon you, so be guarded. In my letter by Bourke and still more by Coltman, I expressed a wish for you soon here Stuart and Gale were very anxious on the subject, I now see it myself and have brought them to see it very differently, your obvious policy, as far as we can judge here, if it can be done with safety is to join your strength with D'Orsonnens very early in the spring, you will thus be within the Hudson's Bay boundary and out of the reverence of Sandwich warrants and even Commissioners. Unless you have very strong proofs indeed of the submission and peaceable intentions of the Half Indians, I think you should not advance beyond Lac la Pluie till the Commissioners reach that post, then you would go into Red River in grand state with them. ... Stuart has explained that the sale will not be valid, I earnestly hope you will not remove *any of their goods.* You will of course take all your officers with you who are exposed to the warrant, and only leave a party in Fort William sufficient to protect it from injury. You will learn the tricks of your North West friends in time at present you are but half up to them. Grant is a great personage here, visited by all the North West honourables. ... The enemy has got a bruise but he is not crushed yet, do not lose sight of this truth, for you seem to me to think we are much further on than we really are ... at York they (the Commissioners) examined at no allowance, and sent a large report, but I hear from good authority without cross-examination, mere ex parte statements, this is of little signification now, for Sir John is not to be taken in by one side of a story, be that side which it may. Governor Gore no longer pretends to conceal his North West propensities ... your plan of our joining you this summer is quite 'en l'air'. For Heaven's Sake be less sanguine, you really frighten me, and your 'pleasing visions' were so out of unison with my anxiety and wretchedness at the time that I was quite upset between the two. You must make a point, if it be in anyway practicable, to come back here next fall, we cannot battle through these trials without you. ... I do anxiously wish that you would keep clear of the trade altogether. All the Canadians are fitting out expeditions for the spring, let them reap their harvest in the Indian territory. It will help the fall of the North West and your popularity in Canada will be greater than ever. You must really be satisfied with the Hudson Bay winterers and such Meurons as we can send you. The

finance is most difficult. I have seen Garden today, he is
to write you on his account and the demands that pour
in from all quarters, the amounts will horrify you, but it
is necessary you should know them, and I wish it would
have the effect of making you try to wind up, and refrain
from further outlay, the difficulties at home are dreadful, Mure has not been able to bring forward above half
what you expected, I wish you would now make some
terms for yourself with the Hudson's Bay Company. I
think you might fairly say that you have fought their
battles, and laid their enemy on his back, and that they
must assist in what remains to be done. If you would do
this manfully and threaten to give up the settlement if
they will not, you might bring them to terms. And really
it will be little short of ruin if you go on on your own private funds. I acknowledge I cannot swallow the exchange
of St. Mary's Isle for your kingdom on Red River. Could
you deprive Daer of his title you have a right to prefer
that exchange if you like, but as it is while he lives you
are in duty bound to leave him independent at home,
and you must allow it is not *to him* that the settlement
will begin to pay what has been laid out upon it, whatever
advantage his children may reap from it. This subject
always gives me the blues, because I never can get you
to open your eyes to it, some sanguine calculation is always ready to answer me, but year after year passes, and
we are always deeper and deeper in the mire. The transaction with C [*recte* D] Mackenzie vexed me very much
at first, and does so still. I hope you will give up to
Stuart's opinion on this point. Mackenzie having been
your prisoner is so glaring a fact, that no 'conscious innocence' should have tempted you to brave it, however
it will do good as justifying the detention of the furs. I
am a little provoked at this moment by a letter from
Madame D'Orsonnens, in which she implies that she is
very miserable and that she has much more reason to be
than me, the woman is living in the midst of her family.
... You know I had sent Archy Macdonald by York to
Drummond's Island to give you warning of the Armada....

195

As Lady Selkirk sat writing, the bearer of Coltman's dispatches to Sir John Sherbrooke sped down the St. Lawrence River. His skates rang on the hard ice as he swung along, bent forward, nearing Quebec. In the early hours of New Year's morning he reached the Lower Town and made his way up the hill to the sleeping Château. There, under orders, he hammered on the door with his urgent business and confronted the awakened Governor with the report of Lord Selkirk's resistance to Dr. Mitchell's warrant.

The Selkirk house at St. Mary's Isle, Kirkcudbright.

Thomas Douglas, fifth Earl of Selkirk.
From the portrait believed to be by Raeburn.

Jean, Countess of Selkirk.

Colin Robertson.
Portrait probably by
Gilbert Stewart Newton, 1821.

Portaging between York Fact

Colonists of the Red River poling and tracking York boats.
From a water-colour by Peter Rindisbacher.

Red River. From a water-colour by Peter Rindisbacher.

Miles Macdonell.

Fort William about 1812.
From a painting by Robert Irvine (real name Cruickshank or Crookshank

Two views (above and right) of Fort William in 1816.
Probably by Lord Selkirk.

Lord Selkirk.
Portrait assumed to have been done
during his time in Canada
1815-18; artist unknown.

Archibald McDonald in later life
when Chief Factor of the Hudson's Bay Company.

Fort Douglas in 1817.
From a pencil sketch by Lord Selkirk.

The Red River Settlement in 1817.
From a sketch believed to be by Lord Selkirk.

Indians hunting buffalo.
From a water-colour by Peter Rindisbacher.

Colonists on the Red River. Swiss woman, man,
and children, de Meuron soldier,
Scotch settler, French Canadian.
From a sketch by Peter Rindisbacher.

ishing through the ice at the forks
the Red River in 1821;
artially rebuilt Fort Gibraltar
the background.
rom a water-colour
y Peter Rindisbacher.

A sergeant of the de Meuron Regiment.

Departure of colonists for Red River from York Factory.
From a water-colour by Peter Rindisbacher.

The two Company forts at Pembina.
From a water-colour by Peter Rindisbacher.

The *Prince of Wales* and the *Eddystone*
of the Hudson's Bay Company fleet
meet Captain Parry's arctic expedition in 1821.
From a water-colour by Peter Rindisbacher.

Chapter 8

THE SPRING TIDES

I

Those who are wakened with disturbing news do not easily recover sleep or judgment, and Sherbrooke was not cut out to be the exception. The affidavits of McKenzie and McRobb accompanied by Coltman's rather flustered report confirmed his worst fears. Already in November he had sent to Lord Bathurst a gloomy letter full of worries, about the country around Red River being 'in arms', and the dangers of the Indians (controlled by the half-breeds) being exasperated at the failure of supplies to come from Fort William. This, he said, represented a threat to the whole white population in the Indian Territory and parts of Upper Canada. Out of all this might even come American intervention. It was North West Company propaganda at its most blatant, accepted for lack of knowledge.

Now Coltman advised him that Selkirk had further inflamed the condition and taken the law into his own hands: not only had he refused submission to the King's warrant, but he was said to be preparing to move the goods – which he had obtained under his doubtful transaction with Daniel McKenzie

– from Fort William into the Hudson's Bay Company territories. Coltman added, and seemed to think it reasonable, that the partners of the North West Company expressed the apprehension that they might be obliged to call on the Indians to help prevent such a measure.

Sherbrooke had judged his limitations nicely in saying a year before that he felt quite unable to command military operations or control constitutional problems. He had the authority and the means to prevent the frontier war that was said to threaten by firmness with the North West Company. And he had at least as much time as the Nor'Westers to prevent Lord Selkirk from removing the goods from Fort William, and could accomplish it with no aid from the Indians. But it was all too much for him. This experienced soldier was so ill or so lacking in firmness that he seemed to forget both his responsibility and his training. His report implied no recommendation as to action of which he would have been the best judge; instead he feebly asked to be favoured with 'particular instructions' for his future conduct. He might have added what it was his duty to know, that the half-breeds, far from controlling the Indians (always the whipping-boys for the North West Company), were themselves controlled by the North West Company.

Sherbrooke, moving through the rooms of the Château St. Louis, writing in his dilemma to Lord Bathurst on January 1 and again the next day, was a man to be pitied. He lacked the knowledge to challenge his informants, and the wisdom to wait for calm counsels. He seems to have realized that he was out of his depth – driven beyond his strength and judgment. The man whom Wellington had described as 'the most passionate man I ever knew' – the man who had led the Guards in a glorious victory charge at Talavera and almost thrown success away by not knowing when to turn back – wrestled now in good faith with matters too big for him. His genuine regard for Lady Selkirk, and by proxy for the man he had never met, seemed to impel him at moments of stress to lean over backwards – a doubtful posture in a man of uncertain balance.

Some word of all this stress seems to have reached Lady Selkirk at Montreal. But she could not have known – would not perhaps have believed – that the man who was not to be fooled by mere *ex parte* statements had already fallen into this trap, and within two days of her confident assertion. Perhaps it was as well she did not know, for on Saturday, January 4, her baby was born; it was a girl and therefore Katherine, god-daughter of Lady Sherbrooke. Almost from the first the little girl was pronounced to be remarkably like her mother. But this pleasant piece of news was not to reach her father until April, and it could have been little comfort to Jean Selkirk, weak, worried and desperately alone – in spite of the affectionate Katherine Sherbrooke, and the well-meaning Sir John.

And she had reason to worry. All around her was evidence of varied activity directed towards Fort William or at Lord Selkirk. Operating across the blinding distance and the silence, it was like a grown-up game of pin-the-tail-on-the-donkey. Stuart, acknowledging Selkirk's letters of August, September, and October, was writing to expound the law. He was pleased at the evidence found at Fort William against the Nor'Westers, but in the criminal prosecutions affidavits would not serve – there must be witnesses and oral testimony. Moreover, he was disapproving (much, it appeared, beyond his measured words) of the arrangements with Daniel McKenzie. Maitland, Garden and Auldjo were following up their letters of October on financial problems, which had not been answered (had not, indeed, been received as yet), with further bad news. They realized that the alarming expenses were far outrunning Selkirk's expectations and probably his convenience. In October his account with them had risen to £12,000, for which they had been obliged to draw on Andrew Colvile. Now it was rising again, and stood already at £7,000; some of this was a Hudson's Bay Company obligation but no one was sure just how much. And finally, with difficulty and at great expense, a further party of de Meurons and *voyageurs* was being collected to go to Red River in the spring.

The tangled skein of unhappy events seemed to roll backwards on itself as spring letters, too long delayed by winter, sought to overtake misunderstandings or to correct errors already compounded. No wonder that Selkirk, in April 1817, having to acknowledge mail written between October 12 and January 26, groaned in bewilderment, between happiness and distress: 'What a mass of intelligence ... and how chequered of good and ill.'

Meanwhile he had again exposed himself to censure. Winter still lingered and only lengthening days promised that its grip must shortly loosen. Selkirk had hit on the project of an improved winter road to the interior and attacked it with almost boyish enthusiasm. He was away from Fort William with a work-party on March 8 when the first canoe of the spring arrived with mail; it carried Bourke, who had left Montreal in October – and was therefore late rather than early. The letters he bore from Lady Selkirk had been written only three days later than those that had reached the fort in November. But two days behind him came a North West canoe carrying the letters about which Coltman had written in December: announcements of the appointment of the Commission, a letter from Lieutenant-Governor Gore revoking all other Commissions of the Peace for the Western District as of November 25, and declaring everything west of Sault Ste. Marie to be Indian territory for the purposes of the Commission. Four senior Nor'Westers were in the party, and with them was the deputy sheriff from Sandwich – Smith – come to arrest Lord Selkirk and to restore Fort William to its rightful owners. Smith went briskly through the form of declaring the fort restored, and gave himself airs that left the occupants surly but with confidence shaken. When a carefree Selkirk returned, and while he was arranging for some extra comforts to be drawn on his charge for his work-party, he found himself declared under arrest. Cautiously, he asked to see the warrant, and, finding it dated previous to Gore's letter annulling all powers for the area west of the Falls of St. Mary, he calmly declared it illegal. Smith, momentarily uncertain, attempted to argue, and Selkirk pointed out that it was a great impropriety in him while carrying news of the Commission to attempt to act without its sanction; the balloon was pricked. Smith capitulated and announced he would await the commissioners. The fort breathed again.

But Smith, who was to show an ungovernable temper and a strain of brutality later on, changed his mind after two days. In all probability his North West companions, having listened to his loud talk on the upward trip, found amusement in reminding him of his rash promises. It was too much; Smith in violent terms asserted that his warrant was legal and would be executed at once. He forced his way into Selkirk's room and announced his new decision. Selkirk took him firmly by the arm and turned him out, and when Smith became violent he was placed under an armed guard. The North Westers philosophically started back for the Falls of St. Mary, leaving behind Smith and Campbell, a North West Company half-breed. The unhappy man, who had been pursuing his $800 reward since October and had already suffered shipwreck on the schooner *Invincible*, sat nursing a hatred that was to pursue Selkirk without pause for two more years and finally to yield Smith a measure of vengeance. His companions, to more immediate purpose, carried away the tale of yet another resistance to arrest by Lord Selkirk.

The first resistance to Constable Robinson had already produced results that were grave, perhaps graver than anyone had foreseen or intended. The Colonial Office had in the past preferred to follow a policy of salutary neglect in dealing with the fur trade; its problems had seemed to work themselves out. This was rough justice, but any other policy promised immense trouble and expense for perhaps the same practical result. Now a succession of events forced the reluctant Lord Bathurst to act, probably in a mood of irritation and prejudice. He had already said more than once that he considered Lord Selkirk's Red River Settlement scheme 'wild and unpromising'. His under-secretary, Henry Goulburn, seems to have disliked it for the opposite reason; he was a friend of Simon McGillivray and of Edward Ellice, London agents for the North

West Company. Presumably from them the Colonial Office frequently had news of events at Red River before official dispatches reached them; and they in turn were well informed of Colonial Office views. Moreover, Goulburn had the same confused idea of the Selkirk-Hudson's Bay Company relationship that the North West Company persisted in. Then, in the autumn, had come the news of the Seven Oaks massacre (which might or might not blow over), followed by news of Lord Selkirk's 'sack' of Fort William and the arrest of the North West partners. Now some notice would have to be taken, since the whole judicial machinery of Upper and Lower Canada was the responsibility of the Colonial Office. Sherbrooke's panicky report of November the eleventh was a further goad. Things began to stir.

About February 4 Simon McGillivray and Edward Ellice paid an unlooked-for call on the senior officials of the Hudson's Bay Company at Fenchurch Street. They were received stiffly and made heavy weather over stating their business, which approached a proposal for compounding their differences and a suggestion that Lord Selkirk should be curbed. Governor Berens explained coldly that Lord Selkirk had no official position with the Hudson's Bay Company, nor had they any control of his actions. The North Westers smiled politely and insultingly, voices were raised, and the forms of severe politeness barely survived Ellice and McGillivray's departure.

Berens and Colvile were still speculating over the precise reason for the call when, on the following day, Berens was sent for by Lord Bathurst. Colvile suddenly understood; once again the North Westers had learned what was about to happen in the Colonial Office and had moved to head it off. Bathurst spoke from the first as though Lord Selkirk's and the Hudson's Bay Company's policies and interests were identical. He told Berens that he had ordered sent 'home' for trial in England the men apprehended or accused by Lord Selkirk, and went on to talk of the responsibility Selkirk would incur if he failed to substantiate his charges. He had written to Sir John Sherbrooke, he said, to urge Lord Selkirk to come home to attend the trials. He added that the Hudson's Bay Company should 'order' Selkirk home, and if he refused they should dismiss him altogether. Once again Berens embarked on a patient explanation of the relationship between the company and Selkirk – of the differences in interest – and the history of the settlement.

For just that brief moment it must have seemed the battle was won. The taking of Fort William and the arrest of the partners had secured the sort of attention that the death of more than twenty people could not command. It seemed exactly the result Selkirk had dreamed of.

The pleasing vision was there, and overnight it was gone. The mail from Quebec, arriving within a day or two, changed everything; it contained Sherbrooke's dispatches of January 1 and 2 with the affidavits. Rumour also said that a North West clerk had been sent to England by John Richardson and – presumably through Goulburn – conducted direct to Bathurst.

Selkirk was perhaps at this moment the victim of special circumstances. England, full of demobilized soldiers who had come home to high prices following on poor crops, seethed with hunger and discontent. The ministers believed, as they had believed periodically since the outbreak of the French Revolution, that revolution was imminent. There was probably no time and less patience for the nice calculation of distant problems, stirred up by a member of the House of Lords who should have known better.

However it was brought about, the result can only be seen as in part an explosion of pent-up irritation. Bathurst, too long disturbed by Selkirk's concerns, turned on him in the same mood and with the same carelessness as Henry turned on Becket. Doubtless Selkirk's resistance to arrest – if it was as it appeared to be – represented a grave misdemeanour, especially in a man of his station. But the steps taken against him seemed to treat his action as more serious than the variety of capital crimes with which his opponents were charged. On February 11, Lord Bathurst, finally roused but ill-informed, signed a letter to Sir John Sherbrooke – a letter in which we may assume the hand of Henry Goulburn, of which Bathurst could not fully have foreseen the results, but for the results of which he was nevertheless wholly responsible.

Having advised Sherbrooke that he had further information on the case 'from different quarters', he outlined a form of proclamation to be issued in the name of the Prince Regent requiring the two companies to abstain from acts of hostility and mutually to restore captured property; neither Selkirk nor his settlers were recognized, apart from the inclusive reference to the Hudson's Bay Company. (The Colonial Office had had no fewer than seven communications from Simon McGillivray or his associates since January 1, six of them addressed to Henry Goulburn.)

After regretting the failure of the commissioners to reach Fort William before winter, Bathurst went on:

I am fully sensible of the danger which may in the interim result to the commercial and political interests of Great Britain, from the opening which the conduct of Lord Selkirk appears calculated to give to the admission of foreign influence over the Indian nations, to the exclusion of that heretofore exercised by the subjects of Great Britain; and feel the necessity of putting an end to a system of lawless violence, which has too long prevailed in the Indian territory, and the more distant parts of Upper Canada. By resisting the execution of the warrant issued against him, Lord Selkirk has rendered himself doubly amenable to the laws, and it is necessary, both for the sake of general principle, for the remedy of existing as well as for the prevention of further evils, that the determination of the government to enforce the law with respect to all, and more particularly with respect to Lord Selkirk, should be effectually and speedily evinced. You will therefore, without delay, on the receipt of this instruction take care that an indictment be preferred against his Lordship for the rescue of himself, detailed in the affidavit of Robert McRobb, and upon a true bill being found against him, you will take the necessary and usual measures in such cases for arresting his Lordship, and bringing him before the court from which the process issued. Surrounded as Lord Selkirk appears to be by a Military Force which has once already been employed to defeat the execution of legal process, it is almost impossible to hope that he will quietly submit to the execution of any warrant against himself so long as an opening is left for effectual resistance. It is therefore necessary that the Officer to whom its execution is entrusted should be accompanied by such a Civil (or if the necessities of the case should require it, by such a Military) force as may prevent the possibility of resistance.

It was to be months before this wave of official wrath could roll through the two Canadas and break over Red River. In its passage it would sweep up into its purpose the members of the judiciary and the law officers of the Crown. The views and intentions of the Colonial Office, 'more particularly with respect to Lord Selkirk', were in the result to appear unmistakable.

2

But at Fort William, for the moment, everything promised fair. In the first week of April the inscrutable silence from Red River was broken at last. Nothing had been heard of D'Orsonnens and Miles Macdonell since they had led their men out of Lac la Pluie on October 27; but the long wait was over. A letter from Miles described how, on January 10, on a moonlight night of crackling cold, they had advanced with scaling-ladders against the sleeping Fort Douglas. In the early morning his men had dropped like cats within the stockade to capture a trouserless Archie McLellan and fifteen men. And when the rising sun glanced along the dazzling miles of snow-covered prairie it revealed to freemen, half-breeds, and Indians that on the flagstaff the North West Company pennon had been replaced.

The report from Miles Macdonell came hard on the heels

of great batches of mail from Montreal. In February Selkirk had poured out some of his concern in a letter that could not move eastward for weeks: 'I was very anxious about New Year's Day but now the time is gone by I persuade myself all *must* have gone well.' And so, the mail now told him, it had. He was able to picture his wife on New Year's Eve sitting at her desk showing him some of her anxieties – the nagging worries of years; and showing him, if he had ever doubted it, the courage and loyalty and skill with which she fought his battles.

It would not, he believed, be needed much longer; the eternal optimism of which she complained would certainly not down at such a moment. All was well in Montreal; the colony was on the way to being restored and his own next move, which had until now remained in doubt, was clear. Knowledge that commissioners were on the way completed his satisfaction. He knew he had something to answer for but he had no sense of serious guilt to weigh against the established crimes of his adversaries. Both to his own people and to Hudson's Bay officers he recommended complete co-operation in the work of the Commission. 'The benefits to be expected from this interference of Government', he wrote to Miles Macdonell, 'are so great that nothing ought to be wanting on our part to give effect to acts of the Commissioners.'

The Commission seemed merely to hasten what he had looked on as already assured. Months before, writing to Lord Melville, he had spoken of contending against 'a set of men "whose tongues are a thousand, whose hearts are one" and who at the same time are as great adepts as Bonaparte himself at misrepresentation'. He implied that he did not expect to be hastily condemned by those who knew him on the word of such men, whose conduct would shortly come before the courts, 'and a scene of wickedness will then be developed which will excite astonishment'.

To an intending settler, alarmed by rumours of lawlessness in the Indian Territory, he had written: 'The measures which I have taken for bringing to Justice the authors of these troubles afford a fair prospect that it will soon be as tranquil as any other part of North America.'

Well might a worried wife, watching events from Montreal, write: 'For Heaven's Sake be less sanguine.'

But if he was over-sanguine he was not heedless of what he had to answer for. A crisp note from Sherbrooke dealing with his oft-repeated plea for troops to maintain law in the North-west dashed that hope once again. 'It will not be in my power to comply with your Lordship's wishes in this matter.' The note of coolness was unmistakable.

Answering the April batch of letters, he met the warmth and frankness and sweet concern that sprang from every sentence of the Hogmanay letter. For the moment he faced events squarely and with humility.

The consequences so naturally arising from my wretched-ly ill-judged conduct in September, give room for bitter enough reflections, but on the other hand I have the cordial of knowing that my own love is safe and well, about which I have had many an anxious fit since New Year's Day. . . . I hope the letter I sent for Sherbrooke may have been of some use in apologizing for the measures I have so much reason to regret. Though it was but an impudent avowal, I think it was better to take the responsibility frankly on myself than to attempt to evade it and hope that my letter would at least show that my error was rather an exception than a specimen of my general conduct . . . though the Sherbrookes may still remain partial to you, I cannot doubt that I must have sunk in their esteem. . . . I enclose a fragment of a letter for Daer, I had a great deal more to tell him about snow-shoe expeditions and encamping in the woods in the middle of winter, which I find on trial to be a much less formidable undertaking than I had imagined. I must however have my mind more at ease before I can go on with a performance of that kind. This fragment may serve as a remembrance. Kiss the dear babes for me, and the little stranger I have never seen. The name is delightful.

For a few days the rich harvest of letters must serve, must be searched for everything imagined and longed for. And in the answers written at intervals as he prepared to turn his back on Fort William – to widen further the gap between him and peace and love and absolute support – he tried to catch up every loose end. There were letters from the children to answer and he asked their mother to tell them he was glad they could write so well. It called up scenes of home, of Jean bending over the small heads, the serious faces, encouraging, chiding gently; a mere glimpse across the gap.

He had to challenge her on her plea that he should not meddle in the fur trade. 'It is a business that I hate from the bottom of my heart.' Perhaps he did not really know the truth of that even as he wrote. But what he would not have denied, at least not to her, was that he was now ready for anything within the law, and a bit beyond, that would rout the North West Company; and this was hardly to be accomplished without involvement in the fur trade.

There was a growing excitement throughout the fort as departure approached. Under Stuart's and Lady Selkirk's stern admonition, they were taking only essential supplies and their own trade goods. These now began to move up the steep portage trail. Nine or ten miles above Fort William, on a point formed where the Slate River flowed into the Kaministiquia, Selkirk's men had built Point de Meuron, an outpost in enemy territory and now a staging-camp. A few miles farther on, the river plunged towards them over a 100-foot cliff, in the Kakabeka Falls, and rebounded in a great plume of spray from which drifted a perpetual rainbow. The Kaministiquia swept on, gathering the waters of the Slate and swinging around Point de Meuron. Where it came from they must go, and now they were eager. They were shedding Fort William and the long winter. Behind them, John McNab and John Spencer, with a few men, waited to guard the fort against marauders and to hand it over to the commissioners. They held the keys, the inventory of North West goods and furs and a careful accounting of whatever had been made use of. They also had a long memorandum for delivery to Colonel Coltman. On May 1, exulting in a rude health such as he had not known for a long time, Lord Selkirk took a last look at the ice that still clogged Thunder Bay, wrote a final line to his wife, and faced towards Red River. The *voyageurs* lifted their paddles, the scarlet blades dug deep into the swift water, and the canoes moved out into the current.

3

The approach to the Kingdom of Red River challenged both cunning and strength. It was a maze of lakes with a tangle of streams and connecting portage trails. The trails established by Indians in the dawn of history and rediscovered by the explorers and fur-traders centuries later were the best routes to circumvent dangerous water, or the shortest passage from one body of water to another. They might be a few yards long or more than a mile, but they represented the tested experience of endless travellers in an otherwise unmanageable wilderness, cut and scored out by the great Ice Age. The canoes drove on across silent lakes, where deer and moose lifted startled heads in the deep bays, or slipped into the quiet corridors of rivers running between red granite walls as kingfishers flashed and dived and sandpipers minced along the water's edge. After long days on the water, fires were built on the shore of some island above a beach on which the canoes rested. The flames flickered and hissed under fresh trout or venison or moose-steaks and flung shadows against the encircling trees. When the cooking was done, green cedar-boughs were tossed on the fires; the smudge of sweet, white smoke drove back briefly the clouds of hungry mosquitoes, and the weary travellers sought sleep before their return. On still nights the unimaginable silence was broken only by the splash of a leaping fish or the wild, echoing laughter of the loons.

Day by day the splendid country flaunted its challenge to the advancing party. It was a challenge that could be met directly, with courage and skill and endurance, for it hid no secret menaces. Though the waters could narrow suddenly into swift and dangerous rapids, they were still clean and invigorating. It was tough and exhausting work but had it been the summit of Lord Selkirk's problems all would have been well. Steadily the swinging paddles and the songs of the *voyageurs* cut down the distance. Once over the height of land, though they were still a long hard journey from Red River, things went better. By fur-trade tradition the act of crossing the watershed conferred a distinction: they became men of the north, men of the Upper Country. The waters flowing towards distant Hudson Bay were helping them forward as they at last shipped their paddles beside the landing-stage at Lac la Pluie.

Here, as they rested, checking gear and repairing damage to the canoes, mail overtook them. The weight of the conflict which had been shed a little in the past three weeks settled down again. While others strolled beside Rainy Lake, or fished, Lord Selkirk drafted and rewrote, checked records, and gave careful directions to Michael McDonell for the handing over of the post to the commissioners, and to no one else. He was everywhere at once and taking thought for everything. The tall, spare figure seemed tireless, driven by mysterious sources of energy. Did it occur to any of them to speculate how differently things might have turned out had they reached this far forward by this date the year before? Selkirk might then indeed have entered into his kingdom without a struggle. He entered it now under quite different conditions, almost under sanctions.

The mail that had overtaken them here and at Arrow Lake was not reassuring. Lady Selkirk's letters contained more than a hint of North West successes in Quebec and in London. And a letter from a Lake Huron captain, Robert Livingstone, which apparently reached Selkirk here, contained the first suggestion that the Commission might not be quite the august instrument it appeared. Livingstone had talked with the commissioners in January about transporting them to Sault Ste. Marie. In writing of this he added that the two gentlemen 'did not hesitate to declare their prepossession in favour of the North West Company course and announced their approbation of the independent Spirit (as they termed it) of the *Broulets*.' Was this really the view of Coltman, to whom Selkirk had written just a month before? 'Nothing could have given me greater pleasure than the intelligence of your appointment ... the just sense which you entertain of the importance of your mission and your determination to spare no labour in the investigations which it is necessary to make. ... I have too much confidence in the equity of your mind to suppose that you will prejudge the question.'

This was the spirit in which he had directed his own and Hudson's Bay Company people to give the fullest possible assistance to the commissioners; even questions of Hudson's Bay Company jurisdiction were to be waived. He believed – or he had believed – that there was everything to be gained from a full and objective investigation. But now – how objective was it going to be? Did the commissioners seek the truth or only a solution? How could there really be a difference?

A letter from Sir John Sherbrooke, in acknowledging letters written by Selkirk in November, referred to the transactions with Daniel McKenzie as 'what may be called the weaker parts of your case',

> ... your Lordship has no doubt been fully apprized of the conduct of Mr. McKenzie on his arrival at Drummond's Island. This circumstance will have induced your Lordship to have changed the opinion you appear to have entertained of that Person at the time you wrote.

He had not needed this reminder of how the McKenzie episode appeared to others, and the pleasant references to Lady Selkirk with which the letter closed did not conceal its irony and a warning note which, if not hostile, was less than reassuring.

But if ever there had been profit in crying over the milk he had spilled at Fort William there was none now. The bitter reflections on his 'wretchedly ill-judged conduct' had been confessed and put in their place; they must not be allowed to rock his judgment or weaken his effort again. What he had done he would answer for if his enemies would do the same; meanwhile, hope and opportunity led north-west to Red River. The place he had seen a thousand times in his dreams, had heard men describe – the great flat plain of his land stretching to the horizon and far beyond in all directions, with perhaps a herd of countless buffalo browsing as it drifted across the broad prairie – it was there his enemies could be answered, his lapses made good. For the answer lay in proving that the colony was no wild and unpromising scheme, in turning evicted and wretched cottars into contented settlers and the wilderness into prosperous farms.

The splendour of the country grew as the canoes made a quick run down Rainy River and the green and blue wonderland of Lake of the Woods opened before them. It was beauty to make the most insensitive catch his breath, but the brigade drove steadily on through the maze of islands, past rocky shores and sandy beaches; they pushed off before dawn to a chorus of bird-song and a gay restlessness of flashing wings among the evergreens; and they slept as the night-hawk went booming out on his evening hunt and the mysterious whip-poor-will slipped invisible among the trees, calling like a lost soul through the short night.

With the lake thrust behind them, they faced the Winnipeg River, last and sternest of tests. Here in the swift river they dare not miss the portage paths, for the canoe that was not lifted out soon enough might be swept out of control and on to deadly rocks in a moment. It was all in the day's work for the *voyageurs*, who flung themselves down at the end of it, often in wet clothes, and slept without moving until the cry of the steersmen woke them before dawn.

There was a brief pause at Fort Bas de la Rivière Winnipeg (Fort Alexander) – the North West post now manned by Selkirk's people. The brigade swept out into Lake Winnipeg on June 20, a day's journey from Red River and Fort Douglas. They had won through without mishap and, they believed, well ahead of any hostile party that might be following. But they were mistaken. As they paddled south along the shore of the lake and towards the river's mouth, a light canoe appeared far astern and came on at a racing clip. As the canoe came leaping after them with the reckless energy that had carried men first across the continent, the watchers must have known it was a North West express; it could be no other.

The canoe bore Angus Shaw, a partner of the North West Company, and Under-sheriff Smith of Sandwich, but lately left in custody at Fort William. As Shaw's canoe drew alongside Lord Selkirk's, he handed over a copy of a proclamation from the Prince Regent, dated at Quebec, May 3. As the two canoes drifted together in silence, his Lordship read the paper spread out before him. We may guess at the deepening line of disapproval and the disciplined hardening of the lips as he read the preamble:

> ... whereas divers breaches of the peace, and acts of force and violence, have lately been committed within the said Indian Territories ... from contention between certain merchants ... under the names of the Hudson's Bay Company and North West Company, respectively, and other persons, their servants, agents or adherents, of whom some have entered into and seized, and occupied by force, and with strong hand, lands, goods, wares, merchandize and other property ... others have met together in unlawful assemblies ... committed murders, riots, routs and affrays, and appeared, gone and ridden in companies in military array, with armed force and have rescued themselves and others from lawful arrest and custody.
>
> We do, therefore, in the name and on behalf of His Majesty ... calling upon the said merchants ... their servants, agents or adherents ... to desist from every hostile aggression or attack whatsoever.

Jean, reading the proclamation in Montreal, had cried out bitterly in a letter to Andrew, 'And this is Lord Bathurst's Justice.' Though Selkirk was to protest later against the injustice of treating all the troubles as a quarrel between traders and weighing his alleged misdemeanours in the same scale as murder and arson, he would not argue the case with men like Angus Shaw and the malevolent Smith. There was only dignity to be salvaged from this encounter. Almost too readily he agreed to restore Fort Bas de la Rivière, without even first removing Hudson's Bay Company furs.

As Shaw's canoe dropped astern, the brigade moved on towards the mouth of the river. It was a moment Selkirk had waited for since 1812 – the completion of a journey begun a year before – and it seemed now that nothing would be as it had been planned. But still, as they drove through the narrow channels between marshes thronging with every kind of waterbird, he must have been filled with hope and excitement and pleasure. It was Red River at last, and just above their heads, over the lip of the bank, stretched the endless prairie. Before them lay Fort Douglas. And when they came abreast of the settlement and the canoes turned towards shore the guns of the fort gave them a salute like thunder. As Selkirk came ashore he was halted by the sheer eagerness of those gathered to welcome him. Among the excited, thrusting crowd were a number of Indian chiefs who flung aside all reserve and sought to touch his hand, calling him their 'Father'. He had waited for this moment for five years, but so had they.

Chapter 9

SUMMER AT RED RIVER

I

The long struggle had left Red River a good deal less than fit for a king; yet it was a goodly kingdom Selkirk had entered, and by entering restored. The buildings so bravely begun five years before were all gone and in their place as yet stood only a mean collection of hastily built cabins. The fort was none too strong and none too clean, and the Governor's House – pinnacle of the settlement – contained only two rooms that were finished inside. 'It appears rather, Mr. Attorney, to have been habitations, than a settlement,' Chief Justice Powell was to say later from the bench at York; and those who might have explained chose not to, and those whose duty it was were not sufficiently informed.

But the kingdom was in the great plain that ran out into the unbroken distance in all directions. Assiniboia, land of unbelievable goodness as the crops proved, lay in a vast circle around Selkirk and far beyond sight. Near at hand, the colony fields were showing crops that would repay fiftyfold the hardy men who had crossed almost 200 miles of the ice of Lake Winnipeg to put them in, as soon as it was known that Fort

Douglas had been retaken and Lord Selkirk would soon be there. Thanks to them it was difficult to believe that the colony could ever have been hungry or would ever be hungry again. Peas, potatoes, pumpkins, wheat, Indian corn, and barley were springing from the ground under a relentless glory of sun such as had never been seen in Galloway. Similar fine crops at Fort Alexander had been handed over to the North West Company.

The colony still lacked people and it lacked livestock. But the people would soon be there. Near Norway House some 150 of them, who a year before had sworn never again to return to Red River, were chafing with impatience. The livestock problem would take longer since only the original bull and cow, Adam and Eve, had survived the half-breed thefts and killings of two years before. The costly Merino sheep and breeding-cattle and sixty horses were all gone. In their place a few horses had been purchased already. There were also a precious cow and an ox expropriated from the North West fort at Lac la Pluie, and famous for having broken trail through the blizzard in which D'Orsonnens' party had fought its way north from Pembina to recapture Fort Douglas. These were farmer Laidlaw's pets; he had got them over the winter with difficulty, fed them through the spring on wild potatoes which he dug for them, and their survival was his triumph.

This was the colony, this primitive shoot that might one day grow into a city. And, if Selkirk's problem consisted only in watching over and guiding its growth, life would be simple and success assured; but a host of questions pressed in on all sides. He had to quench the Indian title to the lands or come to some satisfactory arrangement; this promised no great difficulty. In spite of all the dire predictions, the Indians had always welcomed the settlement and old Peguis, chief of the Sauteaux, was still its champion. He had to face the commissioners and somehow help them to see – make them see – the truth of what had gone on; this would be more difficult, and already he was learning how widespread and cunning were the efforts to hide or distort the truth. And beyond the commissioners lay the government in England, the courts in Canada, and the public of both countries who would make their own estimate if not given a satisfactory accounting. If the truth would serve, he saw no reason to be apprehensive, but what frustrated almost to madness was the web of lies, of misrepresentation, put forward under such distinguished auspices that doubt could be treated as grave discourtesy.

Meanwhile he waited eagerly for the commissioners, for in spite of any hints he could not doubt that he would have vindication at their hands. He was armoured by a passionate certainty of wrong neither intended nor done. Any misdemeanours on behalf of his settlers he would answer for. Meanwhile he guarded a mass of incriminating documents carried away from Fort William. They formed an unbroken chain dating from Simon McGillivray's first letter written in 1812 about Lord Selkirk's colony: 'he must be driven to abandon it, for its existence would strike at the very roots of our trade.' 'We . . . are anxious for the arrival of the Commissioners,' Selkirk wrote to his wife. 'We have a noble mass of evidence to greet them with. Lord Bathurst shall have my accusations substantiated to his heart's content.' This seemed to him then and later the simple truth. Meanwhile an explosive situation had to be contained until the commissioners' arrival.

A few miles away across the prairie Angus Shaw, North West partner, camped among the assembled half-breeds, one of whose leaders was his own son William. John Allan, riding over on the day after arrival, had studied the mixture of resentment and fear that pervaded the camp, each man's gun lay handy and horses stood ready saddled. They had been told that commissioners were coming out – appointed at the request of the North West Company – and that if all went well in their investigations the colony would finally be swept away. The effect of this story spread among half-breeds, Indians, and freemen was twofold: if the Nor'Westers were once again to be the only power in the land, no wise man would dare to testify against them; if the commissioners were virtually the tools of the North West Company, careful answers to questions could avoid punishment for the past.

On the other hand, Selkirk's evil genius, William Smith, the under-sheriff, had been seeking to succeed at Red River with the warrant that had failed at Fort William. If the warrant had been illegal at Fort William it was meaningless here; but if it could give colour as a pretext for arrest, Selkirk would not be available when the commissioners arrived and that end would justify any means. Smith had shown himself an undisguised North West partisan from the first. He had led them in cutting a way into the fort at Lac la Pluie, a practical exercise in restitution. At Bas de la Rivière he had seized Hudson's Bay Company furs and impounded them even as the North West furs at Fort Douglas were being given up. Back of him now stood the men of the North West Company, and the half-breeds, spoiling for a fight. The de Meurons for their part were not less eager.

That Selkirk could be arrested on his own ground was a ludicrous possibility, but it would only have to work once and most of what he had been contending for would be lost. It was an old trick and a dirty trick but it had served before. Spencer's arrest on a bogus charge in 1814 had begun the colony's rot. Miles Macdonell's surrender to arrest on a promise of safety for the colony had cleared the way for its destruction in 1815. Selkirk must not be taken. Smith, breathing violence and rashness, made the mistake of coming within reach of Miles Macdonell. Miles's reasoning was simple and unanswerable: no warrant from the Western District of Upper Canada had any meaning here. Either the commissioners' writ ran here, or that of the governor of Assiniboia. The ridiculous and dangerous William Smith was arrested for the second time as a disturber of the peace and detained pending the arrival of the commissioners.

Selkirk wrote a full account of this and of his apprehensions lest the commissioners be detained, on June 28, and sent it off by express canoe. He begged them not to allow the encumbrance of any military retinue to delay them. What was needed, and quickly, was the prestige of their arrival in person – 'your own presence, with the authority which you hold will be sufficient for every purpose of Justice ... if it be necessary to resort to force in the meantime there will be no want of men to execute your orders'.

Now there seemed little to do but remain on guard. Selkirk himself could go nowhere unless surrounded by a file of soldiers of the 37th supplemented by the de Meurons. It was not left to him but insisted on by Matthey and D'Orsonnens and by Miles Macdonell. If anything happened to Selkirk, there remained no one of sufficient weight to argue the colony's case before the commissioners against the formidable pressures to which they would certainly be subjected. If Angus Shaw was a fair sample, they were right. The long account he had sent to Halifax of the Seven Oaks affair, of how Governor Semple had had to build a fort because of the quarrels between the colony and the Indians, was the document either of an irretrievably stupid man or of one who would stop at no twisting of the truth to accomplish his ends; either way, this minor cog, this skirmisher in the North West phalanx, was an index of danger.

Into the period of uneasy waiting swept the advancing wave of Colonial Office wrath. Whatever casualness was in it could not be detected after an interval of four months and at a distance of 5,000 miles. Moreover, the advance warnings had not been recognized. The Prince Regent's proclamation was one – and Selkirk had been shocked at the view of affairs it seemed to suggest – but the arrival of the commissioners would surely make clear the true state of things, the persecution and murder of confused and helpless people. A few days previously D'Arcy Boulton, Attorney General of Upper Canada, had written James Woods of Sandwich, 'The fact is I am under orders to prosecute criminally his Lordship, on his return' – but this his Lordship could not know for months.

So the canoe that arrived from Montreal on June 30 was greeted with joy in which there was no apprehension. Letters from home, manna in the wilderness. There was a letter from his wife which opened like any comfortable, heart-warming budget of home news: 'Dearest Love ... last week was hot, this week is hotter still', but then at once it moved into menacing intelligence. It described the sending of a clerk by John Richardson to the Colonial Office

> ... who went with his story to Lord Bathurst, and found a ready ear from Mr. Goulbourn who to all appearances desires no better than to find something to lay hold of against you. This clerk has returned as quick as possible with the Government bag and the most peremptory instructions to Sherbrooke. ... Be the most dutiful obedient subject to the laws however unjust, but be sure to give all the stage effect possible to the submission. ... It was not until I was shutting the desk and going to bed that it came upon me like a flash of lightning that our whole success depends now on your playing off properly these nefarious warrants. ... If you come to Sandwich and there is time I will meet you there. ... Never mind Lord Bathurst and Mr. Goulbourn ... but think how deep is the interest of all that are attached to you ... oh that I were with you to help. I could be a thousand different things in a minute. ... God bless and support your health. O.O.L.

He had not long to wait tor its meaning. If the enclosed letter from Sir John Sherbrooke was not perfectly explicit, its general drift was clear enough, and threatening beyond anything he could account for:

> My Lord,
>   His Majesty's Government having thought proper on the representations laid before them of the general measures pursued by your Lordship, and particularly of your resistance to the execution of legal process – to convey to me instructions to adopt certain measures in support of due execution of the laws – I think myself bound in fairness and candour – as these measures will seriously affect your Lordship, – to apprize you of my determination to carry my orders strictly and fully into effect however painful that duty may be.

The next paragraph implied that the proclamation would make the position clearer and the letter went on to declare the authority of the special commissioners throughout the Hudson's Bay territory as well as in Upper Canada. A postcript crisply directed the handing over of his bodyguard to the commissioners.

What could it mean – in effect? He accepted without fully understanding it that his resistance to Robinson's warrant was the main offence. But nobody had heard his side of that story; even the sketchy account in his letters to Sherbrooke and Gore had not arrived in time to be given any weight.

Believing that Samuel Gale was approaching, and travelling with the commissioners, he wrote him at length, permitting some of the apprehension which Sherbrooke's letter had caused to show through the surface of his calm. He proposed further assurances to the commissioners of his complete submission 'whatever may be the measures which are more particularly to effect myself'.

Then he stated the creed that was to become the rallying cry of his supporters for the remainder of the struggle and until it seemed to have proved a delusion: 'Truth must prevail in the end, and in the confidence that justice will ultimately be done to me, I put little importance on any wound which may be aimed at my personal feelings.'

He worried chiefly about two points. Somehow the commissioners must understand the efforts being made and that would be made to suppress the truth. In view of those efforts and especially the North West pretence that the Commission was its creature, Coltman's first acts on arrival would be watched with great interest and might be decisive in confirming or changing that impression.

With the letter dispatched, there was nothing to do but wait. The colony had only one real worry – the bountiful crops desperately needed rain. The day after his letter was forwarded came the blessed rain; the springing up of the crops demonstrated once again the goodness of the soil. And simultaneously came news that Coltman's party along with some

Nor'Westers led by Simon McGillivray were in the river, would arrive directly. They must have a fitting reception. This was, after all, the King's Commission and Selkirk a Representative Peer of Scotland. Within the fort the guard was drawn up and the guns loaded. It was of no consequence that two of the guns had been retaken from the North West Company and that Selkirk had refused to restore them. He had promised the commissioners that the guns would be yielded to them at once.

On came the flotilla, while the officers at the fort on the river-bank gave their commands in low, crisp voices. The gunners' matches glowed near the touchholes. Coltman's canoe was close now and the first guns in a seven-gun salute crashed out their welcome in flame and smoke. As the movements of the gun drill proceeded and the guns spoke again, everyone in Fort Douglas watched the canoes and the stout man who sat uncomfortably there, a reluctant *voyageur*. And then, in a moment, without a sign, the canoes had swept past; there was only their wake and the rising and falling of diminishing paddles. Coltman, without acknowledging the salute, had gone on to dine with the North West partners. By evening the whole of Assiniboia would know, and draw their own conclusions.

2

The commissioner had not been the first to leave Montreal in the spring. Before him had gone a strong North West brigade led by William McGillivray in person and accompanied by most of the partners who had been arrested the year before. The town was full of rumours of what they intended, but above all they would have Fort William back on any conditions; watching these men who had smouldered all winter to little purpose, no one could doubt it. If it had not been for the imminent departure of the special commissioners, Montreal would have trembled for what must follow.

Already there were rumours about the return of forts, about mutual restitution all round. To Selkirk's friends – above all to his wife – this seemed monstrous. They had felt so sure that, on the record they had exposed, Fort William at least would never again be allowed to operate without controls; this would be required by any government, for the sake of its own honour. They saw and expected others to see Fort William as a rendezvous of murderers and the receptacle of their plunder and could not understand how anyone could view it otherwise. The persisting government notion that they were merely one party in a trade war remained incomprehensible. 'It is really cruel to think that after all, Lord Selkirk may be foiled and return mortified, disappointed and humbled. After having struggled so hard for him, I cannot bear to think of it.' So Jean Selkirk wrote in bitterness to her brother Andrew at the end of April, and added a final frustrated cry: 'I fear the Colonial Office is even more the scene of North West influence than the Council here. Who could have believed that the mere scum of Scotland could have attained to this.'

McGillivray was to be followed by two parties. Coltman's included Samuel Gale as legal observer for Selkirk and for the Hudson's Bay Company and Henry McKenzie, a North West partner. In all but the technical sense, it also included the stout Major Fletcher, splendid in scarlet; but he being a slow traveller had always a head start with the hope of arriving about the same time. Close behind them was to come Archie McDonald's brigade of de Meurons and some *voyageurs*, to reinforce the colony in every sense.

As departure time arrived, Coltman was bothered by persistent North West reports that the de Meurons intended to make trouble. He gathered them together at Lachine and solemnly read the Prince Regent's proclamation which they heard in courteous silence. When he finished, they gave three cheers for Lord Selkirk. And as this seemed to be the extent of their trouble-making the voyages began auspiciously enough.

At the bow of Gale's canoe flew a little pennant bearing the arms from the Selkirk seal and the proud motto, 'Jamais arrière'. Once the notion had seized him he had set his youthful heart on this, and Lady Selkirk with affectionate amusement had caused it to be made.

In the early stages there was nothing to impede progress, no examinations to be made, no troops to command; all went well and swiftly until Sault Ste. Marie. Here a detachment of the 37th Regiment joined them and Major Fletcher seized on it eagerly; it was to him the special privilege of a special commissioner. Several times a day the fat and sweating major, accoutred with sword and pistols, drilled his little command in full marching order under a broiling sun; he even staged one special parade for some of the ladies of the Falls. Parades were preceded and followed by liberal libations of shrub, which maintained the major's military ardour at a burning intensity, and by meals at North West House. Coltman also took his breakfast with the partners, but left the military exercises to his colleague. He did not have to expunge the uncomfortable memory of Ensign Fletcher, who in the recent American war had gained a certain notoriety for an engagement recorded in no history books. Fletcher and his soldier-clerk in Quebec had spent a comfortable day drinking Jamaica toddy. Late at night, as might have been predicted, one of them sighted the enemy attacking the Lower Town and they had wakened and alarmed the peaceful neighbourhood by firing for some time into the darkness the while they encouraged each other with heartening cries. Perhaps the humiliating memory had dictated the switch from Jamaica to shrub.

Samuel Gale, watching this performance with both amusement and horror, turned to Coltman as his only hope. Too much hung on the views and the verdict of these two men, and plainly Coltman would have to withstand not only North West pressure and blandishments but Fletcher as well. What Gale saw did not encourage him much. Coltman was not a fool and probably not a knave, but it was clear that he did not approach his task entirely without prejudice. Major Fletcher had announced at one point that Lord Selkirk was surrounded by a damned bad set, all following the 'Selkirkonian system';

224

if they couldn't get what they wanted by law they had immediate recourse to arms. When one of the officers asked Coltman whether Selkirk had not produced impressive evidence against the North West Company, the latter answered contemptuously that as to that he had sent a great number of reasons for what he had done already – 'as many as would make a pudding for Christmas'. Plainly, he was determined to give no weight to such stuff. Moreover, he made no secret of his own disbelief in the validity of the Hudson's Bay Company charter. The whole case for the colony was grounded on the charter, which, it appeared, the Commission proposed to set aside in the face of the best legal opinion in England.

Nevertheless, Coltman was getting on with his work while the ridiculous but dangerous Fletcher played at soldiers and published Orders of the Day for his fourteen-man squad. With a very short pause at Sault Ste. Marie, Coltman was ready to go on, travelling with Henry McKenzie. Gale was inclined to go too, but decided to wait; he was finding the trip a strain and, besides, he wanted to be sure Fletcher also was leaving. He was not, and it appeared that his purpose in lingering was to delay, if not to stop altogether, Archie McDonald's brigade. He may have believed, as he asserted, that the de Meurons were a military force and a threat to peace in the Upper Country, a defiance of the proclamation. But Gale watched helplessly while their effects were searched (they were unarmed but their trading guns were impounded) and Archie McDonald arrested for daring to protest. All this was accomplished by the major's troops who operated at all hours with loaded weapons and fixed bayonets. The de Meurons bore it with admirable patience, and Gale, between written protests, watched in uneasy silence, knowing that one ungoverned temper would provoke a bloody riot.

While this farce was being played out, a further detachment of forty soldiers arrived to supplement the commissioners' guard. Captain Bruce, in charge of them, seemed not to like his task. Within a day or two he and Fletcher collided sharply over who was to give actual orders to the troops; Bruce insisted that he must do so. The major was outraged; his reading aloud of the Prince Regent's proclamation and his frequent assertion of the importance of his office appeared to have been quite misunderstood. 'Sir,' he shouted, 'I have forts to storm.' The soldiers listened in silence; the commissioner, after all, was drunk and inclined to be violent.

Gale was by now too involved to go on without Fletcher or without doing what could be done to help McDonald's brigade forward. A few days after Coltman left, Spencer and McNab arrived from Fort William, under arrest and in the custody of a North West *voyageur*. They had passed Coltman in Lake Superior and appealed to him to bail them; they were doubtful of the validity of the warrant under which they had been arrested and, remembering Keveny, more than doubtful of their jailer. From them Gale learned of the taking back of Fort William by McGillivray's brigade. McNab, on Selkirk's orders, had at first refused to give up the keys, saying that he was charged to hand over the fort only to the commissioners. McGillivray had made it clear that he would have the keys, and at once, by force if necessary. McNab had then given up the keys and he and Spencer had been placed in arrest by Under-sheriff Smith on the warrant already declared illegal by Selkirk. Smith had tacked up a notice of a reward for the arrest of Selkirk and Matthey, and left for Red River with Angus Shaw.

Gale listened with growing perplexity, and watched with amusement Major Fletcher's determined refusal to meet these adherents of the 'Selkirkonian system'. A few days later McDonald was released and his brigade allowed to proceed. This move appeared to be as pointless as the original stopping but was far more welcome. Gale went forward hoping grimly that their troubles were at an end.

At Fort William, Major Fletcher quickly established himself in the style he obviously enjoyed. His intention seemed to be to take statements, but, since at Fort William there were now only North West adherents, the process did not seem to Gale promising for the work of a commissioner of inquiry. The uneasy feeling persisted that genuine inquiry was not the Commission's object. Describing these events in a letter to Lady Selkirk, he threw out a guess that was shrewder than he knew. He had not yet received Selkirk's letter about the menacing communication from Sherbrooke, and yet he wrote:

> Does it not seem probable that orders have been received from England for something like a hunt against the Earl of Selkirk through the influence of the *under* friends of the North Westers at home. – But other hunts such as that of the Colony and of Keveny will open the eyes of the public in Britain – and in Parliament at least where alone everything must finally be settled it may be hoped that all which has happened will be productive of good.

He wrote on the evening of Coltman's arrival at Red River, and though he couldn't have known it he did realize that he was far behind. Observing a two-man Commission was proving a trial which in other circumstances he might even have enjoyed. Four days later he was still pinned down above Fort William, waiting to make sure Fletcher would impose no more delays on the de Meurons.

Archie McDonald went down to Fort William in search of a final clearance. He found Major Fletcher in his tent, guarded by a sentry with bayonet fixed. The major, squinting owlishly from behind a table covered with glasses, the Prince Regent's proclamation, and decanters of brandy, shrub, and spirits, was describing the high and unprecedented powers conferred on him. They were superior to those of a German prince, he said, who could hang, draw, and quarter upon his own estate. Carried away by such splendour, he told young McDonald he could cause him to be hanged within an hour on a gallows eight feet high. Archie, startled and not sure that he had heard correctly, asked the major to repeat himself, whereupon he was charged with impudence and impertinence and arrested. As he was led away, the voice of the special commissioner could be heard repeating his gallows threat and talking of irons and flogging. In the morning Archie was released. The commis-

227

sioner had tried to write out a warrant but couldn't quite manage it; his reach had exceeded his grasp. The de Meuron brigade departed unhindered for Red River, and Gale followed.

'If it were not for a little personal ill health and vexation,' he wrote, 'and the serious injury done to the interests of those for whom I have come hither, this would be the most curious and ridiculous journey that ever was performed by mortal.'

3

The state of near-war between Selkirk and the North West Company, though widely known by rumour, had yet retained a measure of privacy. Now, raging out of control, it became public, and both sides appealed for understanding and support. During the autumn of 1816 the papers that Selkirk sent down from Fort William – including, it appears, some affidavits which he had taken purely in his capacity as magistrate – were copied and passed on to John Halkett in London. He had used them in arguing Selkirk's need of support with the Colonial Office. In January he went further, and, apparently without consulting Selkirk, assembled them in a small volume for private circulation. This he called *Statement Respecting the Earl of Selkirk's Settlement upon the Red River in North America; its destruction in the years 1815 and 1816; and the massacre of Governor Semple and his party*. It was a persuasive statement of Selkirk's aims and of all that his people had endured at the hands of the North West Company in the latter's infatuated determination to prevent the success of the colony. But it was open to attack on certain points. It was less than candid about the pemmican controversy and it skated over the more provocative acts of the colonists.

The answer prepared by way of North West counter-attack was not all designed for private circulation but admirably conceived for public damage. They had in their employ a hack writer, Samuel Hull Wilcocke, with a fine gift of invective and otherwise equipped for their purpose. He now wrote *A Narrative of Occurrences in the Indian Countries of North America, since the connexion of the Right Hon. the Earl of Selkirk with the Hudson's Bay Company, and his attempt to establish a colony on the Red River; with a detailed account of his Lordship's military expedition to, and subsequent proceedings at Fort William in Upper Canada* – and he wrote it with evident gusto. It was printed in the spring of 1817, though without any author's name, and began at once to find its way to influential people.

Halkett now arranged with John Murray for publication of his *Statement Respecting the Earl of Selkirk's Settlement.* To the first edition he added 'Observations upon a recent publication entitled a Narrative of Occurences in the Indian Countries etc.' The public battle was now well joined and each side fought with appropriate weapons. The *Statement* was logical and outwardly calm, though its passionate earnestness was apparent enough. The *Narrative* had more flair to point the naked wrath of its injured innocence, but back of that initial thrust there was a deficiency of substance.

Halkett had in May sent proofs of the *Statement* to the illustrious Dugald Stewart, professor of moral philosophy in the University of Edinburgh, a friend of Selkirk's but not a supporter of his colonization schemes. Stewart had written:

I am particularly delighted with your strictures on the documents which serve as the groundwork of the assertions of his adversaries. Some of them, I own, had puzzled and vexed me not a little, when I first read them in their *Narrative* (a copy of which was, some time ago, forwarded to me from London by Mr. Simon McGillivray); but what you have stated in reply to them has placed matters in a light much more favourable to Lord S. and, in my opinion, much more damning to the agents of the N. West Company than anything that has before appeared. Some parts of Lord S's conduct, I agree with you in thinking, do not admit of a complete justification, although much may be said to apologize for any errors in judgment he may have committed, from the urgency of the case and the extraordinary combination of circumstances in which he was placed.

This was likely to be the opinion of those who made an earnest effort to understand before judging, but they would not be many. The two books became the accepted doctrine of partisans, to be printed in due course in Montreal in both French and English, and to be planted wherever there was promise of growth.

4

That summer at Red River was a kind of watershed in Selkirk's affairs and indeed in his life. The summer showed him the colony as he had dreamed of it and as it might truly be, and, in the same moment, the reality of the menace under which it must live – unless he could remove the menace. The innocent and well-intentioned Coltman represented the danger. He was the law, giving unwitting support to the North West Company's stern pledge: 'there shall be no settlement'. If he could be made to see – as it was his duty to try to see – the true state of affairs, all would surely be well. For Selkirk and his adherents believed that the North West Company could not survive the firm enforcement of the law. Perhaps naïvely, they were inclined to forget their own misdemeanours, simply because they had not murdered people and burned their houses.

From the first, Coltman's attitude, though business-like and proper, was a shock. He arrived suffering from fatigue and fresh from his first severe trial at Bas de la Rivière. There he had found a large gathering of Nor'Westers, led by Archibald Norman McLeod, seemingly ready for a descent on Fort Douglas; the ostensible reason was the arrest of Under-sheriff

Smith by Miles Macdonell. It took all Coltman's *bonhomie* and firmness to establish the fact that it was now for him to right wrongs in the Indian Country. But he couldn't establish it without being reminded frequently that this was the way the 'Selkirkonian system' worked. It was not an auspicious beginning and probably explained his apparent discourtesy in ignoring Selkirk's welcome to Red River.

Within a day, Coltman had established himself between Fort Douglas and the North West camp on the site of Fort Gibraltar. Selkirk received a memorandum of how the commissioner proposed to set about his work; the proclamation required mutual restoration of captured property and he called on both parties to meet this demand. Selkirk agreed in principle but reminded Coltman of the wholesale capture of Hudson's Bay people and goods that had gone on in Athabasca the previous winter; restitution should be simultaneous and complete throughout the Indian Country. At first, Coltman appeared to think this reasonable and transmitted the substance of the argument to Simon McGillivray, spokesman for the North West party at The Forks.

The answer was a sharp document that hardly stopped short of bullying the commissioner and thrust the principle contemptuously aside. The North West Company had always found difficulty in getting a concrete proposal from his Lordship, who preferred long, abstract arguments. They could agree on a formula for restitution on receipt in distant areas; meanwhile let restitution begin at Red River. He called attention in no flattering terms to goods taken from Fort William and Lac la Pluie under the guise of purchase. He had only to add that he must leave Red River by the following Sunday – the implication was not to be missed. Coltman was overpowered. He wrote to Selkirk that Mr. McGillivray's leaving was not of course a reason for haste; still, he, Coltman, was acting in a military capacity under Sir John, a soldier, and obedience was a first duty. The proclamation called for restitution – he hoped his Lordship would co-operate.

But the exact application of restitution proved absurd and

231

vexatious. Selkirk and his people clung to the notion that Coltman ought to be seeking murderers and witnesses. Instead, days went by in impassioned bickering over the details of restitution. The colonists had a fine field of barley growing on ground that had once adjoined the North West's Fort Gibraltar; in the name of restitution and in spite of protests, the North West horses were turned loose to browse in it. In a colony that had never been far from starvation, this seemed merely wicked folly, but protests were of no avail. The cow and the ox 'purchased' at Lac la Pluie were demanded. Coltman heard the evidence about breeding-cattle slaughtered in the previous two years by the half-breeds, but no one could restore what no longer existed. The Nor'Westers had no use for cattle at Red River and no intention of driving these back to Lac la Pluie, but they stood by their rights. The cattle were taken out of the yoke and killed before the eyes of Laidlaw, who, having nursed and saved them, was stunned by grief and incredulity.

'Be the most dutiful obedient subject to the laws,' Jean had said, 'however unjust.' But this was legal madness. Meanwhile, though Coltman had asked Selkirk for a list of crimes, suspects, and witnesses on July 9, he took no effective steps to arrest even those already indicted. Across the plain, wanted men in the Métis camp were slipping away – men who had played a leading part at Seven Oaks and in Selkirk's view were known murderers. D'Orsonnens offered the services of the de Meurons to arrest anyone Coltman wished, but the offer was brusquely declined.

It appeared that the longed-for Commission, the means of making the truth known, would end in futility or worse. Coltman didn't want the truth – he wanted peace and quietness. Yet, for all his seeming wrong-headedness, he was learning much that the Nor'Westers would prefer to have kept hidden. The myth of Indian hostility to the settlement was exploded in the first few days, and Coltman acknowledged to Selkirk that it appeared to him the Indians wished the settlement for their own advantage.

He was also learning respect and even liking for Selkirk and his 'damned bad set'. The question of granting them bail was going to arise, but he wrote that he would have no hesitation in taking the responsibility of this 'from the cheerful and frank appearance of all persons accused among your Lordship's adherents'.

Meanwhile, he stood off Smith, the deputy sheriff, who pressed Coltman to endorse the warrant issued at Sandwich or provide him with another for the 'escape' from arrest at Fort William. Coltman refused both, on the ground that Smith was not legally entitled to them. Even if the legal position had been otherwise, he said, he would have 'felt much hesitation in putting in the hands of a man apparently so violent, the uncontrolled authority conveyed by a warrant if not bailable'. He had himself bound Smith over to keep the peace on his release from Fort Douglas, but it was an uneasy peace.

The Earl was entitled to feel he was gaining ground, and Coltman's reports to Sherbrooke did in fact do him justice, though at first grudgingly. Fletcher, by remaining at Fort William and beyond conversion, reported only second or third hand to Sherbrooke; Selkirk's co-operation he ascribed to his Lordship's appearing to be overawed. Fletcher was not going to abandon his theory of the 'Selkirkonian system' so easily.

When Gale arrived, still shaken from his experience with Fletcher, he was agreeably surprised at the complexion of affairs. He found Selkirk in good health and spirits, and, himself moving about with Coltman, listening to the examination of witnesses, he felt certain that the ugly story of what had gone on would no longer be hidden or disguised.

> The proofs I think will be convincing of the North Westers having effectually laboured to induce their *bois-brûlé* servants to destroy the Colony after having laboured in vain to induce the Indians to do it. – And I believe proofs will be equally satisfactory of their approving and rewarding their servants after the deed was done. – McLeod and a number of the partners with many of the *bois-brûlés* rode from Fort Douglas then in North West posses-

sion to the field of slaughter where they greeted the mangled and half eaten corpses, some of them with shouts and others with kicks and told the *bois-brûlés* that they had done well. . . . Whatever be the result of the capture of Fort William it is certain that without that measure the truth of the Red River transactions would never have been known.

He came also to the conclusion in talking with Coltman that had Lord Selkirk not left Fort William and come on to Red River – for which he had been criticized – the commissioners would not have thought it necessary to do so.

Yes, progress was being made – great progress. But there was much to do, and with Montreal eight or nine weeks away already there was talk of turning back. Fortunately, however, the summer was not wholly taken up with the law's delays. The object of every effort was the success of the colony. Whatever tended to this was of the first importance.

Soon after his arrival, Selkirk had opened negotiations for a treaty that should quench the Indian title at least to the lands of the colony. It had all to be done in due form. The land belonged historically to the Crees and the Assiniboines but had been occupied for some fifty years by the Sauteaux; all had to be consulted, each must be shown proper deference. In a preliminary conference Coltman paved the way for an agreement.

The final meeting, on July 18, was a good deal of a triumph for Selkirk, not merely in the treaty arrangements, which were satisfactory, but in the degree of personal approval he won from the assembled chiefs. He had a sense of occasion and managed in his own dress and demeanour and that of his supporters to invest the event with the ritual and dignity that the Indians regarded as appropriate. Their liking and trust, their naming of this quiet slim man with the auburn hair, so different from themselves, The Silver Chief, were to become part of the lasting folklore of the settlement.

The following day, July 19, the settlers came back to the Red River to which a year ago they had vowed never to return. Since early July, Sheriff MacDonell had found there was 'no keeping them'. And, even as Selkirk sat in solemn powwow with the Indians, their ragged little fleet of boats was making its way down Lake Winnipeg in pell-mell order, the boats racing each other, so reckless of seamanship that one man was drowned – wildly eager to be back. No one at the settlement knew just when they would arrive but look-outs were posted. The nineteenth had been a fine summer day; in the evening the boats reached Frog Plains and Alexander MacDonell rode up to Fort Douglas and joined Lord Selkirk for dinner. When MacDonell had gone out through those gates, it was under the eye of Cuthbert Grant and his men, still in war-paint and wearing the clothing of the slaughtered colonists.

These things and many others must have pressed on Selkirk's mind next morning as he went down in the rain to meet the settlers – down by the road Robert Semple had travelled. This could not be as carefree a meeting as that along the beach in Prince Edward Island years before when he was making his first venture into colonizing. Alexander MacDonell was to record only that 'about 11 o'clock forenoon he came to the Frog Plains and conversed with the settlers'. But it was a meeting none forgot. It may have been the blunt physical experience of looking into those faces, holding those roughened hands, noting the gaps in the ranks, that gave him a realization of these people's suffering which for all his sympathy he could not have known before. It was a realization he never lost; it both armed him for the last fight and perhaps rode him to his death.

In future he fought less for the settlement and more for the settlers. Henceforth his pleas were on behalf of suffering people. He had not been unaware of his responsibility, but short of this he could not have understood it so deeply and inescapably. A host of misadventures had made the burden heavier but it none the less was his place to see these men, women, and children settled in reasonable security and happiness. He would continue to work for the settlement as he had planned it, but if that dream must go his people must still be taken care of.

The following morning the camp at Frog Plain melted away

as the settlers moved up the river, leaving their belongings along the bank at the front of their farms. In very truth they had now come home.

Summer ran into August and the return home approached with alarming speed. Selkirk longed to be back, but before going he must do whatever desperate determination could accomplish to leave the settlement secure. He intended to return to Red River soon, but many complex matters would have to be dealt with first, and clearly he might be delayed. All summer he and Coltman had talked about the arrangements for leaving soldiers to guard the colony. At first, as usual, agreement had not seemed difficult, but then the problems began to appear, and there was no time to solve them. Matthey, in Selkirk's view the ideal commander, was to have stayed, but in the end his apparent pre-eminence in the resistance to warrants seemed to make his return to Montreal necessary.

And, since Coltman approved the Indian treaty, he continued to insist on the North West Company's rights to lands they had occupied at Red River. This, with the incident of the barley-field and its relationship to title in the land, meant continuing danger and uncertainty for the colony. The de Meurons would defend the colony if necessary, would perhaps relish the opportunity to do so, but a colony forced to live as an armed camp was – as a settlement – a contradiction in terms. With bitterness he wrote Coltman that if the proclamation sustained the North West claim to land in the settlement the settlers had better be moved out of reach of the North West Company. 'It may perhaps be the most prudent course to allow these people to seek asylum within the American lines, where at least they will not have to apprehend hostility from subjects of the same Government and where if they be liable to be attacked it will not be considered an offence to be prepared for resistance.'

Until near the end, he had believed he could at least give his people clear title and security, taking it for granted that the picture of North West guilt at Red River must exclude the traders from the area. And, happy in this belief, he had gone about settling the people and making plans for the future. At a great gathering with his settlers on August 10, he had announced that those twenty-four families who had improved their lands and lost the improvements were to have their lands free. At last, the improving land-owner coming into his own, he had walked about with them suggesting sites for a school and a church, a mill and a bridge. Peter Fidler was continuing a survey begun long before and the de Meurons were being settled east of the river opposite Fort Douglas. Ten thousand acres were also set aside across the river for the Roman Catholic Church in the hope that missionaries might control the half-breeds and freemen and reclaim them from savagery.

It was the practical working out of his dream and it, too, passed into the folklore of the settlement, so that, long after, they liked to remember it and to consider that 'so correct and unerring was his judgment' nothing he then decided 'could in after years be altered to advantage'. And, if it cannot have been quite true, it had both a general truth and the shape of the thing his people wanted to believe. He knew and loved land and the planning for settled living in the countryside, and to build something from the ground up was an immense satisfaction – save for the poison at the heart of all his arrangements – the uncertainty.

Coltman was maturing his own ideas about control of the settlement from Canada (which would void Selkirk's claim), and he would promise nothing. Meanwhile he was a commissioner seeking to tranquillize two parties who had in his view been equally guilty. Having at last had inescapable evidence of the guilt of Alexander 'Whiteheaded' Macdonell and A. N. McLeod, he issued warrants for their arrest; but Macdonell was well out of reach, a thousand miles to the west; McLeod had gone east, and a warrant sent to Fletcher at Fort William failed mysteriously to be served on McLeod.

Selkirk, on the other hand, and all those similarly charged, were close by, submissive to Coltman's orders, and on them he clapped an astounding bail for their appearance at Montreal; Lord Selkirk £6,000, Captain Matthey £2,000, Captain D'Or-

237

sonnens and Dr. Allan £1,000 each. This, for a misdemeanour, was more than the total bail exacted from the combined North West partners charged as accessories to murder. Both as a lawyer and as a partisan, Gale was outraged and wished to protest. It was absurd and wrong for Coltman to exact bail of any size in the Indian Country for an appearance in Lower Canada to answer a charge from the Western District of Upper Canada. 'I shall not hereafter be surprised if I hear of some Irish magistrate requiring bail for the appearance at Washington, of persons charged with having committed [crimes] at St. Petersburg.' But Selkirk would permit no protest. He had promised that the bail would be forthcoming and 'it appeared to be a point of delicacy with the Earl'; Gale fumed and for the moment subsided.

There was to be one more act in the farce of Deputy Sheriff Smith. Campbell, a North West Company half-breed, deputized by the deputy, made another attempt to arrest Selkirk in his own house. Though it was stopped short, it was perhaps the thing that finally determined Selkirk to return through the United States. It was known that there would be another attempt to arrest him in Lake Superior, which Coltman would not prevent. Moreover, there was a shortage of boats for carrying witnesses and some of the returning de Meurons to Canada. He wished also, sooner or later, to find out in Washington about his title to the portion of the Assiniboia grant which, since the Treaty of Ghent, fell within the U.S. boundary.

For some reason, this decision shocked and angered Coltman, who regarded the trip as a sight-seeing jaunt. As for the Nor'Westers, they took it for granted that this was the final escape; the Earl, they said, would not be seen in Canada again. Selkirk explained patiently and gave a pledge of his good faith: 'I well know that the laws of my country require that my conduct should be submitted to the judgment of a competent tribunal, this would have been done ere now had there been any within reach. ... I shall lose no time in submitting my conduct to that inquiry which the law requires. ...'

He had had enough; and, in spite of all objections, arrangements went forward for his journey south. Red River carts were to take the baggage to the height of land where it would be transferred to Mississippi river-boats.

There were final leave-takings and promises of an early return; meanwhile missionaries and a Presbyterian clergyman would be sent. Cattle would somehow be forwarded across the plains. De Graffenreid was to command the de Meuron defence force under agreed arrangements. He took a last long look at the splendid fields and mounted his horse. Matthey, D'Orsonnens, Dr. Allan, and the others were mounted and ready. They turned south and rode rapidly away.

Chapter 10

LORD BATHURST'S JUSTICE

1817 had been another interminable summer of waiting for Lady Selkirk. The uncertainties were perhaps not quite so dreadful as they had been the year before, yet she lived always in the possibility of desperate news. And, following the proclamation, there remained no balancing possibility of goodness to match the bad. This was 'Lord Bathurst's justice'. They could lose now, but they couldn't win; there was to be no triumph.

Meanwhile, she accepted a little triumph of her own. The Sherbrookes were spending the summer on the St. Lawrence at Sorel and pressed her to join them there. There was every reason for being out of the city in summer-time, above all the health of the children – or every reason but one. She would be just that much more out of the centre of things, slower to hear news, slower to act. Still, with the distances involved, there was in any case no possibility of influencing events directly. All news from England or the Upper Country was six weeks old, and tragedy might be piled on desperate circumstance long before she could intervene or even know. What could a day or two matter?

So, shortly after Lord Selkirk reached Red River, as it happened, she set out from Montreal with the Sherbrookes to prospect for lodgings or a suitable house at Sorel. There had been comfort or at any rate a kind of peace in the bustle of preparation, for there was much to think about and see to. In addition to overseeing the selection of clothing and furnishings, she had to do what she could in Red River affairs. She had to arrange to see all incoming letters and reports as quickly as possible, and she had also to try to stem the flow of ruinous expense. Alexander Wood at York was to have his heavy outlay for Lord Selkirk paid by draft to be honoured by Maitland and Garden but was to be more firm in outfitting the parties going up and down; they must have what they needed but no more. Then, the day before she left, came encouraging news. A canoe arrived from Fort William bringing the wretched Sergeant de Reinhart, confessed murderer of Owen Keveny; better still, it brought dispatches from Lord Selkirk at Arrow Lake dated May 16. A little over five weeks ago all had been well with him. That was something – the little cold comfort on which she had learned to live.

There was, however, some relief from immediate pressures, with even a touch of wry comedy, provided by Daniel McKenzie at this stage. 'Poor Dan Mackenzie', she wrote Halkett, 'is on the high road to unsay all he has sworn and go back to what he said to Lord Selkirk. ... He is sending me the most tender messages, by every person he thinks will have a chance to send them round to me, assuring me that Lord Selkirk will be quite safe with his people, that Lord Selkirk is the first of human beings, that all the North-West have made him say is false, no ill usage, no compulsion, no unfair transactions, that he wishes his Tongue had been cut out before he said anything against Lord Selkirk.' But that damage had been done and she knew no one was going to allow poor Daniel to undo it.

In a few days at Sorel she had made satisfactory arrangements and sent for the children and servants. On July 10 they set out from Montreal in the *Malsham* (on which the year before she had made her momentous trip with the Sherbrookes) and presently it came splashing happily in to the wharf where she was waiting. In such a quiet, pretty scene it must have been hard to believe that all was not well, or would not speedily be put right. In this countryside of fishing villages and old farms, surely the children would be healthy and happy. They could have picnics along the river and go for drives; she was going to buy a curricle. Daer and Isabella (now known as Poucette) would make progress in their French. It could be a good summer for them away from the interminable grown-up talk about Red River, and an atmosphere of worry.

For her there could be no real peace, but between the express canoes with their messages good and bad there would at least be other things to think about. Her devoted Samuel Gale with his good brain and warm heart – and his cynicism bred of a young man's too-deep involvement with the law – would keep her closely in touch with the commissioners' progress and attitude. She had already had his amusing and startling accounts of the trip up, and of Fletcher's outrageous behaviour at the Falls of St. Mary. Coltman's attitude, though not ridiculous, was more sinister. To match Fletcher's dangerous array of pistols and swords, the unarmed Gale carried a Bible, some law books, and a prayer book. And there was another piece of information, which had come from Lieutenant Moir of the 37th: that the military observing the conflict tended to support Lord Selkirk, but that they believed Sir John Sherbrooke favoured the North West Company. This must have been troubling to her direct and loyal nature – unacceptable, indeed. Sir John was merely upright and he had what he himself called 'the distinguishing faculty'. She had already written her brother Andrew that he was 'the only character with firmness and rectitude enough to do justice', so that he showed the old intrigues for what they were by 'mere plain dealing'.

And, except for Gale's letters, which grew fewer as he too receded to the north-west, the summer was almost empty of news. The very little that came was not reassuring. Coltman's first letters to Sherbrooke in early July gave a very different view from Gale's of the vexatious farce that had occurred at the Sault. Coltman described the impounding of the de

Meurons' cases of trading guns as the disarming of an armed party by Major Fletcher.

Another report from Coltman, embellished out of whole cloth by Fletcher, arriving in early August, told nothing she did not already know and nothing that she wanted to hear. But the summer was passing rapidly. She and the children would return to Montreal in September with the hope that her husband would be there soon after. That was how the talk had run in early summer – that he would return for the September term and the opening of the trials – but she was quickly to learn that it was too good to be true. When at last they all boarded the *Malsham* on September 20 – the Countess, three children, five servants, and a curricle – golden days were shortening into cold nights. Mist hung over the river in the early mornings, and summer was only a memory to be recalled in the brown faces of the children.

It was over a month before she learned that the men from Red River were actually homeward bound. Spread widely across a map that was imperfectly sketched, the three parties were crawling towards her down the endless waterways. They would not now arrive much before the winter, might indeed be trapped. Gale was being forced to travel slowly, conveying witnesses whom Lord Selkirk wanted in Montreal. Coltman was probably moving faster, and with him came Cuthbert Grant in a strange kind of open arrest – like a companion, sharing the commissioner's tent and his meals. From her husband's party there was silence and she could only guess wildly at where they might be. The Nor'Westers were loud in their guesses and wagers; wherever he was, the Trading Lord would not be seen in Canada again: he dare not. She knew better – if only he were safe and well.

While the principals were making their appearance, a variety of lesser figures, bit players and character actors, were trooping in to take their places on the stage at Montreal. In late August Colin Robertson, under indictment for larceny, slipped into town early one morning from James Bay, was taken to Chief

Justice Monk's house by James Stuart and there bailed, to the astonishment and wrath of the Nor'Westers. About the same time, Angus Shaw returned and was bidden to dine with Sir John, when Jean was also a reluctant guest. In October, Archie McLellan, Seraphin La Mar, and Bostonois Pangman arrived under guard and went straight to jail.

Meanwhile, warning of the long and complex legal tangle to follow was sounded when early in the term, at Stuart's urging, Colin Robertson and others were called for trial. On the bench, Chief Justice Monk was supported by Mr. Justice Ogden and Mr. Justice Reid. About these two there had been much murmuring among Selkirk's supporters. Montreal, though accustomed to grim tales of the fur trade, had been shocked at a story that had circulated with a wealth of horrifying detail the year before about the murder of an Indian by Peter Ogden, the judge's son. And though Mr. Justice Reid was a respected man he was a brother-in-law of William McGillivray and therefore an interested party. These circumstances came to their logical conclusion at a peculiarly embarrassing moment as the court opened. Into the expectant silence Judge Ogden announced that he had heard some unpleasant stories about the fur-trade struggle and did not wish to have anything to do with it; he disqualified himself from judgment. A moment later Judge Reid did the same and the work of the court was rendered impossible. In the circumstances Reid returned to the bench long enough for the deferring of trials and renewing of bail. So far as cases from the Indian Country were concerned, the looked-for September term had been brought to a full stop.

In addition to the two judges who had stepped down, a third, Judge Faucher, was facing impeachment, and it began to appear that justice could not be done. Very quickly rumours spread of the trials being moved to Upper Canada. It was said the North West Company had already asked for this and made representations about being subject to prejudice in Lower Canada; moreover, it was claimed that many of the witnesses were in the upper province.

Lady Selkirk wrote about this possibility to Gale in late

October. The letter reaching him at York on the last lap of his journey seemed to crown his exasperation at the direction of events:

> In such a case Lord Selkirk would have little chance of justice. ... Ogden and Reid have done well to discover that they were interested; it would have been only decent to have made the discovery some years ago. But this cannot make it necessary to transfer the trials to U/C: there still remain seven judges in the Province of Lower Canada and there are but two (Powell and Campbell) in this province. ... Can the 'Canadians' who merely contend for the rights of their predecessors during centuries fear a Canadian jury?

It was apparent that he found the North West Company's special pleading as a 'Canadian' company both irritating and contemptible.

> If the administration at home should consider the North West Co. and the Canadians as one and the same, a fear of irritating the latter might render it more difficult to obtain justice. But if the mask be torn off ... it will be seen that the North West Company are, and are also considered, the enemies of the Canadians and really exclude them except as their hewers of wood and drawers of water from the very countries they pretend to claim for them ... the best mode of conciliating the Canadians will not be to skreen but to visit the North Westers with the punishment they merit ... the distinction between the Canadians and the Scotch renegades ... should be forced upon the unwilling minds of various official characters at home.

Gale's natural resentment of the 'Scotch renegades'' claims as Canadians missed the point. It was true they were masquerading shamelessly behind a title they would not otherwise have claimed; it was true that Scotland or Britain was 'home' to most of them and that they took their vacations, bought houses, and frequently retired there. Yet many of them had been born or had spent most of their grown-up lives in the Canadas, and among them and their friends grew the first seeds of a nascent Canadian nationalism – unrecognized and so far only acceptable in their expediency. In general usage, Canadians were those of French blood whose ancestors had first conquered the wilderness. But all those who lived in Canada were finding common bonds and common resentments. That the ancient Hudson's Bay Company charter, traditionally resisted by the French, could be revived by people who knew nothing of the Canadas; that an immense tract of land, always a common hunting-ground, could be alienated to the uses of a Scottish lord to the exclusion of those who had spent and risked their lives there – these were grievances on which traders could meet and be supported by others, moved only by a common and scarcely understood resentment. This unformed sentiment drifted like smoke across party lines, so that the 'English party' (made up largely of Scots) found itself unaccountably voicing Canadian views, while for once interference from Britain was welcomed by many 'Canadians'. The odd juxtaposition tended also to divide Gale from his partner James Stuart, long one of the most bitter of the Canadian party leaders. The generous-minded and explosive Gale seemed as yet to understand none of this, and recognized only that those to whom he had become devoted were about to be pilloried in the name of the law.

The explosion was but the last in a series. Ever since he left Red River, brooding at what had been accomplished there and at the magnitude of the failure to get at the truth, he had dashed off numerous letters to Lady Selkirk, thinking aloud as the gliding canoes slowly closed on Montreal. The necessity of sitting still mile after mile, week after week, left him too much time. Coltman's attitude, the lack of vigour in the Committee of the Hudson's Bay Company, the mysterious, intangible opposition of government – all these things coursed endlessly through his mind, and the spectre of the injustice he saw approaching drove him to angry and sometimes bitter comments. 'You will remember,' he wrote, sitting hunched in his canoe not long after he left Red River, 'however good a man Lord Selkirk may be, that his character must suffer unless his adversaries be known, and they cannot be generally known without great efforts.'

Above all, it was the essence of what he remembered most vividly of his talks with Coltman that worried him. The mood of satisfaction at what was being discovered on his arrival at Red River was all gone, swallowed up in the knowledge that it would not be given due weight. For Coltman had only sought a measure of truth, enough to prove his thesis. 'He is so anxious to show that both parties have alike been criminal, so eager to equalize matters on both sides.' Gale knew now only too well the form Coltman's report must take. 'Like a Scotch Arbiter', he sought a formula for splitting the difference, because he took it for granted that the government regarded both parties in the same light, and like a good subject he hoped to carry out the government's wishes. The crimes at Red River were merely incidents in a trade war.

Jean Selkirk realized that his comments had been made even though he knew he might reach Montreal before the letters did. But they had burned and taken shape in him, so that he had to get them down.

'Private War' is not within the limits of my law, it is a species of offence I do not rightly understand. The Proclamation of the Prince Regent was supposed to insinuate that that had been the crime committed, and the Commissioner was to be guided by the Proclamation. It is somewhat unusual to establish before investigation the nature of the crimes to be inquired into. It is likewise unusual to see the crimes of arson and murder committed by subjects against fellow subjects raised into dignity by giving to them the name of 'Private War' instead of their proper legal appelations.

Undoubtedly, Gale's trip had tried his temper and constitution. At the last, his party had faced very severe cold and the real possibility that they might not get through. Having waited at the Sault as long as he dared for his following canoes, he pushed on lest winter catch him there; and as they crossed Lake Huron in bitter cold they had to break their way in through ice two inches thick before reaching French River. They had planned on descending the Ottawa as the quickest way home, but, meeting a party that had taken four days to travel twelve miles crossing over from the Ottawa, Gale decided to turn south for York where there would be roads and horses if all else failed – as in the end it did.

Coltman had been a few days earlier and correspondingly fortunate. By a narrow margin he had beaten winter home. As word came of his approach to Montreal, Lady Selkirk had considered what her moves must be. James Stuart was to talk to Coltman as early as possible and verify or perhaps change Gale's report of what they faced. They began to feel that, if justice was not to be anticipated from the report of the Commission, the Commission itself should be impeached – and this meant Coltman, for Fletcher had returned early and under somewhat mysterious circumstances; it appeared that his glorious hour of hanging, drawing, and quartering was over.

Sunday, November 9, was a bad day and Jean Selkirk stayed home from church. Right after the service Mr. Garden called in excitement to tell her that Henry McKenzie had arrived from Red River and that Coltman was expected the following day. When he did arrive, she learned, he quickly denied the rumours that Selkirk had fled from Red River into the United States by night, leaving him only a note; still, she thought he ought to have denied them with more indignation. She learned also that Stuart's meetings with Coltman on Monday and Tuesday had made the commissioner nervous about his own position. Nevertheless, this was a somewhat new Coltman who carried himself with an unaccustomed hat-on-head brusqueness, where he had been given to 'bothering one with bows'. The tough attitude towards Coltman went against her nature, but she thought advantage had been taken of Selkirk's 'civility and meekness' and in his support she was prepared for anything. 'The petticoats have been a sore hindrance to me for these 18 months now,' she wrote later to Andrew. 'Yet I am dreadfully sick of wearing the other apparel, which you must acknowledge however I only put on in my husband's absence.'

Yet, when Coltman sent word that he would call on her Tuesday about six, her confidence fled and she found herself 'exceedingly nervous'. Mr. and Mrs. Garden arrived unexpectedly just before he did, and would have left again, but she begged them to stay and support her. The visit was pleasant but gave her little enough information and reassurance; besides, she knew that every amiable thing he said would be matched by some comfort to their opponents soon after. The canards against the de Meurons, spread by the Nor'Westers, he answered bluntly, saying that no one could reproach them for their behaviour. The long, two-hour visit was at once too short and indecisive. After he left, she still clung to the Gardens and, seeing her comforting piano and harp, played to them 'to drive the big man out of my head and lay the evil spirit'. And late in the evening after they left she was still walking about the room to 'cool' herself and consider what was to be done. She must see Coltman again.

Although there was some sharpness to their exchanges, many things he said to her when he came again on Thursday and the following Monday would have given her confidence had she believed he would make them the basis of his final report. For one thing, he acknowledged the richness of the soil at Red River, but added hastily that as a speculation it could never be successful. At this, Lady Selkirk's eyes widened and she answered that if he meant a speculation by which her husband was to make money she supposed there could not be two opinions on the point, but wasn't that Lord Selkirk's affair? Coltman's brusque confidence deserted him. He told her later that with the de Meurons he felt the settlers were safe for the next winter unless they were very imprudent; beyond that he would not pledge himself. She answered dryly that she had hoped his mission would provide for their security, if nothing else. He admitted readily that Selkirk and his people had co-operated fully and submitted to arrest and bail (though Matthey was furious), while the Nor'Westers sent away their most seriously accused servants. Many of her most pointed assertions were put forward 'half-laughing' and she hated herself for being so sharp, 'but I am like a cat watching a mouse on this subject, ready to shift my position at every turn'. Still, 'after all the talk we parted very good friends he all civility and I all courtesy' – but she was little the wiser and little more comforted. She could not doubt that Gale's guess as to the Commission report was sound. They would get no help from Coltman, not even what she believed to be bare justice. Stuart's efforts to shake his settled view and initial prejudice, against the Hudson's Bay charter and Selkirk's actions at Fort William, seemed to have had no effect. Coltman's trip had apparently served only to fill in the rough outline he had sketched before leaving.

This sense of fatal disability combined with a desperate ignorance of Lord Selkirk's whereabouts and welfare to make early November the worst stage of a trying autumn. And then news began to come in – brief bulletins, but heartening: Selkirk's party had reached the Mississippi and descended to St. Louis by river-boat; an agreeable trip and all well. Matthey would go on down to New Orleans to dispatch the de Meurons returning to Europe, then go on himself to New York. Selkirk and the rest would now travel east to Pittsburgh on horseback; local guess said the trip would take twenty to thirty days. That had been written the first week in November; where were they now? Twelve days later he wrote again. They had reached Vincennes on the Wabash, fighting their way against heavy rains that had swollen the creeks and made roads impassable, so that the carriages had broken down and the baggage had been left to follow. But the point she seized on was that, in spite of everything, that frail and delicate figure reported himself 'perfectly well'. (Did she remember the innumerable days in London when he dare not venture out because of a cold?) It would still be a long, trying wait, but alongside that good news nothing mattered.

Just over a week later he reported himself 'out of the woods' from Lexington, Kentucky. Here, after two months of travelling, were to be found some of the comforts of civilization. But then came his own lament at the long delay and hope sickeningly deferred. 'There is nothing now to keep me from my love except distance and dirty roads, but wae's me many are the miles and deep the mire that are to be passed before I can hold somebody in my arms, and I am sick of calculating how long it will take me to reach Montreal.' That call across the distance was enough to stop the heart. He so seldom allowed himself to unbend. 'He is so laconic,' she was given to saying, and, 'You know how laconic Lord Selkirk is.' It was a remarkable trip, made up to now by few if any Europeans, but she wished he had taken it on his travels twelve years before.

She longed for his return and perhaps dreaded it, knowing how much the disappointments he must face would upset him. It seemed all too certain that in spite of protests the cases would be moved to Upper Canada. Stuart had directed a strong protest to Sir John Sherbrooke, on the grounds of the ruinous expense involved and the improbability of securing justice. A letter from Andrew Cochrane for Sir John on December 3 merely said that the measure was already 'complete and in execution'; Cochrane added that it was considered necessary for the ends of justice and by the local situation. There was some hope that Selkirk's own protest might carry more weight, but it was slim. They seemed to be swimming against an unpredictable current, consistent only in its being always against them.

There were heavy snowfalls in November and, overnight, Montreal became a winter city. The streets filled with carrioles and the jingle of sleigh-bells. Prancing horses and people in bright-coloured blanket-coats and toques brought gaiety to the sunny mornings about the markets. The Glengarry men would soon be coming in with their sleighs full of produce for the Christmas larders: great hams, geese, and sides of pork, tubs of butter and cheeses, turkeys and barrels of apples.

Samuel Gale came home at last at the end of November and after the first glad welcomings and exchanges of news they went straight to conferences; there were important questions of strategy in the larger struggle and of immediate tactics – especially for Lord Selkirk who was past Washington now and intended only a day in Philadelphia and New York, then on to Albany and to Montreal. The children must have their Christmas; but with the very streets calling 'Rejoice' Lady Selkirk and Stuart and Gale could scarcely give themselves to that attractive summons.

At Sault Ste. Marie, Gale had opened a letter for Lord Selkirk from Woods of Sandwich. It was the letter that told of impending criminal prosecution by the attorney-general for escape from Dr. Mitchell's warrant. It explained also the basis of the other warrants from Sandwich that Smith had attempted to serve. Selkirk and all his principal officers had been charged with the theft of eighty-three guns at Fort William on the oath of Vandersluys and McTavish. These were the guns found and taken on a search warrant after Selkirk had been warned of an attempted uprising. And, since the clerks knew the guns had been picked up on a warrant, this was perjury, under the simple and time-honoured practice of finding any pretext for the arrest of a North West opponent. But, however infamous the practice, the effect was that Selkirk, who believed himself at most guilty of a misdemeanour, stood charged with a felony.

There came a terrible moment in their conferences when they faced the fact that he must not come back to Montreal under these conditions. If the North West Company could not arrange for his arrest in Montreal, which they would most certainly seek, they might manage to humiliate or even to disgrace him publicly; it was the balm to which their wounds would best respond. He was only days away and his advisers must come quickly to a conclusion. 'I shall feel it when it is decided,' she wrote Andrew on Christmas Day, facing her disappointment. 'I wish you all a Merry Christmas, I have been at church, it is necessary to use all means to keep down the bitterness of spirit. . . .'

And on Christmas Day Gale sat down to write at length to

Albany, reviewing the cases and the dangers of an immediate return to Montreal, turning Selkirk away. They considered it better he go on to York and perhaps to Sandwich, to face and refute the charges, and then to come home in triumph. Public opinion, at first shocked by the North West version of events at Fort William, was changing in his favour as it became better informed. Spencer and McNab had each been required to give £250 bail at Sandwich, Miles Macdonell a few months later only £100. He might find himself fairly, even leniently, dealt with at Sandwich, if he went there now.

Jean's letter was different, but she did not allow herself to say half of what this delay meant to her. The letters met him at Albany on New Year's Eve. 'I am more vexed at this than at all the other delays,' he commented. He had written from Washington that he looked to be home at the latest in the first week in January; now it would be weeks later. But their arguments were unanswerable; and he was the more easily persuaded because at the hotel in Albany he found Richard Grant of the North West Company, apparently waiting to report his arrival. He was sending William home with the baggage while he went on at once to York and Allan perhaps to Sandwich.

So New Year's Eve had come again. The year before, with him in possession of Fort William and his affairs seeming to turn out for the best, Jean had sat writing to him in a mood of measured elation. Could she say as much now?

The excitement of William's return a few days later was still the occasion for rejoicing. He had been with Lord Selkirk every step of the way and could fill in all kinds of details. William, stimulated at being back and having an ever-ready audience, revealed a talent for story-telling, so that the slightest thing would set him off with the children or the servants or m'lady – launched on a reminiscence. And it appeared that Lord Selkirk was one man who was a hero to his valet. William positively asserted that Lord Selkirk had completely conquered Indians, freemen, and half-breeds, so that if anyone had dared to arrest him his captors would certainly have been killed and he set free. The Indians believed he was as wise as they were, and were quite sure he could find his way in the woods without a guide – tributes they paid few white men. Then there was the story – one of William's favourites – of Lord Selkirk being carried by eight Sioux warriors on a painted buffalo-skin while he smoked a long pipe – this on the trip through the dangerous Sioux country. And in Washington, according to William, Lord Selkirk had had the greatest reception from the President ever given to a British visitor; rumours in Montreal supported William in this. Oh, William had tales to last him a lifetime, and to last them perhaps until Selkirk came home.

Jean, passing on some of these marvellous tales to Andrew Colvile, seemed to shake her head in affectionate amusement. 'I don't suppose he has told you of this, he is so laconic.'

Having accepted the necessity of going farther, Selkirk's party wasted no time. They pushed ahead the same day and by nightfall he was writing her from Schenectady, pouring out some of the ideas and questions on their problems which he had been saving for Montreal and now could save no longer. 'Pray write to York when the trials are intended to be brought on, I long to be on the offensive.'

In spite of the exhausting and dangerous trip now nearing its end, the struggle had roused him slowly to a pitch of excitement that could comprehend all obstacles but not contemplate defeat. From New York he had written Andrew Colvile that he had had from Jean good news of the family but less good about 'our affairs at Montreal'. He counted on the evidence with which Gale would return to change all that, to offset even Coltman's official and predetermined report.

He had written to Andrew of another matter that gave him great satisfaction and relief, with which he was doubtless glad to soften the news of further heavy drafts for the expenses of his trip and the returning of some de Meurons to Europe. It was not his way to lament the great sums being poured out on the settlement or to reduce his complaint against the North West Company to those terms. But the letters from Jean and the worried note in the reports from Maitland, Garden and

Auldjo had been constant and uncomfortable reminders.

But it was like him to be wholly seized by the new and big idea he expounded to Andrew which might solve completely the financial problems of the settlement. As the westward-sweeping tide of American settlement had come to meet him on his return trip, he realized how quickly it must reach his own lands; and a large section of his grant now fell within the United States boundary. There was still the problem of establishing his title with the American government. That done, he saw the way 'it may be made without further outlay, to repay (and well too) that which has already been bestowed upon it'. It meant abandoning his original plan, which envisaged a solid European enclave in the Red River country. With that change accepted (for an area over which he could now in any case have only reduced control), 'facilities appear that I had previously no idea of, and I believe that as a speculation it may turn out much beyond any idea I ever entertained of it'.

So he had much to occupy his active mind as the successive stages jolted over rough roads through the winter darkness towards York, when sleep was not to be found save in uncomfortable snatches. He had hoped to travel incognito, but soon after crossing at Niagara into Upper Canada he was recognized; and any chance of slipping unnoticed into York and out again was gone. Worse, his hopes of finding a quick and perhaps an easy solution to his immediate problems at York were in any case soon to be blasted. In his present mood he would be slow to recognize it, but he was moving into the outer fringes of the web of official disapproval from which he was never to escape, where his own frantic struggles could serve only to wear him out the more quickly.

Eight days' hard travelling brought them at last into York, and Selkirk went at once to the home of the Chief Justice, who was now William Dummer Powell – submitting himself to the law. There had formerly been a cordial relationship between the two men and their meeting now seemed at first to be on the old footing. But the things that lay between those days and now had changed Powell's view of Selkirk, and the latter's fatigue and preoccupation with his immediate objectives dulled his perceptions. Meeting superficially as friends divided by problems, they were ripe for misunderstandings which were to embitter their memories of each other and to sow a fatal doubt in Selkirk's mind about the process of justice in Upper Canada. The meeting began as Selkirk had intended, with his declaration that he was here to answer the warrants and charges against him with a view to standing his trial or being bailed (though he was already under Coltman's dubious bail of £6,000 on the same charges). Powell replied that, since the charges had not come officially to his notice, he could not act unless Selkirk wished to plead guilty. However, in that event, since resistance to legal process was not bailable, Selkirk and his associates would have to be held in custody until the next assizes. Then, hearing something of the long roundabout trip through the United States, Powell, contemplating the weary figure before him, either suggested that Selkirk should return to the United States until his trial was due or said on impulse that it was a pity his Lordship had not stayed there for the present. Afterwards, he was hard put to it to say just what he had said or meant. Selkirk, in bitter retrospect, was inclined to believe the Chief Justice had tempted him to an impropriety that would have done him great harm.

In the midst of their talk Mr. James Baby of the Executive Council arrived and, shortly after, D'Orsonnens and John Allan. It was nearing dinner-time, and they were invited to stay while the Chief Justice sent word to the Attorney-General, D'Arcy Boulton, that Lord Selkirk wished to wait on him. Selkirk later wrote his wife that he had met a cordial reception from both Powell and Boulton 'but could get no business done'.

Certainly Boulton had no comfort to offer. The warrants must be answered at Sandwich whence they issued; the Quarter Sessions for the Western District were just finishing, and if they hurried they might be in time. Gone once again was the hope of turning towards Montreal. Sandwich lay 250 miles to the west over roads that were little better than tracks and would be rutted and slippery, if not drifted deep with snow. Before they parted, Boulton told Selkirk that 'he had received orders from Lord Bathurst' to prosecute him criminally for the 'escape' from Dr. Mitchell's warrant. The mysterious web drew a little tighter, but, though puzzled and worried, he had as yet no notion of its strength, or of his comparative weakness. Sandwich was to provide no fair test of either – in spite of D'Arcy Boulton's son, Henry John, who rode hard on Selkirk's heels to act as solicitor-general and to perform that office with an almost indecent gusto.

The first charge to be faced was that of having feloniously stolen eighty-three fusils which Selkirk claimed to have lawfully seized at Fort William. The warrant had been sworn by Vandersluys and McTavish, who according to Selkirk's statement had been shown the warrant under which he acted; they therefore knew the guns had not been stolen, and they were perjured. In the absence of witnesses, it appeared to be his word against theirs until a second statement by Vandersluys differing from the first was produced. The magistrates then set aside the warrant and discharged Selkirk and the others from arrest on that count.

In the face of such testimony, Boulton's task had been impossible, though he had not given up easily. He then asked for an adjournment until the following day, when he looked for the arrival of important witnesses. The court, which had to try the forcible-entry charge under Dr. Mitchell's warrant, the resistance to Dr. Mitchell's warrant, and the assault and false imprisonment of Deputy Sheriff William Smith, agreed to adjourn.

Next morning, Boulton asked Selkirk to agree to do away with the large panel of magistrates of the Quarter Sessions and to be tried in private by two or three only. Selkirk agreed, subject to the bench's concurrence, but the magistrates declined to accept what they considered an improper proposal; a protracted wrangle threatened, until Selkirk, to save time, assured them of his willingness to submit to the suggested procedure. Boulton then chose two members of the Sessions and added a Mr. McIntosh, an agent of the North West Company.

The results of the trials that followed, if not a triumph, were not wholly unsatisfactory. There was frustration, in that nothing more was cleared from the docket for lack of proper evidence, but the bails fixed were so trifling as to provide a curious commentary. On the 'escape' from Dr. Mitchell's warrant, Selkirk was bound over to appear at the next Quarter Session in the amount of £50, Dr. Allan for £25. (This was the offence the Chief Justice had considered not bailable.) On the charge of forcible entry, bail was fixed at £200. Thus bail of £250 in all was fixed for offences against which Coltman had set £6,000. In a sense, the trials had settled little, but they appeared to have restored perspective.

With his sense of innocence unimpaired, Selkirk at last turned homeward.

Chapter II

I

Twice had the North West partners returned, diminished, to Montreal; now it was Selkirk's turn. The contrast with his starting out could hardly have been more complete. Then, he had been following his brave flotilla of more than a hundred men in *bateaux* and canoes, gay in the near-certainty of approaching triumph. Then, he was himself untouched by the brutality and chicanery of the fur-trade war. But now he returned almost alone, with his single-minded generosity called in question – perhaps a buccaneer like the rest; worse, a wolf in sheep's clothing.

There was room for some bitter reflections as with D'Orsonnens he rode down the winding road beside the St. Lawrence and Lake St. Louis, the last freezing miles of the journey. The severe cold, which froze the breath on his upturned collar and whitened the horses' chests, was Montreal's coldest spell in years. Above the glistening tin roofs of the city, the smoke stood up in white columns as though petrified. But one of the columns was from the home he had missed these eighteen months. For the moment the fur trade must wait. The trip to

259

Sandwich had been a wretched detour of a thousand miles over miserable roads, through deep bush, until Montreal and home and family had seemed a mirage. Now, on the last day of January, it was a reality. There would be time now for the stories he had promised young Daer about Indians and bivouacs in the snow; he would see the new baby, Katherine, whose first birthday he had missed by having to go to Sandwich. Here were the children, the comfort of home – of being snug indoors while the thermometer stood at thirty-two degrees below zero – above all, the wife he was longing to see. With so much of happiness in prospect, bitter reflections could wait.

Let winter and the Nor'Westers do their worst! Let the cold crouch frosting at the windows, splitting the tall trees and booming in the ice of the St. Lawrence. Let winter pile the ice of Thunder Bay in great pans against Fort William. Let the Red River freeze in a solid block. If his success had not matched his hopes, at least he had not failed. And now he was home.

The sharp cold that had greeted Selkirk on Saturday was over by Monday, and his holiday lasted little longer. For eighteen months he had lived hard in bivouacs and forts, usually in discomfort, often in danger, and he needed rest. Yet had his sense of duty been much less stern he could not now have turned away. He had set the machinery of the law in motion and was answerable for the result. Moreover he had always known, and realized again with growing force, that he was not acting for himself alone, for his family, or for the Hudson's Bay Company. He was the instrument of justice, if not of vengeance, for his settlers.

The house the Selkirks had taken from Colonel de Chambault was headquarters for a cloud of witnesses, retainers, and advisers, and life quickly became a continuous procession of arrivals and departures. Bourke, Pritchard, Spencer, Colin Robertson, Louis Nolin, Miles Macdonell, and Samuel Gale – all eager to welcome him and convey the latest news or rumour. Sitting in his own house, he must sometimes have found it difficult to remember that there were other problems in the world or that the citizens of Montreal had anything else to talk about. In certain circles the colony and the struggle had been an absorbing topic for at least three years. Doubtless Selkirk's return and the imminence of the prosecutions had again fanned general interest to white heat, so that every hour brought fresh rumour, speculation, or opinion. In the midst of it all, the problem was to keep calm, to maintain perspective.

Two themes were prominent in the discussions. One was that the trials would be moved to York in Upper Canada, the other that there would be no trials. This latter view was based on a widely believed report that the Prince Regent had decreed a mutual return of property and the dropping of charges. The obvious and crushing comment on this had come from Alexander Wood in York the previous spring. Writing to James Woods, he had said dryly: 'The North West Company can hardly obey in the case of the lives they have taken away. On the other side there is not even a charge of the kind as yet against his Lordship's part.' To Selkirk and to all his people, the matter was now as simple as that. The idea that there could be a saw-off seemed monstrous, and yet the rumour persisted.

There seemed little doubt that the trials would take place in Upper Canada. Though it was not generally known at the time, the North Westers had applied for the move in the spring of 1817, partly on the doubtful grounds that many of their witnesses came from there. The Executive Council had recommended the measure and in November the Colonial Office had granted approval. In spite of the complete rejection of Stuart's protest, Selkirk embarked on a general presentation to Sir John Sherbrooke, which he marshalled in calm, reasonable, and persuasive tones. Among other things, he doubted that a competent jury could be found in the raw settlement of York, no larger than an English village.

There was no suggestion that he looked for favourable treatment from the Governor; it was rather the letter of one gentleman interested in the public service writing to another of like views. Before it could be delivered there came news of Sherbrooke's serious illness. He had suffered a paralysis of his left side, though his speech and brain were unimpaired, and for some days his life was in danger. In the circumstances, Selkirk's protest was not sent. It would in any case have been much too late. On the ninth of February, N. F. G. Uniacke, Attorney-General of Lower Canada, wrote that the trials were to be transferred to Upper Canada and asked Selkirk as committing magistrate to communicate the evidence in his possession.

The very next day, Commissioner Coltman transmitted a proposal from the North West Company for a compromise of the differences between the two parties on certain points. Broadly, this suggested the withdrawal of the Nor'Westers from Assiniboia and of the Hudson's Bay Company from Athabasca, and an agreement on either side not to press legal charges. Though it seems probable that Selkirk discussed this matter with Gale or Stuart, there is no evidence that acceptance was ever considered. Without consulting the Hudson's Bay Company, Selkirk turned it down out of hand on February 12. On the fourteenth he wrote simply to the Committee of the Hudson's Bay Company: 'Their suggestion came so near a proposal for compounding a felony that it was impossible to entertain for a moment.'

Yet it must have been tempting: at one stroke Red River was to be made safe and the ruinous burden of uncertain litigation lifted from his back. But the price was to overlook the shocking past, to abandon the dead and the wronged. It was too much. Was it also an objection, that neither he nor Colin Robertson could suppose the offer made in good faith? On the record, the agreement would only hold until the Nor'-Westers felt safe in breaking it. However, there was little doubt that the proposal had the approval of the Executive and an agreement might thus have had more force. Still, the Executive's actions had not been uniformly reassuring.

Coltman, consistent always in his hope for a peaceful arrangement, wrote:

Although never sanguine in my expectations of a favourable result it is with regret that I perceive every appeal to conciliation apparently rejected.

Mr. McGillivray delivered his letter in person and at the same time expressed himself much hurt at a report which had got abroad and had even as he told me been repeated by Nolin to his half-brother Cadotte that the North West Company had offered to give up Red River country in consideration of the prosecutions being abandoned: this he continued, exclusive of its inaccuracy as to times to be an unfair representation of their proposals respecting the prosecutions as to which putting both papers together, there could be no doubt of their intentions being merely to acquiesce in the propositions made by me.

Although perfectly aware that the report in question must have arisen without your Lordship's sanction . . .

Selkirk, no doubt irritated by the familiar picture of McGillivray's too-easily-wounded feelings, answered brusquely on February 21, noting the North West Company's 'singular facility in disavowing the acts of their partners'.

With respect to the expressions ascribed to Mr. Nolin it is very possible that he may have misapprehended the matter of which he was speaking but it would be useless to attempt to rectify every inaccuracy of that kind. Hardly a day passes without some report far more wide of the truth being circulated by persons connected with the N W Co who might be supposed to have better opportunity of correct information than Mr. Nolin. – Within these few days for instance one of the legal advisers of the N W Co publicly asserted that I had applied to you three different times to solicit your interposition for bringing about an accommodation.

Meanwhile in Montreal jail the servants of the Nor'Westers, charged with every crime of violence, held nightly supper parties and drank deep to the music of a piper. The neighbourhood was scandalized by the noise of roistering and by the illumination of the jail windows at night and the gay voices calling greetings into the street. It was even said that the prisoners were aggrieved at being refused a billiard table to ease their unhappy situation.

However censorious, the public could hardly fail to be impressed by this confident demeanour. These were either innocent men wrongly accused or guilty men who stood above the law; either they feared nothing or they had nothing to fear. Nor could Selkirk doubt that this was exactly the impression aimed at. Whoever challenged the lords of the lakes and forests would find that those who could make terms with the wilderness took little account of urban laws. And there was something more: men who had spent their whole lives walking, paddling, fighting, and sleeping in the open were not to be shut up without an explosion.

Like others, Selkirk was affronted at this cocky, heedless behaviour, at this lack of any sense of wrongdoing to be answered for. But, so much the worse for them. When their names were called in court they would be there to answer, and all their exuberance would avail them nothing then. When the time came, they should learn a lesson about the rule of law that neither the fur trade nor the Indian Country would ever forget. Meanwhile, whatever could be done to ensure that result must be done. In talking and writing, he reiterated the need to insist on a respect for the law – a truism to him but one that he was beginning to see could not be taken for granted.

But the first round went well and seemed to promise all he hoped. On Saturday, February 21, a session of the Court of Oyer and Terminer opened before Chief Justice Monk and the Honourable Mr. Justice Bowen. For a week it sifted evidence against North West and Hudson's Bay servants, and it brought in a series of findings that must have sounded like the hammers of doom in McGillivray's ears. Seventeen true bills were found on indictments for the murder of Governor Semple, and on a variety of lesser charges, against Nor'Westers. Of seven cases against Hudson's Bay and Red River Settlement personnel, all were dismissed except for one against Colin Robertson.

On the last day of the preliminary hearings, February 28, the charges against Cuthbert Grant were considered. The vivid young leader of the half-breeds had been a centre of interest, indeed a focus of special consideration, throughout. Now his dark, watchful quietness and the air of command about him caught the imagination of all. There was much that was dangerous in this young man, nothing that was mean. Through the long winter afternoon the case continued. There was a pause while the lamps were lighted and then the case moved inexorably on to a finding late at night: a true bill on the indictment for murder and an appeal for bail not granted. Grant, who had shared Commissioner Coltman's canoe and tent on the long journey from Red River, was led away to his cell. The sober Montreal *Gazette* reported these results on March 11 with quiet satisfaction. Selkirk's followers showed no such restraint. As February closed, it seemed the issue could not be in doubt.

With the opening of the case, however, came a whisper of cautious wisdom. Selkirk had written to James Woods of Sandwich about the probable transfer of the actual trials to York, and the handling of his affairs. The old man replied, begging to be excused court appearances on the grounds of his failing eyesight and lack of confidence in his abilities. He recommended the retaining of the Sherwoods, Samuel, and Livius – advice Selkirk was to have cause to remember. A few days later Woods wrote again about the impending appointment of young John Beverley Robinson as Attorney-General for Upper Canada. He regarded him as a young man of 'strict probity', yet it would be hard for him to believe the worst of his friends in the North West Company by whom, moreover, he had been retained. 'He would no doubt find it difficult to divest himself of his first impressions as to the innocence of his present clients. . . . I may be and I hope I am mistaken; but, if the prosecutions are at York, I fear the result.'

The year moved into March, with its heart-breaking rhythm of hope deferred, of warm days and hints of the awakening earth, followed by the slap of winter roaring back in bitter winds and black cold. Winter was in its death-grapple with spring; there could only be one outcome, but the cost of the struggle was incalculable. In the distance on still days could be heard the beat and lash of the mighty Lachine Rapids where, already, over-venturesome ice was being ground to pieces on the unsleeping rocks. There was a channel through the rapids, and there was a channel for Selkirk through the rocks of indifference, avarice, expediency, jealousy, and coward-ice. But the channel was neither for the reckless nor for the faint-hearted – only for the watchful, the steady, and the bold. He would need to be all three.

2

Whatever the gains, they were being made at a heavy cost; and even their reality seemed much in doubt. The Selkirk who had come down the front road at the end of January looked more solid, bronzed, and hale than he had for years, but by April the outward signs of rude health were all gone. Lady Selkirk and John Allan in affectionate concern urged and even badgered him to get outdoors, to take time for riding and walking. It was all to little purpose. Whatever time could be stolen from the numerous conferences and the inter-minable writing was not enough to overmatch the rage of frustration and the burning sense of injustice that fretted his strength. Outwardly, Lord Selkirk gave little sign of this dan-gerous wearing process, but an edge crept into the tone of his letters, and grew. And with growing irritation came diminished effectiveness, and then diminishing hope.

The first sharp set-back appeared, cruelly enough, in a mo-ment of triumph. The day before the Court of King's Bench concluded its sittings, Uniacke, the Attorney-General, handed Lord Selkirk two bundles of papers relating to the Keveny murder case and the approaching trial at Quebec of Reinhart and McLellan. On going through the papers later, Selkirk found one in Advocate-General Pyke's handwriting that had nothing to do with the case. It was dated February 11, 1817, addressed to Sherbrooke and signed by Lord Bathurst. So this, at last revealed, was the Colonial Secretary's response to the unsupported account of his 'resistance' to Dr. Mitchell's warrant.

The extraordinary document explained much but improved nothing. From this must have come the crushing bail, the hints from D'Arcy Boulton and others of further unspecified prosecutions; hence, too, the stiff note about Sherbrooke's intention to do his duty, however painful it might be. But it was easier to see in this the beginnings of mischief than to guess the end. Who had seen this? To how many people, from Lord Bathurst or Sherbrooke, had it become an instruction? Above all, how was it to be answered? The magistrates of the Western District at Sandwich, in reducing his bail from £6,000 to £250, had made their own comment on the charge of resistance to arrest. But Uniacke was even now moving to maintain the huge bail on the same charge in a different judicial district. Selkirk and his counsel could make nothing of it. If this was the rule of law it had little enough to do with the law he knew; and it mocked his conscious innocence.

At the first opportunity Selkirk asked the Attorney-General if he had been meant to see the paper. The answer came sharply 'no indeed', and the blundering Uniacke seemed to blame Selkirk for his own ineptness. To further questions he answered reluctantly that the paper belonged to Coltman who had brought it from Quebec and was greatly upset on finding it had come into Lord Selkirk's hands. Uniacke added that he himself had known the substance of Bathurst's dispatch (indeed, it was the reason he was now moving about the bail), but it had not been officially communicated to him. On finding that Selkirk had made a copy of the document, Uniacke asked him to give it up; this Selkirk refused to do.

It was futile to object, as Selkirk's counsel did, that this confusion of jurisdiction and of charges was 'vexatious, oppressive and unnecessary'. The bail was renewed at £6,000 without their being able to get any explanation. Samuel Gale wrote cynically that Commissioner Coltman had justified his course privately to the judges and won their support – 'one of the judges to injure Lord Selkirk, one of them to screen Coltman and both of them to please the powers that be'. Judge Reid had refused to sit on Miles Macdonell's case the previous autumn because of his North West interest, and the case could not therefore be cleared from the docket; but that interest did not now prevent him from confirming the monstrous bail on the North Westers' opponent.

It was some comfort that hostility to the North West Company and sympathy for Selkirk, covert until now, began to declare itself with growing boldness. The Montreal *Gazette* gave a lead and, in discussing the Attorney-General's refusal to bring on the cases in Lower Canada for fear of injustice, concluded tartly that wherever the cases were tried it would doubtless be hard to find a jury with which the guilty would be satisfied.

But there was little time to pause and contemplate the improving situation, as it seemed to be. All was bustle as Selkirk prepared to join Samuel Gale in Quebec for preliminary hearings in the Keveny murder trials. John Allan was setting out westward at the same time, to stand his trial at the Quarter Sessions in Sandwich for resistance to arrest. There was still enough winter left to provide hard footing for horses, and ice in the ruts of the highway to let the runners of the carriole hiss and bump easily along. As Lord Selkirk sped down-river, the St. Lawrence ice lay bland under its sparkling cover of snow, apparently undisturbed by the waxing sun. The cold nights would delay its final destruction a little longer, but daily the brown fields crept imperceptibly upwards towards the light. Presently, long blue channels would spatter the white expanse of the river; for a little longer the ice would cling, then struggle and clutch desperately at the banks, and then be gone. Behind the clopping hooves and the soothing harshness of the sleigh-bells there was time for contemplation and there was peace. The snow flowing by the carriole flung back the sun, but opened and sank steadily to sugary ruins with the dazzling effort. Selkirk had long believed that the North West Company was similarly honeycombed and rotten at the core – little more than a brave show.

On April 1, writing to Lady Selkirk from Quebec, the Earl was optimistic: they were well on the way to a true bill being found against Reinhart for the murder of Keveny; an important witness, La Pointe – simple, honest, and troubled – had given his evidence well and had stood up sturdily under a severe cross-examination. 'I have little doubt the public at Quebec will soon be of the same way of thinking as at Montreal.' He did have the caution to add, 'In the meantime however, we have need of your steel jacket and a large doze of Stubborn Patience. O.O.L.'

The next afternoon he was in his carriole again and heading back towards Montreal over nearly 200 miles of winter road. Just as he was leaving, he received word that the Attorney- and Solicitor-General had released Archie McLellan, Cuthbert Grant, and Cadotte on bail. The first two were under indictment for murder – Grant on two counts, under one of which he had already been refused bail in Montreal, while McLellan's case looked so black that McGillivray had thought it policy not to seek bail. At first he felt too stunned to think and merely ordered his driver to start. Through the long night, as the carriole slid westward, he raged and brooded over the meaning and the effect of this shocking decision.

In the morning during a stop for rest and refreshment at Three Rivers he called for writing materials and hastily wrote to Lady Sherbrooke, 'so that it may be communicated to Sir John without the formality of a letter to His Excellency or the least expectation of an answer'. He assumed she had heard of the releases by the law officers of the Crown and referred to them as 'a proceeding so grossly improper that I conceive it must ultimately lead to their cashiering'.

Until now Lord Selkirk had not thought Uniacke dishonest, only incompetent with the irreparable incompetence of stupidity. His knowledge of *voyageur* French was inadequate and his grounding in the cases faulty, yet he had steadfastly refused all real assistance from Stuart or Gale and repelled hints of his inadequacy with pompous bluster. This had driven Stuart back to Montreal in a bad temper and left Gale to write acid comments to Lady Selkirk. But all that was as nothing alongside this inexplicable and dangerous act.

However, he could only hurry back to Montreal and seek to repair the damage. If this had been his only concern it would have been enough, but he was conducting a battle on several fronts and trying in quiet good temper to watch over a variety of administrative problems as well. He was contemplating a libel suit against Archdeacon Strachan and being encouraged by many who were more cheered at the prospect of Strachan's discomfiture than informed as to its probability. He had reports to deal with, difficulties over titles to his lands in Prince Edward Island, and reports from William Mure and from Marshall, the estate agent and factor at Kirkcudbright. John Spencer, ex-sheriff of Red River, was facing what closely resembled a shot-gun marriage in Montreal and needed both money and advice. Selkirk's personal bodyguard of 1816 from the 37th Regiment had not been given the pay and allowances they thought due them from the army on their return to Drummond's Island, and Selkirk was at once in correspondence with Colonel Addison and with Captain Stephens requesting their 'good offices to obtain for these men ... favourable consideration of their claims'.

He was also in consultation and correspondence with Bishop Plessis about a Roman Catholic mission to be established at Red River. Gale had started a fund in support of the cause, to which Coltman and Sherbrooke had subscribed. The Nor'-Westers had angrily refused to do so, suggesting instead that the church should be at Fort William. They were ten years too late.

A less satisfactory and more worrying problem had arisen during the winter and hung over him all through the spring. There was to be a general election in England which must shortly be followed by an election of Scottish peers. Knowing that, Basil Hall had called on Lord Sidmouth at the end of January seeking to learn whether affairs in Canada had changed the government's attitude towards Selkirk. In all but one particular the word was wholly reassuring. Sidmouth spoke of the matter having been before the cabinet, where there was no feeling against Selkirk. It appeared he had even spoken to Bathurst on Selkirk's behalf, going so far as to state his 'positive conviction from personal knowledge of you, that your conduct must be such as you would justify to the country'. This was satisfactory – even bracing. The only condition attached to the government's support of him in the peerage election was that he should be there – 'on the spot'. This, as spring wore on, appeared increasingly difficult. The date of the election was not known, but under pressure Sidmouth had hinted that he should be home by May or, at latest, early in June. 'In the event of your not being able to return so soon as you propose,' wrote Basil Hall, 'your writing to intimate your intention of doing so as soon as possible might have great effect.' It might. But here was another pressure, and a frustration, because there could be no certainty. Things in the Canadas were dragging on – yet the peerage election probably meant more to him now, in 1818, than it had since he first stood for election.

In spite of all these distractions, Selkirk had to keep an eye open for trials being called in Upper Canada while with difficulty he held his witnesses together for trials as yet unfinished in the lower province. His letters to Uniacke in Quebec and John Beverley Robinson in Upper Canada had a note more than once of quiet desperation. Simultaneously, he sought through correspondence to find counsel of sufficient weight for the approaching trials in Upper Canada; for the moment, it appeared he had been successful with Washburne of Kingston and Barnabas Bidwell. Everyone else of standing, including the Attorney-General of Upper Canada (and the Solicitor-General of Lower Canada), had accepted retainers from the North West Company. A group of North West partners led by McGillivray was said to be on its way to Upper Canada in the hope of bringing on their trials there.

The month of April was dribbling away in futility in spite of all his efforts. Stuart had persuaded Uniacke to issue a warrant for the rearrest of Cuthbert Grant, but he was not to be found and there were rumours that he had already set out for the Northwest. Under the pressure, his Lordship exploded in a long, complaining letter to Sir John Sherbrooke, forwarding petitions from his people under bills of indictment, begging that they be tried. Their cases had been thrown out of the King's Bench, but new bills had been granted for the next session of Oyer and Terminer. By such procedures had Miles Macdonell been tied down, on charge but without trial, for nearly three years. In the same letter, some of his complaints against the law officers were voiced – also his concern that since two of the King's Bench judges had disqualified themselves because of North West interest the court must be unable to act unless further judges were appointed.

None of it seemed to yield helpful results. The letter to Sherbrooke being passed to the law officers brought sharp rejoinders from both. If his Lordship had complaints, let him complain to the home government to which alone they were accountable. John Beverley Robinson, also pressed by Selkirk, wrote with cool imperturbability on the nineteenth: 'I can only say (what I trust is scarcely necessary) that I will on this as on other occasions do my duty to the Crown in the prosecution of the offenders, as well as I may be enabled from the means placed within my reach, but without *any* consideration of *any* interests but those of public justice.'

One thing he seemed to be spared for the moment: the spectre of overwhelming expense was less immediately pressing. But, if his creditors seemed less clamorous, it was only because local outlay had abated somewhat, and Maitland, Garden and Auldjo were at hand with quiet vigilance to cushion the blow. Remorselessly, his host of witnesses ate, drank, and made merry at Selkirk's expense, like an army of mercenaries in no hurry for a war to begin. In England, heavy expenditures on account of the colony continued, but there Andrew Colvile, probably with tightened lips, handled affairs.

Among the vexatious claims was one from John Jacob Astor for high wines taken over at Fort William and for the seizure of stores and men at Fond du Lac. Astor took rather a high tone about the latter as a transgression of United States territory; but as the boundary was not absolutely defined this fact was not yet certain, and so could wait. Besides, Astor's concern for national sovereignty varied with his interests, and his injured employees had taken a hand in the most deplorable aspects of the North West offensive: the attempt to raise the Indians against the colony, and the trapping and beating of Lagimonière. So neither Selkirk nor Astor appeared to take the protest very seriously; it was merely a shrewd move in a rough game.

Meanwhile, as the sun gathered strength and spring came on, the fur-traders made ready once again for the long trek to the interior. By day, the area surrounding the North West offices in St. Gabriel Street began to fill with the gathering *voyageurs*. Singing, drinking, dancing, and fighting when they were not required to unload cargo or pack trade goods for the Upper Country, the Pork-eaters carried themselves with a swagger in Montreal; in Fort William they were more modest before the Northern men. Now, as they frolicked roughly, they gave little sign of concern for the future, but there were whispers all the same. Selkirk was not a wholly unpopular figure among them. Having been schooled in rough-and-tumble methods and rougher justice, they were more likely to be admiring than critical of the man who had so quietly and completely silenced the guns of Fort William, who had sunk the unsinkable. Accustomed to partners who ruled with their fists and hoarse curses, they delighted in the growing legend of the tall, unruffled Milord with his cool, intimidating gaze and quiet voice, who never laid hands on a servant, cared for his men like a good officer, and was obeyed without question.

The shadow of worry over the activities of the McGillivray expedition to York grew darker; then it disappeared. Washburne wrote from Kingston that the party had passed there after spending two or three days. In addition to William Mc-Gillivray, they had also their counsel, Mr. Speaker McLean, and others. And, knowing that travelling time would be short, they had booked all the accommodation on the steamer just in case Selkirk and his witnesses might arrive *en route* to the sessions of Oyer and Terminer at York. However, a letter from young George Ridout written at York on April 22 brightened the horizon. The Attorney-General had announced that he was not ready to proceed with cases from the Indian Country, and the session had adjourned. The next day, the *Frontenac* had docked with the North West partners, whose 'disappointment was great' at finding they had made their trip for nothing. To anyone who knew this masterful group, there was amusement in the spectacle of their futile chagrin; for a long time now both servants and opponents had been wont to disappoint them as little as possible. Ridout added that in all probability the trials would now be postponed until October.

Most important and ominous was Ridout's news that an act was in contemplation to remove Indian Country cases from the Western District assizes at Sandwich to York for trial. He believed it had passed the House of Assembly but had not been dealt with by the Executive Council or the Legislative Council.

He expressed two further opinions, both of them unwelcome to Selkirk's party, and both sound. He doubted that Stuart and Gale would be admitted to an active part in trials at York as Lord Selkirk's counsel, because similar courtesy was not reciprocal in Lower Canada. Strong reasons might overcome this objection, but he was not optimistic. Also, he had heard from Allan about the proposed libel action against Dr. Strachan; for technical reasons, having to do with origin of the printing of the alleged libel, he doubted that the action could be successful. George Ridout, who was always spoken of as 'young' – too young and inexperienced – seems often to have been better informed and more clear-headed on events than those more deeply involved.

At least it seemed that winter's hard grip was broken, and there was a lifting of spirits, especially for those who were beginning to worry over Selkirk's health. The mild days of early April had reduced the snow and brought spring on. Then, in the early morning of Saturday the eighteenth, wet, heavy snow began to fall. By evening, roads were blocked and still the fall continued, almost silencing life in town and country. By late Sunday it was over and with it the winter, but the effects were not thrown off at once. Rivers were swollen to the danger-point and roads turned into quagmires, though it was only a question of days now.

On the twenty-ninth the *Gazette* announced the appoint-ment of the Duke of Richmond to succeed Sir John Sherbrooke as Governor General of Canada. The Military and the socially ambitious welcomed the news, and the North West moguls bethought themselves of some welcoming event in keeping with their station – and their policy. Only Lord Dalhousie, Lieuten-ant-Governor of Nova Scotia, fumed at the news. He had suc-ceeded Sir John in Halifax and had been given reason to expect the succession at Quebec. 'I have been very ill-used,' he wrote to the Duke of Buccleuch. It was little satisfaction to him – or to anyone – to be told that Richmond's financial straits were so grave that his brother-in-law, Lord Bathurst, had been obliged to help him out with the appointment. But the cynical act might have brought cool reason to any who counted at this stage on the Colonial Office for scrupulous or deep con-cern over events in the Canadas.

Meanwhile, the exacting struggle went on. From Sandwich Dr. Allan wrote in triumph that he had been acquitted. Be-tween Quebec and Montreal bustled the conscientious but slightly absurd Coltman, taking last statements, trying to be at once impressive and agreeable to all. Archibald Norman McLeod in 1817 had both arrested Hudson's Bay people in Athabasca as a Justice of the Peace and terrorized Indians in his own right, while announcing that these were merely re-prisals for Lord Selkirk's actions at Fort William. Coltman – with apparent satisfaction, though fussed because the Gover-nor was awaiting his report – accepted a statement showing that McLeod couldn't have known about Fort William when his campaign was at its most brutal, and his law most farcical. A few days later, Coltman implied to John Allan that Selkirk might have cleared up everything had he only been reasonable and willing to compromise in February. Meanwhile, George Campbell, a prisoner and a key witness, arch-traitor of the colony in 1815, was conveyed from his prison to hospital on a plea of illness. While there, he was bailed and liberated in secret and smuggled over the frontier into the United States. The order for release was signed by the accommodating Judges Ogden and Reid.

Behind a mask of calm Selkirk worked on. Only his growing reticence provided a gauge of the growing tensions in him. He could still find time for a long, careful letter to Fowle in Kentucky about the delivery of cattle for Red River, with precise directions as to cost and method of payment, type, age, and various alternatives even down to colour; they were to be dark – black, brown, or dark red, without any spots of white. From this he turned to correspondence with Sir Charles Bagot, British ambassador at Washington, about a book of 'anonymous' letters circulating in the United States and said to be ascribed to him; as these were scurrilous and aimed at official characters, he was anxious that Bagot should take every opportunity of quashing the rumour.

But the admirable calm was brittle, and Lady Selkirk, flanked by Dr. Allan and Samuel Gale, stood by in alarmed solicitude. Even these devoted confidants were finding that taut nerves seldom permitted easy discussions of their joint problems now. The clear-cut triumph that must issue from simple justice and be a condition of future good government seemed to tremble and recede before him like a mirage. In this state he was ill-conditioned for the exasperations to come. Yet such was now the set of events that he alone might have drawn the poison that was infecting all who touched the evil circle of controversy. He could not have made Uniacke intelligent, but he need not have driven him to hostile and obstinate fury. He could not perhaps have won over the youthful and slightly pompous disapproval of John Beverley Robinson, but he need not have so offended Robinson as to lose the possibility of cordial dealing on which so much depended. He could not erase Bathurst's hasty indictment of him from the record, but, once disclosed, it might have been rendered less harmful by more conciliatory behaviour. The sick and unhappy Sherbrooke would almost certainly have welcomed an easier atmosphere in which to help a man he was disposed to like, but Selkirk was beyond any of the gracious gestures that in times of less strain came easily to him. As his situation worsened, he lost his capacity if not his willingness to improve it. There was in him at the moment much of the baited and confused Shylock crying: 'My deeds upon my head I crave the law, the penalty and forfeit of my bond.'

Chapter 12

JUSTICE IN UPPER CANADA

I

It was clear that the situation could not long continue without an explosion that might frustrate all their hopes, and the alternatives seemed no less disastrous. Under the constant stress, Selkirk's health was visibly deteriorating, and through the lengthening nights when his active brain refused him sleep he was increasingly racked by coughing. Ironically, in the distance, for the first time in Montreal's history, watchmen were calling into the still darkness, 'Two o'clock, a fine night and all's well!' – 'Four o'clock, a cloudy morning, and all's well!' Rain or shine, he probably heard all hours until the sun climbed above the horizon and flamed along the St. Lawrence. Jean Selkirk, who had so long worried over his every chest cold, watched and listened as each morning was greeted with a fit of coughing that was painful and alarming to witness.

It was taking a toll of his strength, so that some of his affairs suffered, but nothing reduced his vigilance over the trials that were proceeding and those he sought to bring on. Gale and Allan took turns observing the trials of Reinhart and

McLellan at Quebec. Selkirk, in constant communication with James Stuart, watched events from Montreal, meanwhile carrying on a tireless correspondence with Uniacke and with John Beverley Robinson. In his unrelenting drive, security for the settlers had become synonymous with the exposure, if not the destruction, of the North West Company. And, in his grasping at anything that made a case, there perhaps crept an element of vengefulness for his own impugned honour. Henry McKenzie, a partner, tried discreetly to tamper with a witness at Quebec: charge him before the Grand Jury! Shaw and Smith at Red River had claimed as restitution, and obtained from Coltman, provisions which they knew belonged legitimately to Selkirk: charge them with riot or some description of misdemeanour! In the event that the murder charges seemed likely to fail against Reinhart, McLellan, and Cadotte, charge them at least as receivers of stolen goods – the dead man's clothing and effects! 'For God's sake do not make light of these charges,' he wrote to Gale, 'because they are matters of an inferior degree of atrocity. It is of essential consequence to the peace of the interior to procure a *conviction*, upon any capital offense; and not to allow these miscreants to be discharged as innocent men, so that we should not neglect to bring against them charges for any description of felony which can be distinctly proved.'

Outwardly, life went on steadily and in calm dignity. Sundays found him in his pew at St. Gabriel's with Daer and Isabella, while round about many of the North West partners joined him in praising God from whom all blessings flow.

Once more, matters took an upward turn in June with the conviction for murder of Reinhart. But it was only momentary, for Archibald McLellan, the major connection of the North Westers with the case, was acquitted. 'It is painful to see perjury so successful,' wrote Allan from Quebec on June 16, adding that Chief Justice Sewell's charge to the jury was 'shamefully false'. 'A gentleman who sat behind me said that it seemed as if Sewell were delivering an oration composed by the counsel for the prisoners. ... I had no right to expect such want of integrity on the bench ... we must indict for perjury, nothing else will do any good.'

But that ended matters at Quebec. The Attorney-General, with scores of overlapping cases waiting, was unwilling to bring on lesser matters, and Cuthbert Grant, Cadotte, and Desmarais, also indicted for Keveny's murder, were far away. Only Grant, it appeared, had been released on bail with Uniacke's consent, but Pyke, the Advocate-General, who had been given special powers as a legal assistant to Coltman, had released several others.

Colin Robertson, who had been discharged in May and had started for Athabasca, reported that 'Bostonois [Pangman], Desmarais, Severight and others have been sporting their persons both at Michipicoton and the Sault smiling at our feeble efforts to bring [them] to justice; while they boasted of the *great service* rendered them by Col. Coltman.'

There was a final gesture to mark the end of the trials at Quebec, a grand dinner-party given in the jail by the Nor'-Westers. It was said the sheriff was of the party, as was the condemned murderer, Reinhart. It was also said that William McGillivray had announced he would take steps to see that Reinhart should not hang. Whatever there may have been of legend in all this went only to prove Selkirk's point, that the North West Company could appear to be beyond justice and infallibly to protect its own people. Already about a dozen key men, both prisoners and witnesses, had been released quietly and had disappeared, forfeiting their bail.

In May he had begged Sherbrooke to act in the rearrest of those released. 'If no efficacious measures for the arrest of the culprits should be seen to follow, it must be evident that the traders in the interior will be taught to despise the restraints of law, and the authority of Government.'

And with Uniacke, whose tone of cold dislike had become unmistakable, he had managed for the moment to adopt a note of conciliation. 'You are aware that I am acting here not for myself alone but for a number of people. ... It is not only my right but my duty to remonstrate when I see a public officer pursuing a line of conduct which appears to me inconsistent with justice.' The bench warrants for the new arrests were interminably slow in coming and Uniacke defended himself over the delay by saying the Council had not yet decided on the measure. Allan thought it futile in any case. 'It is in my humble opinion, needless to send any warrants into the interior. For what purpose give these vagabonds another party of pleasure to Montreal to be again set at liberty?'

Disillusionment seemed complete. Allan thought better of Uniacke than Selkirk; at least he didn't believe him a North West partisan and felt he had done his poor best at Quebec. Gale, more knowing in the law, thought him stupid and inept, having done his case more damage with his cross-examination than had the defence with their examination-in-chief. Gale had added: 'I am glad to be as unconnected with Government as heretofore; for I certainly should not think it an honour to possess a commission of any kind from a Government which I conceive to have conducted itself with an impropriety amounting to infamy.'

May and June had seen little gain and much loss; but there was always July. It wasn't possible that such a calendar of open crime could go unpunished; it must not be. Selkirk, in the faint hope of a special session of Oyer and Terminer at York, prepared to go up, and the effort with its renewed hope seemed for the moment to improve his health. On July 4 he cleared up some letters on other matters that had waited for weeks.

One had to do with a somewhat embarrassing ghost from the dead past. In the spring he had had a long letter from Thomas Halliday, a settler in Prince Edward Island, who reminded Selkirk of the promised 200 acres of land which he was to have been given, half the land being in trust for Halliday's ward, Mary Cochrane. He had occupied the land for many years but could get no clear title. Slyly he had added one or two malicious stories of his neighbours; one had asked whether the red-headed girl was really his child. Still another had boldly asserted that Selkirk was the girl's father and identified the mother as being from a parish near Kirkcudbright.

281

In answering him, Selkirk ignored the innuendoes but expressed concern at Halliday's difficulty. To make up for it, the grant was to be increased from 200 acres to 300. And by the same mail he wrote sternly to his agent William Johnston, giving effect to the promise and requiring him to clear up the matter of title for Halliday and his ward. 'I am extremely disappointed that any just claims on me, should so long have remained unsettled.'

The next day he left for York, driving to Coteau above the rapids where he was overtaken by his canoe. The change of air and scene at once improved his spirits, so that even a dinner of eggs and bread and cheese at the wretched inn had been acceptable. He slept that night in the canoe very comfortably; it was like stetching out on the sofa at home, he wrote from Cornwall the next day, only the more pleasant for the open air.

Two weeks later, having reported his arrival to Attorney-General Robinson, he was writing his 'Dearest Love' a letter which must have much relieved her worries. He referred to a report on his health which Allan was sending to Dr. Robertson.

> I have not seen it but it ought to be a great deal better than when I left Montreal. I have begun to take little rides on the Old General and find it very pleasant. The coughing and expectoration seldom troubles me at night – but generally there is a fit, in the morning, sometimes more sometimes less, but never so bad as usually at Montreal. I feel ready for my bed early in the evening, but this is almost the only symptom of want of strength. O. O. L.

Within a few days it was clear the court was not going to sit until October, but with his improved spirits he could accept the fact cheerfully. He did not blame the Attorney-General and the time had not been lost. The gain in health alone was worth while.

In his absence, Jean had not been idle. Probably thinking of his health and the children's, she had taken a house for the summer on the Lower Lachine Road, near the head of Nun's Island. The cry of the watchmen would be well traded for the soothing rush of the mighty Lachine Rapids. There was nothing to be done now about the cases until September; doubtless she hoped for some recovery of his peace of mind and tranquillity beside the timeless and unhurried river.

And probably a little relief was purchased, but delay itself was a frustration in his present frame of mind. In mid-August he wrote to James Stewart in Halifax: 'I have been immersed in the perplexities of the law aggravated by every circumstance that could well be added to render them more irksome and vexatious. . . . In addition my health has been very indifferent this summer; from what cause I know not. . . . The fatigue and privations I met in the Indian Country I felt as nothing, and willingly would I undergo ten times as much to be out of the pettifogging atmosphere of this Province.' He added that a more interesting letter would have to wait until he was washed clean of 'the mud of the law'.

His worry had become twofold. Not only were prosecutions against the North West partners and employees maddeningly slow and uncertain, in spite of massive circumstantial evidence, but he was facing prosecution for 'various acts of injustice and oppression in the months of August, September and October 1816' – the haunting echoes of Fort William. So much he had learned from Beverley Robinson. It didn't give him enough on which to prepare himself, but it was enough to worry over. Somehow, unaccountably, the shoe had got on the wrong foot. He realized now how much offence his behaviour at Fort William had given even to friends. He had been careless in crossing the line between actions as a magistrate and as an individual hostile to the North West Company, taking it for granted that in both capacities he was acting in the public interest and that all reasonable people would share that view.

But his uneasiness was probably lulled as, in something of a holiday spirit, a party of them set out by steamer for Sandwich in late August. Jean was taking Daer and Isabella, and although Dr. Allan had faced the Quarter Sessions in April and had been freed, he was going along with Samuel Gale and D'Orsonnens. The latter was joined with Selkirk in the charge of forcible entry to Fort William, but had not to face the charge of resistance to Dr. Mitchell's warrant. The steamer *Charlotte* to Kingston and then on by the *Frontenac* to Niagara took a week of peaceful travel through the Thousand Islands and the slow traverse of Lake Ontario. Above the falls of Niagara they transferred to a new steamboat, *Walk on the Water*, and for another five days progressed sedately through Lake Erie to Detroit and Sandwich.

On a calm Sunday, *Walk on the Water* eased into the wharf at Detroit. No sooner had she done so than the sheriff of Wayne County stepped on board and served a writ on Selkirk at the instance of James Grant, who had been in charge of the Fond du Lac post and arrested by Selkirk's order in the autumn of 1816. This was the same James Grant who by turns was a Canadian and an American, a partner of the North West Company and an employee of the American Fur Company, a recruiter of Indians to attack Red River and to stop and beat Lagimonière and rob him of his dispatches. He now appeared as an injured plaintiff, charging that his post had been robbed of goods and provisions to the amount of $50,000. Across the river, in sight, lay Sandwich, where the assizes for the Western District were about to begin. It was a bad moment. However, kindly advice produced an able counsel, and sureties, and presently the party was allowed to proceed with one more baffling case hanging over Selkirk. It was not surprising to learn that this latest manoeuvre was the work of Simon McGillivray. His brother William was busy in Montreal arranging a dinner for the Duke of Richmond at which, though under indictment for murder, he was to preside.

Once again, as the cases opened in Sandwich, appeared the familiar pattern of progress followed by sharp set-back. The first case on the docket was the by-now-famous resistance to Robinson's service of Dr. Mitchell's warrant, the tale of which had produced Lord Bathurst's devastating memorandum of February 1817. After a brief consideration, it was thrown out by the Grand Jury; the cause of Bathurst's peremptory instruction to prosecute was not considered worth a trial.

Selkirk's party felt confident that the charge of assault and wrongful arrest of Deputy Sheriff Smith would meet a like fate. The circumstances had been fully explained at the time to Lieutenant-Governor Gore, whose own direction, on the suspension of magisterial powers beyond Sault Ste. Marie, had rendered Smith's warrant invalid. True, Gore had never replied to this or any of his Lordship's communications, but the reasons for the action were fully and officially documented. Selkirk faced the event with calm confidence. Then, at the last moment, the Attorney-General directed that the indictment, being somewhat irregular in form, be quashed – a step that he had told John Allan in the spring he never took without direction from government. The magistrate refused to quash the indictment and renew bail, but still the case did not go on; it remained on the docket, as did that for forcible entry.

Instead of proceeding with these cases as the Chief Justice advised him to do, Attorney-General Robinson now, without immediate warning, brought his case for 'various acts of injustice and oppression in August, September and October of 1816'. It was presented in the form of a charge against the Earl of Selkirk for conspiracy to injure or destroy the trade of the North West Company. It was 'a masked battery', Selkirk said later, for though he knew something of the kind was coming he had not anticipated the charge at this time and had few witnesses; the Attorney-General had forty, most of them partners or clerks of the North West Company. Long afterwards, Robinson claimed to have based his actions on Coltman's report. But Coltman had specifically said that he did not believe a charge of conspiracy could be made out against Selkirk. It was the last in a series of upsetting circumstances, and at this crucial point in the struggle it caught Selkirk off balance.

Those who knew him best, those who had watched him with devoted concern, must have guessed that the massing of events at Sandwich had swiftly undone the improvements of July and August. The shock of the writ at Detroit had been capped by a scurrilous pamphlet printed to meet him at Sandwich and purportedly written by Daniel McKenzie. The satirical little eight-page document, putting the transactions at Fort William in their worst possible light, was an effective and wounding shot; either it was not written by McKenzie or he was far from the senile fool his partners claimed.

The attitude of John Beverley Robinson throughout added fuel to the dangerous flame. As a law officer of the Crown, his duty to prosecute effectively was recognized and accepted, but the fact that he had been retained by the North West Company made Selkirk's supporters uneasy, and the virulence of his attack ended by making him suspect. Soon after their arrival, John Allan had requested him to lay a charge of perjury against Vandersluys and McTavish for swearing to the stealing of guns which they knew to have been taken on a warrant. Robinson refused, saying that it was natural that knowing the guns belonged to the North West Company they should regard them as stolen. Besides, the warrant, 'if legal', was for search and seizure 'within' the fort; the guns were seized outside. Not content with the irritating aside, he went on to a lofty lecture in his best youthful manner.

> If in these conclusions they have been mistaken ... they have but fallen into an error of which too many instances appear in the conduct of all parties.
> I feel that I shall be acting unjustly in singling out these Gentlemen for an infamous crime, for a mistake of the laws which in my opinion is general throughout this unfortunate contest, and with such a consciousness I will not be instrumental by straining criminal charges beyond what the law will bear or justice requires, in heightening that feeling of recrimination which already prevails too much.

It was a proper position if it had not been contradicted by Robinson's every act in seeming to strain criminal charges against Selkirk beyond what justice required, and Allan's enraged answer was probably a reflection of Selkirk's views.

When you proceed to speak of the conduct of Lord Selkirk and his people at Fort William as if you were in possession of the evidence on both sides of the question you will permit me to observe that you deceive yourself and may be led to do injustice to others. . . .

It was probably through an equal mistake of the law, although of another kind that the houses of the Colonists with the schooner at Red River were burnt, that Governor Semple with twenty others were put to death and that nearly two hundred men, women and children were driven from their homes. . . .

The mothers may lie down in the dust, and the womb forget the slain, but the memory of these deeds shall not pass away. Even should the Government order all prosecutions against the murderers to be dropt, and insist only on the prosecution of those who have laboured to prevent the continuance of their crimes.

Selkirk's case, in human terms, had come down to this cry of outraged injustice. Doubtless it made Allan feel better, but it seriously damaged relations with the shocked and ruffled Attorney-General. He said later that no one had ever spoken to him in such a manner and he did not consider the fact of Allan's having been a sailor to be a sufficient excuse.

But the unkind fates that were driving Selkirk towards dangerous shoals had still another blow for him. Unwarned, he saw in a newspaper the results of the election of Scottish peers and learned he was not elected; it was the first time since 1806. It was one more blow to his pride, one more triumph for the enemies who were pressing him hard. And it seemed to be incontrovertible evidence that the government in London were to be counted against him; this was more of Lord Bathurst's justice.

And now he faced a charge of conspiracy.

The accounts of what followed are confused and contradictory and painful. In spite of the Attorney-General's concern not to heighten the feeling of recrimination, the event accomplished nothing else, and both he and the Chief Justice were now drawn within the angry circle. It was the disastrous explosion of feeling that was bound to come.

The case began by Selkirk objecting to two members of the Grand Jury – an agent of the North West Company and his brother. The objection was overruled by Chief Justice Powell who said that if the gentlemen felt their interest to require it of them they would doubtless withdraw; they did not do so.

After the Chief Justice had explained the nature of the charge of conspiracy, Mr. Robinson, saying that the evidence was voluminous and complex, suggested that Mr. Simon McGillivray should examine the witnesses before the Grand Jury. To this strange proposal the Grand Jury itself objected and the Chief Justice assured them that at least there could be no objection to the Attorney-General's conducting the examination for their benefit, though he would not, if they did not wish it. This suggestion was accepted.

On the following day Lord Selkirk rose in court to complain against the unusual procedure being followed, and suddenly all his pent-up fury at the injustice he felt burst out. The unseemly wrangle that followed brought him close to contempt, if not beyond the bounds, and only the firmness of Gale and Woods, his counsel, checked what must otherwise have quickly become a shameful incident he could never have forgiven himself. There was a moment when Selkirk and the Attorney-General were shouting at each other, with Selkirk pounding the table, but the ill and goaded figure was silenced at last and the examination before the Grand Jury went relentlessly on. A number of the witnesses called had already perjured themselves in previous cases.

The court waited through Thursday, Friday, and Saturday while the Petit Jury grew restless, uncertain whether they were to be required or not. On Monday at one o'clock the Chief Justice, having had no satisfactory answer about the Grand Jury's approach to a conclusion, adjourned the court *sine die*. It was finished, with once again nothing settled or cleared. The Chief Justice defended what he had done on the ground that the Grand Jury had begun to hear defence witnesses and would give him no answer on their progress. Selkirk believed that he was about to be cleared and that the Chief Justice had intervened to save the Attorney-General the humiliation of losing another bill. The only certainty is that it ended in great bitterness and heightened recrimination.

The prospect was bleak. Were they to go on into the indefinite future, returning to Sandwich, solving nothing, getting no answer – like a Flying Dutchman unable to enter port with a clear name? In its sense of utter futility, it was the lowest point they had yet faced.

Had they but known, they might have salvaged some grim satisfaction from a letter that William McGillivray in Montreal was even then writing to Lord Bathurst. Uniacke, weary of North West complaints and with a full knowledge of the pressures put on him, had burst out irritably that the partners of the North West Company must be sensible that justice had been done them. 'To this I shall only reply', wrote the masterful McGillivray, 'that the partners of the North West Company are *not* sensible that justice has been done them and that Mr. Attorney-General need not cherish the hope that either the great power of his office or his attempt to identify himself with his Majesty's Government, will deter them from complaining of injustice by whomsoever inflicted, or repelling misrepresentation by whomsoever advanced.'

The partners were due to get 'justice' at York late in October, and Selkirk's people, however they might try to gather their hopes, had little doubt now of the result. Meanwhile there were plans to make. It was not worth while, all of them returning to Montreal in order to turn back again to York almost at once. Besides, Gale was seriously ill, in part no doubt from the upsetting events at Sandwich. It was decided that Gale and Allan should make their way to York by easy stages. The Selkirks would return to Montreal whence he planned to come back for the trials of those charged with the murders at Seven Oaks. It was perhaps then, as they discussed plans, that the idea of Selkirk's returning to England began to take shape. There was no justice to be found in Canada, and there was none because the home government had decreed otherwise. The result of the peerage election seemed to confirm this. Was it not best to confront his traducers there? When he left Gale and Allan, it was still undecided, though in travelling by York Selkirk let it be understood that he intended to return for the trials. The prosecutions were, of course, to be conducted by Attorney-General Robinson, and in his present frame of mind Selkirk could not have viewed that circumstance with any great degree of satisfaction. Months ago – a lifetime, it seemed – James Woods had said of Robinson, 'He would no doubt find it a difficult matter altogether to divest himself of his first impressions as to the innocence of his present clients. ... I hope I am mistaken but, if the prosecutions are at York, I fear the result.' And now, following on Sandwich, they all did.

One little ray of light shone across the river from Detroit as Allan and Gale left Sandwich. The renowned Judge Woodward, in a lengthy and elaborate judgment, decided against the validity of Grant's writ, because it had been served on Sunday.

The Selkirks' return to Montreal was comparatively peaceful and healing, though the news of Sandwich pursued them in the York papers and was never far from their minds. In York they called on the newly arrived Lieutenant-Governor, Sir Peregrine Maitland, but saw only Lady Sarah, whom Jean Selkirk pronounced 'pretty and interesting looking'.

En route, a variety of reports reached them from Red River, and more were waiting at Montreal, most of them cheerful. The crops had suffered undetermined damage from grasshoppers but it appeared the settlers would have at least 3,000 bushels of wheat harvested, a plentiful supply of potatoes, and a good quantity of pemmican. Colin Robertson wrote that the de Meurons had worked wonders and German Street looked as though it had been settled ten years instead of only ten months. The Highlanders, he said, were working and grumbling as usual; but he added that the heavy crop weighed down a lot of complaints that existed only in their own unhappy dispositions. The two Catholic priests who had gone up, Fathers Provencher and Dumoulin, had been welcomed and were actively at work.

The cheerful news was confirmed at Kingston where Selkirk engaged some *voyageurs* newly arrived from Red River to take the family on by *bateaux* to Montreal. Once into the St. Lawrence River, their progress was swift as, scorning all portages, they shot the successive rapids in their path. Lady Selkirk felt she wouldn't do it again for pleasure but to the children it was bliss. Little Isabella was never in the least uneasy while Daer, uncertain at first, was 'dancing in the boat for joy' as they swung and rose and fell through the roughest water of the Sault St. Louis, the Lachine Rapids. It was work for experts, for between the banks glowing with autumn colours the turbulent water that bore them safely had drowned countless of the unwary in times past.

But without mishap they reached Montreal in the evening of October 13, a week after leaving York. Baby Katherine was asleep but the temptation to waken her could not be resisted. Daer and Isabella, her small playmates, she knew at once, and 'even pa and ma' were soon good friends. After a six-week separation they were delighted to find her quite well, and fondly pronounced her 'much advanced in intelligence'.

Sandwich with its unpleasant memories seemed a long way off.

2

The trials in Muddy York came on at last on Monday, October 26.

In the morning of the long-awaited day the motley crowd of the official and the merely curious, the fashionable and the humble, converged on the Richmond Street court-house. It was not certain just when the trials would begin, but no one who could be present balked at the prospect of long preliminaries: they would merely be sauce to the main dish. For two years and more the struggle between Lord Selkirk and the North West Company had made lively talk from Westminster to Athabasca, and every case to be heard at the York assizes had been prejudged a thousand times; now they would see.

Inside the shabby court-house there was a last-minute bustle of preparation: the stoking of the big, pot-bellied stove, the placing of the prisoners who had been marched up from King Street jail. The lawyers were laying out papers and muttering together at their respective tables as the clerk settled himself and the public crowded in. Robert Simpson, who had come from Montreal to take a shorthand record, had a table beside the bench.

In the final minutes before court opened, there was a shuffling and settling, a last craning of necks to see who was there, to get a look at the tough, impressive group of half-breeds, *voyageurs*, and fur-traders who crowded the witness-benches. It was not hard to find in those lined, brown faces above the thick shoulders and hard, quiet hands evidence of guilt or innocence as sympathy suggested; in the unfamiliar and formidable scene of the court-house, glancing about covertly, muttering together, they looked guarded, guileless, and trapped.

In vain the curious eyes sought for Lord Selkirk; but he was not to be seen at the Crown officers' table or among the witnesses, though late on Friday the Attorney-General had told the court he confidently expected Lord Selkirk's arrival on Saturday or Sunday and asked that the case be held over. The Chief Justice had remarked, though without heat, that the court could not wait on Lord Selkirk, but he did not in any event propose to deal with cases from the Indian Country until Monday.

Samuel Gale and John Allan sat together in watchful silence. Neither had any confidence in this court; Gale because he was scornful of this new province and its system of justice, and both because the memory of Sandwich was still too vivid. Gale was still weak from his recent illness and ready to find fault. Since Saturday he and Allan had known Lord Selkirk would not arrive for the trials.

There was a sudden stir and scraping of chairs and then, with all the dignity to be commanded by his short body and florid, surprised face, his Lordship, Chief Justice William Dummer Powell, took his place on the bench. He was followed by Mr. Justice Campbell and by Mr. Justice D'Arcy Boulton – a new judge and something of an unknown quantity, who but a few months ago would have been leading the prosecution for the Crown, assisted by John Beverley Robinson as Solicitor-General. Now Robinson stood forward as Attorney-General, assisted by the judge's son, Henry John Boulton, the new Solicitor-General.

John Beverley Robinson, the King's Attorney-General, bore himself with the modesty of good breeding but with the confidence of his youth, his striking good looks, and his acknowledged talents. Moreover, today he was pleading a strong case before the Chief Justice who had, throughout Robinson's short career, been his affectionate patron. If Beverley Robinson had a weakness it was that doors opened almost too easily to his persuasive pushing. He usually got what he wanted. Perhaps the doubt was whether his duty and his inclination called for the same thing today.

The crowd heard that clear, confident, young voice; it was the long-awaited moment: 'I am ready, My Lord, I take the charge of murder against Boucher and Brown ... The charge which I now propose to try them on is for the murder of Governor Semple.'

At once the clear, dramatic moment was clouded, then stolen away. Samuel Sherwood of Montreal, leading for the defence, was on his feet moving that one of the accessories in custody, John Siveright, be admitted to bail. There followed a spirited exchange during which the Chief Justice became testy ('state things correctly Mr. Sherwood'). Sherwood, supported by his lean, sharp-faced younger brother, Livius, continued to argue stoutly, and perhaps then the Attorney-General began to sense the stiffness of the door he must open. The Chief Justice refused the application and Sherwood, unruffled, sat down.

As the case commenced again with the swearing of the jury and the Solicitor-General's opening phrase, Livius Sherwood stood up to move that John Siveright, since he could not be bailed, might now be tried.

The Chief Justice, with a characteristic cocking of his eyebrows, scolded the unabashed defence: 'I do like to march on the old beaten road that I am acquainted with' and, after more argument, 'It is really wrong at this time to perplex us with a new question.'

'I do not press the proposition,' said Samuel Sherwood casually, and moved that the witnesses on the part of the Crown be ordered to withdraw. The crowd, which had grown restless during this legal sparring, watched the witnesses file out. The prisoners, stony-faced, stared ahead or looked towards the Sherwoods and McGillivrays. Now it must really be going to start.

The Attorney-General's opening for the Crown was matter-of-fact enough, but the clear, unemphatic story of events leading up to Governor Semple's death was new in its details to many present and full of drama and horror to all. Robinson paused over one point only, that a first shot was fired in accident by a member of Semple's party, but long before the two groups met, and therefore was not the exciting cause of the massacre nor even relevant to it. He described the thirty or forty riders drifting across the lens of Semple's telescope on that calm June evening, the verification and too-hasty decision to investigate, the panic-stricken settlers running towards the fort, calling that the half-breeds had come; then the encounter with all its dreadful consequences. Attention in the court was complete and even Sherwood seemed to be silenced.

Presently he broke silence to a purpose, calling it one of the most extraordinary speeches ever heard in a court-room. In particular, he attacked all reference to Semple as governor; he was, said Sherwood, as much an emperor as a governor. It was the first attack on the Hudson's Bay charter claims and on Selkirk's title to Assiniboia. As the defence started to develop the point, the Chief Justice cut in sharply. 'Do let the trial go on ... he is not to be murdered though he was not a governor.'

Thereafter, the Attorney-General led his first witness, Michael Heden, through the story of Seven Oaks to the taking over of Fort Douglas on the day after the massacre. The story of the plundering of the prisoners was being developed when Sherwood gave another hint of the course he would follow. This was a charge of murder, he said; if larceny and the taking of forts was considered to be evidence he could a tale unfold. The Attorney-General answered that the events following the murder must be introduced to show the *bois-brûlés'* intention. The murder of Semple and his men was only a preliminary to the taking of the fort and destruction of the settlement.

Heden told his story with reasonable clarity, especially on the one point. The first two shots of the encounter killed Lieutenant Holte and wounded Robert Semple. Robinson asked, 'Can you say that you know the two first shots came from the half-breed party?' 'Oh, my God!' cried Heden, 'I could not but know, for I saw all and shall never forget it.'

In the dramatic silence that followed this outburst, Sherwood set about his cross-examination crisply. On the straight question of murder, this was damning testimony. The witness had either to be discredited or the issue widened. While being questioned about land titles, Heden mentioned casually that he had not paid for his land at Red River. 'Then how dare you, or anyone else, go and take lands in that country, any more than this?' Once again Lord Selkirk's title and Governor Macdonell's authority were called in question. Presently, while Heden shifted on the stand, Sherwood was expounding his view of what he chose to treat as a fur-trade war. The young attorney-general's half-hearted objections were overridden. The bench was uneasy but Sherwood was winning attention, winning the permission, at first refused, to show the events leading up to the clash on the nineteenth of June. Only then did he reveal his full defence: that in the conditions at Red River – conditions of a private war such as existed in the time of Edward I between the Earls of Hereford and Gloucester – the resulting deaths could not be charged as murder but only as a great riot or misdemeanour.

Heden, under examination again, reiterated that the settlers did not go out to fight, but he admitted that some carried bayonets. 'Were they to spear fish?' asked Sherwood.

The discomfited Heden was now led through a maze of questions relating to the events of June 19, with recurring sallies about Governor Semple. ('He was no more a governor than he was a Turkish Bashaw, no more than he was an emperor,' said Sherwood.) Then came an innocent-sounding question: 'Do you remember any conversation at the time of your going out with Mr. Semple? Speak of Mr. Semple because he is not to be governor any more. Do you recollect his saying anything about taking of pemmican?' Samuel Sherwood did not linger over Heden's denial. It was known that the half-breeds claimed to be carrying pemmican cross-country for the North West brigades; and much had already been made of the seizure of pemmican under Miles Macdonell's proclamation. A motive for aggression by Semple's party had now been suggested without an objection from John Beverley Robinson.

More general questions followed and then the unprepared-for thrust at Heden. 'Did you ever say to anybody, no matter whom, "We have been disappointed, we deserved what we got, we fired first. . . ."?'

Heden: 'No I did not. I never said anything like it.'

Mr. Sherwood: 'And everything you have sworn to today is as true as this? Is it?'

Heden: 'Yes it is all true.'

Mr. Sherwood: 'I ask you, is it all as true *as this* – that you never said your party fired first?'

Heden gave his agreement with flustered truculence, and the defence let it pass for the moment. But after some further background examination the question reappeared. 'Did you ever tell anybody in *this town*, or anywhere else, that it was your party or the Hudson's Bay people who fired first?' Heden answered sullenly, 'I have told you before.' 'And you must tell me again,' said Mr. Sherwood.

296

When Sherwood at length sat down, he might have worn a tentative smile of satisfaction.

In the hours that followed, there was little to shake that early confidence. Donald McCoy, John Bourke, Pierre Pambrun, and John Pritchard, called by the Crown, all told stories that filled in the growing mosaic of North West violence. But though they left a strong presumption that the first firing had come from the half-breeds, there was little or no good evidence. Moreover, though Boucher's presence at the battle was not in dispute, it was accepted that after his altercation with Semple his horse had dragged him out of the immediate area. As for Paul Brown, no one had yet claimed to have seen him near the battle though he had afterwards boasted of killing six Englishmen.

By now Sherwood seemed to control the court-room. The Attorney-General's objections grew more perfunctory; the confident and radiant young man of the morning now looked dejected and worn. Gale wrote of Robinson's shrugging helplessly as his objections were overborne: 'It is by such tricks that appearances are to be saved.'

Sherwood proceeded deftly to exploit the opportunity he had created. Above all, he was determined to ridicule any notion of Red River as a serious attempt at settlement or even a possible site for it. It was to be seen only as a thinly disguised Hudson's Bay aggression led by Selkirk's agents. He referred to the troubles at The Forks, 'since my Lord Selkirk has been a trader there' – and it passed unchallenged.

The settlement was never referred to save with a jeering contempt: 'this flourishing settlement, where nothing can ever ripen ...' since five or six inches of frost was not unusual, 'even in summer'; 'this settlement forms a rendez-vous for the former servants of the Hudson's Bay Company from which they can most conveniently intercept the supplies and returns of their rivals in the fur-trade.' If Sherwood knew no better than this, Robinson did, but he let it pass.

'This flourishing settlement without a single house', said Sherwood, '– nothing more than a camp of hunters.' The Attorney-General might have countered effectively by recalling that there had been some twenty-five houses, and a mill and a Governor's Mansion and a schooner, until the North West Company's half-breeds burned them all. But for the moment he was beaten from the field and silent.

'It appears rather Mr. Attorney, to have been habitations than a settlement,' said the Chief Justice with a kind of gentle reproachfulness. Again John Beverley Robinson seems merely to have shrugged helplessly while Gale and Allan watched in frustrating silence.

By now Sherwood's masterful confidence led him into successful argument with the bench. He produced Blackstone and read it over the Chief Justice's protests; then, finger on the passage, he handed up the book to William Dummer Powell – and won his point.

The defence counsel could not obliterate the picture of North West lawlessness but he could meet it by pouring scorn on the alleged legality of Miles Macdonell's and Colin Robertson's activities – the pemmican seizures, the interception of mail, the razing of Fort Gibraltar. His grasp of events allowed him to cap each witness's evidence so as to leave an impression of at least matching guilt; and always Selkirk's settlers were so lumped with Hudson's Bay servants as to maintain the suggestion that this was simply a fur-trade war. The court's attempts to insist that background evidence must relate directly to the events of June 19, or at least be part of a continuous state of excitement, were listened to respectfully and respected not at all.

'Do you mean to swear that crops actually ripened?' asked Sherwood incredulously of one witness.

Increasingly, the defence in cross-examination brushed aside the witnesses' knowledge of the affair at Seven Oaks and made much of the Pemmican War and of mutual ambushes on the rivers, and of the futility of the idea of a settlement – the picture of a private war. When late at night the court was adjourned, the Crown had not yet completed its case, but Selkirk's most ardent supporters could feel no optimism. The seemingly simple, clear-cut case of the morning was slipping through the Attorney-General's fingers.

On Monday evening Gale, still below his strength, encountered McLellan in the street. Without warning the latter attacked him and struck him several times with his stick.

On Tuesday morning, October 27, after a somewhat academic discussion of the court's jurisdiction, the Attorney-General called young Louis Nolin, a freeman of Red River. In his precise French, through an interpreter, Nolin described the aftermath of the battle, half-breeds appearing at Fort Douglas the next day in the clothing of the dead colonists. Once again the issue of calculated brutality, of lawless savagery, seemed clearly re-established. Louis Blondeau was called to give evidence of the summoning of the half-breeds from the Upper Country for a descent on Red River. He testified that they had been carefully instructed that if fighting began they must make sure of getting the principals 'or their heads'. The prosecution rested its case.

With deadly effect, Sherwood began at once to roll up the Crown's case. His first two witnesses testified that Blondeau was a drunkard and a doubtful character. The second went on to assert flatly that for the half-breeds to ride about in war-paint and give the war-whoop was by no means a sign of hostile intentions.

All through the morning came witnesses to develop the picture of private war – or a great riot, in which death by violence is not murder. The Attorney-General's knowledge of the case was much less sure than Sherwood's and his cross-examination did nothing to check the fate that was overtaking him. Every Hudson's Bay aggression was magnified, every North West action made to appear merely as self-defence. As to the Seven Oaks affair, an alibi for the defendant Paul Brown was sworn by two witnesses. It was strongly suggested that the half-breeds had really intended to pass by without a clash, and only Semple's rash act had prevented them. Boucher at least was still in much danger because, if it could be proved that the half-breeds began the battle deliberately, the guilt of murder would probably rest on all who were there.

The Crown's first witness was dealt with last of all. Heden, the blacksmith, had sworn that the half-breeds had fired first, and under menacing cross-examination had reiterated his statement. Now, to close his case, Sherwood produced two witnesses to testify that Heden had asserted the contrary to them: 'We cannot blame the half-breeds, we fired first, and if we had got the better we would have served the half-breeds the same.' 'We fired first and they are murdering Brown and Boucher by keeping them in gaol.'

The Honourable William McGillivray, architect of North West policies, testified briefly and with the dignity of conscious virtue to the good characters of Brown and Boucher, and the defence closed.

'Such swearing', wrote Gale, 'compassed about with a cloud of witnesses, tutored on one side not sifted on the other – what result could be expected? or what could be the evidence of one against a host. . . . The Chief is a wretch. Mr. Campbell seems the only unbiased judge.'

The case that went to the jury could only have one outcome. Summing up late in the evening, the weary Chief Justice struggled at first with his notes, pushed close to a flickering candle. Impatiently, he at last put the notes by and instructed the jury to acquit Paul Brown, since his alibi had not been overturned; as to the innocence or guilt of Boucher, they must decide. The jury withdrew, but before the judges even had time to leave the court-house they returned with a verdict of not guilty on both men.

With grim reluctance, Gale decided to stay on for the remaining trials, 'and to submit once more to the torture of witnessing a trial at York, where ignorance and partiality will preside and where the prosecution will be conducted with apathy and defended with acrimony'.

The event proved his fears correct. A series of preliminary trials for theft and arson at the colony in 1815 all ended in acquittals. These were followed by the trials of the partners arrested at Fort William, with the exception of William Mc-Gillivray. Gale listened with mounting disgust to a strange *mélange* of accusations against the Hudson's Bay Company which went unanswered:

> Relations, only on one side, of irritations caused at distant times and at different places are produced combined and confounded together. Dates are confused, hearsay is brought forward where facts are deficient, the charges from the bench increase the confusion till all becomes perfect chaos. In a case of doubt the jury are bound to acquit. It must certainly be a case of doubt where all is unintelligible. It is vain to expect that these matters should be elucidated by an Upper Canada Court, it possesses neither the ability nor the inclination to throw light upon a complicated subject.

Throughout, the Attorney-General had refused Gale any hand in proceedings and had turned his back on one proposal that might have yielded a different result. Gale had suggested that all prisoners might be tried for the murder of Rogers rather than Semple, for Rogers was generally known to have been killed at Seven Oaks while on his knees begging for mercy. In his case the issue of murder was clearer and turned less on the question of who fired the first shot. As the case closed, the North West partners were free to claim that they were completely vindicated.

Gale merely groaned at the wretched and foregone betrayal of so many hopes: 'Can any good come out of Upper Canada?'

3

Selkirk's failure to arrive at York neither much surprised nor at all disappointed Gale and Allan. The final decision had been left for consultation with Gale's partners, Stuart and O'Sullivan, and Lady Selkirk wrote on the fifteenth that both were 'of the same mind with ourselves as to L.S's motions'. Gale answered that he was relieved from a weight of care. 'I have been in great anxiety for some time lest he come hither.' Allan, too, 'rejoiced' in the decision. But it both surprised and angered John Beverley Robinson, who said afterwards that he hoped his Lordship's failure to arrive fooled his own people, for it certainly fooled him. Mr. Robinson didn't like to be wrong and this was one more cause of complaint against Lord Selkirk.

Just before leaving Montreal, Selkirk, who seemed to have recovered his usual iron control of manners and temper, wrote both Robinson and Sir Peregrine Maitland, expressing his regret at not being present at the trials in York, but referring to urgent business requiring him in England. He did not resist the temptation to refer in bitter complaint to the proceedings at Sandwich, and to the abrupt termination of the trials, which had deprived him 'of the opportunity of exposing the perjured calumnies against me'. He went on:

> You are aware that it has been with extreme inconvenience that I attended at that court and that I have incurred great expense in bringing witnesses from a distance; and if the matter has not been brought to issue it cannot be alleged that this has arisen from any backwardness on my part to meet my accusers.

His last few days in Montreal passed all too quickly in writing these final letters and in drafting an exhaustive memorial to the newly arrived Duke of Richmond, on the settlement, the struggle with the North West Company, and the abortive cases.

It could not have been easy to leave Jean and the children, and it was only by calling on all her courage that she consented to stay. He would return in the spring; meanwhile she must manage affairs in Montreal. He knew at least that they could not be in better hands – and Montreal was learning it too. She was a personal refutation of many of the wildest charges aimed at Selkirk. Just about this time the Commissioner-General, J. W. Clarke, wrote from Montreal to Chief

Justice Powell: 'Lady Selkirk is justly esteemed a woman of uncommon cleverness and on all occasions so reasonable and amiable in her conduct that I cannot believe she could so warmly espouse the cause of her husband did she not believe him to be acting an honourable part, however outra he may be in his projects.'

With his memorial drafted, Selkirk quickly completed his travelling arrangements and left in something of a rush, believing he might find a ship in New York and sail almost at once. The journey by boat from Albany went quite well. During the trip he met Greig, an American, an old acquaintance, and with him talked over his plans for the sale of his grant lands that fell within the United States boundary. For the moment, the revival of the project that months before had promised so fair sustained him.

And then in a New York hotel came a physical breakdown to match his nervous collapse. He had arranged conferences with Greig to carry forward their plans and had accepted an invitation to a large dinner at John Jacob Astor's 'with a number of great folks'. But the day of the dinner he coughed blood and the doctor ordered him to bed on water and gruel, and opened a vein. He rested uneasily, worrying over all he was leaving undone, until on November 9 he was judged well enough to sail. His last day was spent writing a number of letters on Red River affairs and arranging for certain of his witnesses to follow him to England. If he dreaded the trip, it was unexpressed, but every sea voyage was a wretched experience for him and the trip out in 1815 had been a debilitating misery. Still weak, but with his business in some measure discharged, he went on board.

He had written Jean describing his attack in the mildest terms possible. It appeared to be mentioned only because the last-minute refusal of the Astor party had attracted a lot of attention and she was bound to hear of it.

His letter produced the answer it must, following like a cry across the Atlantic. 'I wish I had not screwed my courage up to be left behind ... if this cannot be done without your personal exertions for pity's sake make up your mind to let the wicked flourish, they cannot take from us our own good conscience, and if we do not allow them to bereave us of health and tranquility, we can be happy without the right being proved.'

Chapter 13

THE WORN AND DAMAGED SCABBARD

I

On December 1, Lord Selkirk's ship ran into the Mersey and docked at Liverpool. It had been a swift passage but sufficiently rough for a poor sailor to welcome its conclusion. He came home to weather so remarkably mild that flowers were to be seen in many gardens and the newspapers carried stories of birds hatching a second nesting in late November. There would be none of that in Montreal by now; and in Red River, what? At least the settlers were safe for the moment; the de Meurons could guarantee that, and there seemed to be an ample supply of food.

Not far to the north lay St. Mary's Isle and a fast coach from the Duke of Lancaster would leave for Carlisle at seven the next morning. But without Jean and the children the house would be empty and cold. Besides, he had come home to seek justice in London, the only place where it might still be found, though this was no longer so sure as it had seemed even a year ago. Three short years before, when they had sailed from Liverpool, this had not even been part of his concern, elementary justice and the honour of the King's government having been taken as synonymous. So London must be his first point of attack – or defence. He turned south for the long, jolting ride to the foot of the throne.

What a joy in other circumstances to drive once again into London! London, with the great beat of life about it; London, scene of his greatest triumphs and of much of his happiness. But he was ill now and went direct to the Halketts in Seymour Place, out of Curzon Street, certain at least of their happiness at seeing him and their affectionate welcome. Katherine, his favourite sister, had borne three sons since he saw her last and her correspondence with Jean in Montreal had been one of their constant sources of support. John had carried his fight doughtily, bombarding the Colonial Office and the public with Selkirk's side of a story which the North Westers had done their effective best to conceal or pervert. If, in a public sense, he stood at all on good fighting ground now it was John Halkett's and Andrew Colvile's doing.

Whatever steps he had planned on taking immediately were subject to his seriously curtailed strength and to an active illness that responded very little to treatment. With so much to be done, he spent most of December indoors under doctor's orders. But nothing turned his mind for long from its purpose. He still expected to return to Red River in a few months' time and wrote to Greig in New York about obtaining a passport and permission for him to take a large group through the United States. And he had still to deal with incoming reports from the Canadas, from Red River, and from Prince Edward Island. Most of the troubles at the settlement for the moment came from the ingrained discontent of the Scottish settlers; the French Canadians and the de Meurons were far easier to deal with. However, this was not surprising news; he had always known, from the time he embarked on his scheme of colonization, that Highlanders were *moutonniers* – sheeplike – and he had not liked them the less for it; it was the defect of their virtue. From Prince Edward Island, Johnston wrote sulkily, acknowledging the directions about Halliday's grant. 'This person is not peculiarly deserving of your Lordship's countenance.' And he added, perhaps slyly, knowing the gossip, 'at least his conduct in the settlement does not merit it'.

New Year's came again and must have set going trains of speculation and memory. Just a year before, he had been at Schenectady, on the way to York, in robust health, and, though bitterly disappointed at being turned away from Montreal, confident of the future, longing to be on the offensive. And the year before that they had had a celebration of sorts at Fort William, the enemy's keep, while in Montreal Jean – waiting for Katherine to be born – sat writing to him. It was all more than a lifetime away from the night when as a sleepy boy he had been wakened 'with a rattle' to drink the health of the new-born Basil Hall. And what now? Surely the year ahead could not hold as much of frustration and sheer wretchedness as that which was passing. But as it opened there was nothing to do but wait and harvest his strength.

But the time in which so little seemed to happen was not wholly lost. There was at last an opportunity for long talks with Halkett, giving an account of all that had happened, to fill out the bulletins and documents of the past three years. Out of their talks grew the idea of a complete statement to Bathurst on the iniquitous tangle of legal proceedings in Canada, related, as was proper, to the fatal dispatch of February 11, 1817.

The result began to take shape in January and grew into an arraignment of seventy-eight pages plus several enclosures which must shake Bathurst out of his complacency unless he was quite immovable. It was an admirable, closely argued, and forceful paper, and sounded a warning the meaning of which neither Bathurst nor Goulburn could miss.

The two men working together over the immense and intricate document presumably studied to reduce its length, for it was intimidatingly long. Still, it was admirably clear to a patient reader, and the whole wretched story – of bailed murderers, witnesses spirited away, perjured testimony, and apathetic or prejudiced law officers – must have shocked any responsible public servant. Among other summaries, the letter stated that, of fifty-six people connected with the North West Company against whom grand juries had found true bills for felony, only seven had been brought to trial two years later. Against this, all the charges or indictments brought by the North Westers against Selkirk and settlement or Hudson's Bay Company people had up to the moment of writing been dismissed by the magistrates, thrown out by the Grand Jury, disposed of by acquittals where tried, or abandoned by the law officers of the Crown.

Almost unanswerably, the relationship of these baffling events was established to the Prince Regent's proclamation and the dispatch of February 11, based on an *ex parte* statement by a clerk of the North West Company. 'The Law Officers of the Crown ... concluded, and not without some show of reason, that the Colonial Office was not very anxious about molesting the North West Company, but extremely eager to persecute Lord Selkirk and his friends.' The dispatch had taken some care to set out, as to Lord Selkirk, 'how constables might catch and Attornies-General indict him'.

The statement rolled at last in thunder towards its close. '... It is evident that he has been treated with marked and signal injustice – and it cannot be expected that a man who has been so injured is to sit tamely down, and have his rights of Property trampled upon, and, what is of more importance, his character wantonly traduced.'

It took the Under-secretary, Henry Goulburn, just nine days and two pages to compose a reply, in parts a classic example of the insolence of office. Having said, truly enough, that some statements in Halkett's letter were founded on a misapprehension of what had passed, he added that it was being forwarded to the Governor General for inquiry and explanation of certain parts. He paused to note that the paper that purported to be an extract of the dispatch of February 11 was very inaccurate. (The inaccuracies amounted to about twenty minor points, twelve of them in the use of capital letters, two in the spelling of proper names, and none of any significance in the true meaning of the document.)

He did at least trouble to defend the dispatch to the extent of pointing out that it directed no prosecution against Selkirk except that for resistance to arrest, and added that Lord Bathurst did not think it necessary to enter into further explanation of the paper, 'more particularly considering the manner in which Lord Selkirk obtained possession of it'.

However angry, Halkett was Goulburn's match; he had not been a colonial governor for nothing. As to the inaccuracy, he replied crisply, it was evidently not Lord Selkirk's fault – 'the original he never saw'.

'It cannot be doubted however, that the Copy taken by Mr. Pyke may be deemed sufficiently accurate to satisfy every impartial person that the directions given for indicting Lord Selkirk were founded upon exparte intelligence communicated by McRobb the hired Clerk of his inveterate enemies.'

Selkirk could not have known that when, a year before, the dispatch had fallen into his hands, Sherbrooke had sent a hasty and troubled warning and explanation to Bathurst. He had even gone so far as to add that he did not believe Lord Selkirk could use the document to embarrass the government.

Meanwhile, without warning, a vacancy had occurred among the Representative Peers for Scotland; the Earl of Errol had died on January 26. There would have to be a by-election, which provided the possibility of showing officials in Canada, and the North West partners, that he was not disgraced in the eyes of the government. It was just such an opening as his return was designed to exploit, and by February 4 he had a discreet circular ready, inviting the support of his peers. Even before that, without consultation, James Wedderburn had written Lord Sidmouth pleading the suitability of the vacant seat's going to Selkirk.

Selkirk himself wrote to his kinsman, the Earl of Hopetoun, on February 2:

You are I believe sufficiently acquainted with the circumstances which have taken place to be aware of the sensation which the result of the General Election of Scottish

309

Peers was calculated to excite in Canada: – where for a long time past my enemies had been trumpeting forth, that the prosecutions against me were carried on, not merely by the North West Company but by the express directions of Government & where by this & other methods the whole weight & influence of the Provincial Government was directed against me. ... You can easily imagine the effect of such language, held without contradiction with the utmost activity for fifteen or eighteen months previous to the time when the trials were to come on & confirmed at last by the marked stigma, which my being turned out of the House of Lords appeared to convey. – When the circumstance first reached me (thro' the newspapers) after the expectations of support from Government which my friends had been led to entertain, I must own that I thought it could bear but one interpretation, and that I was to find a decided enemy, not in Lord Bathurst only, but in every member of the Cabinet. It was with great surprize, that on seeing Lord Melville, and Lord Sidmouth within these two days both of them assured me that they had never till now been informed of the orders sent out by Lord Bathurst on the 11 February 1817. –

However much it may be each member of the Government should manage the concerns of his own Department without interference of others. – Yet I think that Lord Bathurst would hardly have ventured to take such a step, unless he had calculated that his colleagues took a very faint interest in the individual who he had resolved to persecute.

I am sending my Circulars, without well knowing whether I have to have the support of Government or not. – Neither Lord Sidmouth nor Lord Melville would give me a decided answer on the subject – alleging that the probability of my returning to America would operate as an objection. I told them as I am ready to tell anyone, that if I do go out again to America my stay there beyond a very few months will entirely depend on the conduct of Government itself. – but while the impunity of past crimes, affords so much encouragement to commit new outrages, & no effectual means are adopted for repressing lawless violence & affording protection to my Settlers, I cannot be content to abandon them to their fate.

It must have been a hard decision, yet in the weeks previous to the by-election he showed no inclination to compromise. By late February he had decided that at least he could not usefully go back to Canada until things showed a more favourable turn in England, and wrote Jean of 'every probability that we shall winter together in Britain next season'. In the light of that, he might have given various undertakings: that he would not leave the country for at least a year; that he would even put a limit to any absence found necessary. But much as he wished to be elected there could be no hampering condition. He must be free to stand by his settlers; and he challenged the peers on the propriety of his decision.

To Lord Napier he wrote:

> My going to America three years ago was not a matter of choice but of necessity; and if I go again ... it will be from the same necessity of affording protection to my tenantry and dependents ... if ... nothing is to be done for the protection of these people ... I must in that case go out and see them placed in a state of security in one place or another. – Surely the Peers of Scotland cannot consider it unbecoming in one of their number to exert all his endeavours for the protection of his dependents.

All through February he clung to the hope that he might be well enough to make the journey to Edinburgh for the election. Moreover, there could be little doubt that his presence or absence might be decisive. This time for a variety of reasons he craved success, perhaps more than ever before; there would be a sweetness to that triumph. Until the last, he wrote friends that he expected to be in Edinburgh.

The very strain of waiting defeated its object. Knowing how much hung on his decision, the doctor had to recommend against the journey in the strongest terms, and no one could doubt that he was right. Five days of hard travelling each way in all weathers was a desperate enterprise for a sick man. At the last minute Lord Hopetoun undertook his proxy and Selkirk waited for news with no great confidence. It was as well. When it came, he found that his closest friends and kinsmen had stood by him, but three or four votes had been lost by the misadventures of travel and the like. He had been defeated by Lord Belhaven by ten votes, – 29 to 19 – and more than ever did it appear that his presence might have tipped the scale.

It was one more disappointment at a moment when he badly needed hope and encouragement. Early in March he had four letters from Jean dated from January 18 to February 16. They were packed with news and opinions about their affairs in Canada, but except for the assurance of her affection and unquestioning support they contained nothing to the purpose. The attempts to indict Coltman for malversation and McGillivray for conspiracy against the settlement were blocked and stuck fast in the mire of official reluctance. In each case the Grand Jury had found a true bill, but trials were as far away as ever.

A heart-warming note from his old friend McDonald of Dalilia, asking about the colony, came as a ray of sunshine in a dark spring: 'I am not actuated by idle curiosity but . . . from the personal attachment I shall always entertain for your Lordship and the sincere wish for the success of every matter in which you may be engaged.' And there was balm in being reminded that the Highland proprietors who had so bitterly opposed his emigration schemes had changed their minds and were now as eager to get rid of their people as they had been formerly to hold them. 'But it is too late,' said McDonald; the people who had been held back had consumed their savings and now lacked the means to pay their passage elsewhere. It was the condition Selkirk had foreseen, but the reality was too grim to afford much satisfaction.

By any measure, it was a dark moment. He could not pretend that his appeal to the government showed real signs of progress; his letters to the Prime Minister, Lord Liverpool, seemed likely to remain unanswered. Even one setting out the story of the 'escape' of George Campbell and asking for action against Judge Ogden, who was in London, had not been acknowledged a month later. His financial problems were pressing; income from the estate was alarmingly reduced, as was agricultural income everywhere. He had already commenced the sale of his lands in Upper Canada and now he determined to sell his holdings in Prince Edward Island as well. A deposit of £18,000 to his credit at Coutts from Sir James Montgomery's banker had to be paid out immediately to Andrew Colvile.

None of it was calculated to lift the spirits and help towards better health. At the end of April he was still confined to the house on a low diet. The doctors were cautiously encouraging, but progress seemed imperceptible and he was unequal to the slightest exertion. 'The precautions that are necessary are very irksome,' he wrote his wife, 'but must be submitted to with as much patience as I can muster.' But there was no real danger, said the doctors, unless he had a severe set-back.

The news from Canada, when it came, did not help. The Quarter Sessions at Sandwich had found him not guilty of assault and false imprisonment of Smith at Fort William. But he had finally been indicted at York for conspiracy, the Attorney-General aided by the Chief Justice having taken the precaution of having a special bill passed by the legislature to permit the trial to be moved out of the Western District. This had been attempted the year before and had failed, but now the 'Lord Selkirk Persecution Bill', as Gale reported it was called, had gone through and achieved its purpose.

Attorney-General Robinson, newly appointed and eager to win his spurs, seemed by a good deal to have exceeded his instructions. Bathurst had directed a prosecution for the 'escape' from Mitchell's warrant, in the court from which the process issued. The prosecution had failed – all the prosecutions for which Coltman had imposed a bail of £6,000 had failed. Robinson had apparently decided in his youthful ardour that what was required was not just a prosecution but a conviction. The conspiracy charge he had laid at the urging of the North

313

West partners, his employers, and against the advice of the Chief Justice. And by contriving a change of venue and not being nicely scrupulous in his choice of witnesses, he had at least secured an indictment. He was on the threshold of a long and distinguished career but he had yet to learn the difference between the function of an attorney-general and that of a private prosecutor.

And close on the conspiracy news came word of two successful civil actions against him also at York, for false imprisonment. Daniel McKenzie had been awarded £1,500 and Smith £500. Beverley Robinson had acted against him in both cases. (Woods wrote with an angry snort from Sandwich that Smith would not have been awarded 500 shillings there.) The civil cases called forth an offensive notice in a London paper, and in his anger Selkirk proposed a libel suit and proceeded eagerly with arrangements.

It was the sort of excitement his doctors had warned against, but the accumulated frustration burst out against caution. He could not, would not, 'sit tamely down' while his character was 'wantonly traduced'. But the proof that he could no longer fight his own battle was not long in coming. The excitement and effort produced a severe haemorrhage, undoing the good of the long, irksome winter. It was the serious set-back against which the doctors had warned him; now there was danger, and even he must have recognized it. 'From then on,' wrote Katherine Halkett later, 'he had nothing but anxiety, sorrow, labour of body and heartbreak.'

Some hint of all this was bound to reach the outside world, a small portion of which was watching the sick-room door with ghoulish interest. Though Selkirk himself referred to his health in letters only as being 'none of the best', word left London about mid-May that he was 'far advanced in a deep consumption, and that his Physicians despared of his life'. Colin Robertson heard and reported the news in August from Cumberland House on the far Saskatchewan. 'God forbid,' he said, sickened at the Nor'Westers' glee.

In between the racking bouts and the applications of leeches that increased his weakness, Selkirk went on with his work. Most of the letters had to be dictated or written from his rough notes, but the flow of instruction and suggestion, though it may have lessened, never ceased. The question of cattle for Red River still worried him; there were to be cattle from Scotland as well as from the Mississippi, and he gave careful directions for the conditioning of the former for the long voyage. For the moment, additional settlers from Scotland should only be selected tradesmen required in the colony and a few Lowlanders begged for by Laidlaw. He had suggestions to make, about a specially fortified house for Captain Matthey, the military commander of the settlement. He worked for its permanent security but meanwhile it was to be a well-armed camp. The brain within the weakened body remained clear and tireless, and as always full of sanguine calculations.

The things he still sought for himself would serve equally the cause of the settlement. The clearing of his good name, in his view, turned on proving that the idea of a settlement at Red River had not been a wild and unpromising scheme; that it had been a sensible solution to a grave problem, both in a national sense and as it affected the lives of the people of the Highlands.

The attack he had delivered through Halkett, and equally through Lord Liverpool, on Bathurst and Goulburn seemed to have come to nothing. They were playing the civil service version of catch-me-if-you-can, and it would take more than letters to flush them out. During April the old Whig weakness for pamphlets asserted itself and arrangements were made for the printing of Halkett's letters to the Earl of Bathurst. And a little later, as though any hope of a more discreet solution had been abandoned, it was decided to print for private circulation Halkett's correspondence with the Colonial Office in 1817, 1818, and 1819. It was to have a prefatory letter from Selkirk and to be entitled *A Letter to the Earl of Liverpool*. Simultaneously, a volume of three narratives on the subject of Seven Oaks, those of Pritchard, Pambrun, and Heurter, was commissioned with John Murray.

315

This was throwing down the gauntlet in unmistakable terms, and though the books aroused incredulity and horror in some readers they appeared to others as a breach of taste or an error in tactics. Sir James Hall, having expressed his indignation at the conditions which the *Letter to Lord Liverpool* revealed, wrote that parts of the letter ought to have been reserved for the private ear of a minister, 'since it now stands in the form of direct threat and must enable your enemies to consider you as in a state of open rebellion'. But he had given the ministers every chance to show an interest in the conditions he believed cried out for correction, and to provide the safeguards of law and order for his settlers. Lady Selkirk was on her way back from Canada and it might have been wise to await her judgment. But the calculations of dying men are not those of people to whom time seems endless. Whether or not he recognized the limits of the time left him, Selkirk was clearly determined to force the issue. He had tried the discreet and polite way and failed; now he had nothing to lose. His fortune was crippled and none of this could mend it. His damaged honour, infinitely more precious, seemed still susceptible of reinstatement and worth all the risks.

He must have known that the most he could hope for was effective legislation for the future. The overturning of decisions already taken was not to be expected. The view of the ministers on the principles of government cannot have differed from those of Sidmouth, which were: 'to acquire the confidence of the magistracy, especially in critical times, by showing a readiness to support them in all honest, reasonable, and well intended acts, without inquiring too minutely whether they might have performed their duty a little better or a little worse'.

There was little doubt that Bathurst would regard Canadian officials as having been honest and well intentioned. They would be supported.

Early in June Lady Selkirk came home. Through May he had seemed to hold his own and on sunny days was allowed to go out for an hour or two in the afternoon. It was enough to allow him to reach Mr. Murray's or the Alfred Club, both in Albemarle Street, or perhaps to walk or drive in Hyde Park. Otherwise those who ventured to seek him out were sure of finding him at Seymour Place. In late May his doctor strongly advised country air and a complete separation from his affairs. He wrote ruefully that he was being pushed 'head and shoulders out of town'. They went to the Colviles at Langley Farm near Beckingham.

It was doubly hard to leave now, because his brother-in-law, Sir James Montgomery, had at last undertaken to move in the House of Commons for papers relating to the Red River Settlement and to the legal proceedings arising out of events there. Lord Selkirk's inclination at once was to write to various people, sending them copies of the books on the case and diffidently inviting their support in the House. Jean both wrote letters at his dictation and undertook calls that might accomplish more and save his strength. That his record in Parliament and his reputation for unselfish service in good causes had won him irreproachable friends was at once heart-warmingly apparent. Men like Zachary Macaulay and William Wilberforce were quick to express sympathy and promise support; and yet – Wilberforce, and doubtless other good men, staunch friends, liking him, believing in his principles, had some reservations. Little paragraphs in the newspapers, the gossip of clubs and of Parliament, had left a smear. And he was perhaps beyond realizing that only the most devoted and unoccupied would labour through the complicated papers that told his story.

Besides, it was four years since he had surrendered his place near the centre of events in Britain. Much had happened of which he was little aware and which laid heavy competing claims on the attention of those otherwise eager to serve him. And while his innate good manners begged forgiveness for intruding his problems, his involvement disqualified him from understanding how remote they must seem. England was torn with discontent; radicals were believed to be everywhere and infinitely dangerous. Red River and its troubles could only be real to those few who were devoted to him, to the Hudson's

Bay Company, and to its enemies. In January, while he kept the house and worked with Halkett over the letter to Bathurst, a monster rally took place at Manchester demanding parliamentary reform. Hunger was stalking through a passively suffering countryside, but the great manufacturing centres were beginning to stir threateningly. Once again, though Napoleon was safe at St. Helena, the results of the French Revolution seemed ready to spring across the Channel. And, though the meetings calling for reforms included one in June of 40,000 poor weavers at Glasgow petitioning the Prince Regent for transportation for the unemployed to Canada, it was all remote from Red River and abstract justice.

Yet their cause might in the end gain in some quarters from this. It had nothing to do with forwarding the 'radicals' and 'democrats', and no one was averse, within reason, to helping poor people to help themselves (except by the franchise). The idea of settlement abroad was gaining in popularity. With the threat of war removed, danger now lay in 'redundant population'. These facts, combined with his own comparative freedom from narrow partisanship, won Sir James a good hearing when on June 24 he rose in the Commons to ask for papers. The debate was not long, but it was effective. In the course of it, Henry Goulburn said imperturbably that it was the intention of the government to have the rights of property under the Hudson's Bay charter investigated without further delay and that the charter was now before the Privy Council. (Later inquiry showed that it had been at the Council office for two years awaiting directions from the Colonial Office.) Goulburn justified the February 11 dispatch by saying that Selkirk had both resisted the warrant and arrested the constable. But Robinson had not been arrested and Smith was not arrested until a month after the dispatch. In thus confusing the two incidents, Goulburn was either disgracefully ill-informed or deliberately misled the House.

In spite of Goulburn, the motion carried, and Selkirk wrote happily that Sir James's success had exceeded their 'most sanguine expectations'. Still, time was running out. These little gains which lifted his spirits were not sustained enough to restore the body, if that was now possible. His doctors pressed him to seek a warmer climate for the autumn and winter and he began to talk of Spain and Italy. There was much to be done. Although he must leave the management of his affairs to others, the trip called forth that pleasure in organizing detail to which he could always respond. He was at once busy inquiring about climate and accommodation at Valencia and elsewhere. Daer was to be left in school and to spend his holidays with the Colviles, who had a boy his own age. There was a question of whether a doctor should accompany the Selkirks and this was at first decided against, probably as an economy.

The centre of life was still the controversy. Within two weeks of Sir James's motion, on July 12, the papers asked for were printed and ready. Lord Bathurst, scanning them, appeared to find some embarrassing gaps, for on the tenth he wrote hastily to the Governor General of Canada asking for reports on the legal proceedings arising out of the disputes between the Hudson's Bay Company and the North West Company; among others, he had no report of the Reinhart trial which had taken place eighteen months before. He indicated what was for him an almost unseemly haste in the need for these reports, though for nearly two years the lack had been so unimportant as to remain undetected.

The papers could not have failed to do much of what Selkirk wanted done in Parliament. The part he had played was transparently as he had represented it, even mistakes he was perhaps now prepared, though reluctant, to face stood clearly on the record. And other things, until now mystifying, became understandable, among them the part that the startled Sherbrooke had unwittingly played in unduly alarming the Colonial Office about conditions in the North-west and the danger of American intervention. Mere fairness had now to recognize that this was probably a powerful factor in the tone of the unbalanced dispatch of February 11 – unless someone at the Colonial Office had seized a pretext for the persecution of Selkirk. At least this partially explained what it could not justify.

Most enlightening of all was Coltman's report, submitted to Sir John Sherbrooke on May 14, 1818, and now written into the public record. In a broad sense he had found, as Gale predicted, a measure of balancing guilt. He did more to distinguish between Selkirk's activities and those of the Hudson's Bay Company than the Colonial Office had ever attempted. Nevertheless, he saw the struggle as a trade war.

Selkirk was bound to feel that Coltman's building of the case for Hudson's Bay aggression was more ingenious than accurate: the Pemmican War, followed by notice to the Nor'Westers to quit their posts in the grant, followed by the destruction of Fort Gibraltar, were woven into the semblance of an unfolding plan. It was at least plausible, and with it went a question of whether a charter granted when Canada was French, having lain dormant as to some areas and now misused by Miles Macdonell, might not have been invalidated. It was true that the validity of the charter had been examined and confirmed by high authorities as recently as 1811 but, said Coltman, the questions that had been asked of them were not published and it was not known whether the learned counsel were even aware of the traditional claims acquired by other British subjects as successors to the French traders.

No Hudson's Bay man could like this shrewd assessment of their weakness, but if the North Westers could read this far with satisfaction their pleasure was at an end. The report found that their violations of law had been much greater, and attended by results shocking to the feelings of humanity, '... any pretensions they may have made, as a body ... being completely destroyed by the vices inherent to the system on which they conducted their affairs, and which have ... produced events so fatal, as to appear imperatively to call for the interference of Government.' Coltman went on to discuss the North West system under which success was virtually the only test and the road to promotion and profit, as a result of which 'habits of overbearing violence ... have at length formed the general character of its members ... in their violent and oppressive conduct toward the natives of the country, frequently to their own servants, and still more to their opponents in the trade'. He referred also to the various illegal measures adopted in the past to crush minor adventurers who had attempted to oppose the North West Company; these were 'recorded in the courts of Montreal, and are of public notoriety. . . .'

'. . . although the Hudson's Bay Company may have been the first aggressors, the retaliatory measures of the North West Company have so much exceeded all reasonable or lawful bounds of self-defence . . . as to render the proceedings of their party, beyond comparison, the most criminal.'

If the report was not all he might have wished for, it was at least a larger measure of truth than he had dared to expect. Now, surely, the government must act to put an end to lawlessness in the North-west. He could at least go away feeling that matters might go on satisfactorily in his absence. In that hope he made a final effort to attach Wilberforce firmly to the support of Sir James Montgomery in the House, and in a long and winning letter set out something of his hopes for the colony and some justification of the part he had played, to the man whom he had so often supported in good causes. In discussing his purchase of Hudson's Bay shares, he asserted that his 'calculation of pecuniary advantage went no farther than to secure myself against loss'; there was naturally no complaint or hint that even this modest hope was now frustrated beyond possible realization. For the first time, he seemed ready to admit that the battle was beyond his strength: 'For my own part I have perhaps undertaken a task of too great magnitude for an individual in embarking in these affairs; but the difficulties I have met with could never had been calculated upon. . . .' His hope was there in the final sentence: 'These things cannot surely be allowed to continue and it will be a sufficient satisfaction to me if I find that I have awakened the attention of those who are better able than I am to eradicate the mischief.'

It was not a plea that Wilberforce could have heard, unmoved, from any man, much less a friend but lately of so splendid a promise, now shrunk to this little measure. Prior obligations prevented him from undertaking the parliamentary leadership in support that Selkirk had hoped for, but he would do what he could (and Selkirk knew that even a little from him would be a host). Wilberforce may have sensed that this was a final leave-taking and therefore exerted himself to deal faithfully with his friend, to bring out the doubts raised by rumour and put them in their place.

> I certainly shall take some opportunity of doing justice to your Lordship ... stating that what had formerly passed between us, had convinced me if any doubts on that head could remain in any liberal mind that your Lordship's Scheme had been undertaken with a view to the improvement and benefit of your fellow creatures. But though I never have had any misgivings on that head, yet I know that in the prosecution of a favourite object, men are sometimes led into the use of means they may afterwards see reason to disapprove. And this especially happens, when from the nature of the case, we are obliged to avail ourselves of the services of men, whose character we cannot scrutinize very nicely. Excuse me if I say that I conceived such might be your situation. ...
>
> And now my dear Lord, let me complain of you, for not satisfying the unaffected solicitude I feel about the state of your health. ... I wish the body may not receive some injury from the mind. I fear the sword may wear and damage the scabbard.

Selkirk could feel a little more optimistic about the direction of affairs as the time to leave for France approached. In a letter to Judge Stewart in Halifax he spoke of believing that the public was 'beginning to be sensible of the infamy of the proceedings in Canada'. Once more the buoyant spirit rose as of yore: 'I believe truth and justice will prevail at last.'

In August he made his will, a supplementary trust deed to a will drawn in 1806. To the original executors were added, as was most fitting, John Halkett, Andrew Colvile, and James Wedderburn, Solicitor-General for Scotland. The correspondence related to the will apparently drew a stern protest from his brother-in-law, Wedderburn, as to Selkirk's losses and continuing expense. The rejoinder, though probably dictated, testified that, regardless of financial troubles and the perilous state of his health, Selkirk's spirit was still intact.

> Your observations as to the general state of my pecuniary affairs are undoubtedly just, but I fear the time for establishing a sinking fund is not yet come. I wish to Heaven it were, but my honour is at stake in the contest with the North West Company and in the support of the settlement at Red River. Till that can be said to be fairly out of danger and till the infamous falsehoods of the North West Company are finally and fully exposed, expenses must be incurred which it is utterly impossible to avoid, and to which it does not depend on me to put a limit. I do my best to avoid all that can be spared, but those that are necessary for the accomplishment of that object must be submitted to, even if they go beyond my income. It is to be hoped that this state of things will soon be over, and when that is the case I will retire to St. Mary's Isle and live on sixpence a day till I am out of debt.

Now they were almost ready and his mind may well have turned back twenty-five years to the departure of his brother Basil for a warmer climate in search of health, a journey from which he never returned.

Before they left, still another piece was added to that backdrop against which the drama of Red River had always been played with difficulty. On August 16 a mass political meeting near Manchester got out of hand and, in the resulting panic and attempts to restore order, occurred the Peterloo Massacre. Horror and indignation swept the British Isles.

There had been twice as many people, equally innocent, killed in the Massacre of Seven Oaks. But even the government did not know where Seven Oaks was or what the trouble had been about.

323

2

In the last stages of the family's preparations for departure, one of Selkirk's medical attendants recommended a young doctor graduated only a few months from Edinburgh and himself suffering from a chest complaint. Selkirk at first demurred and then consented to see the young man. The interview pleased both parties and it was arranged that Dr. George William Lefevre should accompany them to Spain.

The first impression of the sick man was one young Lefevre never lost. He had been elated at the idea of having a lord for his first patient – 'Physician to a Lord', he said to himself over and over, and yet in sturdy Scotch fashion braced himself so as not to be overborne by this man of superior rank. But his impressions were not at all what he had expected. He had not prepared himself for the mild and affable manners, the agreeable smile, at once captivating and dignified, or for the marked intelligence of the haggard face.

> There was something, however, restless about him; an agitation of mind, evinced by his bodily movements; and a certain decision in his tone, which, perhaps, bordered upon obstinacy. His was a mind which evidently could not remain a moment unoccupied. There was no approach to a state of rest. Such was my first impression and it was a true one. This was the feature in the composition which alone brought us into contact, for the feverish brain had destroyed the outward man, and was now gnawing at the vitals.

All this the young doctor saw at that first meeting, and something else. He saw with dismay that his first patient seemed already to be past curing. Medical science might ease and perhaps delay his passing; it probably could do no more. The doctor from whom he took over was disposed to agree, but Lefevre was not going to lose his first patient without a fight.

The Selkirks liked George Lefevre; it was, however, going

to be a little bit difficult to take this earnest boy of twenty-one seriously. The distressing symptoms by now so familiar to them kept him in a continual bristle of professional concern. No doubt things would settle down; meanwhile, better too serious than too casual.

A rendezvous with the doctor having been arranged, what Selkirk jocularly called 'our caravan' set out about mid-September, 1819, travelling down the Dover road through a dense fog. Whatever pangs they felt, they could not at any rate regret leaving that behind. The Channel-crossing in the teeth of a hard wind took their small craft seven hours, and both doctor and patient suffered cruelly from sea-sickness. It was a bad beginning; but from the time they rounded the platform at Calais and presently were sitting over a superb *omelette confiture* at Dessin's things went better. As they retired for the night the young doctor gravely tendered a sleeping draught for his patient though he could not escape the conviction that it would not be made use of.

In the morning they took the road for Paris, the Selkirks travelling in a large 'chariot', a servant and the slightly affronted young professional man following in a calash. So they travelled at a leisurely pace for nearly a week, starting late in the morning and moving by easy stages. When they reached Paris the sick man was perceptibly better. Lefevre was quietly pleased and Selkirk dictated a letter to Jean for Lord Hardwicke saying that the travelling appeared to be of material benefit to him. He added that they were setting out for Toulouse by way of Bordeaux. He also sent Hardwicke a letter for Lord Harrowby which might help to bring the Hudson's Bay charter more quickly before the Privy Council, and he spent some time on a French edition of *A Sketch of the British Fur Trade*.

While in Paris, Lefevre sought out an experienced colleague for consultation and from him received a prescription so elaborate that it covered half a sheet of foolscap. When she saw it, Lady Selkirk burst out laughing.

'What is all this to do?' she asked.

Dr. Lefevre answered stiffly, 'To do his Lordship good, my lady.'

In the last week of September the caravan rolled southward out of Paris. It was time to seek the warmer climate, for they travelled now in cold rain, and that night the doctor was much concerned by Selkirk's frequent fits of heavy coughing. Diffidently he knocked at his patient's door and despite Lady Selkirk's smiling assurances he prevailed on her to give Selkirk some poppy syrup which soothed him and reduced the coughing.

Hope sprang up and grew as they travelled south through dry and sunny days. Selkirk's health continued to improve and his spirits mended; the charm of strange towns and beautiful countryside, of unaccustomed methods of agriculture which always caught his interest, combined to drive back the troubles that had possessed him for too long. At Tours they made their only stay beyond overnight while leeches were applied to the sick man and he rested for a day; then on to Bordeaux.

Pleased as he was with his patient, Lefevre wished to seek a consultation here, but the Selkirks would not have it. By now the young doctor had won their confidence. 'You have had a great success and this medicine has done wonders for us,' Lady Selkirk assured him; 'we want no consultation.' The Earl asked grumpily what a foreign doctor could know of his constitution. So, beyond seeking medical advice about weather and climate, they merely rested at Bordeaux, saw the sights, and attended a theatre. The young doctor, visiting the local hospital, had reason to be glad of his patient's improvement, for there he saw with horror the wretched sick lying two and three to a bed.

They moved on south, still with no fixed destination, talking vaguely of Valencia and Toulouse; but these were yet distant, and they must soon get into winter quarters. Pau, in the foothills of the Pyrenees, lay not far out of their path and had been well spoken of; they would at least see Pau before going farther. Except for a brutal day of travel over corduroy roads that jolted the carriage so much as to cause Selkirk both exhaustion and nausea, their journey was a pleasure to them all. The scenery changed to the wild, harsh terrain of the Landes and changed again to more wooded, rolling country. The people, too, were changing. They spent a night at Roquefort, where the annual fair was in progress, and found the town full of people speaking an unintelligible language and wearing Spanish dress. Overhead there were skeins of geese flying south – the Fair Geese, people said; it was a tradition that they always flew over at fair time.

It was another reminder of approaching winter. As they neared Pau, and the Pyrenees, cloud-capped, came into view, it began to rain for the first time since they had left Paris. The rainy season was on them and the need to find permanent quarters pressed hard. They slept the night at Pau in a comfortable inn, being given the rooms just vacated by the young Queen of Spain on her way to Madrid.

The following day was fine and, taking horses, they rode out to look at the mountains. It was a glorious prospect. At their back the old town rose in terraces, while at their feet, winding through a broad green valley, flowed the Gave de Pau. Beyond the valley, the foothills were covered with vines and, higher up, the forest trees blazed in their autumn colours. As they gazed, the sun glanced in splendour through the Pyrenees, lighting up a scene of startling beauty. They turned the horses homeward with their decision made. They would winter at Pau.

Doubtless Lady Selkirk took up the search for a satisfactory house with her accustomed zest, and very quickly one was found. It stood in Rue Royale facing the Pyrenees, and that splendid prospect across the green valley of the Gave seemed of itself to guarantee happiness to the occupants of the house. In sight from their windows, too, was the Place Royale, a park full of beautiful trees, named for Henry of Navarre who had been born in the Château de Pau. The house belonged to a former soldier of Napoleon, Colonel Larriu, who had seen much fighting and for a short glorious period during the Hundred Days had been one of Napoleon's marshals. Under the mon-archy he was once again a colonel, glad enough to rent his house to the first milord who had visited Pau. From the beginning he was full of kindly but unobtrusive attentions, concerned that his guests should be comfortable.

Pau was something of a lotus-land. Here in an equable climate life was quieter than elsewhere, and life was longer; there was less hurry, less excitement, less crime. Even the French Revolution had reached the quiet Béarnaise town in muted form; the 'Terror' in Pau had resulted in three people being guillotined, then things had settled down to their old, gentle pace.

It was an ideal place for someone whose body needed restoring and whose mind was at rest. Selkirk stood in need of the moderate climate but this was not all he required. For too long his mind had been ceaselessly active, and only positive news of a successful issue to his affairs might have enabled him to yield freely to the healing influences about him. The excitement of the journey with its ever-changing scene was over. Now with his depleted strength there was little he could do, or that could be done for him, to keep his mind quiet yet sufficiently occupied in contentment.

Had all the news that came to him conveyed the note of complete satisfaction he received from Prince Edward Island at about this time, all might have been well. In late August Johnston wrote, giving a long account of his stewardship. 'These poor people whom your Lordship brought hither have universally bettered their condition ... are now by far the most independent settlement in this island – they are contented and happy.' It was in statements like this that his dreams were designed to end. But of his three settlements – his three dreams – only the first was ending as it should. Baldoon was finished, a miserable failure. The total judgment must rest on the result of Red River which was still in a balance he was almost powerless to influence.

In November Ellice approached Colvile with a view to purchasing a controlling interest in the Hudson's Bay Company by buying the shares of Selkirk and his friends at their valuation. The purchase agreement would include guarantees to provide to the settlers whatever Lord Selkirk had promised them, or, alternatively, to move them elsewhere, should they wish, at no expense to them. He claimed, in making his offer, to be acting for himself and not for the North West Company, but this claim was not taken very seriously by anyone; Selkirk pronounced it 'all bunkum'. A condition of the offer was the mutual dropping of all prosecutions.

The offer must have had the disturbing effect of a bomb on the peace of the household in Pau. Here, where the chief excitement of the week was the arrival of the goatherds to milk their goats at the house-door, the turbulent world of the settlement and the fur trade burst in to recall itself and show them the grinning face of financial ruin. Undoubtedly the offer was tempting, and the sick man was almost past continuing the struggle. Jean at first replied for him that he did not put an absolute negative on the idea of the sale.

They could not overlook the possibility that matters might be taken out of their hands. In early December, Sir James Montgomery had called on Goulburn to inquire about the Privy Council decision on the Hudson's Bay Company charter. The Under-secretary had urged 'the expediency of a compromise, without obliging the Council to decide, because he thought the decision might be unfavourable to both'. He held out the hope that the government would confirm any arrangement the two parties might make. If Goulburn were right, they had only poor ground on which to fight; and in spite of every reason for distrusting him there were risks in ignoring the warning.

Still, when Selkirk had thought more about Ellice's proposal he liked it less than ever.

You are aware of the repugnance which I feel to any transaction, which would make me the instrument of putting power into the hands of a set of unprincipled miscreants. To hand over to them the sovereignty as it may be called, of an extensive country, where we had the

prospect of doing so much good is a transaction to which
I cannot easily reconcile myself, and I would reckon it
immoral as well as disgraceful, if it were done from any
views of pecuniary advantage. It is only the impossibility
of holding out against the Colonial Department and the
North West Company together that can justify it. . . . But
we are surely not yet reduced to the point of giving up all
in despair.

With respect to giving up the settlement or selling it
to the North West, that is entirely out of the question.
Unless there were a pointed and absolute decision of the
Privy Council against my right of property, I know of no
consideration that would induce me to abandon it. I
ground this resolution not only on the principle of supporting the settlers who I have already sent to the place,
but also because I consider my character at stake upon
the success of the undertaking, and upon proving by the
result that it was neither a wild and visionary scheme nor a
trick and cloak to cover sordid plans of aggression upon
the prosperity of others.

With these good reasons and their joint agreement on Ellice's
'utter want of veracity or any sort of principle', Colvile firmly
rejected Ellice's offer, saying Lord Selkirk did not see how any
security that the North West Company had the means of
giving could justify him in placing his property or his settlers
at their mercy. However, Ellice was apparently too hard-
pressed himself to give up easily. He wrote unctuously, regretting the decision on behalf of Lord Selkirk's family.

Nevertheless, in spite of defiance, Selkirk was close to a conditional surrender. It troubled him greatly that his concerns
had added so much to Colvile's heavy burdens and his holding
out could only increase them. Then, just at the year-end, came
news that opened 'very brilliant prospects', and, as Selkirk
said, 'drove all other matters out of my head'. Colvile forwarded
a letter from Gale written from Montreal in September to Lady
Selkirk. It contained news of the Hudson's Bay Company
going on the offensive at last, ambushing and arresting five

partners of the North West Company. More important, it contained a discreet inquiry on behalf of the North West wintering partners as to whether the Hudson's Bay Company would make a trading arrangement with them if they quit the Montreal agents – the McGillivrays, Norman McLeod, and the rest. Their contract with the agents ran only until 1822 but was due for preliminary discussion at the next summer's meeting at Fort William; there was no doubt of the serious good faith of the approach. Colvile, intercepting the letter, had already written Gale holding out the possibility of an attractive arrangement, provided only that some of the more criminal partners must be excluded. To the Selkirks it seemed that, if they and the hard-pressed Hudson's Bay Company could only stand fast a little longer, the plan would lead 'infallibly to a complete triumph over the great rascals'.

Against this was to be balanced 'the continuance of a troublesome and doubtful contest ... with all the mischief that Goulburn's malice and Lord Bathurst's perversity can do us, and that assuredly is not a little'. And out of bitter experience Selkirk added: 'It would be folly to shut our eyes to the glorious uncertainty of the law.'

Considering it all, and giving great weight to the need of an early and durable peace for his settlers and the natives of the grant, he dictated:

> I am ready nevertheless to fight out the battle, if the only alternative is to submit to injustice and dishonour. But if the most essential points that we contend for can be obtained in a consistent and creditable manner, I am still disposed to sacrifice a great deal for the sake of obtaining them quietly, without further contest, and would willingly give up the prospect of a complete triumph four or five years hence, if in exchange we can have peace and security immediately, and avoid the waste of your time and the harrassment of my mind. ... It is not improbable that the languor of continued ill health may have its share in taming me down to this pitch.

Jean Selkirk, taking his dictation and looking at the ruin of a man who had lost everything but his honour in this struggle, and knowing his mind, which she had never been able to change, wrote fiercely on her own: 'The choice between the adoption and rejection of Ellice's proposal is merely a question between money and principle.'

Three years before, on New Year's Eve, she had written him about her worries over mounting expense. 'You must allow that it is not *to him* [Daer] that the settlement will begin to pay what has been laid out upon it. ... This subject always gives me the blues, because I never can get you to open your eyes to it.' Looking at him, she could not doubt that her prophecy was even truer now, her fears more justified. Whatever was to happen would fall not on him but on her and Daer and their descendants. But considering all that he had endured, facing his mistakes, weighing his life's work, she wrote in the mood in which two years ago from Montreal she had written John Halkett: 'I think we are all agreed that although we must weigh well whether the gain is worth the expense, yet if we are to be poor for three generations we must absolutely fight this out.'

She may have believed that his surrender was designed above all to save something for her out of the ruin which his dream of a kingdom on Red River had brought on them all. Since even this conditional surrender dishonoured him, it was a sacrifice she could not accept.

The household at Pau settled back into its accustomed routine; taking pleasure in the view, in the people who went to and fro beneath their windows – the women hatless but often wearing a dark cloth mantle, the men in their short-kneed small-clothes and coarse homespun stockings. For several days in early January the weather was mild and sunny, culminating in a day of warm, moist wind blowing from the Pyrenees. As evening came down, the wind blew in fierce gusts and almost without warning it burst into the town with hurricane force. The air was all at once filled with the noise of banging shutters and falling branches; and then, as the wind tore at the house, came the thunder of giant trees flung down in the Place Royale, of roofs stripped from near-by houses and flung into the street, and the fall of the conical wooden turret from the Château de Pau.

In less than an hour the storm had passed and the warm air had been replaced by a biting cold which by morning was more severe than the oldest inhabitant could remember. Before their windows, by breakfast-time, all was bustle as the townspeople swarmed over the fallen trees with every type of chopping implement, gathering firewood against the cold. The same thing was going on in the Bois Henri IV behind the Château, and the mayor with his councillors in their robes of office moved uneasily between Bois and Place Royale, for these were royal trees and they must give an account of the damage.

The cold spell, lasting for several days, acted like a tonic to Selkirk; his coughing and expectoration diminished and his spirits rose. He took the improvement to mean that his lungs were not permanently damaged, arguing that had they been he could not have sustained the harsher air.

The news from Montreal had contributed to the tonic effect, but, with the preliminary moves satisfactorily made, there could be no further news of consequence for months. They could only wait. Though February had many warm days, Selkirk was not well enough to be out very much. The January rush of well-being had subsided and little by little he seemed to be losing ground. Through February and into March the distressing cough grew worse and was accompanied by a sharp pain in the side. For the moment the fur trade, even Red River, receded as he fought desperately, refusing to accept the verdict underlined by his emaciated and weakened frame. In March the mild weather was broken by a week of cold accompanied by snow and ice so severe as to kill much of the fruit crop throughout the south of France. This time the sick man did not rally to the cold.

Some local doctors were called into consultation at last and gravely discussed with Selkirk the desirability of a move to Marseilles or even to Toulouse in search of a better climate. Outside the sick-room they merely shrugged; there was none who thought a move now would be of the slightest use – it was too late. 'But who in God's name sent you here for a chest complaint?' they all asked and pointed to the snow-capped Pyrenees. Dr. Lefevre wondered then, and long after, if perhaps Valencia might have been better. The irony was that with youth and peace of mind on his side Pau had cured him of the same complaint of which Selkirk was dying.

But Selkirk was far from reconciled to the inevitable. He talked with some confidence of going to Geneva where a Captain de May was recruiting settlers for Red River; yet even as he made his plans he was past crossing the room without an arm to lean on. He had fastened too on a phrase, 'the stimulus of necessity', and insisted that it would not be wanting when the time arrived for calling it into action. Withal he seemed contented and happy to Jean, who wrote: 'I never saw him more disposed to enjoy life.'

By the beginning of April it was clear that the long struggle must end soon. Jean Selkirk wrote to Katherine Halkett, 'Mercifully there is hardly any suffering except from weakness, perfect tranquillity of mind and inexhaustible patience.' It was a state of grace dearly bought and in itself the proof of how far the invalid had moved from the man he had been. He had hardly known tranquillity of mind since first the vision of the Red River Settlement had possessed him, and where it was concerned he had not known patience. It was to have been a splendid creation after a great design – 'where we had the possibility of doing so much good', he had said sadly – and when it was checked and botched the disappointment had been more than he could support; he had not been patient then.

Neither patience nor tranquillity meant that he had forgotten Red River or ever could. An old sedan chair, the only one in Pau, had been found for him, and in it he was carried daily out into the soft and glorious late March and early April days. Set on a little knoll in a near-by garden, he could look across the twisting and splashing Gave, now in full flood, to the splendour of the mountains, while beside him snowdrops, crocuses, and cherry-blossom in succession provided a change from his sick-room that must have been almost unbearable bliss. He could no longer have doubted that he was looking at spring and the excitement of the reviving earth for the last time. He had stopped fretting about the North West Company and the injustice done him; that was past his mending. But his mind was still clear and full as ever of wide-ranging interests. He had a number of ideas and plans for the experimental farm at Red River, and these, thought out in his garden seat, were later dictated to Jean with all the old concern for detail – the concern of an 'improving' Lowland laird.

A pleasant companionship had developed between the young doctor and his dying patient. Lefevre found great interest in Selkirk's stories of the fur trade and the Nor'Westers, and more than twenty years later he recalled some of them in a medical book. But most fascinating of all was the patient himself. 'Habits and inclinations are not to be put aside at will or pleasure,' he wrote long afterwards, '. . . they are things which are not to be commanded. The ruling passion remains strong in death, and this passion, with him, was political economy and colonisation, and it occupied him in his last moments.'

That first week of April was a kind of reprieve – inexpressible sadness, but within a framework that made it almost bearable. But it could not go on; the thin line that held him to life must snap at any time. Lefevre was now sending daily bulletins to John Halkett; his patient was going fast, and even 'the stimulus of necessity' would not now recall him. He would not again see the far countries about which he still talked, not Red River, or Fort William, or Montreal. He would not again see Edinburgh, riding in past Joppa and Portobello, through the fields of red earth with the gulls blowing like torn paper across the landscape. There came a day when for a few hours his mind wandered, he tossed and struggled feverishly. It passed quickly, leaving him better and in good spirits.

On the morning of the eighth, though he was well enough, the weather prevented the outing in his garden; rain streamed down the window-panes, diffusing the flicker of lightning, and there was thunder in the mountains. Perhaps it would clear later; meanwhile they were comfortable and happy indoors. About ten o'clock the family, with George Lefevre, was engaged in casual chat over a cup of tea. Selkirk was stretched on a sofa reading a pamphlet, Isabella and Katherine played near by. He was suddenly racked with a heavy coughing fit, which was not unusual or alarming. He tried to sit up to clear his chest and throat, and, being unable, signalled to Lefevre for assistance. The young doctor sprang to lift him, but found him already dead. The thread had not even snapped – it had parted quietly.

The long months of waiting, for all their growing certainty, had not prepared Jean Selkirk for the last sad fact. Moreover, her grief was sharpened by a measure of bitterness for which she reproached herself. It was all too clear that the dream that had killed Thomas Douglas had died with him, and that no one would seek to revive it. This called his whole life in question, and it was hard to bear. For she had earned her right to tease him about his dream, through having always given him unfailing support. Now, for a moment, it appeared a pointless struggle and a worthless sacrifice; but this mood of despair passed.

'I feel confident if we have patience', she wrote to Katherine Halkett, 'he will receive ample justice, and when the North West Company are forgotten his name and character will be revered as they ought. For this I would wish to wait although it may be his grandchildren only who are likely to feel it. ...' In that dark moment only the intuition of love could make her certain that though the dream of a kingdom on Red River had vanished, it would never be wholly forgotten.

A MAN'S REACH

The nearest Protestant cemetery to Pau was at Orthez, about twenty-five miles away. Here in due course a large number of people gathered for the funeral service and followed the elderly officiating priest to the grave. It was all much as it might have been in Kirkcudbright, or, had things turned out differently, at Red River. Selkirk seemed to have passed out of the area of bitter conflict to a state in which anyone might pay him respect without raising painful issues. But it only seemed so; the memories of the conflict were too keen and the burden of the struggle could not so easily be laid down.

A letter from John Halkett reached Gale in Montreal on June 9, but the news had already appeared in the Montreal *Gazette*. The obituary notice, with its reservations, perhaps reflected well the views of all but the most passionate North West supporters:

> It may be said of this nobleman that the endowments of his mind as well as his other qualifications made him be as much respected, as the exalted rank he inherited from his ancestors, a circumstance which but rarely happens.
> Perhaps some people would deduct something from his worth on account of his rage for colonization.
> *Sed de mortuis nil nisi bonum.*

337

Express canoes soon carried the newspapers to the Upper Country, where the settlement lay safe under the protection of the de Meurons, but the contest for the fur trade mounted daily, reckless now of concealment. At a portage a short distance above Fort William it reached Colin Robertson and his captor, Archibald Norman McLeod. From being a truculent and unyielding North West prisoner, Robertson collapsed at this 'dreadful shock', and embarked without further protest, wrapping himself in his cloak to conceal his emotion.

At Red River, though the news had been expected, it came as a stunning blow to both settlers and Hudson's Bay Company servants. As George Simpson wrote later to Andrew Colvile, 'It had at first the effect of palsying all their exertions in the late arduous struggle, and the general opinion was that the colony as also the company's interests would in consequence be forsaken and neglected.'

So they might have been, had the sad word come a few months sooner. Now, led by Andrew Colvile, the hard-pressed Hudson's Bay Committee came to the bargaining table in full vigour and knowing their adversary's weakness. It was Selkirk's struggle that brought them there in a position of strength not formerly theirs; the price was his own oblivion. In the new Hudson's Bay Company that came out of the merger with the North West Company in 1821, the immediate past had to be ignored. The settlement was no longer in danger but henceforth no one in power would foster its growth. The more aggressive of the former Nor'Westers were for the present excluded from the new company; otherwise it seemed to be an organization without a memory, save for techniques of the fur trade.

As the new company took form, the characters in the drama that had ended withdrew from the scene or took up unaccustomed postures. Duncan Cameron and A. N. McLeod were spared exclusion by retirement from the fur trade, and Archie McLellan had died in 1819. Duncan Cameron, having beaten his sword into a ploughshare, became member of parliament for Glengarry in Upper Canada. Alexander Macdonell, embittered by his exclusion and by the publicity given his wretched share

338

in events at Red River, publicly abused John Halkett when the latter visited Montreal in 1821, and, holding a whip over his head, shouted that Halkett should consider himself horse-whipped. Halkett had Macdonell arrested and bound over to keep the peace, and thereafter went armed. It was as well, for later the same day Vandersluys, whom Halkett had in print accused of perjury, attacked him in the street with a horse-whip. 'He was preparing to repeat his blow in great rage,' wrote Halkett later to Lord Dalhousie, the Governor General, 'when I pulled out a pocket pistol and shot him.' North West Company training was not easily laid aside but it was apparently still not proof against the more civilized forms of riposte. Samuel Black, Peter Skene Ogden, and Cuthbert Grant, left out at first, were later brought back into an atmosphere that had cooled, and into a goodly company where in time all won renown for courage and determination directed to worthier objectives. All litigation was dropped, but blind justice remained blind. De Reinhart, alone convicted of a capital offence, was never executed because of a doubt concerning provincial boundaries and jurisdiction.

The star of Colin Robertson, though given a place in the new firmament, never again shone with its former brilliance. He paid a heavy price for the essential position of leadership he had assumed at crucial moments in the past. In the new day that had come his old friends could not much help him or his old enemies forgive. He retained his style and the shell of his authority, but as the years went by it was seen at last to be hollow, and a remarkable man – Lord Chesterfield, as they now called him – had become something of a sad joke. When the star at last went out, its disappearance was almost unnoticed.

Miles Macdonell's last days had something of the same pathos, and yet, like Robertson's, some shreds of the quality that had originally claimed Selkirk's attention. Before the Earl's death, Miles had put in through Samuel Gale a large claim for overdue wages and compensation for lost earnings, amounting to more than £4,400. Ill as he was, Selkirk had roused himself in January 1820 to deal with the claim in clear and merciless detail. He was prepared to allow four years' salary less advances plus something for a gratuity, say £500 in all.

> In this letter it might be suggested, (what it may be well that Miles should be reminded of) that the enormous expenses to which I have been subject, in consequence of his errors, and particularly of the proclamation about the pemmican, which he issued in direct contravention of my instructions, must be taken into consideration ... as they have in fact diminished very much the means which I might otherwise have had of acting with more liberality.

As he dictated the letter, he remembered Miles with affection as 'a touchy mortal' and reflected that there were 'many reasons that would incline me to treat him in a friendly and liberal manner ... and make our parting a friendly one'.

In June 1820 when Miles Macdonell received Gale's gentle rebuff, he abandoned his claims, ignominiously and yet with a kind of lame grace. As he had written to Colvile in February, he had too great an attachment to the family 'ever to give their enemies and mine room to exult by uttering a complaint'. He probably meant what he said. But when foolish speculation took the last of his savings and he lived out his few remaining years on the charity of his brother John at Point Fortune on the Ottawa River – an ageing man become slightly simple – local gossip reproached the memory of Selkirk.

Some, a little apart from the struggle, exercised the survivors' triumphant prerogative of having the last word. Archdeacon Strachan, soon to become a bishop, in his cheerful imperviousness to evidence had remained the most consistent figure in the controversy. He had known from the first, as he said more than once, that Selkirk aimed at the destruction of the North West Company, and nothing was permitted to shake his rock-like certainty. Strachan's pupil, successor, and biographer, Bishop Bethune, wrote of these matters long afterwards, attributing Strachan's *Letter to the Earl of Selkirk* to the excitement in Montreal after the Earl's capture of Fort William. But Strachan's pamphlet had been published before Selkirk's departure for Fort William, and written more than a year before the events that were presumed by Bethune to justify it. Bishops should be more careful.

And so indeed should chief justices. In 1854 Sir John Beverley Robinson, nearing the end of a long and splendid career, prepared some papers on its main events. It is not surprising that the cases involving Selkirk and the North West Company should have been given extended notice in the Chief Justice's memorandum. The trials belonged to the bright morning of his career: the year after his marriage in England, the year in which his first child was born at York, and the year in which he became attorney-general of Upper Canada at the age of twenty-seven. Selkirk had been dead for almost thirty-five years, but the sting of those distant contests seems still to have been with the elderly man, writing in his study. His knowledge of the case, imperfect in 1818, had not improved in the interval. Thus he wrote, in part:

On a view of the whole immense mass of evidence, it appeared to me to be obviously the proper course, instead of indicting, as Lord Selkirk desired me, for murder and larceny and arson, to look upon all that had been done by his Lordship and his associates, in a high-handed contest of this nature as so many efforts on their part to ruin their opponents, by possessing themselves of their effects and supplanting them in their trade. I accordingly presented an indictment of that character, prepared after much labour and with great care.

The efforts of his Lordship to prevent the bill being found by the Grand Jury were in every point of view extraordinary, but were unsuccessful.

Nevertheless, as soon as the indictment was found, Lord Selkirk, instead of remaining to abide his trial, withdrew to England, where he addressed to the Government and made in his place in Parliament, the most ungenerous complaints against the Government of this province, and especially the Attorney-General, whom he charged with all kinds of injustice and oppression.

341

Old men forget. It is perhaps not surprising that during the trials one of the jubilant partners of the North West Company had referred to the young Attorney-General as 'an ornament to the world'. Doubtless he was – eventually, and for other reasons.

In time Canada developed a vested interest in the view of the Hudson's Bay Territory put forward two generations earlier by the North West Company. In 1857 Ontario (Upper Canada) began at last to look west, and the Legislative Assembly challenged the company's claim. Obediently the province's Crown Land Department produced a small blue-book with findings satisfactory to the mood of the Assembly. The synopsis of Selkirk's struggle with the North West Company, in spite of the cooling perspective, might have been written by William McGillivray himself, though he had been dead for thirty years.

At his death Selkirk's estate was in debt to the extent of £160,000, a sum which in today's money could hardly be less than $2,000,000. His holdings of Hudson's Bay Company stock, which he had increased to £26,000 after the grant of Assiniboia, became a substantial asset following the merger of the two fur companies. But it was still far short of the guarantee against loss that he had told Wilberforce he sought. In fact, though he took pride in the careful management of his affairs, proper in the holder of an hereditary title and great estates, he had counted no cost once the battle of his life was joined.

In his balance-sheet history can at least place an intangible asset. The relentless pursuit of an important idea has earned the 5th Earl of Selkirk a place among the great experimenters in colonization; alongside Raleigh and Hakluyt and Gibbon Wakefield. Though unsought it would not have been unwelcome.

It seems unlikely that Selkirk had heard the Chinese proverb

> If you plant for a year plant rice
> If you plant for a decade plant trees
> If you plant for a century plant people

yet the same wisdom was in him. He had founded a city and staked out a province, the hinge on which Canada would one day swing open. This had not been mere chance, for he had always believed – when to others it was a foolish vision – that the prairies could provide food for millions. And he had seen his settlement as the bastion against American encroachment which it later became – Canada's most tangible claim to the prairies it had long neglected.

Against this accomplishment, and his dreams, though they fell short, the scratches of denigration made no lasting scar. Almost a century and a half after his death, tradition, vague though it is, does not doubt his sincerity or seriously question his motives. In Kirkcudbright oral tradition still remembers him as 'the Great Earl'.

About Winnipeg in the last years of the nineteenth century there were still a few revered old people who as children had seen Lord Selkirk. They had only little flickering memories which together make a sketchy but affectionate outline. He was 'tall', they remembered, and 'straight' and 'slender', and 'very lordly in appearance, but not strong looking'.

His legend, shadowy but imperishable, outlasted these fading outlines. For in all those years it had travelled and grown throughout Canada, carried in the hearts of people. The name of Selkirk became attached to schools and streets, to hotels and theatres. It was given to a town and to a county and remembered in the christening of children. Most splendidly, it was remembered in a noble range of the Rocky Mountains.

Unknowingly he and his faithful supporters had long before, in stubborn hope, pronounced his epitaph: 'The truth must prevail.'

A NOTE ON SOURCES

The principal source for any study of the 5th Earl of Selkirk is the large group of Selkirk Papers (20,000 pages) in the Public Archives of Canada, at Ottawa. These are transcripts of papers formerly at St. Mary's Isle, Kirkcudbright, Scotland – the Selkirk family home. The Selkirk Papers are on microfilm in Ottawa and copies of the set are lodged in the Provincial Archives of Manitoba and British Columbia. Three other groups of papers, along with the original Selkirk Papers, were destroyed by a fire at St. Mary's Isle in 1940: Correspondence between the 4th Earl of Selkirk and his sons; Correspondence between Jean, Countess of Selkirk, and Lady Katherine Halkett (1808-20); Private Correspondence, St. Mary's Isle. This last group overlaps somewhat the Selkirk Papers, but contains material not found elsewhere; fortunately a selection of transcriptions from it was away being copied, and so escaped the fire; this is now in the Public Archives of Canada on microfilm only (Reel A27). The first two groups exist now only as short quotations in Chester Martin's *Lord Selkirk's Work in Canada* (Oxford, 1916) and J. P. Pritchett's *The Red River Valley* (New Haven and Toronto, 1942).

A few Selkirk letters are to be found in the British Museum, the National Library of Scotland (The Small Collection), and the University of Edinburgh (Correspondence with Alexander McDonald of Dalilia). There are also many relevant official letters and reports in the Q Papers for the period and some in Upper Canada Sundries, both in the Public Archives of Canada. The Miles Macdonell Papers there are also of importance, though parts of them are in the Selkirk Papers. The account of the Paul Jones raid on St. Mary's Isle (April 1778) is given in some detail in a group of letters between the 4th Earl and his Countess, and from Helen, Countess of Selkirk to her sister, the Countess of Morton. Transcripts of these letters are in the library of the United States Naval Academy at Annapolis and certain other American libraries. A small but valuable collection of Selkirk letters, not previously used, is in the McCord Museum, McGill University. In the Provincial Archives of Manitoba are a few useful letters from the 6th Earl of Selkirk to Dr. George Bryce.

I have also consulted with profit the Dalhousie Papers, the the Hall of Dunglass Papers, and the Clerk of Pennycuik Papers in the Scottish Record Office; the Sir George Murray Papers in The National Library of Scotland; and the Classbooks for 1785-91 in the University of Edinburgh. The Powell Papers in the Baldwin Room of the Toronto Public Library are valuable, as are the records of Selkirk's banking with Coutts (1811-20). The archivist of the Hudson's Bay Company, London, has furnished me with the details of the purchases of company stock between 1808 and 1811 by Sir Alexander Mackenzie and by Selkirk and his associates.

Three collections of documents published by the Champlain Society of Toronto have contributed greatly to this study: *Documents Relating to the North West Company* (ed. Stewart Wallace), *Colin Robertson's Correspondence Book* (ed. E. E. Rich), and *Lord Selkirk's Diary: 1803-1804* (ed. Patrick White).

I consulted the numerous books and pamphlets put out by the Selkirk party and the North West Company during the years of their struggle. These are listed in Dr. Stewart Wallace's article, 'The Literature Relating to the Selkirk Controversy'

(*Canadian Historical Review*, Vol. XIII, March 1932).

I have been given access to an extensive unpublished study by Professor Fred Hamil of Wayne University on Lord Selkirk in Upper Canada, a shortened form of which appeared in the Ontario Historical Society Papers and Records (Vol. XXXVII, 1945). The Molson Archives in Montreal are rich in background information about Montreal at this period and have also provided some specific information on the Selkirks' activities there.

The Goulburn Papers in the Surrey County Archives, which should have thrown light on many mysteries, show no interest in the Canadas, though they contain a draft for memoirs.

A spot search of contemporary published memoirs, diaries and letters has provided a few useful pieces of information, as have the newspapers and periodicals of the period.

Finally I have been fortunate in coming on the memoirs of Sir George William Lefevre, who as a young doctor travelled to Pau with the Selkirks and attended the Earl at his death. This book, *The Life of a Travelling Physician*, London, 1843 (Vol. I, pp. 21-75), has provided much of the personal detail of Selkirk's last months about which little has hitherto been known. This work was published anonymously and the name of Lefevre's patient appears only as 'Lord—'. Lefevre's connection with Lord Selkirk is dealt with in an article in *Pyrénées*, Oct.-Dec. 1960, 'Les Véritables Origines du Climatisme Palais' by Joseph Doulomb. It is confirmed by various anecdotes in Lefevre's medical work, *An Apology for the Nerves* (London, 1844), and at one point in the Selkirk Papers (Reel C7) p. 6633 *et seq.*, P.A.C.

NOTES

Throughout these notes the following abbreviations have been used:

P.A.C.   Public Archives of Canada, Ottawa
P.A.M., P.A.O. Provincial Archives of Manitoba, Ontario, etc.
S.R.O.   Scottish Record Office, Edinburgh
N.L. Scot.   National Library of Scotland, Edinburgh
U. of Edin.   University of Edinburgh Library
McCord   McCord Museum, McGill University, Montreal
P.R.O.   Public Record Office, London
F.O.   Foreign Office, London
T.P.L.   Toronto Public Library

The first reference to any book or periodical gives its title in full; thereafter the title is in abbreviated form.

All Selkirk Papers (S.P.) whose source is not otherwise indicated are in the Public Archives of Canada in Ottawa. As microfilm sets of these papers (with the exception of Reel A27) are available in Winnipeg and Victoria, in the Provincial Archives of Manitoba and British Columbia, the number of the microfilm reel in brackets precedes page references.

Chapter 1   *The Seventh Son*

Page

1-5   John Paul Jones Correspondence in the Naval Academy Library, Annapolis, Maryland. Also S. E. Morison, *John Paul Jones* (Boston and Toronto, 1959), chapters 7 and 8. Morison's Appendix 1 destroys the legend that John Paul Jones was an illegitimate son of the 3rd Earl of Selkirk and therefore half-brother of the 4th Earl.

Page

7   (line 7) 6th Earl of Selkirk to Dr. George Bryce, 2 May, 1881; Bryce Papers, P.A.M.

      (lines 10-25) Elizabeth Grant, *Memoirs of a Highland Lady* (Albemarle Library), pp. 237-8. Also G. Fyfe, *Scottish Diaries and Memoirs 1746-1845* (Stirling, 1942), p. 501.

      Sir James Hall to William Hall of Whitehall, January 1789; Hall of Dunglass Papers, II 300/33, S.R.O. Also Betsy Rogers, *Georgian Chronicle* (London, 1958), p. 113.

8   Thomas Douglas to William Clerk, 28 September 1787 and 30 April 1806; Clerk of Pennycuik Papers 3315, 5540, S.R.O.

      University of Edinburgh, class lists, 1785-9.

9   (lines 12-17) Sir James Fergusson, *The Sixteen Peers of Scotland* (Oxford, 1960), pp. 45, 84, 86.

      (lines 18-37) *Narrative of the Life of Sir Walter Scott, Bart.: Begun by himself and continued by J. G. Lockhart* (Everyman's Library), p. 43. See also Chester Martin, *Lord Selkirk's Work in Canada* (Oxford, 1916), pp. 15-16.

11   Thomas Douglas to 4th Earl of Selkirk, 2 May 1792; Boulton Papers, P.A.O.

13   Correspondence of Dunbar, Earl of Selkirk, and his sons; formerly at St. Mary's Isle and quoted in Martin, *Lord Selkirk's Work*, p. 17.

14   Sir James Hall to William Hall, 19 June 1794; Hall of Dunglass Papers, II 300/33, S.R.O.

      Ibid., 25 August and 11 November 1794. Other letters of this period from Sir James and Lady Helen Hall provide news of the Douglas brothers.

      The Selkirk genealogy and an account of the 4th Earl's family are to be found in Sir Robert Douglas, *The Peerage of Scotland* (2nd edition, Edinburgh, 1813), pp. 487-91. It is probable from the author's statement that this information was checked, if not provided, by the 5th Earl.

15   (lines 29-36) 6th Earl of Selkirk to Dr. George Bryce, 2 May 1881; Bryce Papers, P.A.M.

16   Robert Nichol to John Askin, 15 March 1804; Askin Papers, M19-A3, pp. 93-5, P.A.C.

18-20 Selkirk's exchanges with the Home Office and Colonial Office and related memoranda, 1802-3; S.P. (C13) 13839-95.

21-36 *Lord Selkirk's Diary, 1803-4*, ed. Patrick White (Toronto, The Champlain Society, 1958).

21-2 *Ibid.*, pp. 1-12.

23-4 *Ibid.*, pp. 17, 28-35, 55.

25-6 *Ibid.*, pp. 58-60, Halifax, 23 September 1803; pp. 313-16, Halifax, 30 September and 3 October 1804. Comparison of the first entry with the other two leaves no doubt that all three should be dated 1803. This establishes Father Burke's influence on the selection of Baldoon as a site for settlement. The appendix entry on page 344 places Selkirk in Prince Edward Island on 3 October 1804.

27 Selkirk's antipathy to Americans is not consistent with his whig upbringing and principles. He himself believed this attitude had its roots in the Paul Jones raid. Selkirk to Halkett, 21 June 1813: 'This was a momentous event in my life. I was terribly frightened ... and when I was but a youth I developed an antipathy for the United States due almost solely to the buccaneering of John Paul.' From the private correspondence formerly at St. Mary's Isle. Quoted in J. P. Pritchett, *The Red River Valley* (New Haven and Toronto, 1942), p. 17.

27-8 American character, Government and institutions: *Lord Selkirk's Diary*, pp. 122-31.

30-1 York: *ibid.*, pp. 143-69.

32 Miles Macdonell: *ibid.*, pp. 192-5.

33 North West Company: *ibid.*, pp. 203-9.

The text of Lord Selkirk's diary published by the Champlain Society is in the Selkirk Papers (C18-C19) 19384-964.

Chapter 2   *The Years of Success*

38 Selkirk, *Observations on the Present State of the Highlands of Scotland with a View of the Causes and Probable Consequences of Emigration* (London and Edinburgh, 1805), introduction.
Alexander McDonell to Selkirk, 25 September, 8 November, and 30 November 1804; S.P. (C14) 14351, 14331, 14329.

39 (lines 1-9) Selkirk to McDonell, 17 November 1804, 21 February and 21 July 1805; S.P. (C14) 14538, 14540, 14544.
Selkirk, *Observations* (1805 edition), p. 207.

41 Selkirk to McDonell, 2 November 1805; S.P. (C14) 14546.

42 Lady Bessborough to Lord Granville Leveson-Gower, 17 March 1806; *Lord Granville Leveson-Gower Private Correspondence* (London, 1916), Vol. 2, p. 184. Charles James Fox to Anthony Merry, 7 March 1806; F.O. 115/13. Merry to Fox dispatch no. 28; F.O. 5/49, P.R.O. Also Beckles Willson, *Friendly Relations* (Boston, 1934), p. 53.

43 Selkirk to William Clerk, 30 April 1806; Clerk of Pennycuik Papers 5540, S.R.O.
William Knox, Agent for New Brunswick, to George Leonard, 8 May

Page

1806; *The Winslow Papers, 1776-1826*, ed. W. O. Raymond (Saint John, 1901), p. 550.

44-6   Fergusson, *Sixteen Peers*; A. S. Turberville, *The House of Lords in the Age of Reform, 1784-1837* (London, 1958); *Caledonian Mercury*, 6 December 1806.

47   R. I. W. and S. W. Wilberforce, *Life of William Wilberforce* (1838), Vol. III, pp. 292, 294.

48-9   *Caledonian Mercury*, 11 June 1807, report of election.

49   Selkirk to Lord Grenville, undated; S.P. (C13) 14149-53.

       Selkirk to William Young, 9 August 1806, acknowledging part-payment for Baldoon, on Lord Galloway's account; U. of Edin.

50   W. R. Riddell, *The Life of William Dummer Powell* (Michigan Historical Commission, Lansing, 1924), p. 105.

51   Jean Selkirk to Andrew Colvile, 24 August 1816; S.P. (A27) 311 *et seq*. Selkirk to Lady Selkirk, 1 May 1817; S.P. (A27) 407.

52   *Cunningham's Handbook of London* (London, 1850). The Alfred Club: payment of the Alfred Club subscription was provided for in Selkirk's standing instructions to Messrs. Coutts. This payment for 1820 was the last item in the account.

       Andrew Wedderburn Colvile did not shorten his name to Colvile until 1814. However, the shorter form is used from here on to avoid later confusion.

53-61 A. S. Morton, *A History of the Canadian West to 1870-71* (Edinburgh and Toronto, n.d. *c.* 1938), pp. 531-37. Douglas MacKay, *The Honourable Company, A History of the Hudson's Bay Company* (Revised, Toronto, 1949), Chapters VIII and IX. Colin Robertson, Memorandum; S.P. (C1) 530 *et seq*.

57   Selkirk to Miles Macdonell, 6 December 1809, 10 February 1810 Miles Macdonell Papers, MG19-E4, pp. 84, 88, P.A.C.

58   Information on Mackenzie and Selkirk share purchases from the Honourable Committee of the Hudson's Bay Company. See also S.P. (C1) 4, 6.

62   The grant to Lord Selkirk, his heirs and assigns forever, was of a tract of land comprising about 116,000 square miles, bounded by an imaginary line running as follows:
       'Beginning on the western shore of Lake Winipie, otherwise Winnipeg, ... thence running due west to the lake Winnepigoos, otherwise called Little Winnipeg, then in a southerly direction through the said Lake so as to strike its western shore in latitude fifty-two degree north, then due west to the place where the parallel of fifty-two degrees north latitude intersects the western branch of the Red River, otherwise called the Assiniboine River, then due south from that point of intersection to the Height of Land which separates the waters running into Hudson's Bay from those of the

NOTES

Missouri and Mississippi, then in an easterly direction along the
said Height of Land to the Source of the River Winnipie or Winnipeg . . . then along the main stream of the waters and the middle of
the several lakes through which they flow to the mouth of the
Winnipeg River and thence in a northerly direction through the
middle of Lake Winnipeg to the place of beginning. . . . Saving and
reserving to the said Governor and Company and their successors
all *rights of Jurisdiction* whatsoever granted to said Company by
their charter.' Archer Martin, *The Hudson's Bay Company's
Land Tenures* (London, 1898), p. 5.

63   Sir Alexander Mackenzie to the Hon. Roderick McKenzie, 13 April
1812; L. R. Masson, *Les Bourgeois de la Compagnie du Nord-Ouest*
(Montreal, 1889-90), Vol. 1, p. 53.

64   Simon McGillivray to William McGillivray, 25 May 1811; S.P.
(A27) 22. [Halkett], *Statement Respecting the Earl of Selkirk's
Settlement upon the Red River in North America; its destruction in
the years 1815 and 1816; and the massacre of Governor Semple and
his party* (London, 1817), p. 7.

65   Selkirk memorandum; S.P. (A27) 1 *et seq.* Selkirk to Miles Macdonell,
13 June 1811; Macdonell Papers MG19-E4, p. 137. P.A.C.

Chapter 3   *A Most Unfortunate Business*

67-70   Miles Macdonell to Selkirk, 1 October 1811; Letterbook of Captain
Miles Macdonell, *Canadian Archives Report* (Ottawa, 1886),
clxxxvii-ccxxv.

70-2   Macdonell to Selkirk, Letters from Nelson Encampment; Macdonell
Letterbook. Memorandum on Nelson Encampment Mutiny, and
letters between Macdonell and Cook of York Factory; S.P. (C1)
260-84.

Macdonell to Selkirk, 31 May 1812; S.P. (C1) 344-63.

A mock attack by half-breeds on the settlers' arrival at Red River
is described by Alexander Ross. But it is not mentioned by Miles
Macdonell in either letters or Journal, and probably did not take
place. Macdonell to Selkirk, 17 July 1813; S.P. (C1) 764.

73   Selkirk to Macdonell, 23 December 1811; S.P. (C1) 125 *et seq.*

Alexander Ross, *The Red River Settlement: Its Rise, Progress and
Present State* (London, 1856); Chapter II describes how Keveny's
settlers in October 1812 had to walk from Pt. Douglas to Pembina.
Miles Macdonell's Journal describes their arrival by boat, played in
by a piper and with flag flying. S.P. (C16) 16767. Macdonell to
Selkirk, 17 July 1813; S.P. (C1) 764.

74-5   Selkirk to Macdonell, 24 March 1813; S.P. (C1) 292-3.

Page

76   Quoted in Martin, *Lord Selkirk's Work*, pp. 90 n., 91 and n.
        La Belle Assemblée, Vol. III New Series, January 1 to July 30, 1811, p. 324.

77   Correspondence between Lord and Lady Selkirk, Sir James Hall and Dr. Marcel, September 1811 — May 1813; Small Collection, N.L. Scot.

79   Selkirk to Hillier, 18 June 1812; S.P. (C1) 405 *et seq.*

80   Selkirk to Miles Macdonell, 20 June 1812; S.P. (C1) 729 *et seq.*

81   McKeevor, *A Voyage to Hudson's Bay, During the Summer of 1812* (London, 1819), p. 1.

82   Selkirk to McDonald of Dalilia, 9 July and 3 September 1812; U. of Edin.

83   Account of peerage election, *Caledonian Mercury*, 14 November 1812.

83-4   Selkirk to McDonald of Dalilia, 6, 23, and 30 January, 30 April, and 8 May 1813; U. of Edin. Also S.P. (C13) 14358.

86-8   Selkirk to McDonald of Dalilia, 29 June and 6 November 1813; U. of Edin. Also S.P. (C2) 1091.

88   Auld to Andrew Colvile, 10 September 1813; S.P. (C1) 843-64.

89   Macdonell to Selkirk, 10 September 1813; S.P. (A27) 140-3.
        Selkirk to Miles Macdonell, 13 and 14 June 1813; S.P. (C1) 670, 682.
        Jean Selkirk to John Hall, March 1814; Hall of Dunglass Papers, Sec. 2, 321, S.R.O.

90-6   Pemmican proclamation, 8 January and related letters; S.P. (C1) 916 *et seq.* [Halkett], *Statement*, App. B. ii. Journal of Miles Macdonell, 8 and 10 January, and 1 February 1814; S.P. (C16) 16872.

91   Spencer to Selkirk, 8 December 1814; S.P. (A27) 214-22.

93   Auld to Miles Macdonell, 15 April 1814; S.P. (C2) 1054-9. Notes on the Pemmican Affair; S.P. (C2) 1300-7. Also (A27) 2071X.

97   Archibald McDonald to Selkirk, 24 July 1814; S.P. (C2) 1172. Archibald McDonald's Journal, Churchill's Creek to Red River; S.P. (C17) 18178-428.
        Macdonell to Selkirk, 24 July 1814; S.P. (C2) 1179.
        Memorandum by Edwards from York Factory, 27 August — 1 September 1814; S.P. (C2) 1207 *et seq.* Thomas Thomas to Selkirk, 20 September 1814: 'He was so greatly distressed as to excite the compassion of every officer present...'; S.P. (C2) 1240-1.

Chapter 4   *Here Is At Them!*

98-100   Selkirk to Miles Macdonell, 12 April 1814; S.P. (C1) 1006 *et seq.* Also S.P. (C2) 1069 *et seq.* There has been debate (Chester Martin,

Lord Selkirk's Work, pp. 56 and 67, and A. S. Morton, *The Canadian West*, p. 560) as to whether the letter returned to England by Auld might, if received, have cautioned Macdonell sufficiently to have prevented the Pemmican War. The letter of caution from Selkirk, that of 13 June 1813, reached Macdonell on 31 December 1813. The one returned, that of 14 June, contained, Selkirk said later, 'nothing of direct importance to the business in hand, being chiefly taken up with observations on the winter of 1811-12'; S.P. (C2) 1069 *et seq.*

Thomas Clark to Robert Dickson (at Prairie des Chiens), April 1814; S.P. (C2) 1066-8.

100-2 Selkirk to McDonald of Dalilia, 6 August and 17 November 1814; U. of Edin. Latter also in S.P. (C20) 132.

102 Selkirk to Colin Robertson, 6 December 1814; S.P. (C2) 1280. John Macdonell to John McNab, 10 October 1814; S.P. (C2) 1245.

103 James Smyth to Duncan Cameron, 24 December 1814; S.P. (C2) 1292-3.

Duncan Cameron to J. Dugald Cameron, 14 April 1813; S.P. (C8) 8710.

104-5 Simon McGillivray to Wintering Partners, 9 April 1812; S.P. (A27) 28.

104 Dr. John McLoughlin to Dugald Cameron, 16 August 1814; S.P. (C8) 8621-2.

105 John McDonald (of Garth) to J. D. (Dugald) Cameron, 19 July 1814; S.P. (C9) 9008. William McGillivray's questionnaire with answers by Pritchard, 23 July 1814; S.P. (C2) 1162-9. Alexander Macdonell to John McDonald (of Garth), 5 August 1814; S.P. (C2) 1204-5.

105-11 For subversion of the settlement see [Halkett], *Statement*: Depositions of Michael McDonell, App. D; of Neil McKinnon, App. H; of Alexander Maclean, App. P; of James Flynn, App. T; of Hector McEachren, App. L; and many others. See also *Papers Relating to the Red River Settlement* (London, 1819), pp. 172-3. Also S.P. (C2) 2004-43.

Archibald Macdonald, *Narrative Respecting the Destruction of the Earl of Selkirk's Settlement upon Red River in the year 1815* (London, 1816).

108 Duncan Cameron to Donald Livingstone and Hector McEachern, 10 March 1815; S.P. (C8) 8858.

110 Duncan Cameron to servants of H.B. Co. and settlement, 7 June 1815; S.P. (C2) 1534.

111 Semple memorandum, York Factory, September 1815; S.P. (C2) 1657-82. Selkirk to Semple, 30 May 1815; S.P. (C19) 20072.

112 Lord Bathurst to Selkirk, 11 March 1815; S.P. (C2) 1487.

Simon McGillivray to Earl Bathurst, 19 June 1815; S.P. (C9) 9156.

Page

113   Lt. Col. Harvey to William McGillivray, 14 June 1815; S.P. (C8) 8725-6.

William McGillivray to Lt. Col. Harvey, 24 June 1815; *Papers Relating to the Red River Settlement*, pp. 7-9.

Kenneth McKenzie to J. D. (Dugald) Cameron, 10 August 1815; S.P. (C8) 8636. J. D. (Dugald) Cameron to Duncan Cameron, 15 August 1815; S.P. (C2) 1464.

114   McGillivray Statement on transported settlers, Kingston, 15 August 1815; *Papers Relating to the Red River Settlement*, pp. 23-5.

Miles Macdonell's Journal, 8 July 1815; S.P. (C16) 17052.

Thomas Thomas to Hudson's Bay Co., 15 September 1815; S.P. (C2) 1424.

115   Selkirk to Alexander McDonald of Dalilia (from Liverpool on board the *Pacific*), 8 September 1815; S.P. (C20) 146.

Chapter 5   *A Storm to the Northwards*

117-18   S Series, November-December, 1815; P.A.C.

John Molson, Jr., to John Molson, Sr., 27 February 1816; Molson Archives, Montreal.

Selkirk to Sir Gordon Drummond, 'probably 11 Nov. 1815' (enclosing Miles Macdonell's narrative of events at Red River); S.P. (C2) 1763 *et seq.*

119   (line 16) John Richardson to Edward Ellice, 25 October 1821; Ellice Papers, Reel 5, Bundle 7, P.A.C. Martin, *Lord Selkirk's Work*, p. 100 *et seq.*

120   (line 9) Selkirk to Governor Berens, 18 November 1815; S.P. (C2) 1939. Memoranda and Correspondence; S.P. (C1) 188-255.

120-1   Memorandum from N.W. Co., 27 December 1815; S.P. (C1) 254.

Selkirk to John Mure, 1 May 1816; S.P. (A27) 294-6.

123   [Halkett], *Statement*, Appendices of settlers' depositions.

Thomas Clark to Selkirk, 28 March 1816; S.P. (C3) 2111.

124   Colvile to Selkirk, 24 January 1816; S.P. (C2) 2001-3.

Basil Hall to Selkirk, 23 January 1816; S.P. (C2) 1996-2000.

125-6   Selkirk to Colin Robertson, 10 March 1816; S.P. (C2) 1894.

126   Alexander Wood Letter Book, 1816; T.P.L.

127   (lines 1-8) Francis Hall, *Travels in Canada and the United States, in 1816 and 1817* (London, 1818), pp. 105-6.

Narrative of Joseph Leger; S.P. (C12) 12799-816.

128   Drummond to Selkirk, 15 March and 13 April 1816; S.P. (C3) 2218, 2287.

NOTES

Page

De Meurons' Regiment: *Journal of the Army for Historical Research*, Vol. 22, pp. 265-6.

129 Supplies list; S.P. (C2) 12159.

Selkirk to Colvile, 5 June 1816; S.P. (A27) 3116. Selkirk memorandum on Red River and on the de Meurons as soldier-settlers; S.P. (C2) 12604-791. In addition to the de Meurons there were also a few members of the Glengarry Fencibles and Watteville's Regiment with Selkirk.

John Strachan, *A Letter to the Right Honourable the Earl of Selkirk, on his Settlement at the Red River, near Hudson's Bay* (London, 1816). G. W. Spragge, *The John Strachan Letter Book: 1812-1834* (The Ontario Historical Society, Toronto, 1946), pp. 83, 183.

132 Semple to Duncan Cameron, 31 March 1816; S.P. (C3) 2140. Kenneth McKenzie to Duncan Cameron, 27 August 1815; S.P. (C8) 8568-9.

133 James Hughes to John McLoughlin, 24 January 1816; S.P. (C2) 1466. J. D. (Dugald) Cameron to his brother, 14 July 1816; S.P. (C4) 8764. John McDonald (Le Borgne) to Dougal (Dugald) Cameron, 14 February 1816; S.P. (C9) 9009.

134 Duncan Cameron to James Grant, March 1816; S.P. (C2) 1466.

Alexander Macdonell to Duncan Cameron, 13 March 1816; S.P. (C2) 1467-8, also (C9) 9061-2.

Alexander Macdonell to Dugald Cameron, 13 March 1816; S.P. (C9) 9063.

136-7 A. N. McLeod to James Grant and Morrison, 2 June 1816; S.P. (C8) 8610.

McLeod, Henry, and McLoughlin to Grant, Morrison, and Roussin, 3 June 1816; S.P. (C8) 8612.

Robert Henry to Alexander Henry, 3 June 1816; S.P. (C8) 8727.

137 Selkirk to Sir John Sherbrooke, 24 June 1816; S.P. (A27) 304.

140-1 Semple to H.B. Co., 20 September 1815; S.P. (C2) 1445.

142-3 Deposition of Peter Fidler, 31 May 1816; Q Papers 150, Pt. 1, p. 232. P.A.C.

[Halkett], *Statement*: Deposition of Joseph Brisbois, 19 August 1816; App. Z. Deposition of Louis Nolin, 21 August 1816; App. X. Deposition of P. C. Pambrun, 16 August 1816; App. V.

144 Bellegrade: See Coltman preliminary report; MG19-E2, Vol. 1, p. 198. P.A.C.

144-8 There are many and conflicting reports of the encounter at Seven Oaks and the surrounding events. Among the most convincing are the following: Pierre St. Germain, 10 September 1817; S.P. (C15) 16421. Peter Fidler; S.P. (C3) 2509. See also [Halkett], *Statement*:

Chapter 6 *Fort William: Receptacle of Plunder*

Postscript to the Statement. Daniel McKenzie, *A Letter to the Rt. Hon. The Earl of Selkirk* (Sandwich, 1818).

164   Allan affidavit; S.P. (C5) 4608-9.

167   Selkirk to Sherbrooke, 3 September 1816; S.P. (A27) 336B.

169   Fauché statement; S.P. (C12) 12346-58. Fauché asked William McGillivray's advice before attempting the traverse in rough water during which Kenneth McKenzie was drowned. See also [Halkett], *Statement,* App. KK.

170   Allan affidavit; S.P. (C5) 4617-19. Statement of James Grant on stopping of Lagimonière, 5 October 1816; S.P. (C9) 8908.

Selkirk insisted that Grant and Morrison were Nor'Westers and that papers at Fort William showed the name of the South West Company was 'being used only as a juggle to deceive the American Govt. To the gentlemen of the N W or S W Co you are not bound to give an account of your conduct.' S.P. (C4) 3169.

Chapter 7   *Meanwhile in Montreal*

174   Dollier de Casson, *History of Montreal,* edited and translated by R. Flenley (London and Toronto, 1928), introduction.

175   (lines 1-3) S.P. (C12) 12832.

Montreal *Herald,* 17 August, 14 and 21 September 1816; quoted in Lawrence Wilson (ed.), *This Was Montreal in 1814, 1815, 1816 & 1817* (The Château de Ramezay, Montreal, 1960), pp. 127, 138, 139.

176   H. Forrest to Selkirk, 19 March 1817; S.P. (C4) 3292.

176-7   Lady Selkirk to Selkirk, 9 October 1816; S.P. (C4) 4125. John Richardson to Sherbrooke's secretary, 9 November 1816; S.P. (C3) 2912, and (A27) 390N.

177-80   Lady Selkirk to Andrew Colvile, 24 August 1816; S.P. (A27) 310-311L. Montreal *Herald,* 21 August.

180   Sherbrooke's health: Murray Papers, 121, 47.5.2, N.L. Scot.

182   Sherbrooke to Selkirk, 30 October 1816; S.P. (C3) 2885. James Stuart to Lady Selkirk, 31 October 1816; S.P. (C3) 2893-4. Sherbrooke to Bathurst, 11 November 1816; S.P. (A27) 391. Lady Selkirk to Andrew Colvile, 3 January 1817; S.P. (A27) 390.

Gore to Sherbrooke, 27 November 1816, transmitting a revocation of Selkirk's commission as magistrate for the Western District; Upper Canada Sundries 1816-18, P.A.C. Andrew Cochrane to Selkirk, 28 October 1816; S.P. (C3) 2873.

183-4   [Wilcocke], *A Narrative of Occurrences in the Indian Countries of North America, since the connexion of the Right Hon. the Earl of Selkirk with the Hudson's Bay Company, and his attempt to establish*

Chapter 8   *The Spring Tides*

Page

S.P. (C4) 329. Also (A27) 398C. An account of the affair heard by Gale was reported to Lady Selkirk, 27 May 1817; S.P. (A27) 422. Undated memorandum; S.P. (C4) 3307.

201-3   Andrew Colvile to Jean Selkirk, 6 February 1816; S.P. (A27) 390M3.

204   Bathurst to Sherbrooke, 11 February 1817; G Papers 19, p. 62, P.A.C.

205   Miles Macdonell to Selkirk, 6 March 1817; S.P. (C4) 3233-51.

206   Selkirk to Lady Selkirk, 22 February 1817; S.P. (A27) 399D.

Selkirk to Miles Macdonell, 20 March 1817; S.P. (C4) 3296-8.

Selkirk to Lord Melville; S.P. (C4) 3393.

206-7   S.P. (C3) 2805.

207   Selkirk to Lady Selkirk, 23 April 1817; S.P. (A27) 399E.

211   Robert Livingstone to Selkirk, 19 February 1817; S.P. (C3) 3147.

Selkirk to Special Commissioners, 28 April 1817; S.P. (C4) 3365-72.

Sherbrooke to Selkirk, 8 March 1817; S.P. (C4) 3255.

213   Prince Regent's Proclamation, 3 May 1817; S.P. (C4) 3765. Sherbrooke to Bathurst (No. 113A), 5 May 1817; Q Papers 144, p. 8, P.A.C.

214   Journal of Miles Macdonell, 21 June 1817; S.P. (C16) 17294.

Chapter 9   *Summer at Red River*

215-16   Journal of Alexander MacDonell; S.P. (C17) 18168 *et seq.*

Simon McGillivray to the Wintering Partners, 9 April 1812; S.P. (A27) 28.

Selkirk to Lady Selkirk, 28 June 1817; S.P. (A27) 413.

John Allan affidavit; S.P. (C5) 4632-3.

218   Michael McDonell to Selkirk, 14 June 1817; S.P. (C4) 3557. Michael McDonell's deposition, 15 January 1819; S.P. (C15) 16290 *et seq.*

218-19   Selkirk to Commissioners, 28 June 1817; S.P. (C4) 3615-21.

219   Angus Shaw to James Fraser, 14 October 1816; Dalhousie Papers 3/17, S.R.O.

D'Arcy Boulton to James Woods, 23 June 1816; S.P. (C4) 3644.

219-20   Lady Selkirk to Selkirk, 7 May 1817; S.P. (A27) 398M.

220-1   Sherbrooke to Selkirk, 3 May 1817; S.P. (C4) 3406-7.

221   Selkirk to Gale, 3 July 1817; S.P. (A27) 497.

221-2   Journal of Miles Macdonell; S.P. (C16) 17305-7.

A full account of events at Red River from Selkirk's point of view is found in Selkirk to Andrew Colvile, 7 August 1817; S.P. (A27)

Page

538-50. Lady Selkirk to Andrew Colvile, 27 April 1817; S.P. (A27) 390M2.

223   Lady Selkirk to Andrew Colvile, 19 May 1817; S.P. (A27) 414-15.

224   Robert Christie to Selkirk, 19 May 1818; S.P. (C5) 4895-6.

225-6   Lieut. Moir on Commissioners at Sault Ste. Marie, 3 June 1817; S.P. (C4) 3511-28. Gale to Lady Selkirk, 13 June 1817; S.P. (A27) 454 *et seq.* Deposition of Samuel Gale, Sandwich, September 1818; S.P. (C5) 5403-8.

226   John Spencer to Selkirk, 31 May 1817; S.P. (C4) 3490.

227   Gale to Lady Selkirk, 4 July 1817; S.P. (C4) 3660-7.

229-30   Dugald Stewart to John Halkett, 31 May 1817; Misc. Letters and Docs., M546, N.L. Scot.

231-3   Exchange between Coltman, Selkirk, and Nor'Westers; S.P. (C4) 3657 *et seq.* Lady Selkirk to Andrew Colvile, 26 March 1818: 'Only think of Coltman in his restitution, having an ox and a cow taken out of the yoke and *killed* by the North West . . . Laidlaw . . . was ready to break his heart . . .'; S.P. (A27) 760.

233   Coltman to Selkirk, 29 July 1817; S.P. (C4) 3871.

Coltman to Sherbrooke, 15 July 1817; Q Papers 145, p. 33, P.A.C. 23 October; p. 68. 27 November; p. 146. Fletcher to Sherbrooke, 31 July 1817; *ibid.*, p. 38.

233-4   Gale to Lady Selkirk, 8 August 1817; S.P. (C4) 3929-34.

234   Selkirk to Lady Selkirk, 21 July 1817: 'The Indians agreed to a cession of land for the use of the settlement, negotiated under Coltman's auspices and recommended by him . . .'; S.P. (A27) 521.

The text of the treaty which quenched the Indian title to settlement land appears on the endpapers of this volume. It will also be found with comments in Archer Martin, *The Hudson's Bay Company Land Tenures*, pp. 12-13. The unsatisfactory aspect of the treaty was the sentence that guaranteed also the rights of 'traders hitherto established upon any part of the above-mentioned tract of land . . . till his Majesty's pleasure shall be known'. If more than temporary, this condition clouded the rights of the Hudson's Bay Company and Selkirk, and the tenure of his settlers.

235   Journal of Alexander MacDonell, 7 July ('Northwegian Point') to 16 August 1817; S.P. (C17) 18168-75. Miles Macdonell to Capt. Roderick McDonald, 25 June 1818: 'The meeting between his Lordship and them excited much feeling.' S.P. (C5) 5353.

236   Selkirk to Coltman, 23 August 1817; S.P. (C4) 3974.

237   Ross, *The Red River Settlement*, Chapter IV.

238   Gale to Lady Selkirk, *en route*, September 1817; S.P. (C4) 4097.

Gale to Lady Selkirk, 2 or 3 September 1817; S.P. (C4) 4103-5.

Selkirk to Coltman, 7 September 1817; S.P. (A27) 579.

Selkirk to Lady Selkirk, 4 August 1817: 'Dickson tempts me more and more to prefer the route by the Mississippi, and assures me that it will not only be easier and pleasanter but will save time.' S.P. (A27) 519-23.

Chapter 10   *Lord Bathurst's Justice*

241   Maitland to Andrew Colvile, 25 June 1817; S.P. (C4) 3572.

Lady Selkirk to Halkett, 12 June 1817; quoted in Martin, *Lord Selkirk's Work*, p. 159 n.2.

241-3   Information on Lady Selkirk's trips to and from Sorel is to be found in the Molson Papers, the Molson Archives, Montreal.

Alexander Wood to Maitland, Garden and Auldjo, 12 May 1817; Alexander Wood Letter Book, T.P.L.

242   Statement by Lieut. Moir, Sault Ste. Marie, 3 June 1817; S.P. (C4) 3511-28.

243-4   *Robertson's Correspondence*, pp. 3-7.

Ogden murder of an Indian; Q Papers 150, Pt. 1, pp. 206-7, P.A.C. Also S.P. (C5) 4556 and (C15) 16209.

Sherbrooke to Gore, 10 June 1817: 'Several persons confined in prison at Montreal on warrants of the Earl of Selkirk . . . having presented petitions to me . . . for the removal of the Proceedings against them, & of themselves to the Upper Province where their witnesses principally were, it was recommended by the Executive Council . . . that their prayer should be granted . . .'; U.C. Sundries, P.A.C. This removal took place under the British Act 43rd George III, Cap. 138. The succeeding steps can be followed through Upper Canada Sundries for the period and also through the Q Papers. In the result the procedure constricted the trial process in Upper Canada, since prisoners were transferred under specific indictments from Lower Canada and alterations that might have assisted the attainment of justice could not easily be made in the upper province.

245   Gale to Lady Selkirk, 11 November 1817; S.P. (C4) 4201 *et seq.*

247   (lines 1-4) Gale to Lady Selkirk, *en route* from Red River; S.P. (A27) 615.

Gale to Lady Selkirk, Sault Ste. Marie, 23 October 1817; S.P. (C4) 4146-7.

248-50 Lady Selkirk to Andrew Colvile, 19 November 1817; S.P. (A27) 660-77.

Selkirk to Lady Selkirk, 27 October, 24 November, and 16 December 1817; S.P. (A27) 631-6.

Chapter 11   *Return to Montreal*

Page

266   Lady Selkirk to Andrew Colvile, 13 February 1818; S.P. (A27) 740.

267   Lady Selkirk to Andrew Colvile, 19 March 1818; S.P. (A27) 758-61.
Sherbrooke to Bathurst, 28 March 1818; Q Papers 148, Pt. 1, p. 169,
P.A.C.

269   Selkirk to Lady Selkirk, 1 April 1818; S.P. (C5) 4742.

Selkirk to Lady Sherbrooke, Three Rivers, 3 April 1818; S.P. (C5)
4757-8.

Montreal *Gazette*, 15 April 1818, on trials at Quebec. Gale to Lady
Selkirk, Quebec, 27 March 1818; S.P. (C5) 4711-13.

270   William Johnston, Charlottetown, to Selkirk, 31 March 1818;
S.P. (C5) 4739. William Mure, Kirkcudbright, to Selkirk, 3 April
1818; S.P. (C5) 4753-6. Selkirk to Col. Addison, Capt. Stephens,
etc; S.P. (C5) 4776, 4778-9, 4809. John Spencer to Lord Selkirk,
6 April 1818; S.P. (C5) 4769-71. Marshall, Kirkcudbright, to Lord
Selkirk, 30 March 1818; S.P. (C5) 4736.

Sherbrooke to Bathurst, 20 April 1818, on subscription for a mission
at Red River: Father Provencher and Father Dumoulin had already
gone up; Q Papers 148, Pt. 1, pp. 256-8, P.A.C.

Memorandum on subscription; S.P. (C4) 4380.

271   Basil Hall to Selkirk, 30 January 1818; S.P. (C4) 4393-5.

Selkirk to D. Washburne, 16 April 1818; S.P. (C5) 4800. Selkirk
to J. B. Robinson, 8 April 1818; S.P. (C5) 4778-82. Selkirk to
N. F. G. Uniacke, 8 April 1818; S.P. (C5) 4783-5.

272   Selkirk to Sir John Sherbrooke, 13 April 1818; S.P. (C5) 4790-6.
Uniacke and Marshall to A. N. Cochrane, 18 April 1818; S.P. (C5)
4804.

J. B. Robinson to Selkirk, 19 April 1818; S.P. (C5) 4805-8.

273   John Jacob Astor to Selkirk, 16 April and 7 November 1818; S.P.
(C5) 4802, 4803.

D. Washburne to Selkirk, 20 April 1818; S.P. (C5) 4811-14.

274   George Ridout to Selkirk, 22 April 1818; S.P. (C5) 4825-7.

275   Montreal *Gazette*, 22 and 29 April 1818.

Earl of Dalhousie to the Duke of Buccleuch, 20 May 1818, and
Sherbrooke to Dalhousie, 24 June 1818; Dalhousie Papers, Serial 16,
S.R.O.

John Allan to Lady Selkirk, 27 April 1818; S.P. (C5) 4841-5.

Robert Christie to Selkirk, 23 April 1818; S.P. (C5) 4829.

276   Order for liberation of George Campbell, 28 April 1818; S.P. (C5)
4849.

Selkirk to Fowle of Newport, Kentucky, 20 April 1818; S.P. (C5)
4822-3.

Selkirk to Sir Charles Bagot, 5 May 1818; S.P. (C5) 4864.

Chapter 12   *Justice in Upper Canada*

Page

newspaper) after the expectation of support from Govt. which my friends had been led to entertain, I must own that I thought it could have but one interpretation . . .'; S.P. (C6) 5860.

'. . . the Earl of Selkirk only got 13 votes. He was abroad.' *Edinburgh Evening Courant*, 25 July 1818.

287-9   William Dummer Powell, North West Disputes; *Canadian Archives Report, 1897* (Ottawa, 1898), pp. 86-101. Selkirk to Sir Peregrine Maitland, 21 October 1818; S.P. (C5) 5421-7. Powell to Maitland, 10 October 1819; Dummer Powell Papers 1480-95, P.A.C.

The Montreal *Gazette* of October 21st quoted a dispatch from Buffalo on the disorderly scene during the trials at Sandwich. A similar report from Buffalo was reprinted in the *Dumfries and Galloway Courier* on November 10th.

289   William McGillivray to Lord Bathurst, 3 October 1818; S.P. (A27) 739. Also Q Papers 149, pp. 95-112, P.A.C.

290   Woodward's 'very grand speech': Allan to Lady Selkirk, 24 October 1818; S.P. (C5) 5435.

Colin Robertson to Selkirk, 18 July 1818; S.P. (C5) 5182-3. Lady Selkirk, from Kingston, to Gale, 9 October 1818; McCord, M2982.

291   Lady Selkirk, from Montreal, to Gale, 15 September [October] 1818; McCord, M2986.

291-301   The account of the trials at York follows two published volumes on the subject: *Report of the Proceedings Connected with the Disputes between the Earl of Selkirk and the North West Company (at York October 1818)* (Montreal, 1819); and Amos, *Report of Trials in the Courts of Canada, Relative to the Destruction of the Earl of Selkirk's Settlement in Red River* (London, 1820). The former contains a near-libelous preface, presumably written by S. H. Wilcocke, laying all the blame for delay in trial proceedings on Selkirk. Uniacke had already answered North West complaints by attributing delay chiefly to their determination to have the trials in Upper Canada; Q Papers 149-51, pp. 95-112, P.A.C. The *Report of Trials*, which was probably sponsored by Selkirk, gives many examples of the Crown officers' not using the evidence provided for them.

292   Allan to Lady Selkirk, 24 October 1818; S.P. (C5) 5435. Gale to Lady Selkirk, 24 October 1818 (two letters); S.P. (C5) 5440-51. Also in (A27) 851-61.

294-5   Argument over Semple's title, *Report of the Proceedings*, pp. 108-10.

297   'This flourishing settlement . . .'; *Report of the Proceedings*, p. 96 *et seq.*

297-301   Gale to Lady Selkirk, 30 October and 1 November 1818; S.P. (C5) 5488, 5498. Repeated (A27) 862-76.

302   Lady Selkirk to Gale, 15 October 1818; McCord, M2986. Selkirk to

Chapter 13   *The Worn and Damaged Scabbard*

whole property in the Island as soon as it can be affected.' S.P. (C6) 5985.

Selkirk to Lady Selkirk, 28 April 1819; S.P. (C6) 6146-7.

Quarter Sessions, Sandwich; S.P. (C6) 6719, also (C6) 5975-80.

314   Civil cases and indictment: John Allan to Lady Selkirk, 3 March 1819; S.P. (C6) 5975-80. James Woods to John Allan, 17 March 1819; S.P. (C6) 5993-4.

Lady Katherine Halkett, quoted in Pritchett, *The Red River Valley*, p. 218. Chester Martin, *Lord Selkirk's Work*, p. 165, quotes: 'we had nothing but anxiety . . . .' The original letter was burned, but 'he had . . .' seems to me the more probable reading.

Robertson's Correspondence, Appendix, p. 257.

315   Settlement affairs; S.P. (C6) 6214-33.

Correspondence in the years 1817, 1818, and 1819 between Earl Bathurst and J. Halkett, Esq., on the subject of Lord Selkirk's settlement at the Red River in North America (London, 1819).

Selkirk, Thomas Douglas, 5th Earl of, *A Letter to the Earl of Liverpool from the Earl of Selkirk, accompanied by a correspondence with the colonial department (in the years 1817, 1818, and 1819) on the subject of the Red River Settlement in North America* (London, 1819).

Narratives of John Pritchard, Pierre Chrysologue Pambrun, and Frederick Damien Heurter, respecting the aggressions of the North West Company, against the Earl of Selkirk's Settlement upon Red River (London, 1819).

316   Sir James Hall to Lord Selkirk, 30 April 1819; S.P. (C6) 6149-51.

Hon. George Pellew, *Life of Lord Sidmouth*, quoted in J. R. White, *From Waterloo to Peterloo* (London, 1957), p. 113.

317   Selkirk to Lord Archibald Hamilton, 14 May 1819: 'The only hours when there is any chance of my being out is between 2 and 4 . . .'; S.P. (C6) 6190.

Selkirk to Sir James Scarlett, 19 May 1819; S.P. (C6) 6202.

318-19   *Report of House of Commons Debates*, 24 June 1819, pp. 1351-73.

319-21   *Papers Relating to the Red River Settlement*, 12 July 1819. Bathurst to the Duke of Richmond, 10 July 1819; Powell Papers, p. 43, T.P.L.

321   Selkirk to William Wilberforce, 22 July 1819; S.P. (C6) 6338-42.

322   Wilberforce to Selkirk, 26 July 1819; S.P. (C6) 6361-5.

Selkirk to Stewart, 4 August 1819; S.P. (C6) 6433.

323   Selkirk to James Wedderburn, July 1819; S.P. (A27) 923.

324   Most of the detail of the Selkirks' journey to Pau and the Earl's last illness is drawn from [George William Lefevre], *The Life of a Travelling Physician* (London, 1843), Vol. I, pp. 23-57.

[Lefevre], *Travelling Physician*, p. 24.

A Man's Reach

LL.D., First Bishop of Toronto (Toronto and London, 1870), pp. 61-6.

341-2   Major-General C. W. Robinson, *Life of Sir John Beverley Robinson* (Toronto, 1904), p. 141.

Bethune, *Memoir of John Strachan*, p. 62.

342   *Return to an Address of the Honourable Legislative Assembly, dated 16th March, 1857, requiring Copies of any Charters, Leases or other Documents, under which the Honourable Hudson's Bay Company claim Title to the Hudson's Bay Territory or any Maps relating thereto in the possession of the Government* (Toronto, 1857).

A statement on Selkirk's debts appears in the introduction to Vol. V of the Hope transcription of the Selkirk Papers (now on Reel A27 between pages 699 and 700).

343   Charles N. Bell, *The Selkirk Settlement and the Settlers* (Winnipeg, 1887), pp. 36-44.

LORD WILLIAM DOUGLAS
Earl of Selkirk 1646
Duke of Hamilton (for life) 1660
m. Anne, Duchess of Hamilton

HAMILTONS

| JAMES, *4th Duke* *of Hamilton* | LORD WILLIAM | LORD CHARLES, *2nd Earl of Selkirk* | LORD JOHN, *3rd Earl of Selkirk,* *Earl of Ruglen* 1664-1744 |

LORD DAER
d. 1742

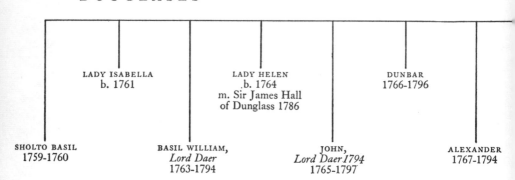

Title passed to grand-nephew DUNBAR HAMILTON

DOUGLASES

| SHOLTO BASIL 1759-1760 | LADY ISABELLA b. 1761 | BASIL WILLIAM, *Lord Daer* 1763-1794 | LADY HELEN .b. 1764 m. Sir James Hall of Dunglass 1786 | JOHN, *Lord Daer* 1794 1765-1797 | DUNBAR 1766-1796 | ALEXANDER 1767-1794 |

Information on female members of the family is quite
incomplete, and in some cases has been inferred.

DOUGLAS *Earl of Selkirk*

A GENEALOGICAL SKETCH

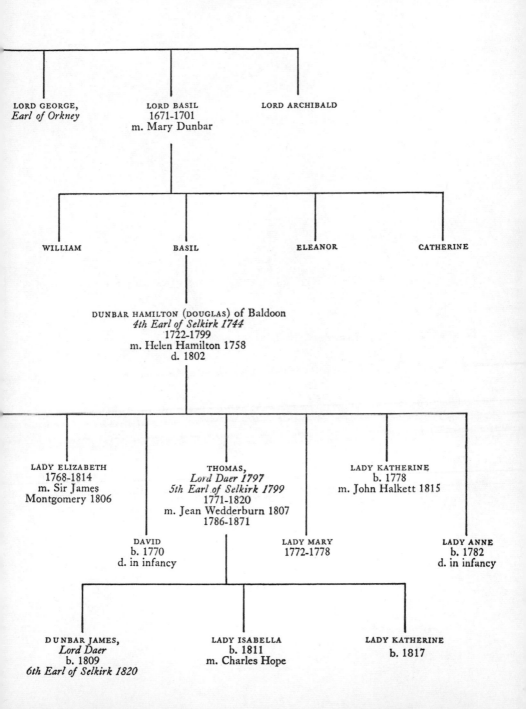

LORD GEORGE,
Earl of Orkney

LORD BASIL
1671-1701
m. Mary Dunbar

LORD ARCHIBALD

WILLIAM

BASIL

ELEANOR

CATHERINE

DUNBAR HAMILTON (DOUGLAS) of Baldoon
4th Earl of Selkirk 1744
1722-1799
m. Helen Hamilton 1758
d. 1802

LADY ELIZABETH
1768-1814
m. Sir James
Montgomery 1806

THOMAS,
Lord Daer 1797
5th Earl of Selkirk 1799
1771-1820
m. Jean Wedderburn 1807
1786-1871

LADY KATHERINE
b. 1778
m. John Halkett 1815

DAVID
b. 1770
d. in infancy

LADY MARY
1772-1778

LADY ANNE
b. 1782
d. in infancy

DUNBAR JAMES,
Lord Daer
b. 1809
6th Earl of Selkirk 1820

LADY ISABELLA
b. 1811
m. Charles Hope

LADY KATHERINE
b. 1817

INDEX

Lefevre, Dr. George William, accompanies the Selkirks to Pau and attends Lord Selkirk at his last illness, 324-36
Leger, Joseph, 127
Lexington, Kentucky, 251
Liverpool, Robert Banks Jenkinson, 2nd Earl of (*Prime Minister*), 77, 312, 315
Livingstone, Robert, 210-11

Macaulay, Zachary, 317
McCoy, Donald, 297
McDonald, Alexander, of Dalilia, 83, 101, 312
McDonald, Archibald, 81, 97, 100, 106, 223
  embarks as second in command from Stromness (1813), 87; sent by Lady Selkirk to Drummond's Island, 195; arrested at Sault Ste. Marie by Fletcher 225-6; goes to Fort William, 227
McDonald, John ('One-Eyed' or 'Le Borgne'), 93, 96, 133, 156-7
McDonald, John, of Garth (*brother-in-law to Wm. McGillivray*), 96, 105
McDonald, Roderick, recruits settlers in Glasgow, 63, 67
Macdonell, Aeneas, 127
MacDonell, Alexander (*Sheriff of Red River Settlement*), 145, 148, 234-5
McDonell, Alexander (*Sheriff at York*), meets Selkirk at York (1803), 31-3; accepts managership of Baldoon settlement, 34; disregards Selkirk's instructions to close Baldoon and move settlers, 40-1
Macdonell, Alexander 'Whiteheaded' (*clerk and partner of North West Company*), 72, 105, 109, 110, 134, 142, 148, 150, 155, 160, 164, 184-5, 338-9
  Coltman issues warrant for arrest of, 237
Macdonell, John (*brother of Miles*), 102
McDonell, Michael, 210
Macdonell, Miles, 83, 88, 99, 100, 298
  first meeting with Selkirk (1804), 32;

Selkirk selects as governor of Assiniboia and brings to England, 57-8; recruits first party for Red River, 63; appointed governor, and warned of opposition by Sir Alexander Mackenzie, 64-5; departure for Red River, 66-8; Auld's hostility to, 73; plans pemmican embargo, 88-9; decides on embargo and posts proclamation (Jan. 8, 1814), 91-3; enforces embargo and collapses under strain, 93-7; Selkirk's criticism of, 100; fails to handle North West campaign, 107; arrested by Duncan Cameron, 110; hears news of Seven Oaks, 150-1; opposes wintering at Fond du Lac, 152; retakes Fort Daer (Pembina) with D'Orsonnens, 191-2; announces recapture of Fort Douglas, 205; arrests Under-Sheriff Smith at Red River, 218; legality of Red River appointment called in question, 295; criticized in Coltman report, 320; last days, 339-40
McGill, Andrew, 130
McGillis, Hugh, 156
McGillivray, John (*of the North West Company*), 163, 168
McGillivray, Simon (*brother of William and London agent for the North West Company*), 112, 204, 217, 231, 284, 288, 294, 331
  warns William against Selkirk, 64; warns wintering partners against colony, 104; friend of Henry Goulburn at Colonial Office, 201-2; arrives at Red River with Coltman, 222; sends *Narrative* to Dugald Stewart, 229
McGillivray, William (*Head of the North West Company, member of Legislative Council for Lower Canada, 1814*), 117, 119, 121, 130, 176, 188, 264, 269, 280, 312
  warned against Red River scheme, 64; brother-in-law of John McDonald, of Garth, 96; condemns pemmican treaty, 105; consulted on colony's safety by Drummond, his lack of candour, 112-14; 'the natural arrogance and violence of

[his] temper', 120; discreet direction of matters of a certain delicacy, 137; his account of Seven Oaks, 153; summoned to give up prisoners and arrested by Selkirk, 155-7; responsibility, 158; interrogated by Selkirk, 159-61; returns to Montreal under arrest, 175; recommendation of Daniel McKenzie, 183-4; sets out to retake Fort William, 222; retakes it, 226; hurt at Selkirk's rejection of compromise, 263; goes to Upper Canada for trials, 272-4; arranges dinner for Duke of Richmond, 284; protests to Bathurst against Uniacke, 289; testifies in York trials, 300

McKeevor, Dr. Thomas, sails with first settlers, 81

Mackenzie, Sir Alexander (*explorer, and partner of North West Company after 1804*), 29, 63, 64, 65, 67, 74
starts buying Hudson's Bay stock with Selkirk, 53; arrangement with Selkirk terminated 1810, 58-9

McKenzie, Alexander ('The Baron') (*North West Company partner*), 156

McKenzie, Daniel (*North West Company partner*), 162, 164-5, 171-3, 183-4, 186, 195, 197, 199, 203, 211, 241, 286
Selkirk attempts to justify dealings with, 188-9; gives sworn statement to Coltman, 190; awarded £1,500 in civil suit against Selkirk, 314

McKenzie, Henry (*North West Company partner*), 225, 279
travels with Coltman's party, 223; arrives in Montreal from Red River, 248

McKenzie, Kenneth (*North West Company partner*), 132, 156, 163-4, 170
drowns while returning under arrest from Red River, 169

Maclean, Alexander (*leading settler at Red River*), 78, 93

McLennan, Archibald, 267, 338
responsible for murder of Keveny, 184-185; is captured when Miles Macdonell takes Fort Douglas, 205; arrives in Montreal under guard and is jailed,

244; released on bail at Quebec, 269; faces trial at Quebec and is acquitted, 279

McLeod, Archibald Norman, J.P. (*Montreal agent of the North West Company*), 106, 117, 119, 148, 230, 233, 275
orders enlistment of Indians against colony, 135-6; treatment of colonists after Seven Oaks, 149-50; rewarded half-breeds for Seven Oaks, 164; arrests Owen Keveny, 184; Coltman issues warrant for arrest, Fletcher fails to execute, 237; retires from fur trade, 338

McLeod, John, 114

McLoughlin, Dr. John (*North West Company wintering partner*), 104, 156

McNab (McNabb), John, 155, 157, 208, 226, 253

Macpherson, Daniel, 155-6

McRobb, Robert, 186, 197, 204, 309
gives Coltman statement on Selkirk's resistance to arrest, 190

McTavish, John Chisholm (*clerk of the North West Company at Fort William in 1816*), 166, 168, 186, 252, 286

McTavish, McGillivrays and Company (*Montreal agents for North West Company, McTavish, Frobisher & Co. until 1804, later McGillivray, Thain & Co.*), 119

Maitland, Garden and Auldjo (*agents for Selkirk and Hudson's Bay Company at Montreal*), 117, 122, 199, 241, 254, 272

Maitland, Sir Peregrine (*Lieutenant-Governor of Upper Canada*), 290, 302
replaces Gore as Lieutenant-Governor, 190

Malsham (steamer), 179, 241, 243

Marshall, William (*estate agent and factor at Kirkcudbright*), 270

Matthey, Captain Frederick (*member de Meuron Regiment*), 151, 157, 190, 219, 226, 236, 249, 315
enlists men as soldier-settlers for Selkirk, 128; bail of £2,000 set by Coltman, 237;